Human Earthquake

To Marsie
To my forite
client Marsie
Ramon Parnell

Human Earthquake

Book I

Ramon Darnell

Earthquake Publications, Chicago, IL© 2017
Copyright 2017 ©All Rights Reserved
ISBN: 0999221302
ISBN: 9780999221303

Throughout the process of writing this book, many individuals took time out to help me. I am eternally grateful for your support and encouragement in completing my first book.

Table of Contents

CHAPTER 1
Grease Sandwiches – The Beginning

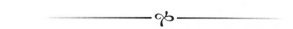

EARLY IN THE morning, the aroma in the air aroused my curiosity. I slowly got out of bed, hypnotized by the smell of freshly fried bacon which drove my nose straight towards the kitchen. I yawned and spoke my first words of the day: "Good morning Grandma," watching her as she cooked.

"Grandma, what's for breakfast?"

"Your favorite, grease sandwiches and coffee."

"Um… my favorite. Yummy, I love it!"

I sat there waiting for her to get the grease hot so that she could swipe the bread across the skillet. We were used to eating grease sandwiches, mayonnaise sandwiches, sugar sandwiches, and syrup sandwiches. My Grandma could make something out of nothing. I would have my coffee, which came from the saucer of my grandma's cup. After finishing breakfast, I watched cartoons, groomed myself and headed out the door to hustle. That was my summer routine at 5 years old.

I spent most of that time unsupervised. In the early seventies, being outdoors until the street lights came on was our babysitter and I observed many things. I learned how to make money by watching older teenage guys who sold Jet Magazines. They seemed to have all the good candy and extra cash, so I asked them how they got it. One of the older boys was my friend Poopie's uncle, Tyrese, who told me they sold Jets they got from a distributor. I asked him where he went to sell them, and he told me downtown. I asked if I could sell Jets too.

Tyrese said that I could follow him to where he got them and take it from there. So, I trailed him to the distributor who told me the layout and explained what to do. After explaining how things worked, the distributor looked at me again having second thoughts because of my age.

"Shorty, you're kind of young for this."

"No, what's wrong with me making some money?" I asked.

He laughed, looking as if he was impressed. "Ok, be here at 12:00 noon to pick up your Jet Magazines and bag. You will owe $1.00 for the magazines and $2.00 for your bag, but you can pay me after your first day of work. Be here on time tomorrow shorty."

"I'll be here on time," I assured him, and ran home excited.

The next day, I picked up my items from the distributor and followed the big boys to the train station. It had one flight of stairs that led up to the pay stations. There were two cashiers who sat inside a small boxed room with a glass window along with a cash slot and turnstile that released once you paid your fare. One cashier sat at the north end near the restrooms and the other at the south end near the paper stand that sold snacks and beverages. You could feel the breeze from the causeway that led to the platform. Once you paid your fare, you walked through the turnstiles and waited for the train on the platform. There was no barrier between the platform and the train tracks so, I was very careful not to get near the edge, for fear of falling on the train tracks.

When the train pulled up to the platform, the conductor announced over the loud speaker, "A Train to Downtown." I saw the "A" on the front as it pulled in. All the teens waited until the last minute and leaped over the turnstile without paying so I went under the turnstile and we all got on the train. I watched my surroundings and made sure that I kept up with the big boys, paying attention to everything. The announcer shouted, "Randolph St. is the next stop." It was a short ride. The big boys prepared to get off the train and so did I.

I watched them as they went in separate directions, agreeing to meet back at the corner of Randolph & State Street at 4:00 p.m. Tyrese walked a block down and shouted, "Get your Jet for a quarter."

I watched him for about 10 minutes and started emulating him as I walked in the opposite direction, yelling, "Get your Jet Magazine for only a quarter." I said it to everyone who walked by. I sold two in the first two minutes.

Then a guy walked up and asked to see the beauty of the week. Not quite sure what he was talking about, I handed him

2

a magazine. He opened it to the middle, looked and said, "This centerfold is nice, I'll take one."

I noticed the photo of the pretty girl in a swimsuit. I asked him if he was buying the Jet because of the pretty girl and he replied, "Yeah little man, if you want to sell the magazines you have to show the beauty of the week." I immediately understood the value of a pretty girl. Now, I carried one magazine open in my hand, showing the centerfold model as I shouted, "Get your Jet, check out the beauty of the week."

I made sure to keep the big boys in my eye sight because I couldn't tell time and I didn't want them to leave me. I made $5 and I was super excited. When we made it back to the neighborhood, I went straight to the distributor and paid him the $3 I owed. I felt like I had a lot of money and couldn't wait to go to work the next day.

I soon started going downtown by myself. I would see the big boys, but I did my own thing. I perfected my selling skills and learned from each sale. When I saw couples, I learned to smile at the lady and she would usually say to the man, "He's so cute, buy a Jet from him." The man would usually buy the magazine and give me as much as $1 tip. It wasn't long before I averaged $10 per day. I was out selling most of the big boys.

I always made it home before my mother except on one occasion. She left work earlier than usual and saw me walking near the train station which was about ¾ of a mile away from my house. I ran home praying that she hadn't seen me but when she brazenly ran through the front door, out of breath from chasing me, without saying a word, she pulled an extension cord out of the closet and gave me a beat down that I never forgot. She hit me so hard that I crawled under the bed and went to sleep when she was done.

I woke up a few hours later. I slowly crawled from under my hiding place and climbed in bed. I could still feel the sting from the whipping that left welts all over my body. As I sat in my bed, I reached in my pocket and pulled out the $5 I had made with satisfaction, thinking how bitter sweet this was. Now my thoughts were, *how will I get downtown without my mom catching me?*" I had a solution; I would have to walk two blocks that would take me out of my mother's path, even if she got off work early.

My brother, Ramell, walked into our bedroom and said in a concerned whisper, "Ramon, we are having pork chops. Are you coming to eat?"

"No," I answered.

"Can I have your chop then?" he immediately asked in a soft tone

"I don't care."

He ran back into the kitchen and said, "Ma, my brother said that I could have his chop."

I could hear my whole family as they sat laughing and talking at the dinner table. I would have joined them, but I didn't want to go in there. I was wishing my mom would break her legs and arm! I envisioned her going to work and falling down the stairs. While enjoying those thoughts, my Aunt Tea came to my room after dinner and said, "Good night. Are you alright nephew?" "Yes," I answered. She gave me a hug and asked, "Would you like me to make you some popcorn?"

"Yes, when my momma goes to sleep."

"Okeydokey," she replied.

My Aunt Tea was the youngest of my grandma's eight kids. Aunt Tea, Uncle Buddy, my mom, my brother and I lived in a three-bedroom apartment with my grandma in the Ickey's Projects. Uncle Buddy was a young man in his twenties and was hardly ever home. Aunt Tea was usually there with grandma because she had Down's Syndrome and grandma always gave her special attention.

My mom was a twenty-five-year-old, single parent who worked as a secretary at St. Joseph Hospital, on the day shift from 9:00 am – 6:00 pm. She enjoyed going out to socialize. She would leave my brother and me, who was a few years older, with Granny. Sometimes she would get sick of watching us. I recall on several occasions her chasing my mom with a broom.

"You're going watch your own kids tonight!" she yelled.

My mom laughed as she ran out the door. My brother and I would also laugh. We didn't mind staying with grandma because we loved sports and music and that's all we did when mom would leave.

I was a very inquisitive kid and always checked my surroundings. One day while taking my new route, leaving downtown heading home, I saw a building called the Cumba Club. It was a performing arts school where a variety of people were coming and going. They were black, white, young and old. Some were as young as eight and some were really old, like in their twenties. It made me curious so, I went inside. I saw a big auditorium with a large stage where people were performing either singing, dancing, or acting. They each had scripts and were practicing their lines. I was captivated by it all and knew I wanted to perform too. I asked the manager if I could join and he told me I was too young but could enroll when I turned eight years old.

Another time on my new route home, I saw the doors of a church open so, I walked in and sat in the back pew, listening to a sermon about Jesus forgiving sins. It was a week day, but I knew that church was on Sundays. I asked an usher why they were having church on a Wednesday and he told me that it was bible study, a continuation of church.

"Can anybody come to bible study?" I asked.

"Is there anybody in particular that you would like to bring?"

"Yeah, my mama."

I was thinking to myself, *'Maybe if she hears that Jesus forgives sins, when I do something else bad, she'll forgive me without a whipping.'* I was fascinated with learning the stories about Jesus and often dropped in on bible study.

On another occasion, while roaming through a nearby neighborhood, I met new kids playing tag and I joined in. When we were playing, I checked my pockets to make sure I hadn't lost my money. An older kid saw me counting it and asked to borrow a dollar. He said he'd give me two dollars back, but I said no. Slightly bullying me, he told me to give him a dollar, he would be my friend and make sure no one bothered me. He explained that if I didn't, he wouldn't help me fight if someone started to mess with me because we weren't friends. He tried his best to intimidate me but I stuffed my money back into my pocket, balled up my fist and stared at him with an angry face.

I stared in his eyes and warned, "I don't need you because I like to fight." He backed down and walked off. I learned to never count my money in front of strangers.

Sometimes I walked to Chinatown to pick up one of my favorite Chinese treats, sweet-tarts, that I purchased from a Chinese candy store. It was a block away from my school and about three and a half miles from my house. On my way back one day, I saw a crowd of kids watching Michael, the toughest guy in the neighborhood, fight. I tried to squeeze through the crowd as Michael rushed the guy. The crowd split and they knocked my sweet-tarts on the ground. While I was bending over to pick up my candy, the guy flipped over my back. As I stood up, it appeared that I had thrown him over my back. I turned around swinging at him because I thought that he was trying to get at my sweet-tarts, but the crowd assumed that I was helping Michael fight. Michael's friends grabbed me and said he could handle it by himself. I was still trying to get to my sweet-tarts, but they thought that I was still trying to help Michael.

From then on, I gained a reputation for being one of the toughest little shorties (kid) in the neighborhood. That was good but also rough because then I had to prove myself all the time and fighting became a norm.

The Ickey's Project consisted of about ten buildings, each having ten to thirteen stories. As I traveled from building to building, the older boys would always find the toughest kid in that building and instigate a fight between us. I didn't mind because I usually won and eventually the boys I fought became my friends. I liked fighting but I liked having them as friends more, so I decided to form a gang that I called *The Vikings*. We were second and third graders who did mischievous things, like fighting and shouting obscene comments at girls, as we hid behind the building walls. I got the idea of having a gang from a TV show called *"The Little Rascals."*

I enjoyed watching cartoons and Sesame Street, but my favorite television show was Soul Train. One Saturday morning while I was watching Soul Train, I saw my Uncle, Syl Johnson, performing and that blew my mind. He was singing a song about his mama. I yelled into the kitchen and told my grandma that Uncle Syl was on television singing about her. My grandma came into the living room and started to do an old lady twist while I continued to do my James Brown dance. Since I was already excited about performing, seeing my uncle on television heightened my desire to be an entertainer.

My mom's other brother, Uncle Jimmy, would come over and visit with the family. He wore loud, colored mohair suits and alligator shoes with a high top, fade-bush hair style and always looked very slick. My Uncle Jimmy and I had a cool relationship. He would open his arms and I'd run to him. As he picked me up, he would ask, "What are you going be when you grow up?" I would say, "A pimp, like my Uncle Jimmy." He would laugh every time I said it. My Uncle Jimmy wasn't a pimp though, he was the popular blues singer "Jimmy Johnson."

I learned the word "pimp" from my Uncle Jimmy. I didn't know what it meant but I knew that it had something to do with women. I didn't know why, but I knew that Uncle Jimmy was very well known, especially with the girls. When he and my Uncle Syl came to visit, all the ladies would come to our door, hanging around constantly trying to get a glimpse or be invited inside. I wanted to be a singer and play instruments so that I could be on television just like them. I started to write songs and began singing, preparing myself for when I turned eight and could join the Cumba Club. Until then, I enjoyed playing sports.

I joined a little league baseball team called *The Baby Earthquakes*. I played three positions: 1st base, short-stop and center field. We played teams from around the city and throughout the suburbs and had a very successful season. One day after a winning game, I ran in the house to change from my baseball uniform into my regular clothes when I noticed something going on. My entire family was in the living room talking and they all seemed sad.

"Your Uncle Buddy is dead," Aunt Tea told me. She took my hand and escorted my brother and me into the bedroom and told us to stay there.

I wanted to be in the living room with my family and everybody else. I understood what death was and I wanted to be a part of what they were going through. When they had my Uncle Buddy's funeral, they didn't allow my brother and me to go. They said we were too young. I was very upset by that. They would only tell us Uncle Buddy died from a heart attack, triggered by high blood pressure because he was drinking alcohol and didn't take his medication.

I didn't know what they were talking about. I just knew that he was gone, and I would never wake up in the middle of the night and watch television with him again. Uncle Buddy would come home late, and I would hear him in the living room, where he slept on the couch, so I'd get up and hang out with him until I got sleepy. In the mornings, he'd wake me up playing the harmonica and I would jump out of bed and do a dance called The Pigeon.

Shortly after my Uncle Buddy died, my Uncle Jerome beat up his wife, who was my mom's older sister Vivian. After that, Aunt Vivian and her three girls, Cup, Chevy and Shady, moved in with us. During that year, we had lots of fun playing all kinds of games. Cup and Chevy were the same ages as my brother and me, while Shady was the baby who was five years younger than me. They were the sisters we never had.

All my cousins' friends seemed to be infatuated with me. A few of them chased me home from school every day. I would fight a boy, but I was pretty shy around girls, especially the ones who liked me. When they chased me, I would run as fast as I could towards a pole and move at the very last minute, hoping that they would run into it. One of Chevy's friends, Keisha, would come over and follow me around the house, calling me clown eyes, a yucky pet name that she gave me. She would say she was going to follow me until I told her that I liked her. I told her that she shouldn't get to close because I had a virus.

I had a secret crush on Chevy's best friend, Twyla. When she visited, she strutted through the house, batting her eyes asking me, "How do I look to you?" She constantly asked me if her dress or hair ribbons were pretty. I'd say, "I don't know, yeah, I guess," thinking to myself, '*That was a dumb question.*' Then she asked me for a dollar and I told her no, girls shouldn't ask boys for money. I don't know where I got that from, but I knew that her asking me for my money didn't feel right.

I told Twyla she should become a girl scout and sell cookies to make money like my cousins. I had ten dollars and didn't mind giving my friends money but when she asked me after parading around trying to get me to tell her how cute she was, it had me feeling some type of way. I knew I wasn't supposed to give her money under those conditions. What was she trying to turn me into? Whatever it was, I didn't like it. I also didn't like her anymore.

Later, my mom notified us that we were moving and would finish out the school year at our old school then transfer the following semester. I was very happy about finishing the school year. My grandma, Aunt Tea, Aunt Vivian and the girls were moving together. My mom, her boyfriend and my brother and I were moving to another location. I thought about all the things that I would be leaving behind: my job selling Jets, Wednesday bible study, my gang and my friends. This was a good life for me. Most of all, I was worried about missing my opportunity to enroll in the Cumba Club. I decided that I would have to figure out how to make it work.

We moved further south into the Englewood neighborhood. We had an apartment on the 11th floor of a high-rise building called the Englewood Terrace. It had 22 stories and there were plenty of kids for us to hang out with. Directly across the street, was our new elementary school. It had a well-equipped playground that included a basketball court and a softball field. After unpacking, our mom allowed us to go outside.

The boys were choosing kids to play on two teams in a softball game. As my brother and I walked up, a kid named Darnell recognized me.

"Hey, didn't you play on the Baby Earthquake Little League team?"

"Yeah," I answered.

He chose me to be on his team while my brother played on the opposing side. I hit two home runs, made the winning catch and we won the game. Each time we played, Darnell always chose me to be on his team, saying, "I'm choosing Baby Earthquake." The rest of the kids started calling me Baby Earthquake as well. The name stuck and from that point on, no one ever called me Ramon again.

We settled into our new neighborhood, and I discovered new ways to make money, which included hustling bottles and carrying customer groceries at the local store. I started a paper route on weekends and was back rolling, making money again. I also got use to my new routine, traveling back and forth to our old neighborhood for school. On the eve of my eighth birthday, I was excited about going to the Cumba Club so I could enroll. It had been my dream for two years and now the time had come. After school that day, I let my brother get on the train by himself while I went to the Cumba Club to register.

I ran all the way there with the songs that I wrote in my bag, thinking about the hours I spent practicing the lines of actors on television. Filled with enthusiasm, I approached the block feeling super excited. My heart dropped as I got close to the door. It was locked and had a thick chain on it. There was a poster in the window that read the Cumba Club moved to Los Angeles. I sat there on the step heartbroken and very disappointed. I walked around to the church and attended the bible study class, not knowing that it would be my last time. It was one of the saddest birthdays I ever had.

When I got home, my mom was very upset with me for not traveling with my brother and gave me a whipping. I cried, not knowing which one hurt worse, the whipping or the disappointment I felt from knowing that the Cumba Club had moved. She still bought me cake and ice cream, but I was on punishment and couldn't go outside for a week. Being an adventurous kid when I did get out, I explored the new neighborhood and spotted a YMCA three blocks away. I walked in and discovered many activities including karate classes and swimming, which had junior life guard sessions. The only requirement was that you had to be at least eight years old. I signed up for both karate and swimming.

We had a great summer and the new school year started out very good. I knew many of my classmates because they lived in the building and were a part of the YMCA activities. The kids at the new school were all Black, the classroom sizes were twice as large and my grades were not as good. I felt that I wasn't smart and was ashamed to ask for help so my grades began to drop. However, there were a lot of athletic competitions and that was good for me because I was great at sports.

The kids at my old school were multicultural; Chinese, Black and White. The class sizes were much smaller, so the teachers provided one on one instruction and I soared from that style of teaching. The school used what they called a "kinesthetic," approach, a hands-on method, which worked better when subjects were physically presented. I was an honor student who enjoyed academics at my old school because things made sense. The teachers at the new school gave verbal instruction rather than one on one assistance, because they had so many students. I accepted that the kids and I at the old school weren't as smart, so I decided to focus on sports.

At the new school, I won the first of three Presidential Athletic Achievement Awards at the Annual Physical Fitness competition. The competition consisted of ten Olympic style games. I became exceptional through my athletic achievements, breaking four school records performing chin-ups, shuttle run, 600-yard run-walk and the high jump.

While breaking school records in physical fitness, I earned "C's" and "D's" in every subject except gym and listening. They were the only two subjects I earned "A's." Although I always scored higher than average in following directions, I sometimes got caught being mischievous, play fighting and practicing my karate on the kids, but I always listened when the teacher told me to stop acting up. I knew I didn't want them to call my mother because that was a guaranteed whipping. Also, I had to gain favor with teachers because my grades were borderline, and I understood they had the ability to pass me. I became very obedient to compensate for my academic shortcomings. Besides, I had physical fitness competitions coming up in a few days and I didn't want anything to stop me from participating.

In class, I took the lead and set the pace because it was easy to get into trouble. My four best friends were also classmates. One was a bully, Cash, another a comedian, Nate, one a girl magnet like me, Chuy, and then there was Wayne, the strong silent type. Wayne was big for his age and a little more mature than the rest of us. He was the only kid in fourth grade with a mustache. He lived in a big, mansion style house on the next block. I used to visit him at home a lot, but never saw his parents.

I went to pick Wayne up on the morning of pre-qualifying trials, very excited and anxious to get to school. He answered the door.

"What's up Baby Earthquake?" he asked.

"I'm good. You're not ready yet? I thought we were going to get to school early. Let's get a move on it so we can practice."

"Ok, my mother is cooking breakfast. Do you want to eat?"

"Yes," then, thinking to myself, *'This is my chance to see his parents.'* I sat on the couch in the living room while Wayne ran upstairs to finish getting dressed.

About 10 minutes later, Wayne came into the living room and announced that breakfast was ready, so we walked down the long corridor and sat at the kitchen table. The table was perfectly set for two so we each grabbed a seat. We had a glass of milk and a plate of hot bacon, eggs, toast and Malt-O-Meal. There was a complete breakfast but no parents. I didn't see nobody. I wondered who had cooked that breakfast?

Wayne ran upstairs to get his books while I finished my food. Suddenly, I felt a lump in my throat as my chest started burning and my heart was beating fast. My hands were shaking as I became dizzy, doing everything in my power not to pass out. I was sweating and getting weaker, gasping for air. Wayne walked into the kitchen, looked at me and asked if I was ok. Unable to speak, holding on to my neck, I was doing my best to get a breath. Wayne stood on my left side and struck me with an open-handed blow, in the upper middle of my back. I let out a loud cough and a big piece of bacon fat flew out of my mouth on to the kitchen table.

I coughed a few more times then said, "Let's go."

"Are you ok? Maybe you need to slow down. Stop being so anxious."

I took my first comfortable, deep breath, and said, "You're right. I need to slow down," realizing that being anxious can cause you to make mistakes.

Wayne walked to the stairway and hollered up, "Everything is alright!" Turning to me, "My mom asked if everything was ok and I was just letting her know."

I stared at him and said, "I didn't hear nobody, not a word."

"Come on, so we won't be late," Wayne said.

I began walking and talking slower, thinking before I spoke. Unknowingly, I started practicing patience and what I came to know as forethought. Wayne and I arrived on the school playground and had about twenty minutes to practice before the school bell rang. Next, we headed to class. We had a one hour reading assignment scheduled for the day, then the teachers took all the kids to gym for the pre-qualifying trial.

My four best friends and I did well, and we made it to the finals. I qualified in every category but got beat in chin ups and the shuttle run. I was curious to know how they did so well. I asked the kid.

"How did you do so many chin ups?"

"I eat horse meat."

I asked what else he did every day and he said that he practiced. Then I asked the other guy how he ran so fast and he told me that he ate spinach every day, like the cartoon character Popeye. I asked what else he did, and he said that he ran every day.

I realized that they both practiced. Since we had two weeks to prepare for the finals, I decided to practice every single day, no matter what else I had to do. I still worked my jobs, played sports and did my activities at the YMCA. I kept thinking about how they beat me and that motivated me to practice even more.

I never looked at size or ability to determine if that made you win. I was short and small. In my class, I was the third shortest. I began to understand that it was your determination that made you win. I seemed to always win even though I was the smallest. I thought about how I won all my fights. I loved watching Bruce Lee movies because I loved karate. Bruce Lee always said, "Concentrate and you can do anything." I followed what he said. This was the second year to win and I decided that no one would beat me — I started believing that I could do anything.

When the games started for the Annual Physical Fitness Competition, the guys that beat me in the pre-qualifying rounds were placed in my category again. I was eager to compete against them, knowing I would win. I beat both and broke two school records in chin-ups and shuttle run for the second year in a row.

They gave me another Presidential Award and a special award for breaking the most records.

My mom attended the awards ceremony, so I was sure to be extra nice. When we headed home, my mom said, "All those little girls kept calling your name. Baby Earthquake! What for?"

"I don't know," I replied. I was thinking about my girlfriend who had just given me my first French kiss the other day. I yelled out, "I don't like those girls."

My mom gave me a stern warning.

"You better not be trying to have sex with those girls because you already been saying that you wish you were taller. Do you know if you have sex with a girl while you are a kid, it will stunt your growth and you will become a midget just like the two midget wrestlers that you watch on television? If you want to be like the big wrestlers, don't be trying to have sex with those fast little heifers." I assured her that I wouldn't, thinking again to myself that kissing and grinding was as far as I was going.

Now that the annual competition was over, I was back to fighting, working, participating in my sports activities and still struggling with the school assignments. During a reading assignment, my teacher left the class and two older students came in looking for her.

"Hey Baby Earthquake, you're in this class?" one of them asked me. He told the other big boy, "I bet he can beat every kid in this room, can't you?"

"Yep," but I would be in a tie with my two friends Cash and Wayne.

One of the boys in the back of the room yelled, "He can't beat me." I immediately ran back to his desk and punched him in the face with five rapid blows then walked back to my seat. I turned and noticed that his lip was bleeding and the kids were all laughing. The two guys chuckled as they walked out of the class. A few minutes later, my teacher came back but he didn't tell that I hit him. After school, I explained to him that I wouldn't have hit him if he hadn't said that. We went over his house and played, and I left a short while later.

As I walked home, I reflected on what happened a few weeks earlier in class, when my friend Nate and I were being bad, and the teacher caught us throwing spit balls. Our teacher eased out of the classroom and called his father. Nate's father walked in 45 minutes later. All the kids stopped and became silent. Nate pretended to be studying real hard, reading as he placed his finger on his temple, burying his face in his work. Nate acted as if he hadn't noticed that his father had walked in. The teacher called his name and he replied, "yes," without even looking up. He continued to write as if he was in deep thought.

"Get up here!" Nate's father growled the command.

Without looking up, Nate pointed his index finger up and said, "Give me a minute," as he placed his hand on his chin, staring at the paper. Nate raised out of his chair and took the tiniest baby steps as he walked towards his father.

"You want to be the class clown?" his father asked. "Ok, I'm going to make you a clown, right now!" He pulled his thick, black belt from the waist of his pants, wrapped it around his fist and started whipping Nate good. The whole class was scared stiff — nobody said a word.

I was thinking, *'Man, I'm glad I didn't get caught hitting my classmate today. I have to think about what I am doing without reacting so fast. I have to be more patient. I could have gotten into serious trouble. I know that I didn't want to get a whipping like Nate. I'm too popular for that and all these girls like me too. That would be too embarrassing. I can't be getting a whipping in front of the class. I'm too cool for that.'*

I finally made it home. As I walked in, my brother was getting a beating because he stole two baseball gloves and a baseball from the local department store. My mom beat him back to the store and made him return the items. He kept saying that Rodney Walls made him do it. I was trying to figure out who Rodney Walls was; I didn't know him.

I stood there pondering: *'Man, this reinforced that I had to think about the consequences of my actions and how to prevent bad outcomes at the same time.'* I went to my room, turned on the television and watched the Olympic male gymnastics competition. I fell in love with it and was fascinated with the art form and began backwards and forward flips on my bed until they returned an hour later.

He came into the room wiping his face. I asked him who Rodney Walls was and he said, "Rocky." Rocky was the neighborhood boy who played with the girls, combed their hair, and jumped rope with them.

"Rocky?!" I asked, shocked.

"Yeah, I had to blame it on somebody," my brother answered.

We both started laughing really hard. I learned that no matter who you blamed, you would still get punished, so the best thing was not getting caught.

The next morning was Saturday. I dressed and went to the YMCA to swim. Ellis, a neighborhood kid with a bad reputation, was breaking into lockers. He was known to be a bully but never tried me. Once, while on the playground, I intervened when he was harassing some kids. So, he punched me in the stomach. I looked at him and laughed, asking, "Is that all you got?" Without answering, he jumped on the monkey bars and started to do chin-ups. And so did I. He jumped off the bars looking frustrated because I did more chin-ups. He walked away with a frown.

I told Ellis to stop breaking into the lockers and he said, "They're not your lockers."

"My friends have lockers and you might break into one of theirs, so stop."

He rooted in position and yelled, "Whatcha gonna do about it?"

As he anticipated my reaction, I tore into him like the wind. The noise from tossing him around drove kids into the locker room. They were hollering, "Get him Baby Earthquake." I hit him in the nose and he busted my lip. Both injuries were bleeding and he surrendered saying, "You got me Baby Earthquake." Ellis left.

Suddenly, we heard music and a coach whistle and walked in that direction. We saw a group of boys doing gymnastics and watched as they practiced, performing so gracefully. I walked over to the coach and asked if we could join the team. He said yes, if we had a valid YMCA card. We joined and had our first practice a few days later.

It was amazing! In two months, I became the best tumbler on the team. The coach and my team members took a special interest in me because I learned fast. Throughout the summer, we were like dare devils flipping off everything. We would flip off swings, buildings, garages, the school roof, concrete, and most of all, on used, thrown away mattresses.

One summer day, Darnell was choosing teams to play a game of softball when his big brother and his crew walked on the field. Wilfred and his buddies were rough. They would rob people and take their money. Everybody feared and respected them. Once, I saw him in front of the neighborhood skating rink. He was with about 30 guys. They would always speak to me, asking, "What's up Baby Earthquake?" However, on this day, they told everybody, "Lower those ends (give me your money)." There were about sixteen of us and they took everybody's money, even my brother's, as he frowned hoping doing so would stop them. They warned him saying, "Get that frown off your face."

They snatched his pocket so hard it ripped, and they took his dollar. Then they walked over to me. I was the smallest one in the group.

"You too Baby Earthquake, give up those ends," they directed their threat straight at me.

I had eight dollars in my pocket from hustling. I told them, "Ain't nobody taking my money."

They posted up, acting as if they were going to rush me. They were acting mad and making gestures like they were about to hit me. I posted up and made gestures back, as if I was going to hit them.

They all got quiet and then started laughing saying, "Baby Earthquake got heart."

"We not going to take your money. Just everyone else's," Wilfred said. He shook my hand and said that I was a cool little cat. Darnell and I were the only two kids who didn't get their money taken that day because Wilfred was his brother.

When I got home, my mom informed us that we were moving again. I was leaving the things that I loved: my friends, flipping, sports and games, being a lifeguard, karate class, and all my hustling jobs. In the middle of the summer, we moved to a townhouse further east, in a neighborhood called the Jeffrey Manor. Now I had to start all over, making new friends and finding a new hustle.

CHAPTER 2
The Jeffrey Manor - A New Life

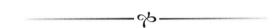

THAT SUMMER, MY mom and her boyfriend Philip got married. We moved into a three-bedroom townhouse. It was much larger than our old apartment. My brother and I had our own bedrooms. The bedrooms were upstairs along with a master bath. On the main floor, we had a large living room with a nice size kitchen and half-bathroom. They purchased beautiful brown suede furniture with matching carpet and hung colorful beads by the stairs separating the kitchen and living room. It was so sharp, we couldn't sit in there. They placed the old furniture and stereo in the basement. My step-father bought a ping-pong table, so we created an entertainment area. It was set it up like our own little apartment with a large laundry room. When we were in the house, my brother and I spent most of our time in the basement.

The neighborhood was quite different. I moved from a building with 22 floors of neighbors, on one block, to a house where the townhouses spread over several blocks, in one community. I explored the neighborhood and noticed that it was clean and well kept. While walking, I heard someone say, "Baby Earthquake." It was one of my old friends from Englewood, who now lived in the Manor. He introduced me to a lot of kids saying, "This is Baby Earthquake from my old hood." I hung out with my new friends in the park and around the townhouses most of the summer.

The summer ended and we started school at Dixon, where most of the kids went. They appeared very cool and reminded me of myself. They all had swagger. At lunch time, we went to Rays, a candy store with a juke box, where everybody hung out and listened to music. That was the fun part; then came the challenging part. It was ironic that they put me in the smartest six grade class and of course, I was struggling. I couldn't wait to go to gym class on Tuesdays and Thursdays, where I was great. In gym class, I started flipping to see if anybody else knew how. My classmates jumped up saying, "Do it again." So, that whole period, I did flips they'd never seen before. My gym teacher was amazed and allowed me to have the floor for the entire period.

The next day, at lunch time, we were all standing in front of the school, just kicking it when this kid walked up and said, "Is your name Earthquake?"

"Yeah."

He looked back and pointed saying, "Isaac is my brother who is in your class. He said that you know how to tumble."

"Yeah, I do."

"Can you do some flips for me?" he asked.

"Naw, not right now."

"Come on just one, I'll give you fifty cents," he said with a smile.

I shook my head no. "Naw, maybe another time."

"What about $1?"

"No."

"Come on, how about $1.50?"

I took a deep breath and said, "Give me $2.00."

"Ok." He reached in his pocket and pulled out two $1 bills.

"What's your name?" I asked.

"Reno."

"Ok Reno, here it goes!"

He stuck his arm out in front of my stomach to block me as I started to run. He looked at me with a grin and said, "Wait a minute, I have to get my money's worth."

Reno started yelling, running around the school saying, "Everybody, gather around," until he had the whole school's undivided attention. As he walked back towards me, he yelled, "Watch this everybody," and all eyes were on me, as if I were an acrobatic spectacle. Reno announced, "This is Earthquake and he is about to turn it up." He focused his attention toward me, "Go ahead, now you can do it." Then he calmly folded his arms and laid back.

I was put on the spot and thought, '*Now I have to give them more than I anticipated*,' but I was up for the challenge. In front of the school, there was a space of grass about a block long, so I had plenty of room. I looked straight ahead and started with a single, round-off flip, straight into ten backhand flips, directly into two, no-hand, backward summersaults, followed by five quick flip flops, to a hesitation, no-hand tuck, where I folded my knees up to my chest, tucking into a ball formation, transitioning into a backwards flip, landing on my feet with my arms straight up in the air. Everyone started jumping up and clapping! I was instantly the most popular student from that day on.

After class, the kids would follow me to see what I was going to do next. I did all kinds of flips including walking on my hands. One day, I walked down the stairs on my hands and down to the corner and a boy started doing it with me. We would compete, trying to see who could walk on our hands the furthest. He became one of my best friends and my brother nicknamed him Babyface because he had a baby-like look. He was cool and slick.

After school, we walked home together we were chased by a loose dog. We were running and saw a fence. I ran up the fence but Babyface couldn't climb up it fast enough and the dog leaped at him. He hollered, hit the dog in the jaw and knocked him down. The dog charged him again and he punched the dog in the head and the dog ran off. *'Babyface got heart,'* I thought. I admired that. By this time, my brother and I met brothers Ralph and Benny and brothers Smooth O, Prescott and their older brother, Bernardo, who stayed in the Manor. We all started hanging out at each other's houses.

I had a lot of good friends and we all became very close. Reno began hanging around me, asking if I could teach him how to tumble. I told him that it wouldn't be easy and asked, "Are you willing to stick with it because you have to be daring?" He agreed so, I took his word.

During school lunchtime the next day, I saw Reno riding down the street on a motorcycle, being chased by a police car. He sped past me saying, "I'll be back." Everyone was watching the chase and Reno was flying. He rode through a tight spot in the school yard fence that had a 4-foot opening. The police car was forced to go around and Reno got away.

Later, after school, he came up there and asked if I was still going to teach him.

"Yeah, if you teach me how to ride a motorcycle. Is that your motorcycle?"

"Yeah."

Surprised, I asked, "Your mother bought that for you?"

"Yeah, I'll tell you all about it later."

I went to Reno's house and met his mother, Jean, and his step-father, Goldie. His parents weren't like mine, they seemed down to earth. They gave him more freedom, so we hung out there most of the time, teaching him how to flip and he taught me how to ride a motorcycle.

One day I was riding and he was on the back telling me not to burn his clutch out when all of a sudden, the police rode behind us. Reno said, "Watch out." He jumped on the front of the motorcycle and we took off. They were chasing us. He kept telling me to lean, when we turned. We hit a gangway to lose them. More police came, and they were saying over the loud speaker, "Stop before you kill yourselves." Reno hit a tight opening through a gangway that led towards his block. We went through the back door of his house and took the bike in. Through his windows, we watched the police ride up and down the streets, still looking for us.

We saw Reno's mother pull into their driveway and the police started talking with her. Reno said, "Let's go get in the bed like we we're asleep." I got in his brother's bed, he got in his and we started snoring. She came upstairs yelling.

"Reno, the police said that you wouldn't stop while they were chasing you."

He acted as if he had just woken up. "Mom me and Earthquake were asleep."

"You are not asleep in the middle of the day. Stop lying. Don't be in those streets running from the police. I am going to get rid of that bike if the police say one more thing about it. That bike is for riding in an open field."

I acted like I was just waking up too, as she walked out of the room saying, "Earthquake still has on his hat and shoes. Is that how you sleep?"

"How did you get your mom to buy you a motorcycle and you are only 13 years old?"

"Easy. I just kept telling her I wanted one and she would say no. When we all sat at the dinner table, I would pick up my fork and spoon, pretending that they were the handle bars, and I was riding a motorcycle, in between taking bites of food. Then I made motorcycle sounds... Rmmmmmrr Rmmmmmm acting like I'm driving and stopping, putting on brakes. As we ate dinner, I would be crying and kept making motorcycle noises Rmmmmmm Rmmmmmm until she finally gave in and got me one. Just try it on your mom, it works, you'll see."

"Ok, I'm going to try it but my mom isn't nice like that plus I'm only 12."

Reno looked at me and said with confidence, "It will work on any parent," and with a facetious grin, we shook hands.

I left Reno's house excited about my plan, while looking at the picture of his motorcycle dirt bike that he had just given me. The photo had a green and a red one and since he had the green, I was going for the red one. When I got to the townhouses, one of my neighbors had a mini bike and he was jumping over crates. I watched as they went from jumping over crates to jumping over garbage cans, but he was afraid to jump so I asked him to let me jump. I had motorcycle fever. He agreed, and I jumped on the bike and took off down the long alley way. I rode up the makeshift ramp and went flying over three garbage cans. I was trying to stop the bike, but it skidded into some rocks. I fell off and my body slid a few feet away. Everybody watching ran down there asking if I was ok. I scarred my hip and burned a hole straight through my pants. My brother was out there too.

He just looked saying, "Boy you will try anything," and went into the house.

I got up. That didn't stop my plan. I went into my house and went straight upstairs and changed my pants after tending to my wounds. It was about 7:30 p.m., dinner time. Here goes nothing.

I went downstairs and showed my mom the photo and asked if she would buy me a motorcycle dirt bike. Of course, she said no. By that time my step-father joined us for dinner. I sat in front of my plate, picked up my fork and spoon and went into my act........ Rmmmmmrr Rmmmmmm as I took bites of food.

My step father looked over at me. "I never saw him act like this. Maybe we should get him one."

I peeped out of the corner of my eye. My mom wasn't completely sold. "I don't know," she said.

"Let's do it. What do you think sweetie?" My step-father replied.

I was in rare performance. It looked like she was about to say yes until my brother came downstairs and yelled, "Mom, don't get him a bike, he's going to kill himself. He just scarred his leg down to the white meat while riding the neighbor's bike. Tell him to pull down his pants and show you. He's just trying to be like that bad boy Reno, because he got one."

I came out of my act. "How are you going to call somebody bad when you're a Chi-town gangsta?"

My brother walked out the front door without saying a word. My mom looked at my step-father and said, "No, he'll kill himself on a bike."

I was thinking, 'My brother spoiled my plan. I can't believe it.' I went outside looking for him. I wanted to tell him off. As much stuff as he was doing, drinking alcohol, smoking marijuana, gambling, shooting craps and pitching pennies. He pitched pennies for big money and every time he popped a liner, he would say "Pow Wow." He pitched pennies so much, everybody started calling him that. Pow Wow grew nearly two feet that year, so now he's trying to dictate what I do. I'm going to check that fool.

Pow Wow was best friends with Prescott, and their crew called themselves the Chi-Town Gangstas. We considered them the big boys and patterned ourselves after them. I was still mad and looking around for him and noticed a family moving in, catty corner from our house. I saw the mother and two boys. Mick was older and the younger boy was my age. His name was Lucky. "I saw you do that jump, it was off the chain," he said walking over to me.

We connected really well and have remained tight ever since. Lucky became my right-hand man and all my crew embraced him immediately. Lucky transferred to Dixon with us. I never found Pow Wow that day and eventually forgot about the bike. I put more time into teaching my friends how to tumble.

My gym teacher learned that I taught three boys how to tumble and asked me if I wanted to create a tumbling team for the school and I could be the captain. I was gung-ho about that because it meant more time out of class. I asked that our practice time not be on our gym days – he agreed. Tumbling practice was always after lunch, twice a week. As the captain, I submitted a tumbling list to the teachers who had to sign it to release us from class. Sometimes we used the list to get everybody out of class when there was no practice.

I spent most of my time in tumbling practice and would ask girls in my class to do my work and they did. By this time, I was in the seventh grade. Reno and I were in the same classroom. He was an impersonator who made fun of all the kids, even the girls. He asked girls for their lunch ticket or one dollar and if they said no, he would signify and impersonate them. Reno was very good at walking, talking and formulating his body to look like anyone. It was amazing. All the kids would be cracking up. The girls catered to him to avoid being his next victim.

I asked Reno how he imitated people so well and he said, "Everybody has quirks. Just find what it is that they do, like a movement or gestures repeated at certain times. For instance, look at the girl in blue, she's shy. She has this little thing that she does when she smiles. She tightens her lips, allowing only her four front teeth to show, kind of like the Joker on Batman. Once I got it, I lock into it and then imitate them."

I laughed so hard. As I looked at her, all I could see was the Joker from Batman.

"Why don't you come to school on Fridays?" I asked when I finished cracking up.

"Friday is my off day."

"From school?"

"Yep, I sleep late because on Thursday nights, I make money."

"How?"

"Well, I rob the grocery store. I go in right before closing time, walk down an aisle, move all the cans of food over, climb on the shelf and restack the cans in front of me, until everyone leaves. Then I come from behind the cans and take all the money out of the registers. I go in the back office and get additional money out of the cash box, unlock the door and leave. That's why I always have a bank roll, buddy."

"Nice, I want one of those bank rolls."

Reno said that he would get me one when we returned to his house. When we got there, he pulled out a pile of newspapers and asked me to give him the $10 that I had. He placed the $5 bills on top of the newspaper, tracing and cutting around them. Now the pile looked like a lot of bills. Reno placed my $5 bills on the top and bottom, folded it up, and put the rubber band over it.

"Here you go, a fresh Willie Dynamite bank roll," he said as he tossed it to me.

I laughed. "A phony bankroll? I want a real one, but this will do for now."

Charm School

I was always doing something different with my two sets of friends. My regular friends were constantly practicing the art of being gangstas and players, while my tumbling friends were practicing the art of flipping. There were many crossroads in our lives. Unknowingly, we couldn't see this at the time because we were irresponsible and immature. No matter how much I learned, my mind was still impulsive. We did things without thinking about the consequences.

The gangstas in the Manor were cool like me, so I resonated with them. I was attracted to that fearless lifestyle. We connected easily and communicated on the same level. We liked the same things and became corrupt in the same way. That was the company I kept.

It didn't matter if I was tumbling off buildings or robbing a store, both roads were pulling me. At times, I could be charming you and at other times I could be harming you. One road could have sent me to the Olympics and the other could have sent me to the penitentiary. My mother took care of me, but the streets were raising me. That was my life in the Manor.

Anybody who visited the Manor and was not associated with our crew could be a victim. Visitors couldn't show any aggression. We welcomed players who were cool if they didn't act like they were trying to run things.

We took anything of value that came through the Manor and wasn't nailed down, including food. After smoking marijuana, we called for pizza deliveries then took the pizzas and the money. Even on holidays we walked around with containers, swiping meat that was unattended. If someone left their backyard with meat on their grill, a portion of it would be gone when they returned to check on it. We took sodas and beers out of coolers, and one side dish off each picnic table until we had enough for everybody. We made our own picnics and had a blast. We had a whole lot of fun in the park. We didn't think about how our actions affected others. My crew and I were young, physical and mentally underdeveloped.

Meanwhile, my tumbling team started having gym shows at school. The Jackie Robin Tumblers sometimes performed with us. They taught us and we taught them. The Jackie Robin team selected me to perform with them on the Westside. I loved flipping, which was my gift and wherever there was tumbling, I was willing to go. I caught the bus and train all the way to the Westside because I wanted to learn everything they knew. They practiced in the park district field-house which had a big auditorium, a basketball court and a tumbling section. The Jackie Robin Tumblers were fascinated with me because I could do a triple in the air. I was fascinated with them because they could do flips through hoops.

After tumbling, we watched the guys play basketball. There was a guy on the court that they called Kat because he played with grace and style. He could leap high and touch the backboard of the rim. When the basketball games ended, they played steppin' music through the sound system. Steppin' originally known as Bopping, is a dance style where partners do a one-two-two shuffle on the beat, while holding hands. As footwork and fancy turns became more popular, the name had recently changed to Steppin'. I loved steppin', it was one of the things that the big boys used to do all the time. Dirk was the best stepper in the Manor and he used to practice with me at our house to sharpen up his moves. I learned everything from him.

When the Westside steppers did their foot moves, Kat stood out. They were calling his name, "Ice Kat" because he was fast and smooth. I did my Manor style shuffle and Ice Kat said, "You're good!" We both started getting down, doing our foot work. Now, every time I went to the Westside, I tumbled, then hung out with Ice Kat.

Ice Kat and his crew were Black Gangstas. That was cool because we were Chi-town Gangstas from the Manor, and kind of the same. Ice Kat was daring, like me. They jumped across two and three-story buildings just to see who would make it and who wouldn't, and I was game for that. It was fun hanging out with him and his crew. Since we had a gym show coming up, I spent a lot of time on the Westside practicing.

Ice Kat was an only child. He lived with his parents in the projects on the Westside, but he spent a lot of time with his uncle who was a pimp, and two aunts, who were prostitutes. He babysat for them when they went out to make money. His uncle was married to one of his aunts. I saw where he got his "Ice Kat Daddy" style. I met his uncle when he came through the projects and he had the same laid-back swagger. I noticed that Ice Kat was pretty smooth with the girls, never frantic, always cool and the girls loved it. The projects were always alive, but it was different from the Manor. The change was good sometimes, but I remained focused on the upcoming gym show.

The African Man

Some of the tumbling moves that I learned out West, I practiced while preparing for my school gym show. At times, I practiced by myself to perfect my skills. I practiced on the lawn, about 10 feet from Lucky's house. I would flip so high that Lucky saw me from his bed, on the second floor. He started coming outside and critiquing my moves. He became my unofficial, personal coach. I learned to defy gravity. I developed a technique where I used my shoulders and Achilles tendon as my guide and I taught my tumbling team many of these techniques. Even Reno adapted quickly.

I tried to adapt to Reno's style of impersonating people. I watched people trying to imitate them, but I got something different from it. I noticed that people made certain gestures at certain times. Whether they were nervous, mad or shy, each one expressed themselves in their own way. I took an interest in learning expressions and what they meant. I even observed this with my tumbling team as I learned their strengths and weaknesses; it made me a more effective teacher.

After practicing tumbling with my new, unofficial coach, Lucky, I walked a few feet to my house. Pow Wow and Prescott were outside. Even the neighbors weren't safe. They were trying to break into our neighbor's house, but they couldn't get across the ledge to the open window. They kept knocking on the door and no one answered. The neighbor's car was gone so they asked me to climb across the ledge, since it was on the second floor. If careful, one could climb across. Since I was agile, I could cross it easily and I was game (able to do it). Pow Wow and Prescott wanted their jewelry. Pow Wow had been watching them very closely. I climbed across the ledge and through the open window and on my way downstairs to open the door, one of the men who lived there came out of his room. I looked at him, not knowing what to say.

"What are you doing in here?"

"I knocked on the door to borrow some sugar and the door was open," I thought quickly.

"It seems that you were coming from upstairs."

"Yeah, I was going to tell you that your door was open. I'm just looking out for you guys. What about the sugar? Do you have any?"

He looked at me with a furious look and said, "No!"

I hurried to the front door, keeping my eyes on him as I unlocked the door and opened it. Pow Wow and Prescott were both standing a foot away.

"What took you so long?" Prescott asked.

"They don't have any sugar," I shouted, as we quickly walked back to our house.

I told them that one of the two guys were home and I was thinking that he didn't buy my story about borrowing sugar. They were an African family of 6 people. A couple with three kids, nine to eleven years old and the wife's brother. The following day, our neighbor told my parents that I was in their home. My step-father punched me in the chest four times and put me on a one-week punishment.

Every time I saw my African neighbor when I was alone, he made threats, telling me that he was going to kill me. He was about 6 feet tall with a medium build while I was about 5'2" with a slender, 13-year-old frame.

"I'm going to kill you Earthquake. I have gun, I have knife, I have dagger, and I have iron, brass knuckles," he would threaten in his Nigerian accent.

After that, he would rush toward me and we would fight. He fought with anger, trying to gouge my eyes out. He went for the kill. When anyone passed by, people started asking him why he was fighting a kid. He would run off without a word. I never told anyone because I felt bad for breaking in my neighbor's house. It was something about them being so close, even though we didn't know them. Still, they were my neighbors.

I wondered if he did the same thing to Pow Wow every time he saw him. The African man often caught me in the mornings, walking to school. Luckily for me I knew how to fight. Prescott taught me how to counter an attack.

"If somebody rushes you, duck and pick them up from their knees," Prescott explained and demonstrated.

"What if you can't pick them up and they fall on you?"

"Drop down and roll over. When they swing at you, block their punch and at the same time, throw a punch at them."

I was thinking that when the African man sees Pow Wow and Prescott, they're going to be forced to use those techniques.

Two months and seven fights later, at about five p.m., I walked into my house. It was apparent that I had just had a fight. I fought off the African man once again. My brother asked what happened to me and I told him the African man was after us so look out for him.

"He better look out for me," Pow Wow said. "There he is right there," as he looked out the window and saw the African man. Pow Wow ran out the front door toward him and the African man took off running, in fear. Pow Wow walked back into the house and said, "Every time he sees me, he takes off running."

Pow Wow was big for his age, muscular with a strong jawline and deep, powerful eyes that told you that he didn't mess around. You didn't bother him because he was wild with an attitude that you knew was trouble. When he walked in a room, he immediately stood out. Guys respected his leadership style because he was fearless and dangerous – you knew that as soon as you saw him. Prescott had those same qualities. As time went on, I didn't see the African man anymore. They silently moved away. I was glad they were gone – what a relief!

I never had a problem like the one I'd just experienced. I made sure that I never got caught again. I realized that it was very important to case out the joint before trying to enter. The African taught me that. We learned that there was a technique to breaking into houses. Burglary is a skill that requires observation. Always scope out the target location to ensure that there won't be any surprises. You must know the prey's time schedule.

There was a moral principle that I lived by from that time on. Under no circumstances, would I ever break into a neighbor's home again. Even though I didn't know my neighbors, I saw them daily, which reminded me that they were regular people, like my parents. That made it feel more personal and anytime you do a crime, it should never be personal. When you are doing wrong, you still must have some sense of value and moral judgement. I started to realize that there were some slight differences between me and my brother. It didn't seem to bother him at all, but that particular burglary didn't sit well with me. So, my focus went back on my upcoming event.

The gym show performance was off the chain! Three of the schools in the district also attended, creating a packed house. The cheerleaders, pom-pom girls and majorettes performed first. Then the crowd got on their feet when the announcer shouted our name. We came out on cue to our song, "Fly Robin Fly." We twirled in combination with perfect timing. We all felt the energy and my concentration was impeccable that day!

I visualized the routine in my head. It just came to me. My coach and teammates didn't know what I was about to do. I observed everything around me then focused straight ahead on the area where we were performing. I saw the basketball rim as I looked to the end of the wall.

"Reno, go tell the coach to stand against the wall under the basketball rim. When I take off, you run to the sideline, then count to ten. On the tenth count, run towards the basket rim and when I go up, you say, 'Two points.'" My face was motionless, but Reno had a grin of confidence.

This was the grand finale. I took a deep breath and started off really slow, hitting the mat. I did a round-off going to a backhand flip in place then another one, in the same place, picking up momentum, going faster and faster, in place, like a spinning wheel. When I got to ten at top speed, Reno was running on the side. My coach was backing up, not knowing what was about to happen. Everybody was quiet and my teammates were frozen, just watching.

I proceeded at top speed, flipping to the end of the mat as Reno ran towards the basketball rim. I was performing one backhand flip after another so fast I wouldn't have been able to stop if I wanted to. I reached the end of the mat and jumped in the air doing a backwards flip. I went up and over, through the rim like a basketball as Reno jumped up yelling, "Two points!" My timing was perfect!

Coach Byron had his hands up, spotting me as I came down through the rim. It appeared that we practiced that routine in advance but of course we hadn't.

My teammates went hysterical as the whole building was on fire, jumping and clapping. The girls were screaming for me but I was a bit shy, so I smiled and trotted off the floor. I got a lot of love letters after that and Reno teased me about them. He was more advanced in that department while I was about being cool.

Coach Offers New Opportunity

The new school year began, Reno and I were in the same eighth grade class. By then, the tumbling team started getting more exposure at Trumbull Park. The park was on the outskirts of the Manor, in a Hispanic and Black neighborhood. My tumbling team performed at gym shows in their auditorium. Coach Pete, head of gymnastics, was the only white man who remained on staff. The park was equipped with state-of-the-art gymnastic equipment including the rings, pommel horse, bars, spot belts and balance beams.

The coach taught us how to use the equipment and I quickly caught on and mastered it all. I preferred not using the spot belt and felt that I never needed it since none of the flips or exercises that I did seemed dangerous to me. Coach Pete always gave me solo performance time at gym shows. Coach Byron attended a main event and discussed my performance with Coach Pete. When I got back to school, Coach Byron told me that he was very impressed with my skills on the equipment.

Coach Byron and the Jackie Robin coach had a discussion and planned to present me to some pre-Olympic trainers at a special school. Coach Byron went on to say that he had never seen a talent like mine.

"You have a gift and you need to share it with the world!" he said.

I asked him who else he was going to present.

"No one just you," Coach Byron said.

I told him that maybe they should also present my teammates.

"The tumbling team is an extension of you. Your teammates are excellent, but you are different. You are a teacher who has mastered precision and timing. This opportunity is made for you, try to understand."

"I understand," I replied, but it wasn't understood.

About a week later, I enjoyed sightseeing on our 3-hour drive to the Olympic school as we laughed and talked about tumbling. I looked forward to it and was excited about performing when we arrived. We pulled up to the two-story brick building that was a half block long with manicured lawns all around the facility and lots of big picture windows. The place was filled with nothing but white people and we stood out like sore thumbs.

I waited in the sitting area of the lobby while the coaches were escorted down the hall. An hour later they returned with the head trainer – Coach Byron introduced us. He was a short, white man with an oval-shaped, bald head that protruded out like a bullet, who looked to be in his fifties. He was wearing a yellow gym suit with a white stripe down the sides. I knew who he was because I saw an article posted on the lobby wall that said he was a key contributor in identifying Olympian talent. My coach asked him to take one look at my performance, but he declined. The Jackie Robin coach tried to encourage him, but he still said no.

"This kid is probably one of the most talented gymnasts that you'll ever see. Take one look at his performance." The trainer declined again so we left, and I didn't ask any questions.

"They're not ready for us yet," Coach Byron said.

"I know," I replied. "I looked in all three of their gymnasiums and watched until a security guard asked me to return to the lobby. I saw them flipping. They weren't all that good. They even had on spot belts," I laughed. "A spot belt is so you don't hurt yourself while you are practicing difficult routines. They were practicing doubles, which are easy to perform." I continued to laugh.

My coach had the saddest look, almost like he was going to cry.

"Coach, you sick or something, what's wrong?"

"You don't get it. Besides, you flip too well for them. Anyway, they couldn't have ever beaten you." He shook his head in despair.

"I would die before I let anybody beat me flipping. That's impossible, for now," I responded arrogantly.

Coach Byron cheered up, as he looked over at me with a slight smile.

"Earthquake you're a true champion. You're going to win at whatever you do. No matter how many times a winner loses, he will still come out a winner. Be graceful no matter what happens, and you will continue to come out on top. That trainer coach knows that you are a true champion. He could see your potential without seeing you perform and he was afraid of that. That's too bad because you would have inspired his whole team to be champions."

Charged up I said, "I know because I was going to show them how it's really done!"

Coach Byron smiled, as he told me I was the greatest gymnast he had ever seen.

"I'm not so good," I said faking a humble voice. We both laughed then he became serious again.

"You graduate this year and I won't ever forget you."

"I won't ever forget you either, Mr. Byron." To lighten the mood, "I was going to do a four fipple for that egg-head coach, looking like a football wearing glasses."

"What's that?"

"Four flips in the air and land on my feet."

He laughed and said, "That's a quadruple."

"Oh, I was going to do whatever you call that."

We laughed again and reminisced about how much fun we'd had with the tumbling team over the past three years.

"The entire team evolved from doing one single flip to becoming full-fledged gymnasts and I am extremely proud of that," Coach Byron said.

We continued to enjoy the drive. Once we got back, the Jackie Robin coach reminded me of the upcoming gym show, as he gathered his things and headed to his car. I confirmed that I'd be out west for practice the following week.

I was about to graduate from the eighth grade. After the Jackie Robin show, it was more difficult to find opportunities to flip. As I weighed my options with Coach Byron, we realized that none of the city high schools had a gymnastic team so the only option for me to continue tumbling was to consider being a high school mascot or a male cheerleader. Being a male cheerleader wasn't even an option and I was way too cool to be a mascot, so I gravitated towards being a player, hustler and gangsta.

Getting Well Groomed – The Jeffrey Manor

As young boys growing up in the Manor, we were watching the older cats (big boys) and took note to how things flowed. We mirrored what they did. Hustling is the art of getting money and when they hustled, we hustled. When they broke in stores, we did too. We learned how to rob and stick people up. They were gangstas who took what they wanted. We learned to be the same way. That's how it went down, getting money.

The big boys were also players, brothers with style and finesse, who taught us to get chose by girls and be lovers who set the tone for relationships, taking the lead right away. A player directs the flow and she adapts to him. They were cool, so we learned to be cool and became stump down players who always dressed with finesse. The big boys had style and good verbal rap ability that was inspired by the music and women loved it.

The music taught us the meaning of words. Music was a part of our daily life. We learned captivating words that we didn't even know how to spell. We were inspired by words and the music that constantly played in our environment. We listened to Bootsy, Parliament, James Brown, LTD, The Isley Brothers, The Jackson Five, The Dramatics, The Moments, Enchantment, Stylistics, Marvin Gaye, Curtis Mayfield, Smokey Robinson & The Miracles, Average White Band, Stevie Wonder, Diana Ross, Al Green, Gladys Knight & The Pips, Bobby Womack, The Commodores and the list goes on!

There were a lot of slow songs and the music raised and taught us. It shaped and molded us and cultivated our minds. We learned how to craft our own style. We listened to the words and realized how they used phrases. We started using words and phrases to express our own feelings, this made us competitive amongst ourselves; seeing who could come up with the most creative ways to express themselves. We created poetry in motion, fully learning the art of expression. We each developed our own persona, which made women gravitate toward us. We formulated our own style. Most of us were a mixture of gangsta meets lover, a raw combination; a unique style developed in Chi-town, by way of the Jeffrey Manor.

The Freight Heist

We were clever little cats, always thinking about money, macking and mo money – focused on ways to come up. One of our hustles was hitting the freights (robbing the trains). One time, we hit the freights and got some nice designer shirts. It was a good caper. My crew, including the big boys, all had designer shirts in multiple colors and sizes. We negotiated with the local clothing stores who purchased dozens of the shirts from us and we all shared the profit.

That was a nice heist but there were so many of us that it wasn't as satisfying to our pockets. We should have planned better. I started thinking if we organized better, we could get a lot more. I determined if there were eighteen of us instead of eight, we could get all the crates instead of what we got. If we calculated what time the train stopped and moved again, we could plan a successful robbery.

We scoped the train schedule out and saw it stopped twice a week, at 10p.m. and moved at 11p.m. I knew that we could be finished unloading and transporting the cargo in 45 minutes, which left us a 15-minute grace period. We kept our eyes and ears open, looking and observing. This time we were going to hit it big.

We noticed that the cargo on the freight trains had a special BB symbol on it, when it contained clothing or shoes. I had our plan mapped out, just waiting on the opportunity. A week later, I called my crew and told them that we were meeting in the park, dressed in all black. Since Smooth O lived a block away from the freights, he was our look out guy. I called him at about 9:45 p.m. He told me that the freight was slowing down.

"Let's go!" he said.

We knew the plan and went to work. We ran onto the tracks, climbed on the train, opened the door, and wow, there were fifty crates. We lined up and ran an assembly line of ten, and the other eight carried the cargo to the park field house until 10:45 p.m. Babyface called time, letting us know that our time was up.

"Let's go everybody."

"Let's get the rest," I replied.

"We have enough," they said, afraid of being caught. I told them to go ahead but I was going to get the last of the cargo.

My crew all left the tracks and headed to the park while I got back on the train. As I pulled the last cargo, I heard a voice say, "Freeze." It was the railroad police agents. Everybody was off the tracks but me. An officer pulled me off the train and I could see everybody running in the distance. I was thinking, *I shouldn't have been so greedy. How do I get out of this?'* The officer got on his radio and called a squad car as he tried to block my path. I acted as if I was crying hysterically.

"Are you going to put me in that big patty wagon?" I asked him, as I pointed. When he turned to look towards the non-existing patty wagon, I took off running and ran all the way to the park.

When everybody saw me, they were excited that I escaped. They were hugging me, slapping high fives and calling my name.

"Ok y'all let's get back to business," I said.

We put all the crates in the field house at the park. I told the entire crew we would meet tomorrow. All crew members, whether they were here or not, still get their share. We put crew members on watch for 24 hours, changing shifts every five hours, until the next day. The next night, we all gathered in the park for our meeting.

We were dressed in our designer shirts, Gatsby pants, and Stacey Adams shoes, topped with our gangsta brims. I orchestrated how we were going to divide everything up.

"We are splitting everything in groups of four, to keep commotion down. Even if you weren't here putting in work, you still gonna eat. That's how we roll around here," I told the crew.

The big boys were laid back watching, admiring our come up.

"You little players got it together," Pow Wow said.

"What are we getting?" Prescott asked.

They continued praising us, as I grabbed my brim with my index finger and thumb, and wisped them across my hat, saying, "Don't worry, the older cats are eating too. Give them ten crates. Now bring the crowbar so we can open the crates," I instructed.

"Lucky went to get it, here he comes," said Babyface.

"Lucky, come on man, we're waiting on you," I hollered.

He gave the crowbar to Prescott while Lucky, Smooth O, Ralph, and I were giving each other dap (fist pounds). Prescott cracked the first crate.

"Y'all did all of this organizing for this?"

Then Pow Wow reached in the crate and said, "Man, y'all got 10,000 baby bottles. You numskulls didn't even check on what y'all were getting!"

"Always check to confirm what you are getting," Prescott said, "cause Earthquake, you almost went to jail for some baby bottles."

We stood there looking at each other.

Prescott said, "Now y'all are going to have to sell all of them baby bottles. There are about twelve girls with babies in the Manor. They might need these bottles."

Pow Wow added, "Never leave a stone unturned. Always check to know what you are getting! Something worthwhile is the only thing that you take risk on, nothing else, knuckleheads."

That stuck with us for life. I really thought deeply about that. Never be greedy, always check to ensure that you are getting what you came to get.

We tried to sell as many baby bottles as we could to the same twelve girls. After a while, they started telling us things like: "I have too many. I don't need no more. I don't want to see another baby bottle as long as I live." We wound up selling them to the neighborhood grocery stores for little or nothing, and used the money to buy alcohol and marijuana then went to a basement party.

I was thinking, 'I have to learn myself. I know that I do things to the extreme. I have to scope out when it's good to be that way and when it's not. It might be good when I'm competing in sports, but it might not be so good when I'm robbing a train. I must always remember to check and know what I am getting, remembering that something worthwhile is the only thing I should take a risk on.' We took a whole lot of risks.

Gas Station Robbery

Pow Wow and Prescott kept guns and I could always borrow one if they agreed that I had good plan. Lucky and I asked my brother and Prescott for a couple of guns. They asked us why and expected an explanation. Fortunately, Lucky and I had it all mapped out. We were going to rob the car wash that was part of the gas station located on the outskirts of the Manor. We had already checked out the scene. There was only one attendant on duty. We were going to enter on his blind side, away from the two mirrors set up for him to view incoming and outgoing traffic. We noticed that they made a lot of cash on Fridays and the attendant took the cash box into the gas station 30 minutes before the car wash closed. We had the whole operation under surveillance from the prairie across the street.

We would observe the scene for 15 minutes and then execute a few minutes before he took the cash box into the gas station. We'd be wearing all black with gloves and ski masks. Lucky would walk in view of one mirror as a decoy, while I ran straight down the center out of view of both mirrors. Before Lucky got to close, he'd bend down and tie his shoe. By the time the attendant turned around, before he could react, I'd be pointing the gun at him, telling him to get on the ground, face down with his arms and legs spread out, giving Lucky a chance to pull his ski mask over his face. Lucky would search him and then remove the money from the cash box while I kept him covered. Lucky would signal me when the coast was clear and we'd run through the prairie and be home free.

Pow Wow listened to our plan and gave us more advice.

"Make sure that you thoroughly check his torso and ankles then lay him face down on the ground."

"I know, robbery is a technique. The objective is for everything to go smooth. It's about timing and accuracy. You must know what you are doing. If not, you can be killed or you can unintentionally kill someone, so you have to know your hustle. We got this," I replied.

"You can't be scared. When you go in there, make sure that you don't have an itchy trigger finger," Pow Wow said.

I boldly answered, "I'm not scared. If I was scared, I wouldn't be doing this."

Prescott expressed some additional advice, "The worst type of stick-up man is a scary one who winds up shooting innocent people out of fear."

"Well then, they're undercover 'marks' who are in the wrong profession, right?" I commented.

Prescott paused, "Cause, sounds like y'all got a solid plan this time." They gave us two gats (guns) and we were excited about the caper.

We executed the plan perfectly, with no problems and got several hundred dollars. We gave Pow Wow and Prescott 10% and returned their guns. Pow Wow and Prescott were impressed. After that, we robbed the gas stations, stores and other local businesses in our area. It goes to show you how the blind led the blind, when we were all young, misguided delinquents.

Lucky and I split the money from the robbery and went shopping the next day and bought new gear. I purchased a sky-blue beaver hat and Lucky purchased a black Godfather style hat. We also picked up the latest shoes from the Stacy Adams collection. I selected the special edition, Johnny Adams, that matched my hat perfectly. We were anticipating dancing in our new shoes, so they had to be immaculate. There was always a weekend party going on so, we arrived dressed and ready to finesse. Lucky and I met my crew at the party. We were all having fun, just being cool, stepping and getting chose.

Lucky was getting his mack on (flirting). The ladies were lining up to hit the floor with him because he had a soft, slick way of slow dancing. The crew and I called his move "the guitar" because he had a sensual style where he danced with a girl, taking her hand and stretching their arms out as if he was playing a guitar, running his fingers up and down her spine, from the nape of her neck to the crack of her butt. Then, in a circular motion, he'd rotate his hand around her butt cheeks, repeating the entire move in sync with the rhythm of a slow jam (record). She'd rest her head on his shoulder and Lucky would lean forward, slightly bending her backwards to get a full grind, pressing against her, as she appeared to be enjoying every moment.

We all did this move and each had our own signature addition to it. I would kiss her softly on the neck, touching her ear lobe with my bottom lip, as I gently breathed in her ear, wetting her eardrum with my verbal rap ability, in coordination with the lyrics of the song, holding her tight, then gently releasing her so that I could stroke her back with the famous guitar move.

After three slow jams, I heard the intro of the well-known steppers anthem, "School Boy Crush" by the Average White Band playing. I headed to the floor with Carla, a petite golden-brown girl who knew how to follow and was very easy to lead as we did the partner dance known as stepping. The beat of the song was perfect for doing the fancy foot work that the Manor steppers were known for.

I had a little extra style because I mixed my Manor foot work with some moves I learned from Ice Kat, who perfected the Westside stepping style. I double shuffled, spinning my partner and as she turned around, I performed a move that my crew named "Amazing Grace." Next, I shuffled my feet, jumped up in the air, crossing my legs and came down in a split to one side, then turned my body to the opposite side and lifted myself up, perfectly in sequence with the drum beat in the song.

After coming home late from the party, I slept in until that afternoon and then picked up Lucky and Babyface. The three of us headed to Trumbull Park. Even though we were known as the little cats, we were masquerading like we were running things and Lucky had to slam one of their big boys from the Trumbull Park crew to prove our point. Afterwards, we were all pumped up as we walked back to the Manor. We ran into the big boys who brought us back down to earth, quickly letting the air out of us.

That night when we got to the park, they did the usual roughing us up. They would box with us so that we were prepared for anything. We would push Lucky out there first because he could take a punch from anybody. He was tough and strong, with muscular arms, a fast runner with powerful thighs and legs. Lucky could almost hang with the big boys, except for Phony Tony, whose punch felt like a Mack truck hit you.

While we were being beat down, we heard a loud pop. Lucky yelled, "oooooooouch," as Phony Tony hit him. We all took off running, knowing that if he hurt Lucky, he could definitely hurt us. They chased us, punching and jamming us up all night.

We both woke up that Monday morning, still sore from those Phony Tony blows. Lucky and I walked to school together and joked as we compared our bruises. Lucky was very comedic, quick witted, and always coming up with something funny to say.

Lucky was so slick that he always stole next years' assignments and books and completed all the work during the summer, so he would have the entire school year to lollygag in class. School was never a challenge, he was extremely smart and everybody, including the teachers, really liked him.

He kept his whole class laughing, always humoring his teacher and this day was no different. I walked Lucky in his class as if he were blind.

His teacher said, "If you did your assignments as often as you made people laugh, you would be ahead of the game. Now, where is your assignment for this week?"

Lucky took out his notebook, "Here you go." The class laughed.

"You need to be finishing your essay for next week."

"Here you go boss," he said, handing it to him.

"Since you think you're so smart, and you've got all this extra time, we have a pre-test due in three weeks. Where is yours?"

"Hold up teach, my ESP kicked in last night and I knew you were going to ask me for that assignment today. I dreamt it. I always wanted to be the teacher's pet because you inspire me, so I already did that pre-test too." Lucky handed it to him saying, "Like Batman and Robin, I could be your side kick, I could be the teacher's assistant."

"Seriously, how did you know to do those assignments because you don't have ESP?"

Lucky said in a genuinely humble, soft tone, as if he were revealing a secret that no one knew, "Honestly, about a year ago something bad happened." The entire class got quiet and listened intensely.

"It was a sunny afternoon and I was walking with my hand blocking my eyes from the sun, not paying attention to where I was going. Suddenly, a force knocked me to the ground, and I panicked as I saw the tires rolling over me and my life flashed before my eyes. Although I was conscious, I couldn't move. My head hit the ground, giving me an insane headache as I laid there lethargic."

The teacher seemed eager to know.

"What kind of vehicle hit you?"

"It was really traumatic, and I don't like thinking about it, but it was a..." he paused taking a long, deep breath trying not to let it get the best of him then finished, "...a tricycle."

His classmates laughed so hard and his teacher was so impressed, that he cracked up too.

"Why are y'all laughing? Seriously, after I got hit, I could hear footsteps coming towards me," Lucky said, remaining in character. "The rider walked up to me and pulled out a gun, pointing the barrel directly at my head. I was terrified. I closed my eyes and he shot me twice and something wet ran down the side of my face."

"What kind of gun was it?" his classmate asked. "Was it a .22 automatic?"

Lucky's voice trembled with fear, when he answered, "No, an orange water pistol. Ever since then, I can predict the future!"

Everyone laughed hysterically, and it took the teacher's focus off where Lucky had gotten the assignments.

Lucky had a knack for taking the focus off what was going on, easily diverting attention. He could captivate people so that we could catch them off guard. He was great in that role, a decoy, allowing us to effectively execute our schemes. That's one of things that I loved about him. He was also genuinely nice and people were naturally drawn to him.

While Lucky was diverting his teacher's attention, I walked in class across the hall and saw Reno. He said that his mom was giving a party on Friday and Lucky and I should come and hang out with him.

"We'll have drinks and everything," he said.

I told Lucky after class and he was down with it.

On Friday, we arrived at Reno's house. It was the first party that his mom had since her husband had been locked up. I don't know why he was in jail, but he had been gone for about four months. She had a full house of cool looking guys and beautiful ladies. She prepared a nice buffet style spread with plenty of liquor. While Reno's mom socialized with her guests, Lucky, Reno and I snuck a few pink Champales for ourselves.

Reno's mom wore a gold outfit, with a short sleeve, fitted jacket and high waist, hot-pants. Hot-pants were shorts that accentuated your butt cheeks. Her outfit was topped off with stylish, gold, knee-high, go-go boots and she wore her hair in a big, curly natural.

Lucky saw those hot-pants and started following Reno's mom around, looking at her shorts.

"Why are you following Reno's mom?" I asked Lucky.

"Look at those shorts, you can see her butt cheeks."

"That's Reno's mom. Why are you looking at her butt cheeks Lucky?"

"Because they're out."

"Stop it!"

"I can't help it; her butt cheeks look good."

"Lucky, you're a sick puppy."

Reno's mom walked over to speak to us. She kissed me on the cheek and went to kiss Lucky on his cheek. He stuck his tongue out, stretching it around his jaw, attempting to French kiss her. She didn't even notice. That's just how little she paid attention to Lucky, barely acknowledging him.

Shortly after the party started, some of her guests went to her bedroom while the rest of them continued listening to music, dancing, drinking and eating. Lucky camouflaged his way to the bedroom with the grownups before they shut the door. I was thinking, 'Wow, Lucky is up there with the grownups. He passed for grown.'

Three minutes later, the door opened and they pushed Lucky out and slammed the door closed.

"Dag, I almost got in. They were smoking marijuana and everything. Reno's mom saw me and told her guests that I was a kid and they threw me out," he explained coming down the stairs.

I laughed as he continued, "They were about to have an orgy. They were getting naked and everything."

They weren't having an orgy, but they were doing something else. I went upstairs and noticed that there were a few people still in Reno's mom's bedroom with the door open. I saw a man with a pipe and a lit torch collecting $20 from each person as they sat next to him. He packed the pipe with a white substance and put it up to their mouths. When he lit the pipe, smoke came out and the person would take a pull, sucking in the smoke. Their heads would fall back and their eyes would be in a daze, as if they were in la-la land.

I also noticed that it had a peculiar smell. I knew that it wasn't heroin because it didn't have a smell. Heroin is brown in color and you snort it or inject it with a needle, but you don't smoke it in a pipe. There were junkies in our neighborhood in the Ickey's Projects when I was five-years old and I became aware of dope. It was the first time that I saw people free-basing (cooking cocaine). I knew it was free-basing because I'd heard about it in the streets. It had just hit the scene and they called it "the rich man's high."

It seemed to be the main attraction of the party. Some of the guests came out of the bedroom after an hour or so while others stayed and never came out. Still, other guests went back and forth. With all that traffic, I saw the way that the money was moving. They were sucking on that pipe like it had sugar in it. At $20 a pop, with people coming back repeatedly, I realized that drug dealing was a lucrative business.

The pipe had a hold on one particular lady. Once she went into the bedroom, she never came out. She had a bank roll, and kept giving him money until it was spent. It appeared to be the only function she had left. I knew the value of a pretty lady and watched how the pretty lady valued cocaine. I saw how her value went down while the value of cocaine went up. This made free-basing scary to me. Dope (heroin) was known as a poor man's high while free-basing was known as a rich man's high and I could see why.

It was a live party and we had a good time. Lucky and I left at about 2:00 a.m. and headed home. We shared the lines that we kicked to the older chicks and how some of them were digging it. They were telling us our rap was strong to be so young. A few of them said that they were going to marry us when we got older while we tried to convince them that we were ready now.

When I got in from the party, Pow Wow and Prescott were in the basement, so I went down there to tell them about the party. My brother had his gun on the table and I asked what happened. Pow Wow explained that all the boys from six nearby neighbor-hoods attended their high school. Some were rivals and some were allies and they fought all the time.

"You'll be attending that school next semester, so I want to hip you on who to look out for," Pow Wow explained. "Earlier today, our rivals, 83rd and 87th street, jumped on Prescott in school. They had caught him by himself."

I looked over at Prescott and he had a blood-shot red eye. He started telling me how he was beating down one dude when three more jumped in.

"I was handling all of them and they only got one good lick in."

Pow Wow interrupted him and said, "When I heard about it, the Manor and 93rd street crew stormed into the lunchroom and blazed everybody in there. We shut it down, fighting all the 83rd and 87th street crew for what happened to Prescott. We beat them with anything we could find."

My brother was only 15 when he was expelled from high school. Prescott and the rest of the big boys got kicked out as well. Now they all had plenty of time to be hustlers. Our allies, 93rd Street crew, was led by Keith Brown. They were nuts and would do anything when the Manor and 93rd Street crew got together. Keith Brown and his crew liked fighting – they enjoyed shooting more. When they saw their rivals from 83rd or 87th street, they would gun them down and I was a witness to that.

CHAPTER 3
The Westside Prodigy – Ice Kat

LATER THAT WEEK, I traveled to the Westside to tumble at the gym and visit Ice Kat. After tumbling practice, I walked over to Ice Kat's building since he and none of his crew were at the gym. That was kind of strange because usually there would be at least a few members of his crew there.

When I got to his block, I saw Ice Kat. He motioned me to come to the vestibule. No one else was outside. Normally there would be a lot of people hanging out. He was dressed in all black, sporting a jacket, zipped up, and the hood on his head, with a brown towel tucked in the neck part of the hoodie. There were about fifteen of his crew members standing in the vestibule.

"What was going on?" I asked.

"My crew member baby sister got molested and she pointed out the perpetrator. We beat him down, broke his legs and arms and threw him in a dumpster. One of the chiefs of the Vicky Lous came through with his crew and accused us of beating the molester down. He started talking crazy about what they were going to do to us, so I cracked him in his jaw. We all started fighting and we were smashing them. They upped a missile (pulled out a gun) and started shooting so we shot back. One of my crew members got hit in the leg and one of their crew members took one in the shoulder. So now we are at war, so be careful."

"I'm down with y'all. Whatever is going down I'm here," I said.

"That's cool, but we are gonna walk you to the El station (elevated train) before it gets too late," Ice Kat said.

As Ice Kat walked me to the El I asked, "You broke dude's legs?"

"Yeah, he's a rapist and I don't like rapist. If you got to take it, you a mark (looser)."

A few weeks later I went back to the Westside. Ice Kat and his crew were in the gym. "Are y'all still at war?" I asked.

"No, their chief called a peace treaty because he didn't know the true situation. Come to find out, dude raped a Vicky Lous member's little sister, so the Chief apologized to us. Everything's cool now."

"What happened to the dude?"

Ice Kat shook his head. "They found him under the stairs with his throat cut."

"That whole ordeal was jacked up. Two little girls got raped, y'all went to war, two people got shot, and dude got killed over committing a foul act. Ice Kat, that's nuts!"

"Everything has a chain reaction," he agreed.

I pondered then asked, "If you do something sick, you need help before something wicked happens to you. What kind of person would do that anyway?"

Ice Kat grabbed my shoulder and said, "A maniac."

From then on when I visited the Westside, I hung out more with Ice Kat and less with the tumblers. Ice Kat started working for a key hustler selling quarter bags. He told me that he made a five-dollar profit off each bag that he sold, and business was starting to pick up. I learned that drug dealing would get you paid. I knew that it was a sky rocketing business, easy money and Ice Kat would be on top in no time.

He gained control of one section of the projects, generating a bank roll, working hard, handling business and was still fun to be around. Ice Kat was analytical and calm, very soft spoken but fierce. He had a sense of loyalty, whether it was business or personal. If he had one dollar, I had fifty cents.

Ice Kat rode with me (ride or die) and when something went down, I could always count on him. He was a smart decision maker, very visual, able to understand a situation from observing, checking out the scene, knowing what was about to go down, and many times, able to avoid conflict. Ice Kat knew how to handle atrocities, able to hold his composure, and maintain his cool, keeping his emotions in check, while always being pleasant.

Personally I wasn't into selling drugs, but Ice Kat had just started his business and I had his back. On one occasion I went over there, and Ice Kat and four other crew members were outside with hoodies on and towels again. The towels were used to cover their faces so they wouldn't be identified. A crew member handed me a towel and I put it in my shirt and they gave me a .25 automatic. He told me that he had just gotten robbed by two known stick-up guys. They called one of them Lil Loco and the other one Dex. They were members of a crew called the War Lords.

Ice Kat told me that those two War Lords had stuck up their own members' drug house twice. Then the War Lords decided to give them a dope spot of their own. The dope spot was about a mile away, in the Vicky Lous territory, on the first floor of a Project building. We got word that Lil Loco and Dex were on their way to their new dope spot so we headed that way. As we approached the building, we heard rapid gunfire. Someone beat us to it! They got gunned down, right there, in front of the building.

Covering our faces with towels, we ran back to Ice Kat's building. Later, we found out that the War Lords set up Lil Loco and Dex, deceiving them into thinking that they were giving them a dope spot, luring them to that building, to keep them from sticking up other War Lord locations. Greed made them fall into the trap and both Lil Loco and Dex got killed by their own people.

I stayed over Ice Kat's house that weekend just to make sure that he was straight. I realized that the dope game had pitfalls too. You have to be alert and aware of your surroundings at all times, keep your circle tight and be careful who you trust. For those idiots, it most definitely was a bad idea to stick up people that they knew. That was the fastest way to create enemies. I learned that from the Africans.

That Sunday before I left, we congregated on the bleachers in Ice Kat's territory. Sometimes the neighborhood girls came and hung out with us. They flirted, telling us how cute we were, just meddling around. It was cool to kick it with them but then they started taking photos of themselves. A pretty, tall, slender girl named Towanda, got up on Ice Kat and took a photo of him. He grabbed her camera and took the film out, gave her five dollars and explained to her that he didn't take photos.

Towanda stepped up, looked him up and down, put her hands on her hips, as she jerked her neck and said, "I just wanted to take a picture of you because I told my girlfriend that you were a tall, chocolate, smooth-skin brother with muscles, and long hair that you wear in loose curls with waves. You got incredibly warm, brown eyes and a Hollywood smile, but gangsta. I described you perfectly, so I just wanted her to see for herself, how cute you are."

"Yeah, thank you for all of that but we are about to handle some business so y'all are gonna have to cut out," he said.

Ice Kat shortened their visit and two of his crew members escorted the girls away.

"Why did you take the film?" I asked.

"Having photos out there is the quickest way to get set up. Girls take photos of you, especially when you are wearing jewelry or showing off your money and then give them to your opposition. You can become a target. Not saying that's what Towanda was doing, but better safe than sorry. You can never be too careful," he explained.

From that day on, I was very selective of who I allowed to take photos of me.

"We aren't at war with anyone right now, but there are always renegades out here trying to come up (capitalize). So, in times of peace, I always prepare for war, just in case," Ice Kat reiterated.

"Yeah, Ice Kat, you have to have all angles covered, being aware of the police, stick-up men, shady customers, competitors, stool pigeons, traitors, haters and most of all, women."

As Ice Kat and his crew walked me to the El station, we discussed the pitfalls of hustling and how to stay under the radar. I said goodbye and told them I would see them in three weeks, after I graduated from the eighth grade. Ice Kat handed me half of his earnings.

"Buy yourself something slick for graduation."

I smiled, gave him a hug and dap (fist pounds) and said, "Good looking out, chief." With that, I got on the El and headed back to the Manor.

CHAPTER 4
The Sack Race – Kyle is a Champion

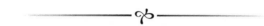

TWO WEEKS BEFORE my graduation, my family attended my mom's job's annual picnic where all the staff and their families were treated to a full day, festival style celebration. There was a pie eating contest in Pow Wow's age group. Since he was so greedy, he competed but didn't win. Fast eating Lenny, who won the previous year, took home the trophy and $50 cash prize. He was a bubbly, chubby white kid that hung around our table, grabbing snacks the whole day.

In my age group, there was a 3-legged sack race. Since I loved competing in sports, I decided to enter the contest for the $50 prize money and I was determined to win. The announcer told all pre-teen boys entering the race to line up. I hurried and secured a spot. Two assistants were choosing partners for us.

I immediately sized up my competitors and potential partner. There were two tall white dudes, a plump Hispanic boy, and a short Asian kid. There were also two Black guys and one of them was short, but strong looking. It appeared that I could win with any one of them, but they were all partnered off with other boys. The pickings got so slim that I was the last fellow standing in the line and there was only one more kid from the second group. I said, "Oh my God, shorty is just standing over there wheezing, sounding asthmatic with every breath."

I was in shock to realize that we were the only two kids left and that he would be my partner. He was a scrawny little white kid with pale skin and stringy black hair, wearing black bifocals that were attached to an eyeglass cord. He had a bit of an over bite, with a full mouth of braces, which gave him a lisp when he spoke. One of the assistants grabbed the little boy's hand and started walking him towards the right, in the opposite direction and I thought to myself, *'Thank God!'* Then suddenly the assistant made a quick turn to the left and said, "Here's your partner," and walked away fast.

I looked at the boy and said, "Hey, how are you doing?"

He said as he breathed heavily, "I'm Kyle."

I thought, *'Hold up, something's wrong with his breathing. How is he going to run?'*

"I'm Earthquake."

"Wow, what a cool name!"

Kyle put his leg in the sack while the officials lowered the bag so that they could tie our legs together.

"You don't wanna race, do you?" I asked.

"Yeah, I wanna race."

"You don't have to race if you don't want to."

"I wanna race. I wanna race like everybody else."

"Oh, ok. Well, you know that I'm gonna try to win."

"I wanna win too."

"Have you ever run a race before?"

"In school, I run pretty fast."

"You do?"

"Yeah, I run really fast. I run surprisingly fast. I'm serious."

"Now you are my partner and we're gonna win. Hold on to my belt and don't let go, ok?"

"I sure will."

"Look at me Kyle. We are gonna do whatever it takes to win."

I was looking at how frail he was and thought, *'Man, I gotta get a jump on our competitors because I know I might have to pull him.'* That was ok, because we were determined. I kept thinking, *'I need that $50.'* Second place was a gift certificate and a trophy. Third place was a ribbon and two apple pies. I thought, *'I only want that 50 bucks.'*

"Kyle, we are getting that money!"

We lined up at the start mark for the race. The referee raised the flag and I positioned myself to take off. "Hold on tight."

"I'm ready."

"Are you sure Kyle?"

"Yeah, I'm ready to rumble."

The referee called, "On your mark, get set, go!" Man, I leaped out there and told Kyle to hold on as he grabbed the side of my belt real tight. I was running at full speed. Kyle's body was jerking, his head went in all directions, like a bobblehead while he sighed with a sound, "eeerrrrrr". He fell in the grass, getting his pants stained, his arms flapping, and his glasses were dangling all over. I was running and I saw two teams passing us up. I was dragging him, and he was flopping around like a ragdoll. He felt like the scarecrow in the Wizard of Oz, boneless and raggedy.

First, I saw the black dudes passing us up, then the white boys. I thought, *'Man they're beating us.'* I was dragging Kyle, going for broke. I looked over at him as he dangled in the sack. He told me to keep going so I kept running at full speed. I could see two ladies out of my peripheral vision, running fast along the sideline. It was his mother and grandmother.

I saw the winners cross the finish line and the second team followed. Then I leaped up and we were flying in the air as we hit the ground. I rolled over him and he rolled over me, right over the finish line. He fell out of the sack but his leg was still tied to mine. Kyle's hair had dirt all in it and his clothes were covered in grass stains. He could hardly breath. His mother ran over and untied our legs. I stepped back so that his mother could get to him. She took his asthma pump, put it in his mouth. Two doctors came over and checked on him while the announcer shouted over the microphone, announcing third place. I thought to myself, *'Dag, we lost!'*

I walked over a few feet to see little Kyle. His mother looked up and mean mugged me. I asked if Kyle was ok but she turned her head without answering. I walked toward my mother, who was watching with a look of disgust and embarrassment.

When I got close to her, she asked, "Do you have to win everything?"

"Well, yeah!"

"Can't you lose sometimes?"

"Well, I don't know how to lose! How do you do that?"

"Earthquake, do you know that you dragged that boy in the dirt and the grass and had him flopping around like a wet noodle?"

"No, I didn't know that I did anything wrong. I thought that we were in sync. I felt him holding on to my belt and he didn't let go."

"You knew he couldn't win. Look at him."

"I didn't know he couldn't win. He told me that he could. Mama, I believed what he told me. He said he wanted to win."

"That was cruel the way that you dragged him. You did it on purpose. That boy knew that he couldn't win and you did too."

"When I wanna win, I believe that I can and I do. I was pulling him to victory so he couldn't hold me back. Why is everybody mad at me? If I hurt Kyle, it wasn't intentional. I did it on purpose because we had a purpose. We had planned to win, and a winner can see that! I gave him the benefit of the doubt and took his word. I saw his will and determination. I wasn't looking at his looks, I was looking at his outlook, which dictates a person's outcome. Is believing in someone wrong?"

"In some cases."

"Are you trying to make me think I was wrong for trying to win?"

"Everybody is not capable of winning."

"I would rather partner with a person not capable of winning, who wants to win than a person capable, who's not trying to win. If they're not trying to win, they should get out the way. Why doesn't anyone see that I was pulling Kyle to victory, not holding him back? Yes, I was the leading partner and if you're trying to win, then you have to endure the pain, struggle and consequences. Kyle was willing to sacrifice that. He has the heart of a champion. That's what makes a winner, mom. I got that from Kung Fu and Coach Byron said it too."

While my mom was lecturing me, Kyle ran over with his mother trotting behind him.

He stuck his chest out as the wheezing sound came from his screeching voice with strength and courage. "Earthquake, we won! This is the first time that somebody believed in me and gave me a chance."

He reminded me of a young, fearless lion. "Kyle, we lost."

"No, we won, we won 3rd place." Kyle pointed towards the platform.

"Look, they have our ribbons on the stage. Let's go and get them!"

I was thinking, *'Actually Kyle won.'* Since he felt that he won, then I guess I won too.

"Yeah Kyle, we did win!" I raised his hand over his head with pride.

Kyle said with his new-found confidence, "Next year we're gonna do it again. I'm gonna try everything now! I know I can do anything! I love to win!" Kyle grabbed my hand and pulled me to the stage as a few people patted him on the back and congratulated him.

I thought that Kyle was in my way but realized everybody who cared about him was in his way. At that young age, I understood that you have to be around people who make you stretch yourself. I knew then, no matter what anybody said, Kyle was a champion. We went on stage. He held me by my neck so tight while the photographer took photos of us with our ribbons and this was better than all the times that I won first place!

That day, Kyle became my little brother from another mother. I learned a lifelong lesson. When you limit people, you cut off their ability. Kyle's mother came over to thank me.

"Thank you. I've never seen Kyle this happy and proud before. You saw something in him that we didn't see and that made a world of difference. You're a good kid."

"You're welcome Ma'am."

"You've got a great kid," she said to my mother.

My mom shook her head and said, "Thank you, but you don't know the half of it."

"Earthquake, let's go to the bounce house," Kyle said.

"Ok, I'll be there in a minute," as he and his mom walked off.

"See mom, I told you, Kyle is a champion and he got in the sack race to win! I think you were right about your theory, but wrong about Kyle."

"Well, I guess I was."

"If someone gets in your sack but isn't planning to win, then they're holding you back and keeping you from achieving success.

You judged Kyle by his looks and not by the content of his character. I learned that in my black history class last year. Even his mom didn't believe in him. Maybe his mom needs to get out of his sack. Maybe she will now."

My mom looked over at me and said, "Boy, I don't know what I'm gonna do with you!"

This experience was a poignant time in my life and I learned a lot. In any relationship, the sack race can refer to parent and child, husband and wife, siblings, cousins, friends, etc. I can think of times when we get into their sack race, they strive to be victorious, and we stagnate them. We are not aware that our actions only benefit us and for our own selfish reasons, we hold them back. If not, get out of their sack! I decided I would always apply this code of conduct from that day on.

That was an extraordinary day. I wished it had never ended but at 7:00 p.m., my parents were ready to leave. Kyle and I had lots of fun. I introduced him to Pow Wow and he warmed up to Kyle as well. We both were crazy about little Kyle. I gave Kyle my number and took his, said my goodbyes and we parted ways.

CHAPTER 5
Graduation Time – Meeting J-Hawk

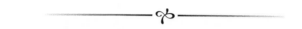

WHEN WE ARRIVED home, Pow Wow and I immediately left and headed to the park where my crew was hanging out. While in the field-house playing ping-pong, Smooth O mentioned that he was going to his father's boutique the next day to pick up a graduation suit and asked if I wanted to come. Of course, I was game (ready to go).

I met him at his house at noon the next day. We took two CTA (Chicago Transit Authority) buses to 75th Street and headed to the boutique. Smooth O said that he was going to ask his dad to give him a gold ring with diamonds as a gift so that he could flex (show off), since his father also designed and sold jewelry.

We walked into the spacious boutique with racks of the latest fashion for women and men. Everything was jazzy – it had all kinds of jewelry along with suits that could be tailored on the premises. Everything in the shop was boss (nice).

When we walked in, Smooth O's dad was dressed real sharp, in off-white from head to toe. He had on a baseball style cap with a suede bib and buckle on the back, a long sleeve, button down shirt, with pleated slacks and suede shoes.

Smooth O's dad was a slick looking older cat. He had a deep brown complexion with very distinguished features, slanted eyes with a strong nose, broad shoulders and a husky build. He told Smooth O to wait in the front of the store as he walked to the back. A minute later, he returned with a nice brown suit, trimmed in or-ange stitching with a square pattern design. He handed him the suit, telling him to try it on.

"Ok, dad. This is my homie, Earthquake. He is Pow Wow's lit-tle brother." Smooth O's dad stood there in a wide legged stance with his arms crossed, looking at me.

"This is my dad, J-Hawk."

I slowly walked over to shake his hand.

"Hey Mr. J-Hawk."

"Your name is Earthquake?"

"Yes sir, Mr. J-Hawk."

"Yeah, you look like an Earthquake, a cute li'l dude," he said half smiling. That was the only man I ever heard call another guy cute, and it didn't seem fruity, it sounded cool. He asked if I was buying a graduation suit and I told him no, I already had a suit. He asked me what kind of suit I had.

I described my attire as a double breasted, three-piece, peach colored suit, a white button-down shirt and Godfather hat, laced with a turquoise blue band and a striped tie, with matching peach colored Stacey Adams shoes. Mr. J-Hawk scowled, shaking his head, "You are gonna be sharp as a razor." He tickled me. He was so fly; the coolest adult that I ever met.

Smooth O walked over to the dressing rooms and tried on his suit. The pants were too long and Mr. J-Hawk called for his tailor, Matthew. He was an older guy with a tape measure around his neck and tailoring chalk in his hand. As Smooth O stood there, the tailor asked him to hold the pants at the waist, took some chalk and drew a line, a half inch from the ground. He took the pants off, gave them to Mathew who went in the back to make the alterations while we talked to Mr. J-Hawk. We were shooting the breeze, looking at clothes, for about two hours until the suit was ready.

Smooth O started telling his dad that I taught his two-year-old granddaughter, who was his oldest daughter Nene's child, how to count and say her ABC's. Mr. J-Hawk smiled. I told him that I loved babies and kids. I liked teaching them things. Smooth O said, "When he comes over, he plays with Tobbie for an hour and she always cries when he leaves."

"Dad, Earfy can flip off buildings too."

I told Mr. J-Hawk that I was sort of an athlete and loved to tumble. In a braggadocios voice, Mr. J-Hawk said, "I use to be an athlete also. I used to do fifty pushups. How many can you do?"

"Well, more than fifty. I can do over one hundred," I replied humbly.

He swelled with anticipation saying, "Let me see you do it now."

I jumped five feet in the air, landed in a Chinese pushup position and easily did one hundred of them. Mr. J-Hawk laughed hard and said, "Earthquake got inner strength. This li'l dude is bad."

I enjoyed talking to Mr. J-Hawk. Before Smooth O could ask, Mr. J-Hawk gave him a gold ring with a diamond in it along with his suit and we headed back home.

When I got home, I grabbed something to eat and then walked outside. The kids were playing in front of my house and they gave me a big greeting. I loved children and often performed tumbling shows for them.

In the morning on weekends, I taught them how to count and to say their ABC's. Something in me enjoyed teaching them, even though I didn't like school. I also showed them how to fight so they could protect themselves. I didn't know why I loved them so much, but they were fun to be around. Their parents always knew that they congregated at my house but my mom complained that there were too many little kids hanging around, making too much noise.

I had so many little friends and they all felt like family. Smooth O's eleven-year-old sister, Toya, would bring their niece Tobbie over to visit. We played hop scotch, four squares, red light – green light, and Simon says. We sang nursery rhymes and did patty cake routines. That was the youthful, untainted part of me.

I had friends of all ages, from babies to the big boys and truly enjoyed hanging around a variety of people. I macked (talking) to the girls all the time and it was my claim to fame. Even though I liked girls, had a strong rap, was a good kisser and loved touching and grinding on them, I wasn't frantic and didn't lust for them.

I was sexual but I wasn't over-sexed. Girls never let me grow into the excitement to thirst for them. It was thrown at me so much that it lessened my desire for it. It's like having one thousand of your favorite cookies. After a while, your craving for them will decrease but certainly not cease.

Money and macking came natural to me, so I spent the most time with my crew. We slowed down on hustling while we prepared for our eighth-grade graduation and practiced our stepping footwork for all the upcoming parties.

We all graduated! It was Babyface, Lucky, Moe, Reno, Smooth O, Ralph, Buck G and me. The ceremony was held in the huge auditorium at Chicago Vocational High School (CVS) on a warm summer day. As each of our names were called, we marched across the stage with the hardest pimp walk that we could do and I could hear screaming and yelling when we received our diplomas.

With all the mischief that we caused, we were reasonably well behaved in front of our parents, so we acted respectfully until that night. We each spent a few hours with our families, having dinner and then we all hooked up, except for Reno, who did his own thing. They got alcohol, marijuana and turned it up (partied). I didn't drink or smoke anymore because I decided it wasn't for me.

Buck G's mom allowed him to use her car. I don't know what he said to her but we all piled in and went downtown to the Ascott Hotel's graduation party. When we arrived, there were graduates and non-graduates from the North, South, East and West sides of Chicago in attendance. The music was bumping and the scene was jumping in the grand ballroom, filled with multiple chandeliers and a large dance floor that was packed with steppers.

My crew and I walked around, just checking out the scene and sizing everybody up. The whole crowd was sharp, and the graduates stood out with their graduation ribbons pinned on them. The girls were all dancing with each other and the guys were doing what they do, competing in groups, and displaying their footwork against each other. The party was cracking (fun) but everybody was clicked up with their own schools.

There were pretty girls all over the place and we were revved up to get chose (selected). Babyface was first to grab a pretty girl's hand and lead her to the dance floor. We each grabbed a girl single handedly putting our Jeffrey Manor style in effect.

As crowded as it was, you knew the Manor was in the house because you could feel our presence on the dance floor. Being well groomed, filled with confidence, never overly cocky, like fish in water. We were known for the special way that we jacked our slacks, popped our collars, and strutted around in sync with the music. Captivated with flare, we knew how to bop to cop (dance to get girls).

All the guys followed suit. After seeing us, they stopped comparing footwork and started pulling the girls from dancing with each other. Soon dudes from everywhere were dancing with girls from everywhere. Now the party was on "10".

After escorting the girls off the dance floor, we hit them with our verbal rap ability. Any subject that they brought up, we knew how to capitalize on it and that seemed to intrigue all of them. We could easily come off the top of our head with a play on words. For example: when a girl said something like, "It was nice meeting you," we would reply with something like: "Ain't no time better than the present and us meeting is just a gift, the special kind that money can't buy."

We also had perfect timing. Our style was to hit a girl with a line and then back off, letting her marinate on our conversation, while we walked around and socialized. We recognized that the further away the gift appeared, the more drawn to us she became because she wanted to get back to us, the "present."

We decided to compete, seeing how many phone numbers each of us could get. Seven was the magic number. With that in mind, I made my way toward the restrooms to freshen up, which led me into a big hallway area where a large crowd had formed. I was curious to know what was going on. They appeared to be watching someone, so I got closer and noticed that the guys were lining up, while someone was dancing in the center of the crowd. To my surprise, it was Ice Kat and his crew.

Ice Kat was teaching people how to do a stepping turn for a dollar and they were eagerly waiting. His crew members saw me and asked, "Earthquake, What's up?" Ice Kat looked up, stopped in the middle of a dance, trotted over, gave me a brotherly hug as his eyes shined, his mouth pulled back, exposing his white teeth with a vigorous grin.

"I didn't know that you would be here. Who are you with?" he asked. I told him that I was with my Manor crew and flagged them to come over so that I could introduce them.

After everyone met, I freshened up, Ice Kat finished selling turns for a dollar and we went back to the ballroom where we all mingled and danced. The song "Flashlight" by Parliament came on and everybody hit the floor, doing the latest dances. We kicked it off doing "The Bump" and you could see the Westside doing "The Feeling." Not to be outdone, the Northside started doing "The Spank" while everybody was shouting out their side of town. Our Southside crew partnered with Ice Kat's Westside crew and did "The Earl Flynn" and everybody joined in, one party, one dance. It was off the chart!

The DJ changed the tempo and played the steppers song, "Cooling Me Out" by the Isley Brothers and a girl walked straight over to Ice Kat and asked him to dance.

"Ice Kat getting chose," Babyface hollered.

Ice Kat popped his collar, winked and said, "This is how we do it."

Meanwhile a girl walked over to Babyface and handed him her phone number and Ice Kat hollered, "Babyface getting chose," and Babyface jacked his slacks, pointed at him and replied, "This is how we do it." We all started laughing, just enjoying the moment.

The music slowed down and the first jam played was "Love Ballad" by LTD. Before I could ask, a coffee colored cutie grabbed my hand and led me to the dance floor. The crew and I hadn't seen Moe for a while but there he was right next to us, tongue kissing a girl.

"Hey Moe, what's up?" I whispered.

"I'm getting married," he answered and started back kissing.

My dance partner held me tighter while she chuckled at what Moe said. After the dance, I cruised around checking on my homies and I slid over by Smooth O.

Smooth O was clever looking, flexed out (sharp) with his tailor-made suit and flashy ring. He was held up in a corner, talking to two slick looking chicks. I walked over.

"Smooth O, what's going on over here?"

All swagged out, holding both girls' hands with a gangsta snare, he said, "It's a sweet, sticky situation, ain't no shame in my game, double the pleasure, double the fun."

"Ok, strength come in numbers, that's what's up," I said, giving him a thumbs up.

Still making my rounds, while mingling with the girls, I unfolded a situation with Buck G and Ralph. I saw them talking to two girls who looked exactly alike, and asked, "What, y'all talking to a couple of Siamese twins?"

"Yeah man and they do everything exactly alike. They're amazing. When we ask one of them a question, they both respond at the same time, saying the same thing. Sometimes, when one says something, the other one finishes the sentence. Not only that, they're models," Ralph explained.

"How do you know that they're models?"

He measured their height according to his forehead as he saluted. He spoke as if he was selling a car off the showroom floor. "Because they're tall, sexy and look how they are sashaying around and wearing those dresses. They're beautiful."

"Yeah, they're tall and beautiful," I said.

Ralph, put his hand over his mouth and whispered, "They gotta be models because they ain't got no booty."

Buck G asked them to turnaround. They both turned around simultaneously, looking over their shoulders, and smiled.

"Yep, there's nothing back there. I don't see no lumps in those dresses, not a one lump, not two lumps. There ain't noooooo lumps back there!" I noticed.

"We are gonna give them some nicknames. I'm gonna call her Pancakes," Ralph said, "and Buck G said he was gonna call her, Brickhouse."

"I understand 'Pancakes' but what's with 'Brickhouse?'"

"Man, I'm gonna call her Brickhouse because her body measurements are 24-24-24."

I had to move around quick, because that was too funny. I didn't get too far when a girl with sandy brown hair and marble size eyes came over.

"My girlfriend noticed that you've been so occupied that you haven't had the chance to come back over to finish talking to her." I looked over at her girlfriend and said, "Oh yeah," as I grabbed her friend's arm and escorted her back to where she was. I remembered that her name was Kim.

"I saw you collect at least ten phone numbers. Why do you need so many?" she asked.

I stood back, casually folding my arms and spoke. "So, what are you telling me, I only need your number?"

"I don't know, maybe."

I told her I was going to give her three dollars so that she could call all the numbers and tell them that she's my new girlfriend. Kim laughed, gave me the googly eyes and said, "I don't need your three dollars, I got it."

Blushing as she batted her eyes, Kim said, "I'm going to let you celebrate your graduation since it's a special day."

I looked down, then slowly starring her in her eyes said, "There ain't no celebration that is more important than you. There ain't enough holidays in a year that could celebrate this moment that I'm having right now."

As she fought to keep her composure, she said, "You got a lot of game to be a little, eighth grader. I'm a sophomore, you know."

I smiled and quickly came back with, "Big things come in little packages; sometimes less is more so don't cheat yourself, treat yourself."

Making a wise crack, her voice simmered with sarcasm. "You mean little things come in big packages."

As I adjusted my tie I responded, "No baby. If I gave you a fifty-carat diamond ring in a little box, or a million-dollar check in a small envelope, those are big things in little packages, pretty girl."

I heard Buck G and Ralph calling my name as Lucky and Ice Kat walked up to me.

"Yo Earfy, we about to break out (leave)."

I told Kim that it was nice to meet her as I joined the fellas. She frantically ran behind me, put her hand on my shoulder and said, "Wait, you forgot to take my number," as she shoved it in my hand and unexpectedly kissed me for about fifteen seconds. "Please don't forget about me."

As I walked off, I answered, "Of course, I won't."

While heading to the parking lot, we chopped it up with Ice Kat and his crew. In the car as we headed home, we talked about how many phone numbers we each collected. Everybody got at least seven but Lucky had eight.

"Earfy, how many did you get? I know you got at least ten," Ralph yelled out.

"No, I didn't," I laughed.

"I got seven too," Moe hollered.

"I don't know how you got any Moe, you spent most of your time with that girl," Buck G commented.

I jumped in saying, "Moe is getting married." We all laughed.

"Nah man, she said she wasn't having sex until she got married so I told her that we were getting married. I took her behind the curtains and I almost got some. She let me finger her and everything. See, smell it," as Moe stuck his fingers under Lucky's nose.

Lucky took a whiff and frowned saying, "Dag Moe, it smells like booty."

Lucky and I were last to be dropped off. When I got to the house, I jumped right into bed, thinking about what strategy I'd use to keep up with my high school classes. I had the entire summer to come up with a plan.

Monday morning my parents went to work and I decided to clean my room. Pow Wow had already left the house, but I didn't know where he went. A few minutes later, I heard the door open and Pow Wow coming up the stairs. He had Erica with him. She was one of Prescott's girlfriends' sister.

Had I known she was with him, I would have jumped out of my window. That's a tactic that I used often when girls who I didn't want to see came to visit because Pow Wow would usually let them in. If I jumped, he knew that I wasn't that interested, then his goal would be to try and have sex with them. Any leftovers that I had, he was on it like a hungry dog on a bone.

Erica came in and sat on my bed as I continued cleaning up. She asked if she could help and I said, "yes." Erica was moving some light boxes from under my bed and opened one, when I briefly left the room to make a fist at my brother for letting her in. When I walked back in, she was reading my love letters.

She peeled her face from reading long enough to look up and asked, "You got all these love letters from all these girls?"

"Yes, I've been getting them since I was in the fourth grade."

"You got one from Renee and Brenda? These are recent, huh?"

"Yes, where is your love letter?"

"I never wrote one. You've got one hundred of them, why do you need one from me?" she asked glaring at me.

"Since you were nosey enough to look in my box, don't come back until you write me one."

She told me that she'd write one tomorrow and I suggested that she bring it on Friday.

"Do you go with them?" Erica asked.

I showed little emotion behind her comment.

"Yeah, some of them but what about you bringing me a love letter on Friday?"

As I escorted her down the stairs to the door, she paused and asked me for a kiss.

"You know my rules, bring me what I told you on that day and I'll see."

She sighed, half disappointed. "Ok."

I was thinking to myself, *'That'll give me a chance to talk to my other cuties.'* It was summer and I had a whole lot of macking to do. Erica didn't live in the Manor. She was from 93rd but some girls from different neighborhoods hung with the girls from the Manor because the girls in the Manor were fly. Erica was a pretty girl with coal black, curly hair, caramel colored skin and a slight case of acne.

The summer felt good, hanging out with my crew with no worries, we were just having fun. That Friday, Erica came back with her love letter and I didn't jump out of the window this time. I wanted to see what she wrote. She rang the doorbell, I let her in and led her to the basement. I asked about the letter again and she stuck out her arm with a white envelope fast, anticipating the results said, "Here Earthquake."

I asked her to read it to me.

"I think about you day and night but at night I wish upon a star, hoping that you like me too. There is nothing more that I want but you. I would love to be your lady..."

Etc....etc....blah, blah, blah.   I smiled and said, "That's nice." She asked if she could have a kiss now.

Caressing her behind the neck, we softly tongue kissed as I glided my hand down to her butt and she laid up against me while I slid my fingers between her legs. We sat on the couch and I reached for the button on her pants, pulling them down as she raised up for me to take them off. I stopped, looked at her and said, "I don't want you for just sex. Pull your pants back up! Do you know what I mean?"

"Yes, I do."

I wasn't really feeling that way about her because girls came a dime a dozen.

"Whatever you want, I'll try to give it to you," Erica went on to say.

I buttoned her pants up and told her, "That's nice to know."

"Are you going to that party tonight, because I'm going to be there?"

"Yeah, I'll be there so don't be giving your number out, you hear me?"

With a grin, she answered, "Ok."

"Let me walk you to the door, I'll talk to you later."

As she walked away, I left the house and jogged over to Lucky's.

It was mid-afternoon on that beautiful day. Lucky was standing outside with Reno shooting the breeze. We heard live music and walked a couple of townhouses down to Scony's place. He was a guy our age who had formed a band that sounded pretty good. Most of my little friends were out there running around listening to music and dancing.

Reno said the drummer was off beat and asked to let him demonstrate. Reluctantly, the drummer got up and handed him the drumsticks to prove that he could do better. Reno was very talented and drums was one of the many instruments that he could play. He switched to the lead guitar and got right on course with the melody. The song was riveting with rhythm and sounded really good. On the next song, Reno played "Rollercoaster" by the Ohio Players and they were jamming.

After a while things slowed down, Reno got tired and headed home to eat. I thought about the party Erica had mentioned and told Lucky, "Let's get ready." I said goodbye to my little friends who we had a blast with. We each went home, changed attire and headed out. We walked to the party which was about a mile away. Lucky asked me about a girl named Gina, who he was introduced to over the phone but had never met in person. She stayed a few doors down from the party. I confirmed that I knew her and described Gina as short, alright looking with a big booty.

"Hey Lucky, I got an idea, tell you what! I'll go in the party, get Gina and let her know that you're outside. I'll ask her if I can cover her eyes with my hands and y'all can meet with a kiss. When she opens her eyes, she will see you and melt."

"Yeah that's what's up," Lucky agreed and gave me a fist bump.

I instructed Lucky to hide behind a car while I went in to get her. Gina was thrilled when I put my hands over her eyes. Lucky walked up and they started kissing, hugging and caressing. They stopped, looked at each other and started back with more passion and intensity. He was sopping her up like a biscuit.

I heard an uproar, looked toward the party and saw a huge crowd. In the middle of Lucky's homerun kiss, I tapped him on the shoulder and said, "Look down the street Luck, what's that?" He stopped kissing and told Gina that he would see her at the party. We saw Babyface fighting off the Trumbull Park boys, so we ran towards the commotion.

Lucky took his jacket off and handed it to me. One of the Trumbull Park big boys was wrestling Babyface to the ground. Lucky forcefully pushed the big dude away from Babyface and Babyface took off, running inside the party, where the Manor crew was. Lucky and I were standing out there, about to explode when my crew came outside in a rage. I threw the jacket over the big boy's head and Lucky pounded him in the face, knocking him out cold and he hit the pavement hard.

The Trumbull Park big and little boys were fighting against the Manor crew little boys, causing a major brawl in front of the house party. There were so many of them because the party was close to their turf.

The brawl got serious when Ralph rushed one and fired (punched) on him. Moe was fighting two of them so I ran over to help. I swung at one guy and he dodged the punch, then he swung at me, but didn't connect. I side stepped, swiftly swinging at him, landing a punch right in the jaw. He faded back to regroup. Buck G came out of nowhere and cracked him on the side of his face, knocking him down.

Smooth O was also good with his dukes (fighting) and he was fighting a couple of their big boys. He rushed one and swept him off his feet, kicking his right leg out, in a sweeping rotation, while throwing a blow. Babyface was hysterical, swinging with a vengeance at any Trumbull boy within his reach. The Trumbull Park little boys started to run, while their big boys remained on the scene, fighting us. Lucky and I took off after the little dudes our age while everyone else was still brawling.

As punches were flying everywhere, their big boys were trying to maneuver and hit back, but we were getting the best of them. One of them got caught with a sharp blow to the chest and hit the concrete. A Manor big boy rode up on a 10-speed bike. He saw what was going on, jumped off his 10-speed and threw the bike, crashing it on top of their guy. As Lucky and I ran back from chasing the little boys, the crowd dispersed and their guy was laying there, with the bike on top of him, and he was not moving.

We heard police sirens and saw blue flashing lights speeding down the street, so we all took off running in different directions. Lucky and I ran to the townhouses and we each went home.

That night, when Pow Wow came in the house, he informed me that one of the Trumbull Park boys that we were fighting was stabbed and killed. Party guests, Trumbull Park boys and other witnesses congregated near the location of the party, where the police were conducting an investigation.

With a serious look on his face, Pow Wow explained, "There was a rumor that Smooth O and Babyface murdered the Trumbull Park guy tonight. Off the record, they also said that you and Lucky were involved, but they didn't mention y'alls' name to the police. I stayed out there, making sure of that."

"But I didn't see any blood on him."

"They said he had internal bleeding," Pow Wow replied.

The next day, the homicide detectives swarmed Babyface's house, bammed on the door, displayed a warrant and arrested him. At the same time, police drove down on Smooth O and went through a similar process. They were both in custody and taken to the Audie Home (Juvenile Detention Center). I was like, "Man, I don't even know why we were fighting."

We got the wire (gossip) on what happened when our crew met at the park that afternoon. The Trumbull Park boys said that Babyface had a knife because he believed that they were going to jump him but they claimed that they were only trying to take the knife. When Lucky and I ran on the scene, the knife was on the ground and a Trumbull Park boy picked it up.

Our questions were, why were the Trumbull Park boys still wrestling Babyface down when he no longer had the knife? Babyface was a gangsta but I knew he wasn't a bully. He didn't start trouble and didn't run from trouble. So, why were Smooth O and Babyface locked up? I was wondering who could've had a knife, Smooth O? Could the Trumbull Park boys have some internal strife amongst themselves and took that opportunity to settle it?

CHAPTER 6
Money, Macking and Murder

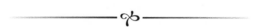

WHILE IN THE park, we settled down, trying to deal with the situation but soon fell back into the swing of things. Even though I was still thinking about my homies, all the girls out there made it a little easier to cope with. One of my girls, Cutie T, was breezing through with her girlfriend. Pow Wow and his crew were chilling, macking (talking) to the girls and playing basketball. Lucky and I went to talk to Cutie T and her friend.

While sitting on the benches, we heard someone do a short flirtation whistle, the kind aimed at an attractive girl. We all looked and saw Creature Feature, one of the big boys from my brother's crew. He had a unique look with coco colored skin, fine, short, curly, dark-brown hair and keen facial features.

Creature Feature headed toward us all swagged out (arrogant), sporting a pair of blue Adidas jogging pants with no shirt, glistening with sweat from the basketball court. As he walked, he lifted his arms, curling them in a body builder's pose, revealing his well-defined biceps. He stuck his chest out, making it expand and jump rapidly, flexing his muscles and exposing his perfectly chiseled body.

The girls secretly looked but could hardly keep their composure. They were gasping for air and mumbling as he walked past, even though Creature Feature never even looked our way. I had to admit, that was a slick move. I thought about it and realized that I had to sharpen my game. Chicks liked muscles, so I might start working out.

The girls appeared to be hot and thirsty, so they ran to the store for cold drinks while Lucky and I stayed in the park, girl watching. I spotted Pow Wow talking to this fabulous looking girl, so I walked toward them. Then I realized that it was Cindy, the sexy little chick that I had been talking to. She walked off and I caught up to Pow Wow, telling him that she was one of my girls.

"No, it's not. She doesn't even know you."

I informed him that she lived down the block and we could go and ask her.

Pow Wow, Lucky and I proceeded down the block where she was sitting on her porch looking like a beauty pageant contestant. When she saw us, she trotted down the steps. Pow Wow stepped to her first while Lucky and I lingered a few feet behind. She walked past Pow Wow and came straight to me. I told her to tell Pow Wow that she was my girlfriend.

"I didn't know that we were dating."

"We are now, so go tell him."

She gave me a warm smile and slowly approached him. "This is my boyfriend and I can't be talking to you."

With a little chuckle and slight grin on his face, Pow Wow said, "That's cool," as he walked back to the park while I finished my conversation with sexy Cindy.

Cutie T had returned from the store and asked Pow Wow where I was. He escorted her a half block and pointed me out, saying, "There he is right there, with the blue shirt on and Lucky is with him, in the Red All-stars gym shoes. He is talking to his girlfriend right now."

When I walked back to the park, I was unaware that Cutie T returned from the store with the cold drinks, talked to Pow Wow and then left. It was a good thing because my girl Adrian had just walked up and greeted me, so we talked for a while. Before I left, told her to call me later.

Lucky and I took off toward the townhouses heading home. I freshened up and kicked back, watching television knowing that Adrian would be calling soon. Pow Wow and some of his crew came in and went straight to the basement. Shortly after, he called me to come downstairs. When I hit the bottom step, I saw Prescott, Bennie, Tony, Creature Feature, Maceo and Mike D.

The big boys started questioning me about how I got the older girls to like me so much.

In an inquisitive tone Prescott said, "We just don't get it, you're so young and little."

I laughed. Bennie followed up with, "Seriously, we really want to know." I looked as confused as them and told them that I didn't know and went back upstairs and made myself a hamburger.

Through the basement door, right off the kitchen cooking area, I could hear them discussing setting someone up. Tony was telling Pow Wow their plan to rob an older guy in his twenties, rumored to have a lot of money. Tony had cut into (chatted with) the older guy a few times. He was scheduled to visit a chick who lived in the Manor. Tony would stop the guy to chop it up (chat) while Bennie would approach them and pull off a simple robbery.

Creature Feature came upstairs while I was eating my hamburger and revealed that he had something to tell me. Reluctantly, he paused and then said, "That's ok, you might tell." I promised that I wouldn't talk about whatever he told me, and he agreed saying it was about my girl Adrian.

"As you know, I have a backyard full of marijuana plants. I was on my porch after cutting leaves when Adrian walked by. I asked if she wanted to smoke some weed with me. At first, she said no thank you but after the third time I asked her, she gave in and said she would smoke one joint. I invited her into my house and took her to my bedroom where we smoked a joint and listened to Teddy Pendergrass. Before I knew it, we had smoked three joints, so I turned on my strobe light and she was so high, laughing and closing her eyes as she shared that the light was making her dizzy. I suggested that she could lay back on my bed and I turned the light off.

She still had on that pretty little skirt from earlier today, so I rubbed her thighs and heard her moan a little. Then I lay on top of her and we kissed. I took off her panties and we had sex. She made me promise not to tell you, but you are my little homie so I'm telling you."

Not asking any questions, I said, "Thanks big homie," and continued to eat my burger.

Creature Feature went back downstairs. I was thinking, 'Dag, that little slut.' I guess he was too big and strong to resist. My phone rang and it was Adrian, asking me to come over and I told her in 15 minutes, I'd be there. Pow Wow's crew was leaving but he and Prescott chilled in the basement.

I headed to Adrian's house. She and her grandma lived there. Her grandma had bad eyesight. She thought that I was a girl because of my long hair and smooth features. She invited me in and walked me to Adrian's bedroom and asked if I was spending the night. I told her maybe if I got too sleepy.

I sat there observing Adrian's behavior for an hour thinking, 'Wow, I've never seen anyone pretend so well.' She was such a good actor, what a flawless performance. If I didn't know the truth, I most certainly would have been fooled. I asked her what she did after leaving me at the park and she skipped the whole experience with Creature Feature, as if it never happened.

Finally, I told her that we were through. She was not the girl for me. She hit me with another stellar performance, crying, begging and asking why. I didn't tell her because I made a promise and I didn't want to go back on my word. I hated what happened but there was no way I could talk to her after what Creature Feature told me. Besides, there were so many other girls to choose from.

I left her house and walked back to the park and the few people out there appeared to be watchful. There were a handful of crew members and even they were cautious. Then I saw Moe laying back behind a set of trees. I asked him what was going on. He had a sad look on his face.

"They locked up seven or eight people tonight. Tony got shot in the head and he's dead."

In shock, I expressed that Tony was over my house earlier. Moe told me that it was a robbery gone bad. I asked Moe if he knew who got locked up and he shook his head no.

Detective cars slowly rolled through, so we ducked and took off running behind the trees. I ran back to the house at top speed to see if Pow Wow and Prescott were still there. When I made it home, I went straight to the basement. Pow Wow was downstairs, so I woke him up and asked where Prescott was.

"Upstairs why?"

"Hold on, one minute. I'm about to wake up Prescott."

He was sleep in Pow Wow's bedroom. I woke him up and told him to come downstairs. We went quietly so that we didn't disturb my parents, who were sleeping in the next room.

I shared the details that I knew about the robbery. I took a deep breath and spoke.

"There ain't no easy way to say this – Tony is dead! The robbery went badly."

Pow Wow took it hard and Prescott was devastated as well. They both looked grief stricken. After grieving for a while, I told them the details of what happened.

The stick-up was going as planned. Tony was talking to the older guy when Bennie walked up and told them that this was a stick-up, commanding them to put their hands up. Tony didn't raise his hands high, so in his quest to make the robbery appear real, Bennie pointed the gun directly at Tony's head. He repeated, "Put your hands up." Tony said, "Man get the gun out of my face, I'm gonna put my hands up but don't point the gun at my head," as he pushed the gun away from his face. At that moment, the gun accidentally went off, shooting Tony in the head. They all stood there as the blood splattered on everyone and then they took off running.

He blew Tony's brains out. We sat there in silence for about five minutes. I never wanted to experience anything like this. I thought about what Pow Wow and Prescott taught me. A gun can be devastating in the wrong hands. You can't let a simple robbery become a huge problem that can't be fixed. It really enforced my thinking on that.

Prescott started up the discussion again. "That's the kind of stuff that I worry about. Things like this happening. These types of mistakes are too sad."

Pow Wow came out of his silence and expressed, "Man, my boy is gone! I can't believe this happened. Man, he should never have pointed the gun at Tony's head. I would have done the same thing that Tony did, trying to push that gun out of my face, but you can't take it back now. Now we have to deal with it."

Bennie was picked up by the homicide squad the next day. Ralph was very sad about Tony's death and to make it worse, his brother was accused of accidentally shooting him. We all were broken up about it. Two big boy crew members gone at one time, one facing life in jail and the other one accidentally killed by him.

We all attended Tony's funeral and it was really sad. My crew and I said our goodbyes in our own way. After leaving the funeral, I went home and relaxed realizing that this had become a way of life for us. Seeing what was happening as I was living through it opened my eyes. We had to understand our consequences and be prepared to deal with them no matter what they were. Moving forward, we gave our undivided attention trying to ensure that whatever we did, there would be no casualties.

I turned on some music, still reflecting and vibing on Marvin Gaye's song, "What's Going On" when my brother walked in with some of his crew; Creature Feature, Maceo, Mike D and Dirk. I chopped it up (talked) with them for a minute.

"Where is that fine girl of yours, Adrian?" Creature Feature asked.

I told him that I didn't know, I quit talking to her. He looked surprised.

"Why? She's a fine, pretty little thing."

"Because you told me that you had sex with her."

"When?"

"You told me that a couple of weeks ago."

He busted out laughing. "I was just kidding. You didn't believe me, did you? Man, she wouldn't even talk to me. I was just testing your game li'l homie."

I shook my head as I was leaving the basement and Maceo shouted, "Man, you know you can't believe anything he says. He nuts!"

The big boys were always testing us when it came to fighting and girls, but this lesson was the most valuable. It would stick with me for sure. I knew right then, believe none of what you hear and only half of what you see from now on out.

Angel Dust

I went back upstairs. Creature Feature trotted behind me sincerely expressing, "Earthquake, I was high when I told you that. Hey, check this out. I have some weed from my home-grown plants. It's the best! I laced it with some angel dust and it had me tripping. That's why I forgot to tell you that I was kidding. Here are five joints for you li'l homie."

I remembered when I got high off angel dust and experienced everything in slow motion, so I told him give it to me. Even though I didn't get high anymore, I thought that others might enjoy it. Creature Feature pointed at me with a serious look.

"Only hit it twice, that's all you need," he warned.

"Ok, I'll keep that in mind." In the meantime, it was too late to think about Adrian but maybe someday I'd make it up to her.

My phone rang and it was a collect call from my dad so I accepted it. My dad was a hustler who was in and out of the penitentiary his whole life. He was so smooth and had swagger. When he got out, we would see him and kick it. Each time we were used to him being around, he'd be arrested and back in jail again.

I understood why my mother didn't talk about my father much because she focused on my step-father, Phillip. My dad and his wife would come and get my brother and me on occasions. I loved my dad and I understood his lifestyle early on. Sometimes my Big Mama (my dad's mom) and grandfather would pick us up and take us to visit with their side of the family. They had nine kids. We all gathered at my grandparents which we called Big Mama's house.

It was fun being with my aunts and uncles. Uncle Billy would always give us money when he stopped by and that was cool. My three aunts and uncles all lived in Big Mama's house. My father was the oldest. He, uncle Billy and Columbus lived elsewhere.

Most of my aunts and uncles had kids so there were many cousins to play with. As I got older, I didn't visit as much but I had great memories of all of them. Talking with my dad over the phone was nice and I looked forward to his calls. It was cool that my parents allowed him to periodically call collect and we talked about twenty minutes each time.

After speaking with him, I got ready to go and visit my grandma (my mom's mother) for a few days. I missed living in the same house with them so I visited frequently, catching the bus and a train to get there. They still lived on 55th street in a two-flat building that my Aunt Vivian owned. I always went upstairs first to hang out with my grandma and Aunt Tea. Grandma was in the kitchen preparing to cook. I asked if she would make my favorite dish, chicken and dumplings.

Aunt Tea was in the dining room watching a television program called "The Three Stooges." It was our favorite program to watch together. We would imitate the three main characters, being humorous and doing minor, silly pranks like pretending to poke each other's eyes out and making funny hand gestures that made us laugh. Even with Down's Syndrome, Aunt Tea was adorable. Every time there was a visitor, she would speak and give them a warm loving hug. I never saw my Aunt Tea sad, or in a bad mood. Her smile and affectionate ways always brightened my day. She always made me laugh and it was refreshing to be around her.

After dinner, I went downstairs to visit with my cousins. Aunt Vivian was headed out, which was perfect because I told my cousins about the treat that I had for them. I knew the older two, Cup and Chevy smoked marijuana. I told them that I had five joints and they each wanted one.

"Slow down, you all can smoke off one joint. It has angel dust in it and will get y'all high."

"So what, we know what angel dust is. We can handle it," Chevy spoke. They lit the joint and I reminded them to only take one pull (breathing in smoke one time). Shady was only nine so she just watched.

Chevy took a few pulls and I stopped her saying, "That's enough, stop trying to hit it multiple times." I finally took the joint from her and passed it to Cup, who followed directions and only took two pulls, like I told her to.

Chevy started talking in slow motion and said, "I can't feel my legs."

Chevy stood in the middle of the floor for at least five minutes with her mouth hanging open. Cup sat down and said, "I'm higher than a kite. It feels like I'm floating in this chair, wow!" We looked at Chevy, she busted out in an Indian Rain Dance and then stopped and started acting like she was Chinese, babbling as if she was speaking their language. Then she got on the floor and started acting like a baby, throwing a temper tantrum, saying she wanted her bottle. She started crying, so I picked her up off the floor and laid her on the couch. I asked, "Shady do you still have those baby bottles I gave y'all?" "Yeah we do." As she ran to get one.

This was weird, so I called Ice Kat and the phone rang about nine times before he answered. After he said hello, I frantically said, "Ice Kat I have a situation. I gave my cousin weed laced with angel dust and she's acting like she's a baby. What you know about angel dust?"

"A little. Angel dust and Sherm stick are two new drugs. They dip the leaves in "PCP" (hallucinogenic drug) that has you tripping. I heard about a dude who jumped out of the fourth-floor window, thinking that he could fly. Some people who take the drug become strong and violent so keep her away from windows and give her some warm milk. That should bring down her high faster. I don't deal with those two drugs because they're too dangerous. Sometimes it's funny to watch them tripping but other times it can be fatal."

"Ok Ice Kat, I'll call you later."

I asked Shady to warm some milk for the bottle and give it to me. She ran and did it. Chevy was kicking and screaming, yelling, "I want my bottle! whaaaaa, whaaaaaaaaaaa." Shady hurried back with the warm bottle and handed it to me. I held it up to Chevy's mouth and she sucked it, just like a baby. I was praying, '*I hope this wears off before Aunt Vivian returns.*' She cried for four hours, requesting multiple food items. I was exhausted trying to fulfill all her needs.

Cup sat quietly in the same chair, without moving a muscle, just looking down at her arm. She sobered up first, then Chevy. I thought, '*How in the world did Creature Feature smoke this?*' I knew that I would never give anybody angel dust, ever again. Cup finally spoke, "That was some crazy stuff. I had to stop myself from biting my hand off because it kind of looked like a piece of chicken."

"I thought that I was a one-year old baby. That angel dust had me hallucinating. I don't want to smoke weed or angel dust ever again," Chevy said.

I didn't tell them that was a frightening experience. After seeing that things were ok, I went back upstairs, flopped on the bed and fell off to sleep.

That afternoon, I went downstairs to see my cousins and they were fine I thought back.

Ice Kat mentioned that most people who take the drug believe only weak people get hooked and that their mind is too strong to get addicted. To me, anything that takes you out of your right state of mind cannot be good. If it alters your performance and controls your thinking, I never want that. I'd rather be in control. It was clear to me what they mean when they said, "A mind is a terrible thing to waste!"

I spent another day with my cousin and then headed back home. It was almost the end of the summer. The murder charges were dropped against Smooth O and Babyface and they were released from the Juvenile Detention Center. The whole crew was around and everything was back to normal.

Often on weekends, the crew would purchase weed and alcohol and consume it in the park. Since I didn't participate, I laughed at them when they were high. Being high always made them hungry. On one such occasion, we walked to the pizza parlor a few blocks away. Lucky and Babyface ordered an extra-large pizza and it was smelling good. We stood outside talking and pitching pennies, a side walk game that we played for money while they prepared the order.

The cashier called out, "Extra-large pizza."

"I got it," I said, as he handed me the hot box, since they prepaid. I walked outside while they were still pitching pennies. I discreetly started walking toward my house and gained a little distance before they noticed me. Then, I took off running. Lucky and Babyface realized that I stole their pizza so they tried to catch me but I had too big of a lead.

I ran into my house and locked the door. Pow Wow was on the phone, in the kitchen.

"Whose pizza?" he asked.

"I took it from Babyface and Lucky," I answered, catching my breath.

We were both eating when they knocked on the kitchen door. I peeped out the small window on the door, eating a slice, snickering. They looked like two hungry buzzards. I went back to the table and continued to eat.

They kept knocking so Pow Wow looked out the window.

"What do y'all want?" he asked as he took a bite of the slice in his hand.

"Earfy took our pizza," Babyface answered.

"Get out of here, there's no more pizza," Pow Wow said. We busted out laughing and they finally left.

We did pranks on each other all the time, but this was the best one. Pow Wow and I ate well that night. My crew and I hooked up the next afternoon. There were no hard feelings, but they warned me that I would get mine someday. A week passed, and my mom had just cooked the family dinner; a big plate of chicken, creamy mashed potatoes and mixed vegetables. She went upstairs, waiting for my step-father to arrive.

I was famished, about to have dinner when Lucky rang the doorbell. I told him I would eat quickly so we would go up to the park afterwards. I went to wash my hands, came back to the kitchen and Lucky was gone. I looked out of the window. I saw Lucky running with our whole plate of chicken.

I was thinking, '*He ain't that crazy. That's my family's food and no one had eaten. Now Phillip won't have any meat.*' I knew I wouldn't be able to catch Lucky since he got a big head start. I could understand if it was my dinner plate that he took but it was my families'.

I waited a few minutes hoping that Lucky would return. He didn't so I called Babyface. He answered, saying, "hello," smacking his lips as if he was eating something. I asked, "Is Lucky there?"

"Yeah, he just brought some good chicken over here."

"That's my families' chicken, don't eat it. Tell him to bring it back!"

"I didn't know that but it's all gone now. We ate that chicken up," he responded, sounding chipper.

I hung up.

Phillip came in from work. I hoped he had eaten before he arrived home because there was no chicken. I went in the basement waiting to face the consequence. My mom entered the kitchen to prepare his plate. I heard her scream, "Earthquake. Where is the chicken?" I walked upstairs, and Phillip was sitting there with a plate full of vegetables. They looked at me, waiting for an explanation.

With a grim look on my face, I said, "Lucky took it." My mom was bursting with fury, picked up an oversized wooden broom and hit me more than a dozen times across my arms, while I attempted to block my head, until the broom handle finally broke. "If you don't get out of here right now, I'm going to break your neck," she huffed and puffed.

Phillip just snarled and shook his head saying, "I'm hungry."

I decided to leave for a few hours until they calmed down. Before leaving, I peeped in the kitchen and saw Phillip eating his plate of vegetables and potatoes. No more food pranks for me for sure!

School was about to begin, and I had no angle (plan) so I played it by ear. Most of the main crew attended different high schools. That was cool because I still went to school with the Manor boys and we were all solid, as one. The other neighborhoods quickly recognized me and so far, there was no trouble.

My high school was in the South Chicago neighborhood and that was a huge crew that nobody seemed to get into it with. One of the main guys from their crew used to go skating in the Manor and we became friends. He introduced me to his crew and his little brother. All the younger crew from each neighborhood liked me too and that set a different tone. I had created new alliances. Now, fighting was not a problem, but school work was. The girls took to me also, but we switched classes a lot and I couldn't gain favor with the teachers because I had eight different teachers. This was a struggle, but I made up my mind to try and make this school thing work and at least finish high school. Thinking, 'If I could, then I can go to college and be a doctor. Yeah, I could see that. Well, here goes everything.'

We had a half day and school ended at noon, so I headed to the house. My step-father was there playing a Johnny Guitar Watson album. It seemed kind of odd that he was home in the middle of the day, but I paid it no mind.

I went to the kitchen to make myself a cheeseburger. I ate then headed out. Since my mom and I planned to go running at a new track today, I would head home by 5:30 pm. She told me about this huge new track where she had started jogging and I was looking forward to trying it out. I wanted to see how fast I could get around it.

I arrived home right before my mom. I was already prepared. She came in and said that she was going to change clothes so that we could head out. She went on to say that she had to be back so that she could prepare dinner before my step-father got home. As she opened the front door, I mentioned that Phillip had been home earlier, and my mom asked, "What time?"

I had a half day in school, so it was about 12:30 p.m. when I got there. She said, "Oh, ok, let's go," but then she stopped in the doorway. She turned around and walked over to his closet and slowly opened the left side, I opened the right side. Then she went into his bathroom and opened the medicine cabinet and closed it.

My mom looked at me, walked to the kitchen table and took a seat. I pulled out a chair and sat with her. She looked at me with disbelief and said, "Phillip left, he's gone." My mom was just sitting there in a daze. I was thinking to myself, *I wonder why he left?* I only heard them argue twice in all the years that they'd been together and that was a long time ago. She seemed to be good to him. I never saw my mom give him any trouble.

Perhaps he left because of me. Maybe he got fed up with us and was tired of me and my brother. I thought back to the things we did.

Like the time when they had to pick me up. We were friends with three sisters who were around my age. They had a father who worked long hours at night; until 5:00 a.m. Sometimes we socialized at their house, eating, drinking alcohol and listening to music.

One night, Lucky, Ralph, Babyface, Smooth O, the sisters and two of their girlfriends and me had a contest to see who could drink the most. I out drank everyone, taking 29 shots of Crown Royal before I passed out. Everybody got drunk but Lucky and I were so drunk, they couldn't even wake us up.

The sisters got so scared that they called my parents to come and pick me up before their father made it home. First, they tried shaking, slapping and pouring water on me. My crew even threw me outside in the snow, but nothing worked. They tried everything!

When my mom got there, she called my name once shouting, "Earthquake, get up right now," and I stood straight up at attention. They were amazed since it turns out that all it took to get me up was mom's voice. Lucky and I stumbled to the car and my parents drove us home. My step-father walked Lucky across the grass to his house. It was hard for me to make it upstairs, to my bed. Everything was spinning and I felt awful.

That morning, my step-father woke me up to go outside and shovel the snow from the front and back yards of our house while I was still drunk. Then they demanded that I go grocery shopping with them and forced me to walk around the store. We loaded the groceries in the trunk of the car and then my step-father handed me two shopping bags full of canned goods and meat and told me to walk home.

We lived over a mile away, it was ten degrees outside and I still had a hangover. I said to myself, "I'm never going to drink again." After that, we attended basement sets (parties). I didn't drink or smoke weed. I was finished with all that, so I watched the crew get high. When they offered alcohol or weed, I'd say, "Nope, I got a natural high just watching you all." I just wished that Phillip knew that I didn't drink or smoke weed anymore.

Next, I thought about the situation when Todd had a set in his basement. He lived in the townhouses a few yards away, so my crew and I attended. Everybody was having a good time steppin' and macking to the girls. We went outside to get some fresh air and saw Todd's uncle standing in the doorway, pushing my crew member Moe out the door. His uncle was irate about something.

We all went over to stop him but as we approached, he took a swing at Lucky. Lucky faded back and punched him. Babyface ducked and grabbed his legs. They both tackled him while Smooth O put Todd's uncle in a headlock as Todd screamed out, "Earthquake, don't let them hurt my uncle." Lucky swiftly kicked him in his butt with the side of his shoe, about ten times in a row.

I was asking his uncle if he was calm. "You have to calm down."

"Yeah, I'm calm," he replied.

I told Babyface and Smooth O to let him get up. I warned his uncle to stay cool.

"We don't want to hurt you."

"I'm cool. I used to do this all day long in the penitentiary. Whatever you shorties want to do, I'm with it." I advised him to go back in the house.

Suddenly we heard police sirens and saw the lights so we all took off running. I ran home and took my key out to unlock the front door and I heard a click. Someone locked the top lock, which was a dead bolt. I ran to Lucky's house and he let me in. I went back several times, ringing my doorbell but no one answered even though I knew that my parents were home.

I wound up spending the night at Smooth O's house. The next day, I saw Pow Wow outside and asked if he'd been home and he said, "Yeah, I just left."

"The door has been locked all night and no one answered," I said, with a puzzled look on my face

"I know, Phillip locked you out and told mama not to open the door for you for a couple of days."

I asked him why and he said that my step-father saw us fighting Todd's uncle. "He was looking out the window and saw the whole thing. When the police came, you tried to run in the house and he locked you out right then. You are not allowed to come home until tomorrow."

I told him that was cool with me. I spent the night at Ralph's house. I went home the next day, took a shower and stayed in the basement. My step-father didn't speak to me for a week. I hadn't seen him that upset since we lived on 63rd Street, when I used the word "cock" strong. He thought that I was being funny, but I simply didn't realize that it was an inappropriate word to use. I wished I could take it all back.

Maybe it was a combination of things that Pow Wow did also. Pow Wow used to sneak and wear my step-father's suit jackets. On top of that, Pow Wow stole his credit cards and purchased himself some clothing. One time the police detectives busted into our house, looking for my brother and my step-father woke up with a gun and flashlight in his face as they questioned him about Pow Wow. He was only wearing boxer shorts.

To make matters worse, when my step-father tried to discipline my brother he tussled with Phillip and threw him on the bed. My mom rushed into the room and punched Pow Wow in the face about 50 times and he ran out the house. Then mom called the police on him. Maybe that could have done it.

I wished I could have done something about this. If there was a clue that he might leave, that may have sparked me to change my behavior. I needed to pay more attention to my surroundings, watching everybody's behavior closer. It would have been good to learn this earlier.

In a compassionate way, looking over at my mom, I could see the sadness in her eyes as she sat there for about ten minutes then started to cry. Out of all the things that happened in our lives, this was the first and only time I ever saw my mom cry. I kind of felt sad too. At this point, she was a single parent again. During that time, I noticed that my mom had become quiet, not as talkative. I think that she was trying to digest what happened, but she kept it moving. Everything was about to be different with no step-father.

Pow Wow walked in and asked what was going on. I told him that Phillip left.

"Man, ma, why did Phillip leave? You were good to him. He could stay out all night and do whatever he wanted to do. He shouldn't have left you, ma. You are a good woman, ma. That's ok. I'm going to get a job and help out around here."

My mom, looked over at him with a soft smile and called him by his first name saying, "Thanks Ramell, we'll be alright."

"Ma, what's for dinner?" Pow Wow asked.

CHAPTER 7

Creature Feature

ON THE WEEKEND, I got a chance to see my crew. Since it was still warm outside, we headed to the park. On our way, we saw an ambulance and several detective and police cars. More than a dozen police were trying to pull a guy off someone. I spotted Pow Wow, Prescott and their crew in the crowd, trying to see what was going on.

We got closer and saw the cops pulling Creature Feature off a guy, so we threw bricks at the police cars to divert their attention. The police chased us and we ran and hid behind cars and trees. To my surprise, Creature Feature was in a rage, beating his dad. His father had just done the unforgiveable. He brutally stabbed Creature Feature's beautiful mother twenty-five times and killed her.

The homicide detectives processed Creature Feature's house as a crime scene and the detectives drove him and his sister to the police station to get detailed information. We found out that Creature Feature went into their house.

His parents were in their basement. His father had been drinking alcohol and was arguing with his mom, accusing her of not caring for him anymore and planning to leave. Trying to avoid the argument, she told him that she wasn't leaving, she just wanted to go upstairs. In a jealous rage he shouted, "If I can't have you, nobody will."

Creature Feature heard his mother's screams and desperately tried to break down the basement door which his father had barricaded. His sister and some neighbors had already called the police. By the time he broke down the door, his mother was mortally wounded. Creature Feature went crazy on his father, beating him mercilessly until the police arrived.

Creature Feature was released to his grandmother's custody, but he still spent most of his time in the Manor. Pow Wow and his crew cuffed (looked after) him. He had plenty of places to stay as a welcomed guest in any of our homes. He even stayed several nights with us, sleeping in our basement.

I really didn't know how to approach him about his mom, even though he seemed to be the same suave but humorous person that he was before it happened. I told him that I was sorry to hear about his mom and he gave me a slight grin and replied, "It's cool, li'l homie, she's up in heaven with God now." Pow Wow really loved Creature Feature like a brother and he was one of his main guys. The girls were crazy about him as well. There was never too much love for one of ours, he was a Manor boy.

My mom had a hard struggle trying to hold it down with two teenage boys while I was having a hard time in school. I was trying this school thing, still hustling but staying focused on my grades, attempting to do it myself. Prescott and my brother were doing what they do, robbing car washes, fruit markets and breaking into houses – the regular.

Mom Gets Fired

My mom got another shocking blow. She got fired from her job after 15 years and didn't know what was next. Within the next two weeks, she had two jobs, working from morning to night, seven days a week. Pow Wow and I had a lot of free time alone at the crib (house) so we entertained a lot and often had girls over. His crew would be there when I came home from school.

Usually, it was Creature Feature, Dirk, Maceo, Mike D and Prescott downstairs steppin' while getting high off marijuana. Normally, their conversation would be about hustling but today they were talking about being pimps. As I walked down stairs, I could hear the song, "Pathway to Glory" and Dirk and Prescott were steppin'. Dirk said, "Watch out Prescott, let Earthquake get some of this." I jumped in the dance, displaying the foot work that Dirk taught me and combined it with what I learned from Ice Kat.

They all gave me props for my sharp moves. I chopped it up with them for a spell and then headed up stairs to try and figure out my homework. I could only do my best. It was Friday and I had two days to figure it out. A short while later, my mom made it home, after 10:00 p.m., took a bath and then went to sleep.

The neighbor across from me was a 22-year-old cat named Lou. I stole my mom's car key, went over to his house and asked him to teach me to drive. He was working on music, playing the piano. Sometimes I practiced his songs, singing the bars so that he could determine what pitch the song should be sung in.

Lou lived with his mom and younger sister, who were both quite strange. They often treated him bad and weren't supportive of his music. When he played the piano, they turned out the lights on him. Sometimes they cooked but wouldn't allow him to eat so when my mom wasn't home, we invited him over to cook pancakes and eat with us. We always had food so it wasn't no thang.

Lou taught me how to drive. As we rolled through our neighborhood, we went down Moe's block and saw Babyface, Lucky, Ralph and Creature Feature, who walked out of the crowd, hitting a joint.

I rolled up on him, stopped and said, "What's up Creature Feature?"

"Hey li'l homie, you rolling, huh?"

I answered, "Yeah, straight like that. I like your wide, gangsta brim and cape."

Standing there shirtless, in a black cape and jeans, he shook the dust off his shoulders and said, "I'm Mack Zarro," as he pulled out a long, gray colored, plastic sword with a black handle on it and we all laughed.

Babyface positioned his fingers to look like pitch forks while he pumped his lower body back and forth, as if he were a dog in heat. Lou and I laughed. I enjoyed tripping on them (laughing) when they were high. It was comical, but I warned them, "I hope you all are not smoking weed laced with angel dust."

"Nope, but Creature Feature put some dust on his weed," Ralph shouted.

My thoughts were, '*It was good to see him in good spirits after losing his mom at the hands of his father.*' I guess he was self-medicating since he was smoking laced weed much more than usual. Just seeing him back to what was close to normal, was good enough for now. I reminded myself to talk to Creature Feature later about smoking too much angel dust.

For now, I was cruising and learning to drive, which was fun. I liked flexing like that, I had "drive" fever. Lou looked over at me and said, "I heard that Creature Feature's mom died. What happened to his mom?"

I kind of filled him in, without too much detail. Seeing how Lou's mom often mistreated him, I didn't want to spark any ideas. She used 30 words yelling at him and 28 of them were degrading curse words and I remember him ripping their phone out the wall. So, I told him just the basic facts, that she had been stabbed to death.

Lou frowned and said, "That's horrible." A few seconds later, he cheered up. I could feel the breeze as I stuck my head out of the window, just checking out the view, listening to the radio, lost in the moment.

Stevie Wonder's song, "Mary Wants to Be a Superwoman" came on the radio and Lou sung with his sultry, silky voice, sounding exactly like the song. "You've got that voice, real talent. I need to start singing or lifting weights. Girls like singing and muscles."

Lou said, "I got some weights that you can borrow. I'll bring them to you in the morning." We pulled into the same parking space as if my mom's car hadn't been moved. I eased in the house and quietly put her keys back in the ashtray, then headed to bed. Mission accomplished!

That morning the doorbell rang and it was Lou, bringing his equipment. He had two bar bells and a straight bar with two 25 lbs. steel weights. That was more than enough to get me started. We took them to my basement and noticed Vince, a neighborhood kid, who was a year younger than me, sleeping on the rug. He lived with his mom, who was a minister that had a candy store in their garage, on the next block.

Pow Wow stepped into the basement and said, "His mom gave him a pumpkin head (swollen from being hit) so he and Lou can eat breakfast with us."

I asked him why his mom hit him, and he said, "Because I didn't make it home before the street lights came on. She started beating me with a pipe upside my head, so I took off running out the house and was too scared to go back. I saw Pow Wow early this morning and he said that I could sleep down here once your mom left for work."

We agreed that after breakfast, I would go to his mom's candy store to see how she reacted. Previously, when I went to buy candy, she was always very nice. She looked like a sweet lady with a very soft voice. I know that kids get whippings and I really knew why I did, but this seemed different from what I got. This kid's head was distorted as big as a basketball.

After we ate pancakes, I walked around to Vince's house, purchased a candy bar and asked his mom if he was home. She said, "No, no he's not." I looked her in her eyes and asked if she knew when he would be home? She hesitated and then said in a soft, trembling voice, "If you see him, can you please tell him to come home."

I looked her in her eyes again and asked, "Is he going to get a whipping?"

She immediately said, "No, I just want him to come home."

"Do you promise?" I asked.

With tears falling down her face, she said, "Yes, I promise."

I told her that I would go and get him.

When I got back home, Vince had a look of anticipation on his face as he waited for me to tell them what happened. I told them everything and then Pow Wow and I walked him home. I know that my mom could get mean, because I did bad stuff, but I thought that a preacher wouldn't do anything bad, especially over something so small. She proved to be no different than anyone else. I guess you really don't know what's going on behind closed doors. Even good people do bad things. Looks can be deceiving!

As the days passed by, I continued to steal my mom's car every chance I got, improved on my driving and I even started to work out. The more I lifted weights, the more muscular I became. As the afternoon approached, Reno called saying he was going to pick me up. We wanted to go and check out new leather jackets on the shopping strip near our neighborhood. We walked with two other friends, about one and a half miles away. We went into a department store and took the escalator to the second floor where the coats were.

They had the new "Fonzie" style jackets with the collar turned up in all colors. We each tried them on. They were sharp and fit real nice. I had $50 but the leather cost $150 which was a lot at that time. Reno said that he had $40 and our other two friends had even less than that. Together we couldn't even afford one jacket so we all put the coats back on the rack.

Reno whispered, "We can take off our coats and hang them on the rack. Then try on a leather jacket and put our coat back on, over the leather. We'll take two more (decoy) leather jackets off the rack, pretending to try them on in the dressing room. When we leave the dressing room, we'll put the two (decoy) leather jackets back on the rack, while wearing the new leather jacket on under our own coat."

Skeptical, I said, "Man, we might get caught."

Reno reported that the security went downstairs and no one else was watching. I was thinking that retail theft was not my style, but those leathers were slick and we'd be the first in the neighborhood to have them. I was really unsure about it. The department was too quiet and we hadn't checked out the scene, we didn't know the layout and had not cased the joint, which was something Pow Wow and Prescott taught me and my crew to do.

Reno and I went on with the suggestion while our two friends decided not to do it. Reno announced that you could do whatever you wanted but he was about to walk out. The three of them started walking toward the escalator. I slowly walked behind them, looking around in each direction and then stopped, thinking to myself, *'Never leave a stone unturned, always case the joint'* so I immediately turned around, walked back over to the rack and took my jacket and the new jacket off and hung it up.

As soon as I put my jacket back on, a tall man with a security radio rushed in through a door that was camouflaged to look like a mirror. He ran past me as he yelled on his security radio, heading toward the door. I hurried in the same direction and saw Reno as he nearly made it out of the revolving door.

The security guy reached and grabbed Reno by the back of his jacket collar and led him back through the revolving door, inside of the store. Another security guy ran up and grabbed him by the waist of his pants and hustled him toward the back of the store. They walked him past me, I saw Reno holding up his Willie Dynamite bank roll saying repeatedly, "I was going to pay for it."

The security guard said, "If you were going to pay for it, why were you running out of the door?"

"Because you all were chasing me," Reno replied. He kept flashing his fake bank roll. He looked at me and said, "Tell them Earfy, I got plenty of money. I got this bank roll, why would I have to steal. Earfy, tell them." I looked at the fake, Willie Dynamite bank roll and then walked straight out the door. The three of us cracked up.

I'm so glad that I didn't try to take that leather jacket out of the store. I think that security guy was waiting to see if I was going to steal the jacket and when I put it back, they went for Reno. Good thing that I didn't. When I got back to the Manor, we went our separate ways. I stopped by the candy garage and got myself some snacks and went home, straight to my bedroom, turned on the television and relaxed on my bed. I was still laughing about Reno getting caught.

The afternoon news was on. Just as I was about to change channels, a news flash appeared. The reporter said that a sixteen-year-old boy on the Southside, in Princeton Park, allegedly stabbed his grandmother, Mrs. Betty Johnson, fifty-two times with a hunting knife and killed her. She had wounds in her back and torso areas. Her head was nearly severed, hanging by the neck when police broke into the home after several neighbors called 911 reporting screams coming from the house. He kept insisting that his father committed the crime. You may recall that three months earlier the sixteen-year-old lost his mother after his father, Antonio Johnson, Sr. fatally stabbed is wife twenty-five times.

Although Antonio Johnson, Sr. had been in custody since that time, the sixteen-year-old insisted that his father committed this crime, essentially, killing his own mother. They showed footage of him being arrested, shouting, "My dad did it. You got the wrong man." I was mortified after realizing that it was Creature Feature. I just sat there for about an hour.

Suddenly, I jumped up wondering if anybody else knew. I ran out of the house at top speed, all the way to the park. There were about one hundred Manor folks at the bleachers, so I figured that they knew. I saw Prescott and Pow Wow and everyone. They were discussing what happened. All the Manor girls were present, even Cindy. She walked up to me and went on to explain, "I saw Creature Feature last night and he asked me to keep a big knife until he came to pick it up today. I let him know that I couldn't do that. He was acting kind of weird but harmless. He was wearing a cape. If I knew that something was wrong, I would have come and got one of you guys."

The Letter

I believe that Creature Feature was in a bad place and didn't know how to escape. I think it started before the angel dust. The dust just drove him deeper on the path, never to return. He needed mental help so that he could have found some sort of comfort, enough to deal with reality. He was lost forever, only God could save him.

After that, we all drew closer than ever, always watching each other's back, with a deep concern for our well-being. We even went to each other's schools to ensure that everyone was protected. They didn't have to make trips to my school. There were no worries because I had alliances with key people in each neighborhood.

Everything was good except for my school work. It was still a constant struggle. I was passing some classes and failing others. I looked forward to the end of the school year but for now, I had to deal with it.

Walking home from school one day, I was thinking about my plans for the semester.

I made it to the crib and heard Pow Wow and his crew in the basement listening to music and playing ping pong. I went downstairs and saw Maceo, Dirk, Mike D, Den Den and Prescott. They were discussing Creature Feature, so I asked if anyone heard from him. Everyone was quiet while frowning. Maceo spoke saying, "Yeah he wrote me a letter."

"What did it say?" I asked.

He reached in his pocket and took the letter out, handed it to me saying, "You read it."

I took the letter, thinking, *'Maybe he will explain the whole thing.'* He might have a logical explanation. They stopped playing ping pong and stared at me as I was about to read the letter. The letter said:

Hey Maceo,

Tell everybody that I am ok. Creature Feature will miss everyone. What happened was meant to happen, to set me free from all that I been through. I love all of you but now Creature Feature no longer exist. He is gone forever. I have emerged from that thorn and blossomed into a flower. Now I am a new creature.

As I turned to read the next page, I was thinking, *'Did he turn into a Muslim, Hindu, or a Buddhist?'* He went on to say:

My name is Tonya and it is refreshing. I am a woman now.

I looked up at everyone and they each had smirks and looks of confusion on their faces. I handed the letter back to Maceo and said, "I'll never forget Creature Feature. We had some good times and all the girls were crazy about him. He inspired me to lift weights. I know that he is still a Manor boy in his heart."

The silence broke with Pow Wow saying, "Yeah, it doesn't matter. I could see if he was like that all the time, but he is sick now."

With compassion I reminded them, "Yeah, but he was still telling the truth about his father."

Maceo looked at me strangely asking, "The truth about what? His father was in jail when he killed his grandma, so how in the world can he blame his father?"

In a thought-provoking way I conveyed, "Creature Feature couldn't deal with everything that happened. I believe that his father committed that crime because Creature Feature would never have done that if his father hadn't killed his mom. That's why he said his father did it!"

They all looked at me and then Prescott spoke. "You got a point, Earfy."

"You really think that's why he said that his father did it?" Dirk asked.

"Yeah, just think about it," I said.

After a brief silence, Pow Wow turned the music back up and they began steppin'. Dirk and Den Den started up, as I watched two pros dominating the footwork. Steppin' school was in session and it was always good to watch and learn.

I was thinking I didn't pay close enough attention to Creature Feature's behavior, but I will for sure in situations moving forward. I envisioned, if I didn't become a medical doctor, maybe I could be a psychiatrist because I kind of liked studying people's behavior and habits. Then I could help them physically or mentally. So, let me get up here and do my homework. I guess there won't be a driving lesson tonight. Maybe I'll steal the car tomorrow.

I eased up the stairs to complete my homework assignments, thinking about Reno, hoping he was ok. He was good at observing people and his surroundings. I learned that skill from him, but we both needed to be better at detecting problematic circumstances.

I called Reno and asked, "What happened after you got nabbed?"

In a sneaky voice he answered, "I'm good. They took me in the back to the security office and wrote me a warning slip, took a photo of me and placed it on a wall of pictures. Then they called my mom and she came and got me. She popped me up side my head and made me stay in the house, that's all."

"You're famous now. You made the wall of thieves, a true celebrity in that store and you'll have your own security watching your back every time you enter." I was rolling.

CHAPTER 8

History in the Making

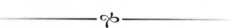

I VENTURED OUT more, socializing in other areas since everything was peaceful between the neighborhoods. I attended stepper sets (parties) all across the Southside of the city and eventually invited Lucky and a few others from the Manor. I became increasingly popular and well known. Suddenly Steppin' transitioned into an underground (not mainstream) dance when the hustlers took it to another level. The main ingredient to a successful Steppin' party was to have key songs played in a sequence that inspired steppers, making the music extremely important. The top deejays were Cousin Danny, Sam Chapman, Herb Kent, Terrible Ted, and Tornado, aka Big Daddy Wu Wu.

Each neighborhood had their own brand of footwork and there were key steppers who stood out as unique. I learned clever moves and slick turns from Dirk. His footwork was perfected down to a science, most captivating, extremely creative, "the boss" who sculpted the Manor style.

My footwork got better each time I went to stepper sets all over the city. I enjoyed attending sets on 93rd Street because Slick Rick did slides across the floor while he popped then jerked his body. Then I would flow to the Wild, Wild Hundreds to checkout Ty Skippy and Tony Dow who I dubbed princes of dynamic footwork. As I traveled to 22nd Street in the Ickeys, I witnessed the illusion of hand movements coupled with fast, but furious, footwork of the stepping ambassador, Tyboo.

At the parties on 95th Street, I was dazzled watching Derrick Nute, who they called twinkle toes, with his flawlessly, fast footwork and flare. When I bounced to the 79th Street Strip, I'd see Tracey Dog and Dre with their smooth combinations of fakes and short step footwork. Then I moseyed through Englewood where Sarg and Black Fred Astaire demonstrated quickness with outstanding shuffling.

Strolling through 39th Street, Kim Bouie would display great hand movement coordinated with complimentary footwork. Also from the low-end Lil Mike, the Wizard of steppin', was breath taking to watch. Mackironi was a heavy dude whose steps looked light as a feather. He was one of the most profound steppers that I ever saw. Kicking it on 55th Street, Larry Joe turned it up with his comical style. He was always very entertaining using fancy turns and swift footwork; a demon on his feet.

Dee Dee and Light Skin Fred Astaire from 71st Street, had a gangsta dance style with intricate turns and a special brand of footwork. Ice Kat held it down on the Westside, for sure. My buddy was the total package with his silky smooth, fast but slow flow. He had a high step that was second to none, the most unique style of any stepper that I've ever seen. Other steppers out west, who were quite clever included Frog, Skip, and Lil Alfred, a masterful artist who was before his time.

Last but not least, Womack from The Gardens. Most all the great steppers copied something from him. Each of these guys were among the best! They were the ones who inspired others to learn the dance and the birth of underground steppin' became more popular. Guys dominate the flow as the girls follow their lead. Steppin' is a beautiful performance where the guys display spectacular footwork, but when a guy and a girl danced together, it was the most innovating, eloquent dance that you've ever seen.

Trends in the City

Steppers were known for wearing dress attire that included Gatsby styled suits, Stacey Adams shoes, and Beaver and Godfather brims (hats). The slick style of dress that the steppers wore caught the attention of the mainstream throughout the city. Players had a certain way of presenting themselves in public. They were well dressed, exerting charisma and swagger. Self-assured with bold conversation, using a slick vernacular.

This is how players were geared up (outfitted) on a daily basis and it set the standard for young Chicagoans. Soon, the bar was raised and steppers were wearing tailor-mades to events. Then everyone started wearing them on special occasions. A few of the swagged-out homies even wore them to school.   Tailoring shops became popular as young folks embraced the fashion. Even though they weren't all players, they gravitated toward that style, reinforcing the Chicago trend.   Being a gangsta and a player definitely came natural to me, so I gravitated more towards the Steppin' community. Most of the hustlers spent their days at home, scheming on a plan, trying to make a come up (robberies or burglaries), working jobs, shooting craps (dice), smoking weed and practicing footwork.

During the same time, the preppy kids and gay crowds created another underground dance called the Mendel and we all respected each other's space, even though our dances and lifestyles were considerably different. Their dance consisted of jumping, hopping and gyrating with lots of arm movement, "jacking their bodies," very energetic.   The Mendel dance was named after the location where it was created, at Mendel Catholic High School on the Southside of the city, in the late seventies. Even though it was an all boy school, they threw some legendary parties. House Heads were crazy for the sounds played by deejays Frankie Knuckles, Farley "Jackmaster" Keith, Steve "Silk" Hurley, Pink House and Darryl Pandy.

After the parties at Mendel became so popular and the crowds outgrew the space, they moved their parties to a warehouse location that was converted into a dance venue for teens and young adults called The Warehouse. Mendel renamed the dance "House" and considered themselves "House Heads." Another popular joint was on the Northside called Club LaRay. House Heads dressed in a more causal fashion, sporting polo and button-down shirts, vests, bow ties, sweaters laid across their backs with the sleeves tied around their necks, Levi jeans, Izod socks and penny loafer shoes.

They stepped the fashion game up, showcasing a new style, dressing more exotic and free. Spicy colors, torn jeans, vests, ripped T-shirts, with lots of spandex dominated their fashion. They wore hairstyles with side fades and shags (long hair in the nape area). Many of them were smart, outgoing with unique personalities, daring to be different and they hung out in clicks. The House Heads spent their days as students, dropouts, retail and fast food workers.

Since a lot of pretty girls from all over the city attended these parties, I enjoyed sliding through every now and then.

These two styles of dance were vastly different. Steppers were mellow and calm while House Heads were wild and sweaty but they both shaped the trends that evolved in Chicago. If you weren't a Stepper, then you were a House Head.

Stepping was a past time but making money was still my passion. The air was changing in every part of my life. As I grew, I looked at things differently and became sharper. I understood my craft more, young but with much experience in the underworld, slowly being molded into a connoisseur of crime.

Even though I was a stepper, education was my number one priority as I tried to pass ninth grade. When the school year ended, I was short a few credits and had to figure out how to get into tenth grade. Spending five years in high school definitely wasn't going to work for me. It wasn't even an option. I found myself in a familiar place again. After the last day of school, I went home thinking about it.

Pow Wow, Prescott, Dirk, Maceo, Mike D and Spivey were in the basement, so I trotted down the stairs. Spivey was styling Pow Wow's hair into finger waves. I asked him where he learned to do that, and he said at school. "I attend Carver High School, majoring in cosmetology, mastering the art of styling hair, for four periods each day."

I interrupted him, asking, "You only have four periods?"

He quickly replied, "No, I also have to take three general classes that include English, Math and a choice between music, art or gym and you know I always choose gym. I earn seven credits each year and 500 hours annually for three years. Then I'll take my state board exam and become a professional hairstylist."

A lightbulb went off in my head, so I asked, "Seven credits?"

Spivey said with excitement, "Yeah, I graduate next year and I'll have my license. It's much easier than taking regular classes."

"I'm already short three credits. Earning seven credits would place me in my sophomore year. Plus, I can gain favor with at least one teacher if I'm in one class each day for four periods. That would be much better than doing work in science, geography and history classes," I told him.

I asked him to show me how to transfer and register at his school and he agreed. He kept his word and I transferred, majored in cosmetology and had all sophomore level classes. That was awesome! I told Lucky about my move and he followed suit, landing in my cosmetology class where we had a ball.

Lucky's family had relocated to what is known as the wild, wild hundreds. His new neighborhood was closer to our school, in an area called The Gardens. A few blocks away was The Dungeon, one of the hottest underground Steppin' venues in the city. Even though we stepped all over Chicago, that was our number one spot.

I kept it player (cool) all the time, dressing and finessing, the usual in what I do. There were others from school who lived in the Gardens who went to parties at the Dungeon. They had their own niche within Steppin'. The Garden crew were players and hustlers as well and I was getting to know them. Some of them who didn't attend our school often hung around outside. They robbed kids who stood at the bus stop, so I stayed alert and aware. If you didn't know the right people, you could become a victim.

Music was my last period of the day. A guy from the Gardens and his girlfriend were in my class. She walked over to my desk, speaking, being overly friendly and trying to hold a conversation. I was short with her, hoping she would walk away before her guy got there. He strolled in, saw her at my desk and told her to, "Get away from him before I have to hurt that mark." She walked away smiling, acting like she hadn't done anything.

He mean-mugged me the whole class period. I wasn't trying to run into any trouble, especially not with anyone from the Gardens. They had a bad reputation. Besides, I didn't want anything to interfere with my goal. This was the best opportunity for me to get through high school and coming up with another plan would be next to impossible.

After class, I could hear him cursing and calling me names, saying to her, "I should whip that chump." When I walked out of class, he stepped to me and yelled, "Don't be talking to my girl."

I turned around, walked two feet in front of him and said hostilely, "I wasn't talking to her, she was talking to me."

"Check your eyes before I have to check them for you, ok," he barked.

Taking a step closer, I teased him, laughing and taunting him saying, "Get your game together because it sounds weak."

His eyes swelled with anger as he spoke in a solemn, deep tone saying, "You better watch your back." I just laughed as we all walked out of school and headed towards the bus stop. They were holding hands as they walked. His girl didn't live in the Gardens. There was only one route out of the Gardens and everybody rode the same bus.

As we waited, he leaned on the fence, with her laying against the front of his body. Six dudes were coming out the Gardens neighborhood toward us. Last week I witnessed those same guys robbing kids at the bus stop.

I glanced over at the guy and his girl and he was wearing a facetious grin. I slowly turned my head away like it wasn't no thang. When the Garden crew approached us, the guy greeted them saying, "What's up fellows?" Barely acknowledging him, they nodded and circled around everyone. I stood there, wearing a new leather jacket and a gold watch with money in my pocket.

The lead crew member (the spotter) stared straight in my eyes, trying to size me up, to see if I was a punk. They all looked at me like hungry lions about to pounce on their prey. I stared back, hoping that he felt my energy, saying in my mind, while talking without uttering a word, *'we're one in the same. I respect your hustle and I hope game recognize' game. There is honor amongst thieves so you better understand that. We're in the same circle. You can tell your own kind but if not, y'all better rob me using a gun. If you do, that's how the game goes but if you hurt me, know that you're going to see me again. I'm sure of that!'*

He unlocked eyes with me and shifted them side to side, landing on a guy a foot away. They knocked him to the ground and took off his Stacey Adams shoes and two silver rope chains from around his neck. They searched his pockets and took his money. He remained balled up in a knot, covering his face with his arms, trying to protect himself. They stole all his possessions and simply walked away.

I looked over at the guy with his girl. He wandered off in space, evasively, trying to avoid eye contact with me. The bus finally came and from that time on, I explored the Gardens often and made friends with some of their crew members. I stood at the bus stop with more confidence, knowing that everything was all good.

Cosmetology in School

Learning cosmetology gave me an opportunity to do the right thing but doing the wrong thing was much easier. Hustling was wrong, but I was good at it. I wasn't really looking for what was easy, I just wanted to be good at something. It was difficult to be good at cosmetology because I was not interested in styling hair. It was simply my big opportunity to get through high school.

I tried all kinds of methods to help me focus at school. I thought if I braided my hair, didn't look so fly and just concentrated on my work, then I wouldn't attract that fast crowd. It helped a little and class became somewhat tolerable, but I had a daily headache from it. I'd leave school relieved that it was over.

Cosmetology was more fun when a few of my homies came through and allowed me to style their hair. I gave one of my friends a press and curl. He walked in with a natural (afro), I washed, pressed and curled his hair and he left with a blowout (a straighter afro).

Lucky allowed me to press and curl his hair and I burnt his scalp at least fifty times. He left school that day with blisters throughout his entire head. Lucky said that he couldn't comb his hair for three days because his scalp was so tender and his head smelled like he spent a night in a burning building.

Finally, I did a successful style when I gave myself an auburn streak, going from the front left side to the back of my head. Lucky liked it so he decided to give me another chance and allowed me to color streak his hair. I determined that I could use a higher-level developer to mix his color and make it spicier. His streak turned out to be more vibrant, sort of bright; a unique color. It was orangutan orange. After that, Lucky didn't trust anyone to do anything to his hair. Babyface gave him the nick name "Orangutan" and the entire crew called him that for a while.

We were learning how to do facials and arch eyebrows. That seemed easy enough. A girl in my class allowed me to wax hers. I used too much and accidentally removed most of her eyebrows, so I used a pencil and drew her some, hoping that she wouldn't notice. Yep, she noticed. First, she loved them but then she realized that they were created with a pencil. I guess this is why no one trusted me.

Lucky and I tried to convince the girls in our cosmetology class to allow us to style their hair but there were no volunteers. So, we reached out to some of the players, trying to encourage them to come and get their butters whipped (fresh relaxers). We had no luck. I saw Womack and before I could ask, he did a spin and shuffled down the hall in the opposite direction.

Then I reached out to family, asking my cousins Cup, Chevy and Shady and they each said no way. I asked my Aunt Vivian and finally she said yes and allowed me to give her a manicure. The manicure turned out well and she liked it.

Back in school, I finally got a candidate, a girl who agreed to get a roller set style. All the girls in class assisted me and it turned out very nice. What a great day that was. It made me so proud that I had successfully styled my first customer.

After school, I went to visit Lucky and we talked about how well I performed today and then I happily headed home. As soon as I walked through the door, my mom called out, "Earthquake."

I hollered back, "Yeah ma, it's the hair styling king."

"Kyle's mom called and wants you to call her back."

My first thought was my little brother from another mother probably wants me to attend the annual hospital picnic festival. That would be fun. Maybe I could style Kyle's hair into an Elvis Presley hairdo. He'll love it!

I dialed the number and Kyle's mom said hello.

"Hey ma, this is Earthquake, where is my little brother?"

After a brief silence, she spoke in a sorrowful voice, "Kyle passed away last night. He fought a rare form of Leukemia, chronic asthma and allergies but he just couldn't fight anymore."

I was quiet, in shock – my heart sank. I'd never felt like that before. I've seen death but this was different. For some reason, it hurt to the core.

She spoke again, "I want you to be at the memorial service."

"I'm there Ma." I could hear her taking deep breaths, trying to maintain her composure.

"Kyle loved you so much. He talked about how you guys won that sack race. It was the joy of his life. At the hospital, he told that story a thousand times. It seemed to give him strength. He never saw color and though he was my only child, you were truly his brother."

"Ma are you going to be alright?"

"I'm alright. The memorial is Saturday and I just need you to be there." I took the address and ended the call.

My mom walked into the kitchen and said, "I'm sorry to hear about your little buddy. When I think about how you flung Kyle in that sack race, it makes me laugh. That was so funny. He loved it. He hung around you and your brother the entire day. He called you all the time, happy to share all his achievements. I liked little Kyle too. God doesn't make mistakes, you'll see him again some-day." She turned and walked out of the kitchen.

My mind stayed focused on Kyle as I trotted up the stairs to my room. I took a short time and sat on my bed. My front door opened and I heard Pow Wow and Prescott laughing as they head-ed to the basement. I said to myself, *'Let me go tell them about Kyle.'*

I went downstairs and they were in the mirror trying on new style ties, comparing them to determine which one looked the best. They both were nice. I had never seen that fashion of tie. It had five pleats in it. One was a gold color and the other one was dark red. They asked me whose tie looked the best. I was think-ing, *'The older we get the more they seem like the li'l boys.'* I told them to hold them up to their necks as they eagerly waited for my answer.

"You both look like doe-doe birds."

With a sad look on my face and in a gloomy voice, I told them, "Lil Kyle died last night."

Pow Wow asked what happened and I told him what Kyle's mom explained. Pow Wow replied with a look of disappointment, "Not my li'l buddy, naw man, my li'l homie. Ah man, he didn't deserve that. He was a little fighter but he's with God now. Kyle is in heaven racing over those pearly gates."

"Cause he's the little white kid, right?" Prescott asked.

"Yeah," Pow Wow answered.

Prescott spoke, "That was the little soldier. Now he can breathe easy. Cause I was hoping to meet the li'l fellow."

Pow Wow asked when the funeral was, and I told him Saturday, up north. Pow Wow said, "Man, we've got a come up planned for Saturday. We're on these two chicks and we can't let them get away." They called themselves tapping into the pimp game.

Since they were already players, they flowed toward their natural element. Being a player was the top of the line (pinnacle) for a hustler. Most all young guys fantasize about being a pimp.

Pow Wow and Prescott knew that they had what it took to be pimps. It was rumored that Prescott's father, J-Hawk, was a pimp and his pimping was off the chain (excellent), so it was easy for them to go in that direction.

Pow Wow and Prescott were approaching seventeen-years-old and the risk factor would increase when committing robberies and burglaries. They could be tried as adults and receive extensive jail time. Perhaps that's why they were trying their hands at pimping. For me, I was uninterested. Just being a player and a hustler was my thing.

That Saturday, I took two buses and the el train to get to Evanston, a North suburb of Chicago, where Kyle's service was being held. It was in an all-white neighborhood. When I walked into the corridor of the funeral parlor, everyone turned to the door and stared at me. I stood out like a sore thumb as the only black person there. It was as if I had the plague. No one even spoke to me. There was a feeling of hatred in the air and everyone stayed their distance. I felt that I wasn't welcomed.

At that moment, I totally understood the experience I had with Coach Byron at the Olympic school. As I approached the funeral, Kyle's mother motioned with her hand for me to come to the front. It was as if she was already alerted that I was there. Kyle's father was already deceased and his mom, grandmother and his nurse were sitting together on the first row. His mom asked me to sit with them and I did.

Kyle's nurse said, "Kyle talked about you all the time. He said that you were his brother. He spoke so highly of you and he really wanted me to meet you."

I smiled and said, "I'll never forget him as long as I live. He will remain my little brother, in my heart."

I stood up and walked over to the casket and saw his fragile little body. He was dressed in a black suit and tie and his stringy black hair was perfectly combed with a part on the side. Over his black suit lay the ribbon he was so proud of. I reached into my pocket and pulled out my ribbon and placed it over my neck. I heard his mom behind me as she began to cry. I said to him, "We'll race again one day my little brother." He laid there so peaceful, looking as if he were asleep.

I stayed until the service ended. As I said my goodbyes, I knew that Kyle's mom and I would never see each other again and I believed that she knew it too. She said sincerely, "I love you. Please take care of yourself and never let hate conquer you." She kissed me on my cheek and I went on my way.

The ride home was strange. I kept thinking about how prejudice those people were. I understood Dr. Martin Luther King Jr. and why he fought for equality. I wished that there was something that I could do to make a difference, helping the races get along. I thought white people hated us.

I vowed that someday I would find a way to do something about this. I'll show them that black people are not that bad. Black people love every race. I never saw black people be mean to other people. I'm bad, but I don't hate anyone. I pray that God gives me the strength to finish what Dr. King started, but for now I've got other stuff to do. When I arrived home, my mom asked me about the funeral and I told her all about it and then went to my room. Since my mom was still awake, I couldn't steal the car so I went to bed.

A week passed and on Saturday Cindy called. She told me that her mom was going bowling and asked if I could come over. Puberty was kicking in and I was feeling a little fresh. Sex was on my mind.

Who better to be with than Cindy? I was thinking about Cindy and Cutie T all week. They both were fine and they were special to me. Cindy happen to call me first, so I quickly headed to her house.

She was home alone but her little brother, Junie, was playing outside. She looked pretty as ever, just smiling in a happy to see me kind of way. We wasted no time. She walked me to her room which was directly off the stairs on the left side. Her bed was nice and soft.

Cindy said, "You can sit down." She turned off the light, walked back to the bed, sat down, put her arms around me and kissed me as I laid her across her bed. I felt that it was going to be good. It was my first sexual experience, with the person I wanted it to happen with. It was perfect! She got up and locked her door, then took off her shorts.

I was super aroused and couldn't wait. I took off my shirt and shoes. As I was pulling my pants off, I heard the front door slam, so I quickly pulled my pants back up and grabbed my shirt and shoes. I asked her who was at the door.

"Wait a minute, I'll go check but it's probably my little brother Junie." Cindy went downstairs, and I heard her talking with him. She walked back into the room and said, "Where were we?"

It was going to be the first time for both of us and we were curious and ready. We undressed again. I rolled over on her as she laid on the bed. She held my back and looked in my eyes. I gently grabbed her legs and opened them as I held my magic stick, ready to insert it, then pressed it up to the lips of her cookie.

Someone started beating on her door and we quickly jumped up. Her little brother yelled, "Here comes mom." I hurried and put my clothes on and headed to the window. There were burglar bars on it. Oh snap, I ran and crawled under the bed while she went out the room. I was getting dressed under the bed when she walked back in and said, "That silly Junie was just kidding, playing around."

"Does he know that it's me in here?"

"Yes, he knows."

Since the kid always liked me, I suggested that I should go out there and have a little talk with him.

"Hey, Earthquake," he said, looking up at me.

"Hey li'l Junie, listen, I'm upstairs talking to your sister about something important so don't be banging on the door anymore, unless your mom is really coming, okay? You got swagger li'l homie, right?"

"Yep!" he smiled. I went back upstairs relieved that the problem was solved.

She held my face and we kissed wild and passionately. Taking our clothes off for the third time, she laid on the bed, invitingly opened her legs while the energy surged through my body. My mind was back on the booty. I came upon her ready to penetrate when we heard Junie beating on the door, shouting, "Here comes mom, for real this time." We jumped up and quickly dressed again. Cindy opened the door and checked downstairs and then came back to the room and announced that it was another false alarm.

I was really mad at that little numbskull. I came out the room and warned him not to beat on the door anymore. "Don't be a little mark." I went back into her room and stated that he was killing our special moment and now I was upset and ready to go. I couldn't take it anymore. I was still excited but also overly frustrated, so I told Cindy, maybe another day. I walked out of her room, looked at li'l Junie and told him, "You are gonna be a great football player because you are an excellent blocker!" I walked out disappointed but knowing that someday it would happen.

I Believe It Was God

Since it was still fairly early, I decided to go and visit my cousins Cup, Chevy and Shady. We ate popcorn and watched television. I was thinking about Dr. Martin Luther King, Jr. It was his birthday and they were playing movies about him on television and airing speeches on the radio. We watched and listened, and it had me feeling some kind of way. I analyzed these experiences very carefully. Studying human behavior remained a part of what I did. Things beyond the human eye made me curious and I was always trying to understand them.

After spending a fun night with my cousins, Aunt Tea and grandma, I headed home. On the bus ride, I remained in deep thought, wishing I was a super hero that could rid the world of these problems. I arrived home. To lighten my mood, I sat in the kitchen watching a comedy called The Carol Burnett Show, laughing and eating dinner. After that, it was my week to wash the dishes then I made my way to my bed to get an early start.

My bed was on the far-right wall, next to the closet and bedroom door. The window was on the left wall next to the dresser. My television, which usually sat on my dresser, was still in the kitchen where I had left it before dinner. I wasn't really that tired, just lying in bed, still thinking and relaxing until I fell asleep.

Something woke me up. I heard wind blowing and taps on my window. I looked over at my window and the tapping stopped. I turned my face toward the wall and went to sleep again. I was awakened by tapping and wind blowing again but I didn't turn around, thinking that it would stop. It didn't. I continued to hear the noise, waking me completely. I turned and looked at the window to determine where the noise was coming from. The wind was blowing extremely hard. What was that tapping?

I opened my eyes and looked at the window and the tapping stopped again. Before I turned back toward the wall, my eyes met the ceiling and there was a bright light shining down on me. I felt subdued as if I was in a trance. Within the light, a huge hand appeared, pointing at me. I was receptive to this vision, not afraid, just drawn to it. A deep, powerful voice spoke. It said words to me.

The vision slowly vanished, and I began to feel an intense fear. My heart was beating fast and I was so nervous, afraid, not knowing what to think. I tried laying there but I couldn't go back to sleep. I got up and went to my mom's room and asked if I could sleep with her. Since I had never, ever slept with my mom, she asked what was wrong with me. I got in her bed shaking and she repeated, "What's wrong?" so I told her what happened.

She sat up, tried to rationalize the situation and suggested, "That was probably the light from your television." I told her that my television was in the kitchen. She asked, "What did the vision call you?"

"It told me that I was Abba," I said.

She said that she never heard that word before, but it sounded evil. I replied, "Me either." In the morning, I got up to get ready for school but felt fearful when I headed to the basement to iron my clothes.

My mom warned, "You better go and get ready or you're gonna see my hand and some stars."

Pow Wow woke up and asked, "Why are you in the bed with momma?" Our mom told him what happened, and he laughed saying, "A big grown dude still sleeping with his mama." That night, I slept in Pow Wow's room, on the rug since my mom told me that I couldn't sleep with her.

On my way to school, I saw a Muslim selling the Final Call newspaper. He was preaching with a bullhorn. I walked up to him and asked, "Can I ask you a question?"

"Sure, little brother, go ahead."

"What does the word Abba mean?"

"Why are you asking?"

"Because someone called me that."

"That's impossible, you can't be that name, little brother. Whoever called you that, called wrong."

"What does the word mean? Is it something evil?"

"No, it's divine, it means Father God."

Well, I was happy that it wasn't evil, so I eventually forgot about it as I went on with life. Getting away from myself, thinking about the world's problems probably sparked that vision. My thought was to focus on other things and as I did that, the fear went away.

During the mid-term of the school year, my mom announced that we were moving again. I kind of knew it was coming. I loved the Manor and it would always be a part of me. It was my home and these guys were my family. Even though Lucky and Reno had already moved, I still got to hang out with Lucky often, but Reno went to live with his grandma and I hadn't caught up with him yet.

Since I was already traveling around the city I'd look at this move as an expansion, but the Manor would still be home base. I went over to Babyface's to tell him and the crew. Of course I would always come back, and they promised to visit me no matter where I was and that was solid.

Walking home, I heard Todd's sister, Camille, calling me. As I got to the door, I looked but didn't recognize her at first. She was always cool and I considered her a friend, but wasn't feeling her. Somehow this day was different. Camille's appearance had changed. She was made up really cute, wearing a nice dress and her hair was styled, just looking fine.

When she walked up, I told her that we were moving. She got sad and I did too so we reminisced in my doorway. At that moment, I looked at her different and was kind of attracted to her. Camille always found ways to let me know that she liked me, but I really wasn't enticed by her until this day.

She asked what I was about to do. I told her not much. Seductively, she said, "Do you want some company?"

My magic stick answered, "Yes," as my mouth uttered the words, "Come on in," as she stood there looking all dreamy eyed.

We went straight to the basement. I looked over at her as she sat on the couch. She was a cute girl with a brown complexion and a nicely developed body. I took a seat on the rug and, with an "I can't wait to get you" walk, she came and sat right next to me. The next thing I knew, I was having my first sexual experience and it felt great. It was the first time that I ejaculated.

Afterwards, I was ready for her to go. I got up and suggested that she put her clothes back on. I told her that I was about to go to bed, so I walked her to the door. I went upstairs and jumped in the shower. On one hand, it felt good and on the other hand, it was crummy because she wasn't Cindy or Cutie T.

We had sex on one more occasion, then I revealed that she was a cool friend but would never be my girlfriend. Camille said, "That's ok, just being friends is cool. I like you as a friend as well." From then on, we remained cool and hung out from time to time.

CHAPTER 9

Discovering Lust

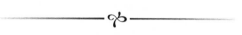

IN THIS EXPERIENCE, observing Camille's behavior as well as my own, analyzing the way that I reacted left me surprised that my feelings had not grown stronger. I thought I would be attracted to her after sex but realized I wasn't. I confused lust with like and then discovered they were two different things. I learned that lust is a strong physical attraction that can quickly go away after sex, feeling no connection. Now I know that you don't have to like or love someone to have good sex.

Camille still liked me after sex and was willing to take what she could get; just remaining friends was cool with her. However, I think that she also confused lust with like. She liked me before we had sex and that was the reason she liked me afterwards.

With Cindy and Cutie T, I enjoyed being around them even when I wasn't thinking about sex. Since my first sexual relations was with a girl that I didn't like, I believe it disconnected sex from like, in my mind. When the physical act was over, there was nothing else to hold two people together. After sex with Camille, I tried not to be lustful because it could be misleading.

Now I understood my friends' behavior when it came to girls. They would hit a broad (have sex) and keep it moving, able to do so because they were physically attracted to those girls, and that's lust. I don't even think that they understood this about themselves, as they also confused lust with like.

After further observation, I noticed when a guy is lusting for a girl, he paints a portrait in his mind of how great she is but after having sex, the physical attraction is gone. He says, "I really like you." Believing that, he tries to bond with her but she's not like he envisioned and regrets that they have nothing but sex in common. He ignores her and she thinks that he purposely did it. When the physical desire returns, he might be attracted to her again.

Just coming into being a man, I was letting my "little head" think for my "Big Head." My little head was telling me that Camille turned out to be everything that I wanted but after sex, my "big head" told me that I didn't like anything else about her, helping me realize that my little head steered me wrong. I couldn't trust the little head to make those decisions.

The 82nd Street Connection

It was early March when we moved on the first floor into a two-bedroom apartment. The eighteen-unit brick building had three floors and was in the Lon City neighborhood. It was a lot smaller than our townhouse in the Manor. Pow Wow and I had to share a bedroom and we now had only one bathroom. It took a little getting used to.

We settled in but my mom was barely home. She quit her second job to attend college at night while working as a legal secretary at a top insurance company. After work, a few nights each week, she drove downtown to Harold Washington College (formerly The Loop) for classes. Money was tight and things got tougher.

One night, my mom came in with barbeque hot links for dinner. "Hey Ma, are you cooking or are we having hotlinks tonight?"

"I'm afraid not. I'm not cooking and you and Pow Wow are going to have to fend for yourselves. I can't afford to pay all the bills and take care of you guys. I'm attending school now so there is no extra money. Y'all have to pitch in and the first way to help is to buy your own meals."

"I'm cool with that. I'll have to get my hustle on around here but tonight I'm gonna need some of those hotlinks." She shared her dinner and I relished in it, my last free meal from my mama. After I ate, I walked through the neighborhood, checking things out. I lived a few blocks from the 82nd Street Strip which was hot 24-hours a day. Nearby was Cottage Grove Avenue, another popular hangout where it was always jumping. There were hustlers from thirteen to thirty years- old throughout the entire area.

The organizations in the city were on the rise, getting stronger as membership increased. There were four established sets that became more powerful. The Rocks, the Mob, the Vicky Lous and the Four King Crowns were the main branches of all the city gangs. Before leaving the Manor, we all turned Mob (joined) and I was loyal to the cause.

Since the Strip was close to my house, I spent a lot of time out there and met all the main players because hustlers recognized a hustler. One side of the Strip was ruled by King Fish and Milton, old G's (original gangstas) from the Rock organization who were drug-dealing pimps. The opposite side was controlled by young Mob members Bull and Creflo, who sold weed. I knew I had to connect with one side soon if I wanted to eat.

I asked Milton for a job and he said yeah but warned if I got caught, to keep my mouth shut and he would get me out of jail. He ran down the job description and explained the pay process. My duties were to:

1. Stay alert and keep an eye on the locations where they hid the work (drugs).
2. Scream "Five-O" (police) when police or detectives approach the block.
3. When a worker is being chased by the cops, grab his drugs from that location and hide the work in another spot.

My job was cool. I made enough cash to buy food, toiletries, pay car fare to get to school and save for emergencies. Milton gave me the night shift so hustling wouldn't affect my school attendance in the daytime. As the summer approached, there was more time to work. My drug dealing skills were good right off the bat because of the experience I got hanging around Ice Kat, learning the ins and outs.

Soon, Milton gave me a promotion and I moved up, selling uppers and downers called Ts and Blues (prescription pills). I also sold "Syrup" aka Aminol or Nol (prescription cough syrup with codeine). My Mob, homies who sold marijuana across the street, Bull and Creflo asked, "Why are you over there with those ancient Rocks (Old Gs)? You're not a Rock, you are Mob, right?"

"Yeah, straight like that, I'm Mob fo' sho'. I'm forever Mob," I told them.

"We see you hustling over there. Come over here and get money with us, sell weed. You hang with us anyway, so you may as well," Bull said.

I agreed and began selling all three, weed, pills, and Nol, just grinding and saving for a car. We all worked and hung out together and my hustling buddies became extended family. I was plugged with the young Mob and worked with the Old Rocks. Everybody gave me mad respect, and no one questioned my loyalty.

One day, standing on the Strip, who did I see walking into the corner store? My buddy Reno! He was a sight for sore eyes to see. He asked, "What are you doing around here?" I told him that we moved down the street. He pointed towards a building right off the Strip and said, "That's where I live."

That was the first time that we reconnected since he had left the Manor a year earlier. It was good to see Reno. He updated me saying he got fired from his bus boy job at the Hilton Hotel downtown and I told him all about my new hustles. I introduced him to all the key players. Lucky was a regular, still hanging out with me and now Reno was back on the map.

Our lives were changing. Pow Wow got a job on the border of the Manor at a fruit market and Prescott worked for a mattress company while they were still hustling at night. Pow Wow set up a robbery where Prescott held up the fruit market at least three times that I know about. His boss told him, "I don't know what it is, but since I hired you we've been robbed three times." With a look of concern Pow Wow replied, "This neighborhood is changing! It's just getting bad around here, that's all." His boss let it go for a little while but eventually Pow Wow was terminated.

Prescott got fired from his job shortly afterwards and they both went back to hustling full-time with a strong emphasis on pimping. Prescott drove one of his father's cars. It was an old-school Lincoln Continental with suicide doors (facing inward) so they now had transportation. They spent most of their time in the Manor but ventured out more to see new sights and further their pimping careers.

Sometimes I hung out with Pow Wow and Prescott. There was no more big boys and little boys, we now flowed together. After hustling on the Strip, they picked me up and we rolled to J-Hawk's boutique so that they could purchase clothing for their girls. He showed them samples that would be best for their women of leisure. Mr. J-Hawk was always cool, and I enjoyed seeing him.

Suddenly he looked at me and blurted out, "Earthquake is going to be the biggest pimp in Chicago." We all laughed.

"He's more of a hustler, not deep into girls like that," my brother said.

"Yeah daddy, cause he's a body builder and he's gonna be my body guard. He likes to fight and can box (fight)," Prescott added.

J-Hawk laughed and insisted saying, "He's gonna out pimp both of you all. Just watch and see. I like the muscles but trust me, he's gonna be a pimp."

I just looked back and forth as they talked about what I was gonna do, thinking to myself Mr. J-Hawk is most definitely wrong because I didn't want to be a pimp, that's not me. They dropped me off at home and headed back to the Manor to prepare their girls for work. I kept thinking about what Mr. J-Hawk said and analyzed the pimps that I knew like King Fish, Slick Rick and Icey Mike who all had girls working Cottage Grove Avenue. Even though they were getting money, I didn't think I would make it my career. So, I went back to work.

This was a good night, standing on the Strip making money. My customers were consistent and I liked most of them. That evening, I sold my entire supply except four pills. An older cat named Pluto walked up and requested his usual, a two and two. As always, I checked my surroundings and then made the transaction, giving him two Ts and two Blues. I saw Five O detectives slowly driving down the street with their lights off. I had spotted them before I did my last transaction.

They rolled up, jumped out the car and showed their badges. I knew who they were. We nicknamed them Detectives Jesse James and Doc. Then they told everyone to put their hands up. Doc picked up the piece of aluminum foil next to Pluto's leg. He opened it and found the Ts and Blues I had just sold. Pluto became extremely upset, crying as Detective Doc placed hand cuffs on him while saying that the foil pack was his.

Half crying Pluto said, "I'm on parole, please it is not mine. I don't want to go back to the penitentiary, please, no."

"Well, whose is it?" the detective asked.

Crying hysterically Pluto replied, "I don't know."

The detective stated that Pluto was going to jail. I thought, '*I can't let him go to jail, they're going to eat him alive. Since I'm only sixteen, they'll send me to the Juvenile Detention Center if I take the heat.*' Then I thought, '*They'll have to call my mom and I can't have that, but I can say that I am seventeen, and they'll arrest me without contacting her.*'

So, I stepped up saying that the pills were mine. Pluto wouldn't have made it in jail. There were rumors that Pluto did a stint in the penitentiary and got raped, which emotionally scarred him. He wasn't the same after that. The detectives looked at me with disbelief.

"We know that you don't take this stuff, unless you sold it to him?"

Calmly, I answered that they were mine. Detective Jesse James asked how old I was, and I replied, "Seventeen, sir."

"Are you going to go to jail for this drug head, penitentiary bound, no account buzzard?" Detective Doc asked.

I replied that the pills were mine, so they placed me under arrest and handcuffed me along with Pluto.

I was charged with delivery of a controlled substance. It was my first time being incarcerated but I wasn't worried. I knew a few of the guys in lock up and my reputation preceded me. I grew six inches and had been lifting weights, so my chest and arms were huge. Pluto was in the cell next to me, throwing up and crying all night long. Part of it was because he was having withdrawal symptoms from the drugs. I hollered out, "Shut up Pluto. Man, they're gonna let you out in the morning, after your prints clear."

Pluto was charged with loitering and released that morning. Milton bonded me out that afternoon and Reno rode with him to pick me up.

"Why did you take that case? I heard you took Pluto's rap," Milton asked.

I explained that I could deal with it better than him. Milton suggested that I work to pay back the bond money because I took a case that really wasn't mine, so that was on me. I understood and told Milton that I would pay him back the bond money once I got home.

The money was good, but it was too easy to catch a drug case and I wanted to keep my record clean. As I gave Milton his money I shared, "Drug dealing isn't for me, I'm done." He extended his hand saying, "If you need anything just let me know. That was a real G move (taking the rap) that you did but I couldn't have done it."

"Yeah, there are things that I could endure that you won't and things that you can handle that I can't. Whatever the situation, I'm still with you."

Next, I walked across the street and gave Bull my supply, telling him that I was finished with selling weed too, reminding him to hit me with some ends (money) when he sold out my stash, before he replenished.

"That's cool. I heard about you taking the charge for Pluto," Bull said. I confirmed that it was nothing. Bull asked if I wanted him to get at (punish) Pluto and I told him no, he's cool.

It was survival of the fittest even when we weren't generating money. Getting to school and providing my own meals were mandatory necessities that I had to take care of. There were so many other ways to get money, I just had to figure out which hustle would work for me. I tried all of them to see what fit me best. Soon I was a jack of all trades and a master at none.

I took my savings and purchased a nice, used Buick Electric 225, known on the streets as "A deuce and a quarter." Now the crew and I could move around, even though I didn't have a driver's license. Lucky and I only had driving permits, so Reno usually drove. He doctored up his birth certificate and lied saying that he was eighteen and obtained his driver's license a few years early.

The Grind

Our general grind was putting effort into making life easier and we had an angle for everything.

We hustled transfers to ride on public transportation without paying. When riders exited from back of the bus, we asked for their transfers which could be used to ride on another bus or train. Sometimes we just entered the bus from the rear door without paying.

We figured out how to eat most of our meals for free. We went to restaurants carrying a bug, hair, glass, or other foreign objects and after we ate a third of our meals, we complained to the waitress that we found objects in our food and refused to pay.

The crew always encouraged me to engage in conversations with girls wearing restaurant uniforms since they seemed to be more responsive to me. Most of the girls who worked at our favorite fast food establishments gave us free meals all the time.

We hardly ever paid party admission fees. One person would pay to get in, collect tickets and bring them outside to the crew or find the back door and let the crew in. After a person got a hand stamp, they went back outside and pressed their hand against another for a two for one deal.

We used miscommunication tactics to get free gas. We played our music loud so that the attendant couldn't hear us clearly. We requested two dollars' worth of gas, quickly corrected ourselves and ask for eight dollars' worth. Once he pumped seven dollars' worth of gas, we would ask the attendant to stop the pump, reiterating that we only requested "a dollar" not eight dollars.

Pickpocketing (The Blister)

I started a relationship with a girl named Smokey who joined our team. She was a con artist who always had a scheme going on. She didn't see herself as a criminal, so her facial expressions were different all the time, aimed at making you believe a lie. We called her Smokey because of her charcoal colored skin.

The next hustle that I tried was pickpocketing which is a game of distraction, requiring fast hands. It was known in the streets as Cannon. One of the easier, fool proof jobs that we worked on hot days, we named the Blister because of the distraction tactic used. While downtown, we spotted a female victim walking with her oversize purse hanging from her left shoulder.

Reno walked six feet behind her on the right side, pretending not to pay attention to where he was going and accidently tapped her shoulder with his lit cigarette. Simultaneously, Smokey walked up on the victim's left side, took her wallet out of the purse and discreetly handed it to Lucky as he past them, heading in the opposite direction. Smokey continued walking straight past the victim.

Totally consumed by what just happened, the victim shouted, "Ouch," as she turned towards Reno and brushed her shoulder, checking for damage to her skin. Reno apologized profusely. This job was a quick come up. She was carrying $1,500 but no identification so we couldn't obtain credit in her name. We jumped on the bus and headed back south glad that the Blister never failed.

We pulled off another pickpocketing caper on a summer evening. For our best results, we organized in a team of four: The Cannon (Reno), The Distracter (Lucky), The Spotter (Me) and The Writer (Smokey). We started this activity about one hour before the bank branches closed.

One experience was a game changer for me. Lucky, Reno, Smokey and I hit a lick (pickpocketed a victim). First, we caught a crowded bus from downtown heading south, then I identified a female victim.

Before Lucky could create a distracting situation, two guys started to argue, and everyone focused on them. Reno slightly brushed his arm across the victim's face, to direct her vision towards the distraction, at the same time blocking the victim from seeing Smokey go into her purse and pass her wallet to me.

A purse could be opened and a wallet taken within two seconds. Other ways that we pick pocketed included lifting wallets from a man's jacket or pants. We also slit victims' pockets with a razor so that the wallet fell straight through, landing in the Cannon's hand.

Check Writers

After the wallet was lifted, we got off the bus two stops later and I handed it back to Smokey. A Writer's job is to take the information that the Cannon retrieves from the victim's wallet, study it thoroughly and then go to the bank as swiftly as possible. Then Smokey opened a bank account in the victim's name, forty-five minutes before the banks closed. She obtained temporary checks and we immediately went shopping.

Writers had to be sharp with a photographic memory, exude confidence, without fear, unflustered when portraying the victim which required nerves of steel. Smokey was one of the best girl Cannons in the game.

The female Writer was a huge commodity, and everyone knew it so those girls were very picky about who they chose to work with and at 17 years old, Smokey understood her value. The Writer also had to look the part. Above all, she had to be an expert duplicating signatures and writing in the exact style of the victim. Every hustler desired a girl like that.

Our game had to be tight and we had to be slick with the appropriate skills. As a Spotter, I had to have the keen ability to select a victim that the Writer could easily emulate, taking into consideration their age, height, weight and size. The Distractor had to be great at getting everyone's attention and Lucky was an expert.

We directed Smokey on what to buy, purchasing big ticket items that included expensive jewelry, high end clothing, furs and electronics. We also drew funds from the bank accounts, used the victim's credit cards to purchase more items and got cash advances.

We always assumed the victim would immediately report their info stolen. The victim's information was "burnt out" (unusable) by morning so we didn't take a chance trying to use it again. The following day, we mailed the victim's wallet back to them.

Diversion

Being a Cannon was short lived. Although we used it to our advantage, the diversion on the bus that day was not created by us. However, it played a major part in my decision not to be a Cannon.

It was extremely crowded and a slick looking older dude was inpatient and rude. He bogarted his way through the people, bumping into everyone without saying excuse me. He shoved an older, heavy-set woman so hard that she almost fell into the seat where a square looking guy was sitting.

The square looking guy commented, "Man, why don't you show a little respect, we know you're trying to get off the bus, but you don't have to run folks over." The square guy got up and offered his seat to the heavy-set woman. The slick dude walked toward the back door, cursing, in an irate manner, pulled out a six-inch blade, threatening to stab him, warning that he better not get off the bus. The square guy reiterated several times, "I'm not looking for any trouble. I just want to get off the bus."

"Then you should have kept your mouth shut and mind your business," the slick dude yelled

The square guy walked toward the front door and the slick dude hurried out the back and ran to the front to meet him, with his knife out. He stabbed at the square guy who stepped back on the bus and walked to the back door. As the bus driver started to pull off, the square guy pulled the red emergency door opener which slows the bus down and ultimately to a stop.

As the square guy attempted to exit the bus, the slick dude kept poking the knife at the door. Finally, he stopped poking the knife and challenged the square guy to get off the bus. When the square guy got off the bus, the slick dude walked towards him with the knife in his hand and before he could raise his arm, the square guy pulled a gun from his waist, under his jacket, pointed it and shot the slick dude in his chest four times.

He took off running north, fleeing the scene fast. The bus driver drove off and all the passengers saw the slick dude laying in the gutter by the curb bleeding to death. People were screaming and crying on the bus.

From that point on, I realized that we didn't know what a person had in their pocket, who they were or what they were thinking. In any caper, I learned to always watch a person's midsection and analyzed all the reasons why being a Cannon didn't work for me:

1. I didn't like lifting wallets without having a gat (gun)
2. I didn't like going into someone's pocket, not knowing if they had a weapon
3. I didn't want to pull a gun out in public when I'm wrong, even if they pulled one on me first

Being a Cannon simply didn't fit my personality. It didn't feel right.

Three Card Molly (Meet Scandalous Trudy)

Then there was Three Card Molly where the object is to catch people who are trying to be slick. We had a 4-man team. We added a
girl named Scandalous Trudy who was down with all the hustles, no
matter what it was. She was a golden-brown skin girl, thick but not
too curvy, who stood about 5'7". She had soft features but kind
of masculine looking. She was rough around the edges but had a
loveable personality.

Three Card Molly was a card game consisting of one red and
two black cards. Each card was folded down the center so that
they were easy to pick up. The object was to slowly shuffle the
three cards while riding the back of a bus, allowing everyone to
see them. During one of our daily hustles, we held at least five
hundred dollars in our hand to entice victims. After shuffling the
cards, we asked if anyone knew where the red card landed.

The team pretended to be spectators who didn't know each
other. After I shuffled the cards, I turned my head away and Lucky
would lift the red card exposing it to all the observers. When I
turned back around, he would bet me fifty dollars and win. I shuffled the cards, turned away as I talked with the people and Lucky
exposed the red card again. Then I invited everyone to make a
hundred-dollar bet.

I chose someone and gave her twenty dollars. Scandalous Trudy
accepted my offer and bet one hundred dollars. I explained to the
girl that I gave the twenty dollars to that if Trudy chose the right card
she could keep the money. I turned to a lady and man who were sitting together and asked them to point to the red card and they did.
She chose the correct card and I passed her twenty dollars and Trudy
won one hundred dollars which I also passed to her. They all won.

Everybody on the bus applauded. I shuffled the cards again,
turned my head to the audience while Lucky lifted the red card once
more. I asked if anyone wanted to place a bet. Reno made a bet,
the lady and man said yes, betting two hundred each. I was ready
to pick up the card. I asked them all, "Are you sure, are you ready to
choose the card?" I made the final call asking if anyone else wanted
to bet and a girl accepted. I said, "Money on the wood make all
bets good." Everyone laid their money on the floor of the bus.

I came back to the cards and right before I picked them up, I shuffled one more time saying, "Chose the red." Lucky, Trudy and Reno pointed to the black card. Everyone else pointed to the black card and they all lost. I got off the bus at the next stop. The team waited and got off a few stops down.

That game taught me a lot. It was the simplest but of all the games, this was my main key to success. In any game, whether I'm doing right or wrong, I always remembered you can draw people in who are trying to get something for nothing. They can easily be tricked.

I understood what the older cats meant by always making me work for what I wanted. They said, "If we give you something without you working for it, we are making a bad hustler out of you. The only time you can be hustled is when you are trying to get something for nothing."

Nobody confessed or told me that Lucky looked at the card when my back was turned. That's how we always knew that we had an audience full of pigeons, trying to get something for nothing.

Deception is the greatest tool used to get over on someone. Showing them what their heart desires at little or no cost, lures them in but there is always a price. If you don't pay in the wash, you will pay in the rinse.

Whether you are a hustler or not, people sell themselves cheap or expensive, both making you think you are getting more than it's worth. On the bus, all the observers reacted the same. Conning is the most magnificent game that I ever witnessed because people are dishonest even when they don't realize it. They always try to beat the system, but it is more difficult to trick an honest person. This knowledge helped me sharpen my game and took it to the tenth power.

Tamar Pays Me Back

Reno and I were standing outside when one of my old customers walked up. Her name was Tamar. She used to buy Ts and Blues from me when I worked for Milton. When she made her last purchase, she was short and asked me for credit until the next day.

Since she was a beautiful girl who already prostituted, I took a chance and gave her credit under the condition that she would work off whatever she didn't pay, she agreed. In fact, she suggested that she go and work it off at that moment. I said I'd watch her back and she got in the car with us.

I looked at Reno and with excitement in his eyes he said, "Let's take her to the stroll on Cottage Grove."

We drove her there while I explained that we would be around and after each time she turned a date, to bring me the money. Tamar answered, "Ok." She got out the car and we sat there observing her as she worked. She walked with a sexy strut, watching each car that passed by.

It didn't take long for a car to pull over and stop. She spoke to the driver through the passenger window and then got in and they pulled off. About 10 minutes later, she walked to the back door of my car and handed me the money. She paid off her debt and then some. At that moment, I realized what it felt like to be a pimp. It wasn't bad at all. It would do for now, but my mind was on other hustles. Reno suggested, "Tamar could be both our hoe, right?"

"Yeah, she can but I'm in charge of her since she owed me money." I told him I'd split the money with him after she finished working. Reno got real cool, acting all fly popping his collar, talking slick and saying rhymes. He said, "Ain't nothing finer than checking loot from a prostitute. Now we're getting hoe money too." It was no big thing to me. I wasn't convinced that we were pimps.

We cruised down the Strip as I talked to her about working tomorrow. I told her to be ready at noon. Tamar replied, "That's cool, let's do it!" I dropped her off at home around the corner from me. She lived with her Uncle Bill who was an old customer of mine. All the dope fiends hung out at their house. It was easy to see how she got involved with drugs. I dropped Reno off at his place and went home. The following day, I promptly pulled up to Tamar's at noon and she was standing outside, ready to go.

I knew my mom would be at work. I drove her around to my house so that we could get a clear understanding of our situation. I took her into my room and she sat on my bed.

I started by saying, "Tamar I'm not a pimp but I'm into hustles that make money. Is hoeing the only hustle that you do because we have several other hustles going on?"

"This is the only way that I get money and it's what I like to do. If I hustle money, it's from a trick. I don't go into banks or do any of that other stuff."

Shaking my head, "I understand. Whatever you do, I see you giving it your all baby. You make it look easy out there. I think it's because you're so gorgeous or is it that everybody on the Strip is ugly?" We both laughed.

"What's your story? Where are your parents Tamar?"

She looked down and sighed, "I don't know who my father is, and my mom died when I was five years old. I lived with my grandma and three uncles. When I turned ten, my grandma died so I continued to live with my uncles."

Tamar's body language told me one thing, but her eyes said something different. She appeared to be cool and calm, but her eyes were very cold. She seemed like a prisoner trapped in a lonely place that only she knew and would never leave.

Maybe I'm wrong. I'll study her behavior more. She was beautiful and that seemed to get her what she wanted. She probably learned early to use what she had to force an advantage. Maybe she was trying to make everybody love her to make up for the people who didn't

After chatting for a few minutes, I grabbed her hand and we headed out. We rode onto the Strip. I parked and walked down the street to get Reno. We stood outside the car conversing and flexing. Prescott pulled up and shouted, "What's up Earthquake? What y'all up too?" Happy to see Prescott I answered, "We just chilling." He parked and stood outside with us.

He asked, "Who is that?" as Tamar got out of car and walked into the store.

"That's my new hoe, Tamar."

"Cause, she's cute. Where do you have her working?" Prescott asked. I told him on the Cottage Grove Strip where she made decent money.

Prescott advised, "Cause you should take her to Indiana where my girls work. She will really make some money, but she can't wear hot pants or booty shorts. Cause she needs to look more sophisticated. It's an incognito hoe club so she has to be dressed looking lady like."

I'm thinking, '*Yeah, he's right.*' I asked Prescott where I could get some nice dresses.

"My daddy's boutique, cause we can go over there right now."

I told Reno that Tamar and I would be back and we jumped in the car with Prescott.

At J-Hawk's boutique, Prescott walked through the door and said, "Hey daddy, Earthquake need some nice dresses for his girl. She going to work in Indiana where my girls are." Mr. J-Hawk asked her age and Tamar replied, nineteen. I was hoping Prescott didn't say my age since I wasn't sure if Tamar knew that I was only sixteen.

Mr. J-Hawk looked at her, then over at me and Prescott and said, "What did I tell you and Pow Wow about Earthquake? I told y'all, don't tell me I don't know what I'm talking about." Mr. J-Hawk got a real kick out of seeing us. He laughed continuously. I still didn't see myself as a pimp, it was just an added hustle. Mr. J-Hawk sold me a dress and gave me one for free.

We chopped it up with him while Tamar tried on her new clothing and then we left. I always enjoyed kicking it with Mr. J-Hawk; he was too clever. Prescott dropped us off at my car and confirmed that he would come back to pick us up at 7:00 p.m.

I told Reno and he was thrilled so we took her to our make shift spot, a storage space located in the laundry room of my building where we built a club house because I couldn't have girl company and Reno couldn't either. We converted my mom's 20X20 storage space and created our own little studio. He nailed sheets of drywall over bland wood, got two mattresses, sheets, chairs, rugs, smell goods and other furnishings from our homes and made it look real cozy and nice.

Reno was very good with his hands. He could build anything, plus he was a neat freak. He was very creative and could design and reconstruct items.

She got dressed while we waited for Prescott. He picked us up and took us to East Chicago which is in Indiana. The club was crowded, filled with men and women of all races. Prescott suggested that I let Tamar go and do her thing while he explained how things operated.

Girls took tricks outside to their cars, turned a date and then went back into the club. I made sure that she had plenty of rubbers. Tamar worked very well that night. There were a lot of prostitutes in that place and we were behaving like we were pimps. They didn't even ask us for any identification at the door.

After work, Prescott dropped us off at my car. Tamar asked if she could get some money to get Tees and Blues because she was feeling queasy. I handed her the money and directed her to buy it from Jimmy Red who worked for Milton. I didn't want to ride with drugs in my car because one jail experience was enough. He gave her a package and we took her to the clubhouse.

We opened the combination lock that we installed. Reno and I sat there and watched while Tamar prepared her drugs.

She pulled a little kit out of here purse. She crushed the pills in the bottle top, added a little water, then took a cigarette butt and put it into a syringe. She warmed the pills by lighting a fire underneath the bottle top and then sucked the contents up in the syringe. While still holding the bottle top, she tied a rubber band around her left bicep. Then she drew blood from her arm using the syringe.

While watching her, Reno passed out for a few seconds and then got up and ran out. As I watched, the blood and dissolved pills mixed together, then she injected it into her arm. It was gross an extreme turnoff, but this was business and that's how I handled it. About five minutes later she was real mellow and her eyes were glassy but everything else about her was the same.

She asked if I was taking her home. I didn't answer immediately but was thinking what's wrong with the clubhouse. Before I could say anything, Reno nudged me and suggested that we take her to his mom's house since no one was there but her. I said, "Ok, let's ride," and we went out to the Manor.

When we arrived, Reno's mom was in her bedroom. He took Tamar to the bathroom so that she could shower and freshen up and I went into the basement.

Reno's mom was cool. He told her the situation and she said that it was ok for us to stay. We spent the night and the three of us slept on the let-out couch which opened into a bed. We laid there just talking. Reno said, "Tell her to have sex with me," and I did. I watched him stroke her down. I was thinking about that needle and how disturbing that was. I knew I wouldn't be having sex with her. He could, but I never would.

The next day we took her to work at the same place and she did well. We split the money again and went back to his mom's house to drop Tamar off. She got cool with Reno's mom. As we were leaving, he decided to stay there with Tamar, so I headed out. I confirmed that I would picked them up at 7:00 p.m. for work tomorrow.

When I arrived the following day, I walked in and heard the three of them upstairs talking so I announced that I was there and then went to the basement. Tamar seemed right at home. After a few minutes, I called up to Reno saying let's go so that we could get an early start. Tamar came down the stairs looking classy and beautiful as ever. She was wearing lipstick and looking super fine.

Reno came down. "I have to tell you something. Tamar wants me to be her man, not both of us. She chose me. We'll look out for you since you're driving, but she with me now."

"Ok I'm cool with that," thinking as long as I get half of the money, he can screw her all he wants. I wasn't going to have sex with her.

"Tell him that you like me now."

"Yeah, I'm going to be with him," Tamar confirmed. "Are we still cool?"

"Yeah sweetie, it is, what it is. Y'all bumped into each other's lives and that's y'alls collision. Y'all are an accident meant to happen."

She smiled, and Reno hollered, "Let's go." We took her to work.

Tamar seemed to be uncomfortable. She kept staring at me like she wanted to tell me something. I wondered what happened. Did she choose him because they had sex or did Reno and his mom sway her? Well, it didn't matter as long as he split the money it worked for me. That night after work we picked her up. In the car, Tamar told us about another location that she learned of, so we went to that club I was thinking the more money she makes the bigger the split.

It was pouring down rain as we headed to the club. My coil wire got wet and my car stopped in the middle of a dimly lit, two-lane road. Reno and I were under the hood drying the coil wire. We finally got the car started but it was raining so hard we could hardly see. We decided to try the new club another day.

Suddenly, we heard loud screeching tires approaching. A car swerved out of control and ran head on into a large oak tree a few yards away to avoid hitting us from the back. They must have been driving about 60mph and didn't have any lights on. Since my car was stalled, we didn't have any lights on either. The driver and his passenger were both bleeding and clearly in a lot of danger.

The driver was unconscious and the passenger was semi-conscious. He mumbled, "Get some help." We finally got my car started and drove to a convenience store about five minutes away. Frantically, we told the 2 clerks in the store what happened. They called 911 and requested police and an ambulance.

"Let's go back, we need to make sure they aren't dead. If they hadn't swerved, they would've killed us!" I told Reno.

He snatched the keys out of my hand and said, "Come on, get in the car now!" Tamar hollered, "Get in the car please Earthquake, let's go."

I jumped in the passenger seat and Reno sped down the road until we reached the freeway. We all sat in silence for a while. We drove the speed limit and made it home safe. Tamar went into the house while we sat in the car. I finally spoke, "That driver saved our lives and I hope that they're ok. Man, Reno, that was a good call. You know we can't trust the police out there. Indiana is known for not being fond of Black people. They might have blamed us for something."

He took out the money and handed me funds for gas. I looked at it and asked him, "Where is my half?"

"She only wants to be with one person so here is a little extra." He peeled off about $30 more. I agreed even though I felt cheated.

I told him that I would see them tomorrow. I couldn't help thinking that she was a dope fiend snake. *'The next time I get a hoe, she won't be using drugs. Reno didn't even split the money, but I'm supposed to pick them up for work? Imma give him a chance to think about that.'* I took them to work the next day and he did the same thing. Stick a fork in me, I'm done! I told him to take his gas money and the few dollars he gave me and take a cab. I'm not picking you or your hoe up tomorrow.

He said that I was wrong and ran down a list of things he had to do. His mom overheard us and came into the basement adding, "Y'all shouldn't be arguing over a woman. When I was young, I liked two friends. I was dating one but liked the other one much more. I chose his friend and he had to accept this is how the game goes. They didn't fall out over it."

"It wasn't about the hoe choosing him. It was about not splitting the money. I know what you mean but due to the circumstances, I'm going to leave and I'll talk to you whenever," I explained.

I decided to drive to the Westside to see Ice Kat. When I arrived at his building, I saw him standing out there with his crew. Ice Kat was immaculately dressed, wearing five gold ropes, with a gold and diamond watch and ring. He was iced out (bling) and had just bought a new black Benz.

He walked up and told me to follow him. As we headed towards his work car, a Chevy Impala, Ice Kat said, "Since we all turned Mob, they gave me a new position. I supply this part of the Westside. This area is my territory and I've got five spots (dope locations) selling ounces and eight balls of cocaine and dope. I also got two bad boosters and a hoe. Life is pretty good right now."

I told him that I had a hoe, but Reno took her. "I really don't want to be a pimp anyway, but if a hoe gave me money, I ain't turning nothing down but some alcohol."

We fist bumped and climbed into his Chevy. I told him about all my most recent hustles. I explained how I got caught with the pills and he laughed and said, "It's not always what you do but how you do it."

He had two twelve packs of Coca-Cola on the back seat. "Earfy, do you want a Coke?" I said, "yes," grabbed a can, opened it and started to drink. A few seconds later a van pulled over, a tall guy got out, walked up to our vehicle and handed Ice a wad of money. He got back into the van and left while we drove to the next block.

"Let me get some of your pop," Ice Kat said. I handed it to him and he unscrewed the can, which was two pieces. One half of the can was filled with Coke and the other half had an eight ball of cocaine. Ice took the drugs out of the bottom part of the can, twisted it back together and handed the pop back to me. "Enjoy your drink."

A short dude casually walked over to the car, Ice handed him the eight ball and we drove off. I was too impressed. The Coca-Cola can looked so real because it contained real pop. It also felt like a real can of soda. To have decoy cans was brilliant. "That was quite clever. I guess it's all about how you do it."

I saw his operation. He never delivered drugs and money in the same place. He also didn't deliver product to the same person who paid him. Ice Kat made five additional deliveries and then pulled up to a compact Audi. He twisted the center of his car horn off and retrieved another package of drugs. A guy wearing a black brim styled hat got out of the Audi, walked over to Ice, and received the package, then we left scene.

Ice Kat was slick. While riding, I heard officer chatter. He and his crew had police radios tuned in on their frequency. They knew where the officers were at all times. His operation was solid. Ice Kat extended an invitation asking, "You want to come out West with me? I've got two apartments that I rarely use."

"Thanks Ice Kat but no more drug selling for me. I got four other jobs going on. I got a full-time job, a part-time job, a paper route and I sell snow cones on the break. I'm a hustler baby!" I responded with gratitude. We were cracking up.

Ice Kat advised, "You have to narrow those jobs down, find your niche and perfect it. Either way, if you need me, I'm here. Do you have any money?" I told him that I was cool and was about to head back South. I gave him a brotherly hug when we got back to my car and said, "You be real careful out here."

I made it back around the strip and heard Reno calling my name, so I stopped. He approached the passenger door kind of agitated and said, "Earthquake, I know we ain't gonna fallout about no hoe. Man, I let her go. You my homie. We should never be angry about a hooker."

I shouted back at him, "Next time we get a hoe, there is no sharing the money, ok?"

He thought for a second and said, "That doesn't go for bust-downs (tramps) do it?"

"No, it doesn't nasty man. You hungry?"

"You know it." We went and got a pizza.

The next afternoon, we were chilling on the Strip. I loved when Reno imitated people, especially girls. He was the most observant person I had ever seen. He was hilarious. He paid attention to every detail, perfection or imperfection, focusing on wrinkles and subtle changes in everyone. He helped me zoom in on distinguishing things about each of them, which led me to concentrate on their body language. Then I would determine what that movement meant.

This pretty new girl in the hood who just moved from Georgia spoke to us. She was light-brown skinned, standing about 5'5" with a small upper body and a perfect hand full of breast. She had a small waistline with a big butt and hips. Her wavy hair was styled into a short curly natural.

"I been wanting to holler at her for the longest but look at how she's choosing you," Reno revealed. "Let's get her."

"She's ok. Why don't you just talk to her yourself?" I asked reluctantly.

He was hyper when he expressed, "Because she's checking you out. Look at how she's throwing it," referring to her sexy, inviting walk.

When she went into the store, Reno imitated her walk and it was too funny. She came out, I beamed in and called her over. As she walked toward us, I tried to see if she was emotionally attracted or just admired me. That would determine my approach.

"I forgot your name. What is it?"

Sounding slightly disappointed, with a southern accent she answered, "Belinda." She looked off to the side and said, "You must not like me, you didn't even remember my name."

With a slight smile I conveyed, "So, if I don't automatically overlook your sexiness, does that make me inconsiderate? I didn't recall your name, but I remembered your unforgettable style. I was thinking about you. Is it possible to miss someone you don't know? Have you ever experienced that?"

"Yes, I have, now that you put it that way," she answered, blushing as her face lit up.

I continued macking saying, "You learn what you really want through experience. I want you to explore me and other things. Then you'll know what you really desire. Can we share an experience?" Spellbound, she said, "yes." We exchanged numbers and I confirmed that we would get together later that night. As she walked away, she swung those hips, throwing that body like she was Miss America.

Reno rushed over wanting to know what she said. I asked myself the question, *'Am I contributing to Reno being spoiled and selfish? This is the eighth girl that I convinced to have sex with him. He was getting lazy. Come to think of it, they're all getting too relaxed with their game, slacking on their macking. All my crew on the Strip have been waiting for me to come up with females instead of talking for themselves. I think I'll teach old Reno a lesson tonight.'* I snapped out of my thoughts and heard Reno frantically hollering, "What she say? What she say?" I told him that she was going to get with us that night, we'd pick her up later. With a naughty disposition he blurted, "She's bodied up!"

We went to get Lucky because it was time to make some money. We did what we do, on our daily hustles and made some ends. Later, we picked Belinda up. My mom went out with her childhood friend who moved on the second floor so, I took her to my house. I could tell that she wanted me sexually and Reno wanted her.

We went into my bedroom while Reno chilled up front on the couch watching television. While we were undressing, I asked her how she knew that she wanted me.

"I know what I want, there is no mistake about it," she said.

I suggested that she give Reno some first to see if she still would want me. "Do that for me?" I said in a softer voice.

"No, why do you want me to do that?"

I tried to convince her that we both would discover what we wanted. She came right out and said, "Let me have you first and then we'll see." As I laid on my back, she slowly rolled on top of me, vigorously pumping. Belinda was a natural born freak. After twenty minutes, I realized that this girl could go all night, so I stopped, got up and gave her a towel.

I walked out of the room and told Reno to take his clothes off and go on in. He removed them so fast that it was crazy. He walked toward the door, I stopped him and said, "Give me ten dollars."

"Come on, she's gonna change her mind," he said anxiously. I shook my head, "Nope, give it here."

"At a time like this?" Quickly, I replied, "Yep, ten bucks Chief." He grabbed his pants off the floor, went into his pocket, gave me ten dollars and ran into the room. I took a shower and when I came out, I heard her saying, "Dag Reno, what are you trying to do, get your balls in it?" I walked into the room as they finished.

I asked her who she like. She said, "I still like you."

Reno got up and went to the bathroom while I laid down next to her for about five minutes. Seemingly concerned she said, "I don't have to do this with Reno anymore, do I?" I laughed and said, "perhaps." She didn't say anything. A few seconds later she asked, "What's next?" I told her that I would let her know. The three of us talked for a while and then I took her home.

Reno's first words to me were, "Why you charge me ten dollars?"

"I should have shared with you right? See how you feel. You need to learn not to be so selfish all the time."

"Can I have my ten back?"

"I could keep your ten dollars for my own benefit but I'm going to lead by example. You shouldn't be so stingy. Think about others. Learn the meaning of sharing and start practicing it. There's honor amongst players, I returned his money and said, "Now who's your teacher?"

"You, syrup head Sammy," he replied and then I dropped him off.

I rode down the Strip and saw King Fish and Milton standing near the corner store, so I parked and hung out with them. We saw a fine caramel complexioned lady with long, reddish-brown hair, built real nice, kind of sophisticated looking. She had to be around thirty years old.

She was headed towards us and I asked Milton, "Who is that?"

"That's Nicky Blaze. That's Poison's ex-woman. Poison was one of the Rock's main fifteen. He ran the Strip territory back in the day. They have a 13-year-old son. They're cool now, just like family. She's been around for a long time," he answered.

He continued giving me the lowdown saying, "She's a gangsta chick. She looks sweet, but she will fight and shoot that pistol. I don't know of her fooling around with anyone else."

As we stood there, I started getting closer to Milton and King Fish, trying to look older. I never wanted to talk to someone that old, but she was fine – she was something. I thought I would just harmlessly flirt. She walked past.

"Hey Miss lady."

"How are you doing?" she asked, with a radiant smile as she gracefully walked into the store.

"Do you know what to say?" King Fish asked me.

"No, but I will."

She walked out of the store and I murmured, "You're extraordinary!"

She stopped. "Excuse me?"

I walked up to her and she had a serious look on her face. "Most people are creatures of habit but I'm a man of instinct. That's the determining factor of my decision making. When I see something or someone I like, I know it instantly and have a compulsion to get to know that person, place or thing. My intuitions haven't failed me yet. This is the right time, I'm in the right place and this is the right thing to do. At this moment, whatever you decide, you won't be wrong. I'm Earthquake."

"Woe, I'm Nicky Blaze," she answered, shaking her head smiling.

"Where do you live?" I avoided eye contact as I could see her staring at me.

"Down the street. Are you going to visit me sometime?"

"Give me a reason," I suggested as I smiled.

"Dinner, what do you like to eat?" Nicky asked.

"I'm not picky, whatever you choose for me. Here's my number, what's yours?"

"Dinner will be ready in two hours," she said as she handed me her number.

"I'll call you," I said, as she walked off.

King Fish and Milton laughed. "We ain't never seen Nicky Blaze smile like that. You just bumped a vet!"

"It's elementary fellows, what can one say," I told them as I pimp walked back to them. I popped my collar and announced, "She's about to fix me dinner." We continued chopping it up and I saw my booster chick, Veronique, walking towards us. We went boosting earlier that day and she was returning from selling the merchandise, so she handed me some ends (money).

I told Veronique she could hang out with me for a couple of hours, but I would be going to dinner later. She saw me talking with Nicky and asked, "With the lady that you were just talking to?"

"Yes baby, you wanna go over there with me?"

With a stank face she quickly said, "I'll see you when you leave her house." Veronique understood that I was a player and a hustler, and she respected that. I liked that about her. When I called Nicky Blaze, she told me that dinner was ready. She gave me her address, which was two blocks down on the Strip.

Nicky Blaze had two children who were almost my age. I never went with girls who had children. It was weird. Her son was fourteen and her daughter was twelve, but I liked her shorties (kids). She had a very nice three-bedroom apartment. She took me into her bedroom where she had a La-Z-Boy chair. I sat in the chair while she put a tray on my lap and brought in a plate filled with smothered pork chops, rice, green peas and red Kool-Aid. I ate well.

We talked, and I told her that I was a hustler and had a few hustling chicks.

"I know, the girls all like you and I can see why," she said.

"I can only handle a few. I know my limit. You are enough for me Nicky Blaze."

She looked at me with those big bedroom eyes and said, "I don't think you know your own strength. When you find out, you're are going to be a force to be reckoned with." I didn't have a clue what she was talking about.

"How old are you?" she asked next.

"Twenty-two."

She relaxed on her bed wearing a simple blue house dress, answering, "Yeah, you're still young. You got a ways to go." I was thinking, *'If she thought that was young, wait until she finds out that I'm only sixteen.'* So, I quickly changed the subject.

"What do you do for a living?"

Nicky answered, "I manage a barbeque restaurant. I'm the cashier, I handle all the cash."

"Why do you handle all of the cash?"

"Because my boss and I have a special relationship. I also have a white, FBI friend. You understand?"

"Yeah, they're your sugar daddies, Santa Claus and St. Nick," I said. We both laughed. I was thinking, 'She's like a hooker with only two clients.'

She was a hustler like me and I liked that in her. She was doing her thing discreetly. I bit into my pork chop and said, "So, your pappies are like having a couple of tricks, right?"

She sat on the bed, leaning back, crossed her legs and answered, "Well, we have an arrangement. I do my part and they do theirs."

"You call it one thing and I say it's another. It's the same string but a different yo-yo. I understand!"

I saw a Samurai sword on the side of her bed with a beautiful casing. I asked her what it was for and she explained.

"Back in the day I was known for carrying it around. Every now and then, a crazy chick would test me, trying to take my spot since I was Poison's girl. I had to be ready for whatever." Nicky Blaze got up and took my tray into the kitchen. She came back into the room and sat on the edge of the bed. I gazed at her sexy body with unblemished skin, looking like the streets didn't scathe her at all.

I told her that she didn't look so tough. I held her wrists and playfully pushed her onto the bed. She gave me an innocent smile. I looked away and she leaped up behind me, grabbed my neck, and wrapped her legs around my waist. I flipped her over my back and she plunged to the bed. She jumped up and attempted to scissor me, throwing her thighs around my neck. I picked her up, over my head and threw Nicky on the bed, got on top and pinned both of her hands down.

"You give up?" she asked looking up at me.

My eyes were focused on her, all sweaty and sexy, breathing hard. "Nope," gently leaned down and gave her a soft tongue kiss. Slowly opening my eyes, I saw the Samurai sword in front of my neck. With a devious smile, she looked at me and said, "Do you give up now?"

Laughing I replied, "Yeah, spare me until our next rendezvous." I took the sword out of Nicky Blaze's hand and dropped it on the floor. She was very interesting. I wanted to see where this was going.

I stayed for a few hours and then headed back down to the Strip and met up with Lucky and Reno. In a swagged out tone, I told them, "I came up with this vet chick and she's fine, she looks cold!"

Reno knew exactly who I was talking about. We jumped in the whip, rode to Lon City and parked in front of my house to discuss some business. We saw about a dozen young mob dudes walking down the street. There were two bad little broads with them.

They all spoke. As they passed us, the two girls were being friendly while reckless eyeballing us (flirting). We finished mapping out our plans of how to come into some big money, possibly robbing a bank or a McDonald's or something. A few minutes later, the two mob chicks were walking back our way alone. We asked them their names and they introduced themselves as Keena and Dana. Keena gravitated to me and Reno rushed over and started a conversation with Dana. Lucky was a little too slow this time.

We went for a drive with Lucky at the wheel. Reno and I were in full mack mode. Both girls were pretty as buttons, kind of erotic, looking like sisters. We took them to our clubhouse and to our surprise they loved it. We told them from now this would be our secret spot. We can always meet here. They agreed, and we planned to meet at the building at noon tomorrow. We dropped them off and went home.

We met up at noon and rode everywhere. We even went out west to George's music room and listened to the latest records. We wanted to hear this new sound called rap music. I was anxious to buy the first rap album by the Sugar Hill Gang. We got there and each one of us put earphones on, just sampling the latest songs. Keena and I seemed to enjoy all the same songs. Reno and I started doing our old dancing group moves that we got from Soul Train while in grammar school.

Reno and Dana started vibing to the old-school jams. Keena recognized a song and shouted, "That's my favorite song in this whole wide world." It was a group called The Fifth Dimension who sang "One Last Bell to Answer." She pantomimed as if she wrote the song herself and sang it to me. At that moment, Keena was a star! After that great performance, we wanted an encore and Keena whispered to me, "You'll get your encore in private."

I grabbed my album and her hand pulling her out the door as Reno and Dana followed suit. We drove back out South. In the car, the girls asked where we were off to next. I started to sing the popular amusement park anthem, "Fun Town Fun Town for the kids and you, 95th & Stony Island Avenue and Reno joined me singing the next verse. The girls got excited and started screaming with enthusiasm.

We rode some rides, bumper cars, played games and bought cotton candy. Reno even won a large stuffed Teddy Bear which he handed over to Dana. We liked those mob girls. They were cool to hang out with. After the sun went down, we drove to Avalon Park, relaxed, just vibing in the car listening to the radio's slow jam hour. We were kissing and getting into each other.

After hustling each day, we spent more and more time with them. Sometimes we would take them to the clubhouse and just chill. One night after my mom went to school, Keena and I spent time at my house while Reno and Dana stayed in the clubhouse. We never had the opportunity to have sex until now. I took her to my room and gently laid her on the bed. She felt so soft and irresistible. Her kiss was nice. I could taste the sweet cotton candy on her mouth.

Keena pulled back and asked, "Are you my man?"

"If you have to ask, then maybe I'm not."

"Well, I want you to be my man. I'm a down chick. You need a woman like me. I got your front and your back."

"I don't need no gangsta chick. I need a down for whatever chick. Straight like that."

"That's me all the way. I'm always down for the cause. Straight like that."

The electricity in her words sent currents through me. She was on 10. We were both amused.

"Earthquake, you know I'm crazy about you."

"If you are crazy about me, then don't be hanging out with those mob dudes."

She hesitated and said, "Ok, but those are my folks. You know I'm mob for life. That's where I come from."

"Ok, I'm mob too, but you got a new chief so there is no more screwing those little dudes. Which one of them are you sexing? You can tell me." Her voice poured out calmly as she pulled me in her truth

"No one. I don't screw just to be doing something. Besides, I'm with you now." I laid her down and she kissed me with emotion as we fell into a love making scene from a movie. After that, they were with us on a regular.

One night after we dropped the girls off, I noticed that Reno kept gouging at the crotch of his pants. I watched him as he continued. We were driving as I kept having an uncontrollable itch. After dropping him off, I went home and took a nice long shower. It was the only thing that sooth the itch for a while.

Before I got into bed, Reno called. "What's up?"

"Man, I got the willy's. I saw some tiny bugs on my pubic hair. I got the crabs," Reno said.

"I think I got them too."

"Are there little spots in your underwear?" he asked.

"Yeah man. We both have them. We've got to go to the clinic in the morning."

That morning, we went and got Lucky, went to the VD (Venereal Disease) Clinic on 22nd Street called the Little Red School House. They gave each of us a thorough check up and diagnosed us with crabs. They gave us Kwell lotion which kills the crabs and its eggs instantly. The doctor provided specific directions to wash all our clothes, bed linen in bleachy hot water and completely dry everything.

Lucky had a ball teasing us. I told Reno that we were through with those nasty chicks and he agreed. After constantly calling, they came over that evening since we never returned their calls. We told them that we were through with them because they gave us crabs. Keena cried. As tough as she was she acted, she cared.

"Please don't quit me. I'm sorry. I love you," she begged.

Reno did the same thing to Dana. He sarcastically told her to get the Kwell lotion and use it. Then we dismissed them.

They kept calling and stopping by the house. One day they saw my car in front of my house. Reno and I were peeping out the window watching them. I suggested to Reno, "Let's get rid of them once and for all. If they want to be with us, then they have to make a difference. Everybody has to do something." We walked outside, and they came running over to us.

"I don't want to lose you, please give us another chance. I'll make it up to you. I'm down for whatever," Keena said.

We allowed them to come into the clubhouse and talked about hustling.

"What hustles do you all know?" I asked.

They said none. Putting them to the challenge I was very clear explaining, "Well we gotta make some money around here and everybody need a job. Everybody has to have a hustle. Y'all wanna learn how to boost?"

"No, I don't know how to steal. I don't think I'll be good at that," Keena replied.

"Well, maybe you can be hoes," I said.

They both got quiet and then Keena answered, "I don't know about that."

"Both of you are having sex with somebody for free, just giving it away when you can use what you got and make it work for us. So, what do y'all want to do, catch grands (money) or catch crabs?" I explained.

Both started talking. "We're sorry, let us make it up to y'all. We're willing to be down for whatever."

This triggered something strong in me with no hesitation. "Baby we're trying to have thousands. Can't you see that you ain't nothing but money? Look at how fine y'all are. You are sitting on a gold mine. I know you all aren't scared." I strongly illustrated to Keena. "How can there be resistance to a gold mine and reject wealth, unless one is poor in the mind and can't see the riches. Are you poor in your heart or can you see the money? We'll do anything to protect our gold mine. We are gonna make it happen one way or another. So, are you all down with that?"

They both were quiet and then Dana spoke. "I'm down with my man."

"I'm willing," Keena replied.

"Being willing is the main ingredient. Can you see the wealth or are you poor in sight, unable to envision the process? See sweetie, all that it takes is love and we are family now, so we got that. We're in good health and you are sitting on the wealth. Straight like that! Love, health, and wealth is unbeatable. That's all we need," I said.

They both listened intently as I went on to say, "When you love your job, you never have to work. When you are healthy in mind and body, you are able to rise to any challenge. When you have a talent that people value, that's wealth. Love, health and wealth are the three keys to success and when applied, you can't lose. In that order! First, you have to get rid of the crabs. It's obvious that you're not Virgin Marys' but from this point on, there is no more screwing for free. There is a fee for everything, even conversation."

That afternoon we took the girls to the clinic to get full check-ups. Lucky rode with us. He constantly teased Reno and me about catching the crabs and it was really funny.

While the girls were being treated, we told Lucky that was ok because we took a bad situation and turned it around. Now we've got two hookers and we are about to make more money. Reno reiterated to Lucky that they we're pimping now. "We got new game. Fresh fish on the line."

"Yeah, you all are serving Fillet Mignon with a side of crab cakes. That has to be scratch-a-locus," Lucky responded in agreement.

We left the clinic and dropped the girls off at the clubhouse so that they could chill while the guys and I rode the stroll, scoping out locations where we could watch them date. Reno and I wanted to look like we really knew what to do, especially when we took the girls to work.

I was thinking, *If this is going to be one of my trades, I'll have to learn everything about this hustle.* That experience with Tamar was good since it taught us the basics. All the major older guys who pimped, worked their girls on the strolls. Slick Rick and Icy Mike were very impressive and caught my attention, so we studied their pattern. Reno, Lucky and I were learning as we went and put together our own game plan.

Back at the clubhouse, I told the girls that they were going to work the stroll on Cottage Grove Street. I gave them proper instructions explaining, "Walk sexy and when a car stops, ask if they want to turn a date. When they ask how much, you reply,' date cost one hundred dollars.' If they don't have it, then give the limited service that covers their budget. You will direct the tricks to an area where we are parked. After you turn each date, bring the money to us and then go back to work."

I warned our girls, "Do not to look any pimp in their eyes because that's called reckless eyeballing and he can break you (take your money). Never get into any cars with 'slick cats' (flamboyant players) because they can claim that you are choosing them."

"What if a trick looks like a pimp and ask to turn a date?" Keena asked.

"That's money that you pass up. It is a tactic that pimps use to trick girls into getting into their car so that they can try to 'gorilla pimp' a hoe," I warned them.

"What's gorilla pimping?" Dana asked.

"Pimping by force." I gave her the lowdown.

The night approached as we drove Keena and Dana to observe all the hookers working each corner. Then we went further down and let them out where it wasn't as busy. As they walked, cars immediately pulled over. Both got into two separate cars and pulled off. They both came back to our car thirty minutes later. Keena had eighty dollars and Dana only had sixty-five. We explained that time was money, and they needed to cut the time spent with each trick down to fifteen minutes.

I noticed when they got back to the car and handed us our first trap (money) they were different. They acted like hookers. Lucky was laid back hollering up to the front seat, "I just thought of new names for y'all, 'Pimp Itchy and Pimp Scratchy' who got the two baddest hoes on the Strip. They're straight royalty 'Scratch-Heiness' and 'Your Scratchy-ness'." We were cracking up.

"Man look at all of those tricks out there. We could be sticking some of them up," I said.

Reno shoved me saying, "No, we don't want to run the tricks off. Then we won't be getting any money, bone head."

Lucky suggested that we get out the car and try to come up with more hoes. I told him and Reno to go while I focused on my one hoe first. They walked the Stroll and Lucky made friends with one girl in particular.

We left the Stroll, ending work at about 11:30 pm. Dana and Keena went on and on about their experience. They told us about the girls they met and who their pimps were. A few girls asked them if they were happy with their man, letting them know that their pimps would welcome new girls into their families. Keena conveyed that she eagerly expressed to those hoes, "I'm happy with my situation. Y'all should get with my pimp."

Keena said that a hoe named Twinky asked who her pimp was and she replied, "Earthquake."

"Oh, I heard of him. He has a hoe named Tamar. Are you his bottom hoe?" Twinky asked.

Keena asked Twinky what a bottom hoe was, and she told her that, "It's his main girl, the number one out of all of his girls." Keena confirmed that she was my bottom hoe, without revealing that she was my only girl.

She continued telling me all that she learned and then inquired, "Who is Tamar baby?"

"She's an ex-hooker of mine," I said proudly.

"Am I going to be your bottom hoe when you get more girls?" Keena asked.

My face raised into a smile as I kicked back. The volume of my voice was soothing, "If you are the most loyal to me, you can." Keena slapped a high five with Dana and remarked, "I'm gonna be, no doubt." I smirked, feeling all pimpish as we dropped them off at their homes and confirmed to meet at the clubhouse tomorrow at noon.

The next day, we took the girls to K-Mart, bought them work outfits and gave them twenty dollars each and they were so happy. For the next few weeks, we dedicated most of our time to them, prepping them for the night. We supplied them with condoms, lubricants and baby wipes.

Let My Hoe Arm Go!

We established a routine. The girls always met us at my building and I'd lead them to the clubhouse. One day when Reno arrived on my block, he saw the Mob dudes with Dana and ran toward them. The Mob dudes had her by the arm. Reno confronted them even though they were a dozen strong. "Let's go," he told Dana.

"Hey this is Mob hoe now. She owes the Mob dues and she's gotta work it off."

Reno forcefully jerked her arm and said, "This my hoe. Let her arm go."

One of them tried to ply Reno's hand away and Reno struck him dead in his jaw. He fell on the ground, jumped up and punched Reno in the face. They started to fight. I heard the commotion, ran out and knocked the dude down that hit Reno.

"We don't have no problem with you Earthquake. It's this hoe that owe us!"

"I don't care, but she's leaving with Reno that's it!"

Suddenly Pow Wow pulled up, jumped out of his car with a Glock in his hand and said, "What are y'all trying to do to my brother?"

The Mob piled up behind me as they all started explaining at once, "Nothing Pow Wow, we were into it with Reno."

"You heard me, leave him alone!"

The energy Reno felt exploded into a scorch that boiled in his veins. He ran over and hit the main dude he argued with. They bagged off real fast and said that the whole situation was squashed. Pow Wow jumped back into the driver seat of his shiny green Cadillac and we all parted ways. Reno, Dana and I went back into my house and the Mob disbursed from the block.

My brother had to be careful because the police were looking for him and being around those kinds of situations attracted police. Reno didn't have any more Mob trouble, and everything was smooth sailing after that. Reno and I discussed what happened.

The Mob fellas reminded me that we were one in the same. The only difference is they had no one to teach them the ropes, not even the right way to hustle. They were traveling in packs, willing to take from one lion when they were strong in numbers.

They would take a meal if they could. I broke it down to Reno using an example I saw on the television program Wild Kingdom (The Discovery Channel). "See Reno, you are Mob from the Strip and they're not familiar with you. They felt that you came into their territory. At first, they didn't mind until they realized you took the honey and turned it into money. Realizing the value of the food, they wanted it back. I live here in Lon City. Since Pow Wow and I are Mob, they wouldn't test us. Catching you alone, they thought you were a sole lion and a pack of hyenas will try to take prey from one lion."

Filled with frustration Reno blurted out, "I don't care about all that. If he ever approaches me again, I'll crack him in the head with a bat and there will be one less hyena, Mob or not!" Reno calmed down and remarked, "Yeah, you're right. We be doing that too."

"One day the Mob boys will become lions but right now they're just hyenas. Human nature versus animal behavior is interesting. It's survival of the fittest. You know how it go! The game is cold but it's fair, big fish eat little fish," I reiterated.

Reno laughed in agreement saying, "Yeah but you know I'm a shark but it's good to have my dolphin buddy backing me up anyway."

"Let's go," he told Dana.

As the days went by, I spent more time on this hustle than anything else. The player game came upon me and I willingly accepted. If pimping should evolve into a main hustle, I wanted to know the ins and outs of it all. Even though I didn't consider myself a pimp, I was determined to make the situation work for me.

Since I was a natural player, automatically I knew what to do and could easily see the similarities in being a pimp. Being a pimp is the same as being a player and the word pimp is a slang word for player. The terms are used to describe many behaviors. The same is true for the word "hoe." Loose women are called hoes, but the real hoes walk the strolls. They're also called prostitutes and the word hoe is a slang word meaning prostitute. Both pimp and hoe are used as connotations.

CHAPTER 10
Pow Wow Goes to Jail

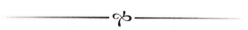

THAT MORNING, PRESCOTT came over driving Pow Wow's Cadillac and Maceo was trailing him in Prescott's car. They walked in the door and Prescott told me that Pow Wow had an outstanding warrant for his arrest. The police had a trunk which was stolen in a burglary and it had Pow Wow's fingerprints on it. Prescott and Pow Wow were riding through the park in the Manor and the police swarmed on them and took him into custody.

"Man, they had my brother locked up. Fingerprints on a trunk? That sounds like he's being railroaded."

"Cause, he don't even have a bond. We have to wait until he calls to see what's up." Prescott said. Then he and Maceo left. I knew that I had to tighten up my hustle to have some ends waiting, in case he got a bond.

After sitting and contemplating about Pow Wow, I left the house trying to figure it all out. I decided to get some input from Ice Kat, so I called and told him about Pow Wow. He suggested we talk in person, so I headed out that way. When I pulled up, he was standing in the vestibule with more than the usual crew members. Ice Kat directed me to park and ride with him. He was in a black SUV with tinted windows while his crew members trailed us.

Once again, he was wearing inconspicuous gear, combat boots, khakis, and a plaid shirt which fitted kind of bulky. Inquisitively, I asked him what was under his shirt.

"This is a bullet proof vest underneath," he pulled up his shirt and showed me. He continued, "Man, it's rough right now. The Mob promoted me and expanded my territory. I run the entire projects now. They're trying to give me a General spot but I'm turning it down even though I would be the youngest General in Mob history."

With enthusiasm, but still puzzled, I asked why he turned it down. Ice Kat paused and revealed, "If I take the position, I'll be responsible for too many lives. I have to be careful of my decision making because it could impact life or death for so many people. Some Mob members are stealing money and not paying debts on time. Those decisions would fall on me. Even though I'm already handling those issues, I deal with them mathematically. We have losses, but we gained a whole lot more. Handling these decisions on a higher scale would be more detrimental because some of the Generals have other agendas. They're greedy, taking money for themselves, not due to them. The Boss wants me to take over two General spots because those guys violated all the rules. The higher you get, the more power you have and the more tempted you are. Some Generals think they're untouchable. I don't want to make those decisions, so I'd rather stay in the middle. It's like a strong tree, the higher you go, the weaker the branches. The strongest part of the tree is the middle, it's solid. That's where I'm staying. The Generals already got the word that the Boss wants to replace them with me, so I don't trust them since they've already went against the Mob. Their lack of loyalty will make them think I'm behind it all because when you are a snake, you think everyone else is a snake too. That's why I'm ready in case they try to come at me, even though I don't want the position and have already said no to the offer. They still have to pay for their dishonor very soon. It has already been sanctioned."

"Did they steal directly from the Boss?" I asked

"Yeah, they were collecting money off the Boss's name and not turning it in, they foul. On top of that, they also got money off my name. They told certain workers in my territory that they owed one day's pay that had to be given to them so they could pass it on to me, they out of pocket. Those two Generals think we're not hip to them, but we been pulled their card. They think their actions are unknown to us. When it goes down, some of their followers might believe that I called the hit. I'm strapped up so, the gear is just a precaution. These incidences come with the territory."

I agreed with Ice Kat saying, "Better safe than sorry. Get me one of those bullet proof vests."

"Ok, no doubt. You found your niche yet?"

I smiled with a little laugh and said, "Nope, but I've been doing a little pimping and I'm kind of digging it. The money is good, but I don't know."

"Yeah, pimping seems like your style. You got the look and the verbal rap-ability. The pimp game is calling you, Quake Quake."

"Leadership calling you Ice Kat. They're feeling your decision making. You got that charisma and are coherent but can also be coldblooded. You would be a great leader but staying where you are, is smart. It's a good thing that you have forethought and are not greedy. That's why everybody loves you."

He laughed in agreement as I continued, "You know I'm just a hustler, trying to make it happen. I'm about to ride to Englewood and check out some Mob buddies." We got back to my car, said our goodbyes and I drove to 63rd Street.

I cruised through a few neighborhoods were my Mob folks were, checking the scenes to see where I could put in work. I was looking for a fast come up, on the grind. My Mob ties were getting stronger and stronger since I became an outstanding member. Being faithful and loyal to the Mob was working out well for me.

I ran into Nik Cannon, a fellow Mob member and inquired about any capers he might know of. He worked three part-time jobs at three different chicken franchises. Nik Cannon said, "Yeah as a matter of fact, I just left work and they didn't even make the usual money drop so the funds were still in the safe. I start work again at 7:00 p.m. so come through right before 11:00 p.m., when we are about to close, and you know what to do. Make me look good but don't hit me with the pistol so hard this time."

"We got a date chief. We'll be those gangstas in black, about to attack!"

I caught up with Reno and Lucky to let them know that we had a caper planned for that night. I told them I wanted to use the bulk of what we got to get Pow Wow out of jail, if he got a bond. They both said, "That's what's up." We rode through Englewood and ran into my Mob buddy, Terrell. He was a rough acting, hard core looking fella and mentioned that he needed some ends like us. He was familiar with Reno and Lucky, but this would be our first job together. We prepared him by explaining how we did it.

Starting with the layout, I walked him through the plan. We would arrive fifteen minutes before closing. There would be eight employees working. To make sure that there are no casualties, just follow my lead. Keep you gun high and your voice low. Once we enter the restaurant, Lucky and I will jump over the counter, take the manager and crew chief to the back while you and Reno stay on guard up front, watching the door and the other employees. Reno is on lead guard because he doesn't miss any details. While in the back, we'll instruct the manager (who is Mob) to open the safe. After they turn the combination, we must wait one minute before we can open the safe door and get the money.

Reno will direct the employees to lay on the floor, behind the counter, while you will back him up. We'll give Reno the signal to bring all the workers to the back, lay them face down on the ground and then we will leave. I asked if he had any questions and Terrell said with confidence, "No, I got this."

We executed the plan efficiently. Everything was going smooth as we walked out of the door. One of the employees came out of the store, saw us and ran towards his car, which was about thirty feet away, in the parking lot. Terrell chased him and I ran to get Terrell. The employee jumped into the driver seat and put the car in reverse, burning rubber and backing out of the space wildly, almost hitting us. Terrell yelled, "Hold it!" as he started shooting at the car. I pushed his hand down and the bullets ricocheted off the concrete.

We ran to our car. I checked Terrell saying, "You goof-ball, what were you doing?"

"That dude was trying to get away, he saw our faces!" he said.

"You dummy! How are you going to shoot at him when we are in the wrong? If you scared, you don't need to be doing this. This is an art. We take money, not lives, fool!"

Reno drove with Terrell in the passenger seat while Lucky and I were in the back. Reno looked over at Terrell and asked, "What's wrong with him? He's a hyena."

Terrell sounded disturbed and blurted out, "Why are y'all coming at me Earthquake? That's cool, I messed up but Reno, what do you mean by hyena?"

"Tell this rookie," Reno sighed.

I explained that a hyena was somebody who doesn't have much training, was ungroomed, hungry, running in a pack. "We're all hungry, trying to eat but a hyena has no finesse and no boundaries. He doesn't know how to stop at the curb, he goes all the way in the street, just to overpower his victim. We don't do that! Even if they can identify us or they're trying to get away, we have to accept the consequences."

"Don't ever shoot at someone when you are taking something from them. If you are scared they're going to identify you or for any other reason, go work at Fun Town."

"I' wasn't scared," Terrell said.

"Then you are a maniac and all maniacs should be put on a rocket and flown to Mars. We hate maniacs. We're stump down hustlers, not lunatics. So get your mind right, homie!"

He was quiet for a few minutes and then said, "You're right, I panicked a little but I'm not a mark. I just didn't think about it like that but now that I know better, I'll do better. Thanks for the game. I ain't trying to be no hyena, I'm trying to be a boss."

"Well, the only way to be a great boss is to first conquer being a great employee. Consider this your first lesson on the job, worker. It's still all love," I explained. We gave Terrell his cut and dropped him off in his hood.

We all headed back, changed clothes and went on the hoe stroll to check on Keena and Dana. We collected our money and then met up with Nik Cannon. Before we could say anything, he shouted, "Why did Terrell start shooting at the employee? Lil dude was scared and just wanted to go home. What if he had shot him? We could of all got a hundred years."

I calmed Nik Cannon down and in a relaxed voice, "I got him straight. I had to take him to school but he's good now." We gave Nik Cannon his cut and headed right back to the stroll, took the girls home, dropped Reno off and Lucky crashed at my house.

CHAPTER 11
Being a Gangsta vs. Being Scary

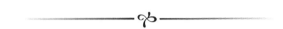

THE RULES OF being a gangsta were well defined and if you didn't follow them, you got violated. Whether you are a part of an organization or not, no one can violate the rules or it could be detrimental. If you did, you were saying that you're bigger than the organization and that is disrespect, which is not tolerated. Money circulated within the organizations when all members paid. When hustling with Mob members or they backed you up, you owed some form of contribution. This is one of many ways of putting in work (paying dues).

Gangsta organizations were originally set up for a group of men to support each other because strength came in numbers, allowing for more resources, more avenues and more thinking power. The rules were in place to ensure structure.

Like any organization, there must be some sort of policing or enforcement that is used to keep order. Leadership roles evolved and the men selected were diligent thinkers. They had forethought and a good sense of understanding. Most were charismatic and didn't show fear. Leaders had to be rational but ruthless at the same time. It's one of the reasons organized crime was kept to a minimum, without a lot of fatalities. If you killed someone without having it sanctioned, you could be killed, if you didn't have a valid reason, like self-defense.

In addition to good leadership, all organizations needed a strong team. Mob members brought other qualities that were extremely important. Some Mobsters were advisors, enforcers, structurers and strategic organizers. A few outstanding members earned a role on the organizations committee and board of directors.

Scary

Understanding that strength came in numbers was a big draw for the organizations and that was very attractive to young men. Some of them made positive impacts and some didn't. Scary people corrupted the organizations the most. They were not loyal, made impulsive decisions and refused to take responsibility for their actions. They hid behind the organization, too scared to carry their own weight and gave the Mob a bad reputation. On top of that, for their own benefit, they made money off the Mob name but didn't give back.

Those members were considered thieves who showed no honor, even though the rule is 'There is honor amongst thieves.' The scary ones claimed to be up to the challenge but usually broke under pressure, causing fatalities in whatever they did. The only thing that you could count on them for was to snitch (also considered rats), which was the worse person ever to have as a member of your organization.

These were the perpetrators who did "drive bys" rather than walking up to their target and shooting them directly. They killed innocent people, including grandmothers and children. The scary ones who did stickups and committed robberies, often panicked and ended up murdering victims.

They even killed victims for fear of being identified, making them cowardly. When frightened members got into altercations, they pulled their weapons first, too afraid to fight. There were a few scary members that made it bad for the true gangstas. Scary members trusted their own fear, easily terrified and often made bad decisions.

Selfishness Ruins It All

Some members use the Mob for their own personal benefit. They got comfortable taking without giving back. Excessive selfishness divided people especially when people allowed selfishness to become a part of their personalities. You had to be both, selfish and selfless simultaneously. Everybody had a bit of selfishness within them but when you want continuous comfort you allow pleasure to fill you with greed.

Greed nearly destroyed the organization and crashed many family structures. The leaders at the top gave so much of themselves and some let greed alter their thinking. They honored their desires more than the rules, hurting others in the name of personal gain. They demonstrated that selfishness was a disease. To be unself-ish took endurance, withstanding emotional pain to give up your desires.

Pow Wow's First Lockup

The next day my mom went to see my brother in jail. I couldn't wait for her to get back. We had a nice stash in case he got a bond. Everyone could put their money together. Prescott now was coming through on the regular. I was just laying back in the room awaiting my mom's arrival. When she came in I immediate-ly jumped up, went into the living room and asked, "What hap-pened?" With motherly concern, she dragged it out as if she had a bad statement from a doctor, saying that he didn't get a bond.

"They offered him six years, but he turned it down. He's going to trial. Trial starts next month," she told me.

"Mom, did you see him? What did he say?"

"Well he asked about you and Prescott. I told him that Prescott brought me down there but only one visitor could come up. Prescott brought his car and parked it in the back-parking lot. Prescott also took me to the north side to pick up my car. It was nice of him to do that. When I saw your brother, both of his eyes were bloodshot. They jumped on him in jail. He said he was ok. That kind of worried me a bit. Jail is a bad place, anything can hap-pen to you in there, but I suppose he will be alright. I'm gonna get my entire church to pray for him."

"My brother got jumped, man, who did that? I need to talk to him. When is he gonna call Ma?" I was angry. She said that he would be calling tonight. "Then Ma I'm staying in until he calls me."

Pow Wow called about 7:00 p.m. I answered the phone and accepted the collect call. "What happened Pow Wow? What hap-pened to your eyes?"

Pow Wow calmly spoke.

"You remember when we use to fight with 87th and 83rd Street, when I went to Bowen High School? They rolled on Prescott, and I went into the lunchroom and we tore it up and I got expelled.

Well, the 83rd Street leader, Mystery Man, is calling the shots on my deck. He's Mob now. They put me on a Mob tier since I'm Mob too. I get in there and this is how it went."

"Hey what's up Pow?"

"Is that you Mystery Man?"

He poured out a happy grin, "Yeah. Hey folks, this Pow Wow. Man, I'm glad to see you. What you been up too? Fellas, me and Pow Wow go way back. Pow go on in your cell and get yourself together. Here are some shower shoes so that you can shower. Man, I'm glad to see you.'

After getting situated, Mystery man came into my cell and sat on the lower bunk, right next to me. He said, 'Pow man, we had some crazy times back in the day. We used to gang bang hard. You were something.' I said, 'we was kids back then, just wild shorties, you know what I mean.' Mystery man laughed, 'Pow, I know what you mean.'

Seven Mob members came into the cell. They stood around while Mystery man explained, 'Pow, I remember when we had that fight at school. Man, you came into the lunchroom like a tornado.' We all laughed and then Mystery Man stated, 'Boy, you snapped off. I remember you picked up a lunch tray and cracked me up side my head and I had a hickey on my head for a month.' Everyone in the cell just cracked up. I said, 'Yeah, we were young,' as he sniggled. Still laughing, Mystery Man looked at the Mobsters and shared, 'I said if I ever see Pow Wow again, I gotta get him back.'

Suddenly, one of them stole on me. I was still sitting next to Mystery Man I thought, *'Did he just steal on me?'* The next thing I know, another Mobster hit me on the other side, right in the eye. I said to myself, 'I'm about to fight my way out of this little cell.' I started letting them have it, throwing blows back at them as I maneuvered my way out of the cell. I fought all of them. Then the guard yelled, 'What's going on, they jumping on you?' I told the guards, 'No, I fell over the mop bucket.'

I told the Mobsters that I wasn't finished with them and when the guards leave, it's back on. After that, we had a meeting and the captain, Mystery Man, called a truce, gave me a lieutenant position and now I'm calling it on my tier. Now, we are all cool. I'm straight, everything is good, don't worry about me."

"Who would have thought that the dude you hit with a tray in high school would be running the prison where you are locked up. You gotta be careful how you treat everyone. The same people you meet going up are the same folks you'll greet coming down." I was flabbergasted.

There could be internal strife amongst Mob members, even in jail. The rules are that all members must aid and assist one another. They must squash all beefs in the name of love.

Gangbangers

Gangbangers are scared, misguided youngsters who were wannabes, trying to act like soldiers in order to fit in.

I had much love for the young gangbangers and they seemed to draw to me. I tried to encourage them to operate with ethics and stop trying to be something they're not. If you want to be down in the game, learn it and follow the moral code of conduct. Don't be an idiot. I always gave to the shorties, but I made them earn it by doing basic chores. As I preached to them, I was preaching to myself at the same time.

I was on 55th street pulling up to my grandma's house. All the shorties saw me and came to speak. I knew that in about 30 minutes the front porch would be filled with Mob members, my buddies. One of the shorties named Chris, stayed directly across the street. He was about thirteen years old, light skinned with curly hair, who stood about 5'5". He was a little gangbanger. He walked over and said, "Hey what's up big homie?"

"Nothing, what's up with you? Are you still terrorizing the block li'l folks?"

Chris looked up at me and said, "Yeah, you know how I roll."

"No, how you roll?"

"Yeah, I'm running things over here. I'm a gangsta."

"Listen up Chris, stop trying to act so angry. Real gangstas don't show what they're thinking."

"I'm trying to be like you. Give me five dollars big homie."

"Here, take this towel and wipe my car down," I replied laughing.

He had a slight bulge in his t-shirt. I walked over and pulled it up and he had a pistol on him. I stepped back and calmly said, "Why do you have that gun?"

"In case somebody violates me. You know how that is."

"Take that pistol back where you got it from. A real gangsta doesn't walk around with a gun for no reason. Don't go on any blind commands. Find out what the situation is all about."

I thought about all the times that I had done the same thing until some older cats schooled me. I listened to them because I respected them. I looked like I was shining but I was grinding, acting like a bigshot, but I was no different.

For some reason, talking to the shorty gave me a sense of clarity about myself. My focus was redirected to all the moves I was making. I had to stop doing stick ups soon and find my niche. I redirected my attention to Chris, as he hit me with another question, "Are you a gangsta?"

"Yeah," I said, thinking, *'I rather him imitate me than be some maniac.'* I was a product of my peers and I knew that he would be a product of his as well. It was important to watch myself and my behavior around the shorties.

"Look li'l homie, Power without wisdom is weak. You gotta be a gangsta for what you love."

"What do you mean by that?" Chris asked.

"What do you love? Do you love your family? Do you love your folks? Do you love what's yours?"

"All of that!"

Then I advised him, "Then don't be a gangsta without a cause. We need young gangstas but you have to operate by rules, ethics and a code of conduct. You can't run around wild and out of control. Don't be robbing and shooting people because you want what's theirs. True Mob members don't respect that."

I wasn't a gangsta, I was still trying to find my niche.

Outstanding Member
An OM is one that is in good graces with the organization, representing high standards. I achieved the status of outstanding member by

putting in work as a tax collector, keeping track of funds from the local businesses and all the other Mob enterprises. I also collected Mob dues from members and provided additional protection to local businesses.

I kept my role as a hustler separate from Mob business. In order to survive, I maintained boundaries. As a Mobster, we purchased wholesale merchandise and sold it on the streets. We also provided security for select entertainers and celebrities who visited Chicago. As a hustler, I was still pimping, robbing and boosting.

While participating in Mob activities as an enforcer and treasurer of the area around 55th where my grandma lived, I became very close with the Mob family there. I loved them all. I was back and forth around the city and 55th became one of my main stomping grounds.

I saw a few local gangbangers who were Mob wannabes, only a year younger than me. They appeared intrigued by my style and they were easy to like because they were young and energetic. These li'l shorties who were from 55th Street, were beefing with the young Rock gangbangers. They were only divided by a few blocks. The Mob and Rock organizations were on good terms and we were not aware that the youngsters were feuding. I decided to speak to the shorties since I knew that I had some level of influence.

Before I got a chance to talk to them, gunfire rang out and everybody took cover. Two of the young gangbangers who I was familiar with, Shron and Fatman, were shooting at the Rocks who they spotted walking across the busy intersection on 55th Street. They were wildly shooting while innocent people were screaming and ducking. The passengers on a passing bus were all ducking as the bus stopped in the middle of the street and the driver took cover. The shooters from both sides fled the scene. Nothing like this had ever happened in the neighborhood. The gangbanger wannabes shot from a distance of 40 yards away and the Rocks returned fire as unsuspecting cars and public transportation buses rode by.

I heard about fifteen rounds ring out. Shooting from a distance led me to believe that they were shooting under peer pressure or they were scared. Then the unthinkable had just taken place. Two stray bullets wounded two female passengers on the bus. Two women got shot, one in the face and another in her left shoulder.

As we were investigating the incident, a few ambulances escorted by police cars arrived so, a group of Mobsters jumped into my car and we left the scene. We drove to the park where the young gangbangers hung out. I saw Shron and reprimanded him.

"What's wrong with you? Why did you shoot like that?" I asked angrily.

"I was trying to get those Rocks," Shron answered.

"If you were trying to get them, why didn't you walk straight up to them and shoot? That's how a real gangsta does it. Why did you do that and who told you to shoot at them anyway?" I asked, shaking my head in disgust.

He paused with a dumb look on his face before answering, "My crew said that we were at war with them. They told our girls that we were marks."

"Man, you reacted off what a broad said?" Shron just stood there shaking. "For what you just did, you are not a mark, you are a coward who just shot two innocent women."

The Mobsters and I walked away knowing that he was in big trouble. I liked the li'l fella, but he was so misguided.

The Mob members and I went to my grandma's and chilled on the front porch. Another member came over and told us that we were having an emergency meeting. We met in an abandoned building across from the Dominick's Super Market. There were about forty members in attendance, discussing what happened. The General spoke, asking if anyone knew where Shron was. His sidekick, Fatman, got caught and was being held in juvenile detention.

No one seemed to know where Shron was. After a few minutes, TJ, a member who was on lookout watching for police through the window, said, "There goes one of those Rocks. They've been acting as if they're running things around here, sneaking around selling weed in our territory and not paying us dues (taxes for making money in our neighborhood). They owe a percentage of their earnings to the Mob. We need to go and holla at him right now."

Curious to see who he was talking about, since I had some respectful ties with the Rocks, I looked and saw Lenizarelly, who was cool with me and was walking with my cousin Chevy. They had been dating for a few years.

"Out of all due respect, may I speak with TJ about this matter?" I addressed the General.

The General nodded his head and said, "No doubt."

I faced TJ and said, "Nobody is touching Lenizarelly or they're going to deal with me. If you approach him, that's where you'll be left." I knew that I had to be forceful because he was known to be challenging. TJ was dark skinned, 5'9" with a muscular build wearing a white T-shirt and blue jeans.

"Earthquake, this is Mob business!" he exclaimed very hostile.

"This is personal. That's my cousin with him and if you even think about putting her in a dangerous situation where she can get hurt, then we will become rivals."

I stared at him with a fierce look and all the Mob members walked over standing behind me, as he stood alone. The General shouted, "Ok, we one love Earthquake so TJ respect his cousin and her boyfriend. He's with family so he gets a pass."

This made TJ humble himself. When we left the meeting, I stayed around 55th Street for a while then headed home.

A few days later, we cruised back down on 55th. Fatman was still in the juvenile detention center but his partner in crime was found dead on the railroad tracks, shot in the face.

I was saddened about Shron. He was just young and foolish. I wish that I could have talked to him sooner. This would have never happened. You can't pretend that you are tough. It could have a deadly effect on your life. Everything that you see is not always what it appears to be. There is an art to what we do. When you don't know what you're doing, it's like playing Russian roulette. Never forget, always think about the victim first.

Gangbangers continued to stand out with their extremely wild behavior, lacking the knowledge of what we were about. Negative behavior always out-shined the positive.

The good Mob members kept the gangbangers in check making the organization leaders very important to the neighborhoods. Locking organization leaders up could cause a calamity and a breakdown in the community structure, leading to chaos and mayhem.

I didn't know why, but I could see the revelation in all of this. Without strong leadership, the blind can't lead the blind. Chop the head off and the body will fall, creating an unstable future in the aftermath. Genocide! Gangbangers had to learn to value themselves. Giving up something to obtain something else was crucial.

The key was to make us work so that we could realize our own self-worth. If we didn't realize our own value, we could never value anyone else. I thought, '*If you don't have anything, then you don't have anything to lose.*' This is why being taught values at a young age was so important.

We operated on principles that some of us consistently followed and others didn't. For instance, we learned that life is meaningful and we stood for loyalty, all as one! Wisdom taught us to be humble and to understand the difference between right and wrong. We knew that having moral boundaries helped us value life and there were certain things that we wouldn't do.

We were taught to have a vision. Rules, values and structure helped to develop morals and built character. It's not automatic like most people might think. Even gangstas had aspirations. You gotta put in work to get your dream out the dirt. It's what you're willing to do to make your dreams come true. You gotta make a sacrifice for the things you earn and never stray far from the teachings you learn. This stuck with me throughout my life!

CHAPTER 12
Life on the Stroll

AFTER THAT REVELATION, I stayed on point with everything that I learned, trying to be sharp at the game. I was thinking about taking my girl on the Stroll, when all the visiting hookers and pimps would be there this weekend. My plan was to come up with some more broads. I thought, *'If I could get Pow Wow's Caddy, I'll really look slick, but I've got to figure out how to get those keys from my mom because I know she's not going to give them up.'*

I made my way to 82nd Street and met up with my other crew. I pulled up and saw Reno, Lucky and the rest of the folks congregating. I hollered, telling Reno and Lucky to get in, revealing the plan to get my brother's car. "We'll look more prestigious when we head to the Stroll on the weekend. First, we have to figure out how to get the keys from my mom. She started keeping them in her purse after she saw me fidgeting with them."

"Why don't you take the keys and get an extra set made. That's how I got a set of my brother's keys. Now he tries to booby trap the car with sticks so that he can tell when the car has been moved. He's not sure, but he is suspicious that his car is being driven," Lucky suggested. We all fist bumped in agreement.

"Good idea Luck," I commented.

"As soon as she gets in, my mom takes a long hot bath. I'll go in her purse and get the keys. We'll run up to the hardware store, make a copy, hurry and put the originals back," I told the crew.

The plan worked like a charm. That Friday we went to the salon, got our hair done and dressed in our best tailor-mades. I wore canary yellow from head to toe, complete with a silk t-shirt, custom slacks and snake skinned shoe sandals. We all looked quite clever!

First, we dropped Keena and Dana off on the Stroll then doubled back to get the Caddy. As we drove the thirteen-block radius, the Stroll was hot. Girls were in and out of cars down both sides of the streets. All the players were out there, including the visiting pimps who worked their girls in the city on the weekends. I pulled up where King Fish and Milton were standing in front of Flukie's Lounge. There was Icey Mike, Country, King Rabbit, Pimp Smokey, Pee Wee Slim, Slick Rick, Money, Mr. White Dawg and Prescott from Chicago. The out of town pimps included Kevin Money from LA, Baby Grand from St. Louis, Dollar Bill from Detroit, Mack Arthur from Minnesota and King London from Baltimore.

I blended in while checking out everyone, observing their physical and verbal communication. I paid attention to details, watching their attitudes and styles of pimping. I knew that pimping was a mind game and the mind controls the body. So, understanding the mind and body simultaneously was the key. I learned to study body language from Reno back in the Manor and it became a part of my observation skills.

Some pimps peaked my interest more than others. For instance, Slick Rick was a pretty boy with an aggressive style and a controlling personality. He talked to his girls' rough with a slick tonality; impressive. Icey Mike was laid back with a nonchalant personality. He walked slow and easy and was calm and smooth with everything that he did. He often gave his women ultimatums.

Money displayed finesse and swag and his movement matched his talk. He appeared to genuinely care about his women; very balanced. Mr. White Dawg was a blue-eyed soul brother. He knew how to play the best of both worlds, being white and talking black. He was more conservative with his girls.

Kevin Money was polite and had good manners, but he moved like a gangsta with a hard pimp walk. His looked matched his behavior with his women. He put it out there, letting them know that they belonged to him and weren't going anywhere.

Prescott let his "pretty" work for him. The girls were drawn to his looks. Everything about him was cool. His look, verbal communication and his attitude all matched well. These guys were impressive on the Stroll because most of them kept four women or better.

Watching the pimps helped me to analyze styles different from my own. There were all kinds of women who gravitated towards certain pimps. That influenced me to get sharper. I knew the image I wanted to project in order to dominate the game.

Mind and Body, Physical and Verbal

While chopping it up with all the pimps, I watched the hookers' behavior as well. I zoomed in on one girl who was near Milton's hoe. She was a renegade broad who Milton said had recently left her pimp after he was incarcerated. I was on it as I laid back, giving her a glimpse that said, I'm the "downest" in the world but I like you. Slowly, I stepped away from the crowd.

She was brown skinned with a pretty smile and long, black silky hair. Standing 5'7" with a medium build, she seemed to be about twenty-one years old. Her left stride was longer than the right which made her walk sexy. She appeared to be shy but by the way she was dressed, wearing black hot pants with go-go boots and a matching halter top, she looked experienced. I observed her movement, saw sensitivity in her body language and got a vision of her personality in my mind. Emotional with gentleness is what I concluded, and I was ready for the challenge.

"You are unblemished in my mind, fine and divine and if I described a perfect girl, you would be it. Even though we just met, I don't see any wrong in you and I know you're meant for me. If you choose, this will be the most perfect thing that happens to us – an earth-shaking collaboration and the best is yet to come," I said, stepping up to her.

"That was touching," she said as she smiled and blushed. She asked me my name and I told her.

Reading her body language, I took a step closer with confidence. Her voice sounded comforting when I asked her name.

"Lonnie." She seemed to be getting relaxed.

"That's good name but it doesn't fit you," I commented.

"I know right. How many girls do you have?"

I counted on my fingers and said, "Two, including you. So, I can include you?"

"That might be nice," she answered with a grin.

"I'm gonna rename you. You are music to my ears so I'm going to call you Poetry."

"Why Poetry? Not that I don't like it, just curious to know why?"

"Well, everything about you is poetic. Your words, your look and your movements are poetry in motion. Your mind, your actions and your spirit tell me a poetic story about you. You are my words! If I described a perfect girl, it would be you. Now, I need a poetic answer so you can fit into your role," I answered.

She was on ten! I gave her my info and let her go back to work. Reno and Lucky came over and Reno said, "You got a real hooker. How did you come up with her?"

I laughed and blurted out, "Cause I'm the devastating international, everlasting pimping rascal and I ain't from Washington, DC. She work for me, my new employee. You see, you never have to beg if you use your head and it will work out perfectly."

Reno came back with, "How many ladies in the place gotta man with a plan that makes them feel great? I don't mean to do nobody wrong... but if you're not about hoeing just go head on." We were laughing and giving each other the pimp finger tips (hand gestures) as Prescott pulled up.

Prescott got out the car and walked over to us saying, "Cause, what y'all doing with Pow Wow's car? Take it back and park it now!"

We all looked at Prescott as I rationalized. "Prescott, we only took the car because I just came up with a hoe. We're just flexing. We only rode the car to the Stroll, seven blocks. That's it! We're only going to ride it this weekend."

Not moved at all Prescott repeated, "I don't care, take it back!"

Trying to reason with him I continued. "Prescott, we are going to take it back when we leave the Stroll. Just let us flex a little bit. We are not speeding or nothing and we are only driving up here and back home. I just want to catch more chicks. There's my new one right there."

Slightly impressed, Prescott looked over and saw Poetry and said, "Cause she' bad. Ok, no guns in the car, no sticking up and only go from the Stroll to home. Agreed?"

"No doubt," I happily agreed.

"Cause, I gotta go. I'll come and get you all tomorrow. I'm gonna check to see if you getting money so make sure you get some dough out of that hoe cause if you don't, you're not getting the car no more," Prescott said as he drove off.

"Let's go and check on Dana and Keena," Reno suggested.

As we rode down on them, we got our money. I told Keena that she had a wife-in-law (another girl) and we rode off. Lucky said, "Let's go to 93rd and Cottage so I can put this little broad, Ida, to work. She's a little chocolate cutie."

"Let's go," I replied.

We picked her up, Lucky gave her work necessities and dropped her off with Keena and Dana.

Appreciation vs. Need

I spotted Poetry and she got in, gave me a nice piece of money and said, "I'm going to try and get my trap up for you baby." She handed me the cash and went back to work. After about three hours, I dropped everybody off except Lucky and we picked up Poetry. I told her that I was giving her a recess as she handed me more money.

"I'm taking Lucky home and I want you to ride with me." Poetry got real close, leaning in. As I put my arm around her, she said, "It's nice to be appreciated."

"You mean it's good to be needed? Sometimes the two are mistaken," I responded, while keeping my eyes on the road.

"What's the difference?"

"There is an uncertainty with one and the other is compelling."

"Which one is uncertain?" she asked, scowling and pulling slightly away.

"Appreciation," I went on to explain that we seek appreciation because we never know unless we're told. "On the other hand, we know when we are needed. That's a duty and need always comes before appreciation."

"I don't quite get it. Can you elaborate?" she asked looking somewhat confused.

I asked her which one would she prefer; to be needed or appreciated. "Keep in mind that appreciation is for validation, because it provides self-satisfaction. Need is necessary and is done for another person."

"I would rather be needed," Poetry said.

"Excellent answer. Appreciation has to be proven, while need is stronger and easily understood. You need love and I need to give it to you," I told her.

With a sexy grin, she replied, "Oh, I get it. It's like, I appreciate a cold can of pop, but I need water. I appreciate a place to stay but I need to pay the rent. I appreciate being here with you but I need to go back to work to get your money, right?"

I nodded and said, "You see, I didn't name you Poetry by chance, that was poetic."

I pulled to the curb and let her out on the Stroll so that she could work a double shift and I could get Pow Wow's car parked before my mom headed out for work. I made it in safe and sound.

I fell asleep that morning and that afternoon Prescott came over at some point and asked, "Cause, did she make you some money?"

Smiling like the Cheshire Cat, I told him yeah as I reached in my pocket and pulled out a small bankroll.

Prescott smiled and said, "I'm on my way home, cause you wanna ride with me?"

Gladly, I did. We arrived at his apartment in Calumet City, on the outskirts of Chicago. All four of his girls were home, three white girls and a black chick. They were very attentive to us. One prepared lunch, another shampooed and roller set his hair, one ironed his clothes and the last one vacuumed the carpet.

They adored Prescott and treated him like a young Prince. We stayed several hours before he dropped me off at my house. I left home, picked up Reno, Lucky and the girls, including Lucky's new hoe, Ida. We headed to the store to get all their work materials which included lubricants, baby wipes, Listerine, soap, wash cloths and plenty of rubbers. Then we stopped at a nearby restaurant.

Over dinner, they discussed their work experiences. I noticed that their eating habits were similar. The girls agreed on the same subjects and they all had the same style of eating, which was remarkable to me. I made a mental note to study that more. We dropped them off at work in perfect timing, as I saw Poetry coming back from a date. She gave me my money and said, "Honey, I'll call you in the morning when I'm ready to end my shift."

We slowly cruised down the hoe Stroll, acting all important as Reno and Lucky talked to the hookers. We went towards Flukie's Lounge where Flukie and his crew were heading inside. Flukie was well known as one of the biggest drug dealers in Chicago. He was very flamboyant with swagger. He had the largest cartel in the city and all his members were sharp. They kind of reminded me of pimps, a little bit.

Look out, here comes Prescott's father, Mr. J-Hawk. He walked up clean on the scene, wearing white tailored slacks with a fitted silk t-shirt that showed his muscles and white summer san-dals, topped off with a white captain's sailor hat, looking clever as ever! Mr. J-Hawk was escorting two white chicks.

"What's up Earthquake?" he hollered. Looking at the women, "Those are young pimps right there. Ain't that right?"

"That's right! Straight like that," I quickly responded.

J-Hawk laughed as they entered the lounge. We couldn't go in because we were too young. I believed once we built our reputa-tion for being players, they would let us in. That was all right for now, there was more action outside anyway. We were having a good time hanging out while making money.

At about 3:00 a.m., we ended the girls work shift and took them home. I dropped everybody off and made it back to the house, took a shower and relaxed while I waited for Poetry's call. I opened the window and felt the breeze gliding across my face, as I laid there thinking, '*I'm feeling everything about her.*' As I doze off, the phone rang.

I jumped up and answered.

"This is Poetry. What's your address?"

I gave it to her with instructions to come through the back door and look for apartment 1A.

"Ok I'll be there at about 5:00 a.m.," and she hung up.

Since my mom woke up at that time, I decided to wait for her in the laundry room, near the clubhouse. I didn't want my mom to hear Poetry knocking and suspect that I would let her in when she went to work. I was wearing a white t-shirt, blue pajama pants and house shoes. I didn't bother to remove the hair net that held my shoulder length, ocean waves in place when I slept.

A taxi pulled up at around that time. I heard her voice as she told the cab driver to wait for her to make sure that she was in the right place. She slammed the door, walked into my building and down the hall. I called her name and she came towards me. Poetry kissed me on the cheek and handed me a large sum of cash.

"I'm tired baby. I'm ready to take a shower and lay down," she said.

"Ok, follow me." I walked ten feet to the clubhouse, took the lock off and opened the door. I stepped in, turned the light on and invited her in.

"Is this a fixed-up storage space?" she asked.

"Yeah, it's our humble abode. You can stay here and relax until my mom goes to work."

"I'm not going in or sleeping in there."

"It's only for an hour," I said with cool confidence despite the circumstance.

Poetry starred at me. Her eyes got wide, then she placed her hands over them and shook her head in disbelief. It appeared that she had just discovered something. While I was still holding the money in my hand she slowly grabbed my wrist and took a few of the bills.

"I tell you what, I'm going to go and get a hotel room and I'll see you later." As she walked toward the door, she yelled out, "Wait a minute taxi."

"Work starts at 7:00 p.m. I'll be waiting," I yelled out.

I could hear her faintly as she said ok. I reiterated, "Don't forget, work starts at 7:00 p.m. sharp." I heard her last reply, "Ok," and the cab pulled off.

At 7:00 p.m. I waited and waited but she never showed up. After an hour, I got the crew and we took the girls to work. For three nights in a row I went to the clubhouse at 7:00 p.m. hoping Poetry would show up. Even on the Stroll she was a "No show." I never saw her again and didn't know of anyone who knew what happened to her. I had a need for things to make sense. It wasn't my style to do something that didn't make sense. Even pimping had to make sense for me to be a part of it.

The next time Prescott came over he asked, "Cause, what happening with that fine chick you put on the Stroll?" I told Prescott that I lost her, and he asked how. "I don't know. I thought I gave her a good message. She was all in and I know that she was really into me but when I invited her into the clubhouse things changed." I told Prescott what happened.

"Cause, it seems she thought you were more established and well off. See, you manipulated the situation, making her believe that you were in a better position. I told you not to drive Pow Wow's car but you too smart for your own good. Cause it's about telling the truth and making it work from the level you're at. That's real game," Prescott advised.

I thought, *'How did all my other hustles work in my favor?'* It came to me – I portrayed myself in a way that was believable for each circumstance. *'From now on, I'm gonna make sure that my conversation fits my situation so that my circumstances work for me. Then my talk will match my walk.'*

Fall was coming and Reno, Lucky, me and all the girls started to prepare for classes. We were back in school and I was short two credits. Lucky and I decided to transfer, leaving cosmetology behind.

Lucky went to a traditional high school to finish up while I learned of an alternative school where I could graduate in five months if I passed the tests required. Reno and I submitted our transcripts and were accepted. I told Prescott about our new school, but he declined. His sister attended and we all had classes together as I was determined to get my high school diploma.

School hours were 9:00 a.m. – 1:00 p.m., giving us plenty of time to prepare the girls for work. Since the girls were also attending high school, we shortened their work hours from 6:00 p.m. – 10:30 p.m. during the week.

As I dropped Keena off one night, her mom approached the car and said, "You're bringing her home too late. You have to get me some cigarettes, beer and give me grocery money for keeping her out like this." Keena had four younger siblings between the ages of seven and thirteen years old.

Keena's mom looked as if she might have been very beautiful before falling on hard times. It seemed like drinking caused her a slew of problems.   I took Keena to the store and picked up the items that her mom requested. I felt bad for her having a drinking problem, so I gave her one hundred dollars and that calmed her down. After that, I would give her a few dollars and she was cool with me.

CHAPTER 13
Nicky Blaze

ONE WEEKEND NIGHT after dropping the girls off, I went to visit Nicky Blaze. She usually cooked me dinner when I visited and today was no different. When I walked in, she was wearing a black satin bath robe with a magazine laying in the center of her bed and the page open to some very erotic photos. There were multiple men and women licking on one woman. I asked why she was looking at that. She said that she enjoyed looking at those kinds of pictures and reading romantic books.

"Do you like that?" she asked.

"I never saw photos like that." I asked why she liked it and she confessed that it was her fantasy. As she laid across the bed, I could smell her sweet perfume and it was inviting. I sat on the bed and kicked my shoes off as I scooted back to the headboard.

"Let me go and prepare your plate," she said flipping the page. "How many pieces of chicken do you want? Is three ok?"

"Yeah that's cool."

When she left the room, I picked up the magazine and looked at the erotic pictures. They were very explicit. She also had three romantic novels sitting on her nightstand. I heard her coming so I placed it back on the bed the way she left it. She entered the room carrying a plate of chicken, spaghetti, cream of spinach and a dinner roll with a glass of grape Kool-Aid. I asked her to turn on the television since she had this new addition called "On TV" which played movies that had recently aired at movie theaters.

She handed me my plate, pulled a tray in front of me, turned the television on, gently laid across the bed and said, "Where were we? Oh yeah, what's your fantasy?"

I thought for a few seconds, '*I really don't have one,*' as I took a bite of my chicken. "What's your fantasy?" Her nose began to slightly sweat, she got up, turned on the fan and then rested on the bed again. Her golden brown, silky smooth thigh came from underneath her robe as she turned to look at me.

"My fantasy is for me to be laying in the bed with both men and women licking and touching me all over my body." She picked the magazine up and showed me a photo and said, "See like this."

As I sucked up the spaghetti, I couldn't wrap my mind around that. I know she was trying to turn me on but that was gross.

"What did you think about that?" she asked my opinion.

I spoke slowly, not wanting to sound too young since I already had one bad experience with a chick. Not that I cared about the subject, I just wanted to perfect my style with women.

I hadn't seen anything like that in the pimp manual and it really turned me off. This was my first time even thinking about something that freaky. Thinking to myself, 'I'm about to leave after my dinner,' so I explained, "Well Nicky, to each his own. My fantasy is to please others." I hadn't thought about my own fantasies much as I picked up my glass and drank some grape Kool-Aid.

Actually, my fantasy was to be a psychiatrist or some sort of doctor, but I wasn't about to share that with her. I also fantasized about her having sex with my two homies, Reno and Lucky, to turn her out but I couldn't tell her that either. I finished my Kool-Aid and set it on the tray, then pushed it toward her. She took the tray and walked right into the kitchen.

I started to feel so tired, like I couldn't get out of the bed. I had never been this groggy and overly drained before. Nicky walked back in the room and said, "You look worn out. Take your shirt and pants off and lay down for a while."

Fighting my sleep with all my might, I couldn't answer. Nicky reached and started unbuttoning my shirt and taking off my pants. I was still uncontrollably sleepy, so I did nothing.

Stretched out on the bed, I was dressed in only in my underwear. I could feel her curling up next to me without the texture of her satin robe. She placed her thighs over my legs and her arms around my chest. I was too tired to even object as I felt her tongue traveling all over my body, even in uncharted places. Finally, I passed out and woke up three hours later with no underwear on as Nicky was curled up next to me smiling.

I heard her doorbell ringing and asked what time it was. She told me that it was midnight, grabbed her robe and then went to answer the door. It was Reno and Lucky, so she called my name as I was getting dressed. I said a quick goodbye and left. Reno told me that all the folks were looking for me on the Stroll.

"I told them that you were being pampered by your grandma," Lucky said as we headed that way.

Meet Bruno

The first face that I saw when we hit the Stroll was Bruno. He was one of my favorite Mob buddies. Bruno was a hustler who enjoyed imitating pimps and he always kept us laughing. Most of the time he bounced to parties with us. He was a stepper, a guy that everybody loved and feared.

Bruno started his pimp talk as soon as he saw me.

"Earthquake, tell these marks that it's all about getting money. Adam got Eve, Samson had Delilah, Ike got Tina and Bruno got to have somebody too. So, when you step up to the plate be ready to turn a date. It's about the money but not to populate."

All the Mob was laughing, kicking it and having a good time. Prescott pulled up and yelled, "Earthquake, cause I'm gonna come and get you tomorrow so you can ride with me." I said ok.

That afternoon Prescott picked me up and we drove to talk to a guy who made threats behind his back. This guy said that he wished Prescott would step to him the way that Prescott did when fighting some dude at the Tiger's Lounge a few days earlier. Prescott was tipped off about the guy's location and we went to holla at him.

Prescott told me to stay in the car until he gave me a signal. "If I raise my hand and touch my chest, that means come over."

"Ok, just give me a sign and I'm there."

We arrived at the house and Prescott blew his car horn. The guy walked out irate, swinging the screen door open hard and then took an aggressive stance.

He was dark skinned, about 6'0 with muscles, wearing a wife beater t-shirt, blue jeans and a white brim. Prescott was talking to him, but I didn't like his mannerism. Before Prescott even gave me a signal, I leaped out of the car, walked over and stood beside him with my arms folded and a no nonsense, killer look that said I'm one second from driving my fist through your skull.

He softened his attitude as he explained that it wasn't him doing all that talking. Prescott inquired, "Cause if you were, then I'm right here."

"No, I'm not looking for you," the guy repeated.

"I'm glad you got out the car," Prescott whispered, as we walked away. "That was on time, you did right! By the way, Jeff and I are taking our broads to Texas and then we are making a few rounds in other cities to bring a bankroll back."

"I wanna go."

"No, because you are still in school. Cause wait until you finish then you can come with us. Well let's go to my daddy's boutique so that I can get a few items before I drop you off."

Prescott described to J-Hawk what happened, emphasizing how I got out of the car. "See daddy, Earthquake is my body guard." Mr. J-Hawk reiterated, like he did several times before telling Prescott to stop calling me a body guard. "I told you, Earthquake is a pimp."

"Cause I know daddy, but he also got them muscles. He's very observant and knows how to handle situations. That's what I'm talking about."

Mr. J-Hawk interrupted him, "I don't care how many muscles he got, he ain't no body guard," as he continued to show me his newest collection of silk shirts. Prescott got a few items from the boutique and we headed out.

On the car ride home, Prescott mentioned that he met a hustling girl who boosted.

"I'm trying to figure out a way to turn her out. I want her to hoe rather than boost."

"She's already turned out," I said letting some wisdom seep through my cracks.

"Earthquake cause, why do you say that?"

"See, some girls come up in a hustler environment, influenced by females that include their moms, aunts, cousins and friends and are attracted to the lifestyle as well. Girl hustlers understand their role, their significance and how to be down for their man. Does she know that you are a pimp?"

"Yeah."

"I do know this much; a hustler chick is going to flow the way you guide her. Like all hustlers operate by rules of the street, girl hustlers adjust like everyone else. Most girl hustlers are talented; you just have to help her find a niche that fits with what you do."

"Cause does that go for her too? She never hoed before." Prescott asked.

"Yeah but girl hustlers use their talents in the best ways that they know."

"She'll make sure to fulfill all the requirements of any chosen hustle. You only have to guide her and put her under your leadership."

Prescott listened and then said, "Cause I think my daddy is right about you!" We continued our discussion until he dropped me off at home.

My doorbell rang, and it was Veronique. She told me that she saw Nicky Blaze looking out of her window and she asked if I was up there. Nicky told her no, that I was probably at home, "So here I am," she said. She handed me one hundred dollars.

Veronique said that the owner of a laundromat that she used asked her to wash dishes wearing only her panties and she agreed. I immediately realized if she will take her clothes off for money, then she was already a hoe.

I took her by the hand and said, "I'm glad you're here."

She blushed and replied, "I'm glad to be here," as I led her to my room where we sat on the bed. I suggested that she show me how glad she was to see me.

As we sat there, I noticed how beautiful her peanut butter colored skin was, just flawless and tight with thick voluptuous lips that were perfect for kissing. She had high cheek bones with deep pretty dimples when she smiled. Her tender brown eyes and full thick brows went well with her soft fine hairline and head full of thick, black silky hair.

I was sexually attracted to Veronique and enjoyed being in a relationship with her. She spoke out, "Give me a kiss." I slowly gyrated the tip of my tongue across her top lip and then tasted the bottom one, as her mouth begin to open and our tongues intertwined. Veronique unbuttoned her blouse revealing her perky breast that looked like they were calling my name. She stood up to take off her pants and her slightly bowed legs stimulated me further as she slid her panties off. I was already naked because I started peeling off my clothes from the moment she stood up.

Veronique turned and starred at me as if she was drunk with desire and said, "Uhh... Your body is chiseled like the Greek God Ulysses."

I was thinking, *'Who the heck is Ulysses? Who cares? I guess it must be good since he's a God.'*

She gracefully coasted down next to me and I observed her every movement. Veronique ran her hand up the inner quad of my thigh as she manipulated and massaged it with care. She slowly looked up with a strong look on her face and expressed, "Your legs are so defined." Veronique continued feeling upward while I laid there absorbing it all as she aroused me to the maximum. She recited, "Your stomach is as hard as a rock, like a washboard."

Her hands climbed up to my chest as she stroked me with a slight trembling touch and her palm gently rotated around my nipples. I impatiently snatched her hand and sucked on each finger as if they were peppermint sticks. My mouth traveled along her arm softly biting gently and arousingly. I slowly turned her on to her back as I slid my tongue on her nipples, sucking and pulling them softly with my mouth.

Veronique frantically reciprocated, pushing me down. I laid back and she got halfway on top of me, kissing my chest while placing her hands in mine, with our fingers entwined. She clinched tightly, taking her hand and stroking my erection. I focused on her breathing as it became more erotic. Veronique turned her face towards me and said, "Laying there with your long wavy hair draping down the pillow, you look like a black Jesus."

I'm thinking, *'Jesus is a spirit! Can she not say that at a time like this?'*

I grabbed her by her hair and aggressively directed her towards my mouth, only allowing us to connect by our tongues.

"I love your tattoos, especially the one on your chest, with the word Earthquake coming out of the world. Does it mean anything?" she asked pulling back a little.

"Yes, see, the places in color on the world are the land. The cracking in the land represents a seismic earthquake that is powerful enough to impact an entire city."

As she remained fascinated by the tattoo, I ran my hand down her stomach to her pleasure zone and felt the overly moist welcome that awaited my arrival. After enjoying that sensation for a few minutes, Veronique asked me to finish telling her about the tattoo.

"I shake up the hood, creating tremors that open the minds and souls of my folks to see our destiny. You feel me! Earthquakes bring lava to create a new pavement, on an innovative journey, cracking the foundation of what you can't do, shaking the fabric of your soul revealing what you can do."

I redirected my energy to her body, kissing her neck, blowing in her ear and squeezing her butt cheeks. I gently pushed her head below my navel and she looked up at me as I whispered, "Do it." She proceeded to pleasure me and I was fully erect, enjoying her, feeling every faint movement.

"Looks like you have a plan right now," she said with a moan.

"I'm always gonna shake a way to make away." Without warning, I pulled her down, turned her over on her back and rapidly fired like a machine gun as her body trembled like a seismic shock.

Feeling her warmth as I gyrated my body every seven strokes, kissing her gently, double stroking and then gyrating as she moaned louder and louder. Veronique's stomach trembled as she yelled out, "Now I know why they call you Earthquake!" she screamed in ecstasy. Making love to the mind and body simultaneously was new to me and it turned me on to the highest degree. I climaxed out of control!

Afterwards, she laid on my chest as I stroked her silky hair and she held on to my seventeen-inch biceps. Veronique lifted up and said, "Oh yeah, the guy who owns the laundromat also wanted me to turn a date for two hundred dollars." I questioned why she didn't do it.

"He was about sixty years old and I don't like old men."

"What, are you trying to fall in love? This is business and there is no restriction on business. He's in the business of cleaning clothes, not sanitizing your mind. Patronizing your body is what he wants. You can pay for his machines then he can pay you for your company. Do you think he cares who comes into his business to wash? He's trying to get paid. If you showed him your breast, you got paid and that's hoeing. So, let's get some money! Call him and tell him you're thinking about what he offered and go and get that two hundred dollars. Just make sure you use a rubber. He won't last but a minute, I guarantee it."

She got up, made the call, went back over there and turned her first date. Veronique went from being my booster to being my hooker. When she returned from her date, I gave her a lesson on the ins and outs of working on the Stroll. Since she was good with jerking a man off, I suggested that she try to give hand jobs whenever possible.

Veronique also attended high school, so I explained the new schedule that allowed us to all prepare for classes each night since we stopped working at 10:30 p.m. We built a weekly routine that allowed each of us to get homework done and study for tests. It cut our money flow, but it was a small price to pay in order to finish school.

CHAPTER 14
Alternative School – Army

———— ✿ ————

THINGS WORKED OUT for the next four months. Reno and I were preparing for the final tests to graduate while the others were finishing up their final semester before summer break.

In class one day, I saw Reno cheating, looking at the completed pre-test hidden under his desk and blurting out the answers. I discreetly snatched the paper from him. When the teacher asked him for the last answer to a simple Algebra question, Reno replied, "I don't know." Everyone cracked up laughing since they all saw him cheating too. Looking like a lost ball in high grass, Reno was saved by a visitor who walked in to speak with the students.

He was a recruiter who gave a speech identifying all the benefits of joining the army. Several of us gave him our undivided attention. When he mentioned free college and trade school opportunities, I was hooked.

Reno and I considered going in under the buddy plan, but he would have to wait three months for me to turn seventeen. I weighed the pros and the cons. On one hand, I could get a free education and become a doctor or learn other skills and if all else failed, I could make a career out of the service. The cons, nothing much. I could just continue to hustle.

The school released our diplomas to the recruiter, qualifying us and we were excited about it. Our Mob buddy, Dee Dee, was also heading to the army.

Since my mom was at work and going directly to school afterwards, we grabbed the girls early, got carry out dinner and headed to my house to chill before their shift started. During dinner, we discussed education and our upcoming graduation.

We asked Lucky to join the army with us to "Be All He Could Be" but he quickly said, "Nope. Y'all will belong to the government, working for Uncle Sam and if a war breaks out, you'll be on the front lines."

I shook my head and said, "I don't care. You can get killed anywhere, even walking across the street."

"Well, let them control you. They're not going to dictate to me. I'm like Muhamad Ali. They tried to force him to fight but he refused to kill people who had never done anything to him. He saw no plausible reason why and I don't either."

"Right, he's a boxer, not a soldier and they should have left him alone. It doesn't make sense to kill people when you don't know the reason why."

Looking somewhat confused Lucky said, "Well that's what you are about to do if you join."

I kept it 100 (real) and said, "Yeah, but I'm a soldier."

"So, you would go and bomb innocent babies and women?"

I stepped back, folded my arms as if I had already thought this through and responded, "But we are not at war right now."

Trying to reason with me Lucky explained, "A war could kick off at any moment. Then what?"

I fired back with sarcasm. "By that time, I'll have my education."

"Seriously, you never know."

Thought provoked by my ride or die homie, I expressed, "You're right Luck, trying to get something for nothing is the quickest way to get tricked. The game is all the same, there are just different players. The government is using the hustling game. I see it clear as day. It's the same soup, different bowl."

"You know y'all have to use the triple cross (when someone tries to get one up on you but you already know the scheme, so you can get one up on them)," Lucky cautioned.

I knew I would have to maneuver my way around in this situation to ensure that I got what I needed, knowing that I might have to give up blood, sweat and tears. There's risk in everything you do. I decided that making it in life the right way was important, so we proceeded. I came to the realization that there are good components of government and bad ones. I shared those thoughts with the group.

Reno looked up from his paperwork and said, "Y'all know how this goes, the world is a hustle."

"You're right pimp buddy. There is good government and bad government just like there are good members of the Mob and bad ones too." I recalled the three main laws realizing that we were still dealing with rules of the game. They are: the art of taking, the art of conning and the art of pimping.

The government built and operated an organized gang, much bigger than any Mob and it was legal. The main difference was that you got a medal for killing as a soldier, when they command you to do so, but you get jail time and sometimes the death penalty, if you kill for a gang. These facts were amazing to me. I couldn't figure out the difference. We'll just be down with a larger organization who has put itself in charge.

Veronique chimed in, "I never looked at it like that but it all seems true. They should take all these guys on the streets who like to shoot people and put them in the Army. That way they kill two birds with one stone."

Keena shared some intimate details about the experiences of her two uncles.

"My uncle Jack went into the Army, was stationed in Vietnam, met his wife, had two children and moved back to the U.S. He retired from the Army after eight years, got a job at a dealership and lives a happy life. My uncle Leroy wasn't so lucky. He got shot in the stomach. His unit was stranded in enemy territory and waited two days before they were rescued. He was in so much pain that he lived off medication, had post-traumatic stress disorder and his life is a wreck."

Lucky asked the group, "So, what do y'all think? Is it a good idea? Should they go into the Service?"

"I believe my man could jump out of a plane and land on his feet. He could create a new pavement for whatever he wants to do but I still don't want him to go," Veronique said.

Dana seconded that thought, "I think Reno could be a good soldier, but I want him to stay here."

I was thinking, '*I'm pleasantly surprised that not only did Veronique remember the description of my tattoo, but she was able to recite the meaning in this conversation.*' That kind of intelligence turned me on. Being pretty always attracted me but in order to keep my attention, you had to have brains.

Suddenly Reno responded to Dana's comment, "No baby, we are going to check out Germany and then we'll send for y'all and bankrupt the country. We taking this thing worldwide. Don't worry, wherever I'm going, you're coming too."

Meanwhile, I watched Lucky's girl, Ida, sitting there eating without saying anything, even though she appeared to be drawn in by the conversation. I could tell by the way she ate that she was going to be committed to Lucky because every other time she took a bite of food, she offered, trying to share it with him.

People never cease to be quiet, maybe verbally they do, but their body language continues to talk. They're having conversations with us in many ways. I noticed this with Ida. Whenever she was interested in the topic, she slightly shook her head as she lowered her eyelids and continued to eat.

I also observed Reno's eating habits and somehow connected it with his selfishness, which showed some form of addictive behavior. When he scooped a spoonful of food, he brought his mouth down to the plate rather than allowing his spoon to come up to his mouth. Lucky asked the girls, "Hey, if they get their legs blown off or something, are y'all still gonna be down with them?" We all laughed as they both agreed saying, "Of course." After we finished our meal, we took the girls to work.

A month later, Reno submitted the remainder of his paperwork and two weeks after that he received a testing date. I suggested that Reno let Lucky to take the test for him since he was the smartest in the crew. We planned and altered Lucky's look in order to fit the description on Reno's ID.

First, we tightened the curls on Lucky's relaxed waves since it was longer than Reno's hair. Then we shaved off his light goatee leaving only a thin mustache. Next his thick eyebrows had to go so we called a master student from our cosmetology class to trim and arch them. Finally, in order to make him look two sizes smaller, we dressed him in all black.

After Lucky's thorough makeover and quizzing on Reno's personal information, we drove Lucky downtown to the Hilton Hotel where the test was scheduled at midnight. All the recruits received a one-night stay which was a part of the testing process. We picked Lucky up at checkout time and he told us all about the test.

"I know I passed that test. I knew the answers to just about every question," he told us.

He was very smart, and I always admired Lucky's level of intelligence. Lucky shared some of the details that were given during the testing process. He told us that the trainer-recruiter warned everyone that if you catch any kind of felony case, you're automatically disqualified and your application is rejected.

Prom Season

That was ok because I wasn't worried about catching a felony case, we were skilled at what we did. I needed a new transmission and would have to hustle to get it. Ironically, prom season was coming up and that was an easy money-making time for us. We robbed prom kids for two years straight. It was one of the simplest capers that we did. This year, we allowed Terrell to be our fourth leg. Since the fast food robbery, he learned and understood how it really went down, even though prom stickups were light and weren't a big risk.

My Army test was in one week. It was on a Friday, the 12th of May. Reno's, Lucky, Terrell and I were dressed in black. We were on location waiting for the proms to end. We always targeted the best dressed couples who drove the most expensive cars and left the affair early. Usually, they were heading straight for the hotel.

We didn't have to do much because a few couples pulled over and parked on the side street near Lake Michigan so that they could make out. Reno was our getaway driver and stayed in the car while Lucky, Terrell and I walked to the couple's car.

I proceeded to the driver's door, showing my pistol which was in my waist and then covered it with my jacket. Lucky was at the passenger door while Terrell got in their backseat, reached forward and took the keys out of the ignition, placing them on the floor in front of him.

"Let's keep this a happy occasion so don't try anything stupid. This is a robbery, hands on the dashboard and feet straight out," I announced.

Terrell did a quick search of both. He also looked under their seats for weapons while Lucky searched the glove compartment. Terrell was taking the guy's wallet and the money from the girl's purse, I asked, "So how was the prom?"

"It was going pretty good for a minute," the girl said.

The guy said it was alright. As if I was concerned, I said to Luck, "Slick, let's not ruin their night."

Then I asked the guy, "Where you taking her? To breakfast and the hotel?"

"I was," he answered.

"Well, today is your lucky day. I'm gonna give you some money back for breakfast and a hotel room."

She sniggled as I said, "If I find out that you didn't take her, I am going come back looking for you. Make this a night that she won't forget." After warning them not to touch their car keys until after 10 minutes had passed, we fled, and I said, "We black history (we're gone)."

We were riding near the boat dock, around the golf course on 67th Street. A prom couple were kicked back, smoking weed and drinking wine with the front doors open. We casually walked up and said, "Chicago Police. Put your hands up!" The young couple turned and faced us with a look of pure panic and then Terrell said, "Psyche! This is a stickup. Hands on the dashboard and don't move."

Lucky slid her over in the front seat and said, "I got good news and bad news. We're taking your money but were going to leave you with your weed and drinks."

The pretty girl dressed in a sky-blue sequin gown was wearing a solid, two carat diamond earing in each ear. Lucky said, "One way to avoid a problem is to give up those earrings sweetie."

An apprehensive look sprung on her face, "Don't take these, please. I just got them for graduation." Her hands slowly traveled up to her ears where she hesitated before taking them off.

The guy was wearing a very nice twelve studded diamond watch, so I asked, "Where did you get that from?"

"It's my father's watch. He let me wear it for prom."

"Y'all can keep the jewels but the money is coming with us."

Terrell searched the prom guy's pockets and looked in his socks where he found a baby bankroll. He pulled it out and tossed it to Lucky who said, "That must be your Great America (amusement park) money."

"Yes, we were planning to go in the morning."

Lucky asked Terrell if we should let them go to Great America? Terrell paused and said, "He look like he's been a good boy this year. Let's give it to him. See, you just won yourself a consolation prize."

I stared at Terrell for him to knock it off, I was thinking, 'He's *getting too happy with this. I'll have to watch him more closely so that he doesn't get too relaxed and careless. I've gotta remind him that this is still a job.*'

"Take the pretty girl to Great America and the next time you take your shoes off in the car with her present, make sure you wash your feet. They smell strange. Your keys are in the back seat but don't look for them for 10 minutes," Lucky advised.

We drove around the golf course to the back of the Museum of Science and Industry where there is a place known as The Japanese Gardens. We saw two people enter that area, so we followed them. The place was filled with trees, flowers, a pond and benches where couples were known to hang out. It was dark, and we lost track of the two people.

As we took a shortcut back, we spotted them sitting on a bench behind a perfectly manicured bush. They turned out to be two guys sitting real close to each other. Lucky spoke.

"I hate to rain on your parade, but this is a holdup. Both of you, get on your knees rodeo style and put your hands up," Lucky ordered.

They cooperated as we went through their pockets and took their money.

Lucky noticed that one guy was wearing a 4-carat diamond ring, so he told the guy to take the ring off. The guy appeared to make one attempt and then said, "I can't get it off, it's stuck."

"Take it off Randy."

"It won't come off Chuckie, I'm sorry."

Terrell began to say something, but Lucky interrupted him and said, "I got this, step away from here. I don't want y'all to see this."

Terrell joined Reno in the car while I walked a few steps and stopped so I could see what Lucky was up too.

"Say goodbye to Randy. I am going to have to kill him to get the ring," Lucky said.

"No Randy, please give it to him," Chuckie said in a trembling voice.

"It won't come off. I'm sorry Chuckie."

Lucky took the gun from the side of his waist and walked closer to him as Randy replied, "Can I try one more time?"

"Go ahead."

Randy pulled the ring straight off his finger on the first try and said in a happy voice, "I got it. Here, take it." Lucky put the ring in his pocket and warned Randy and Chuckie not to move from that spot for ten minutes. Lucky walked over to me and we trotted to the car and left the area.

Lucky showed the diamond ring to Reno and Terrell. Looking somewhat unsure Terrell asked, "Why didn't we take the prom shorties jewelry?"

"Here we go. Earthquake school him again," Reno said looking at me.

"You can get every occasion again, but you only get one prom. I just graduated, but I didn't get a prom and I always thought I would have one. Sticking up prom kids is easy but when they have something sentimental, I'm not gonna take that from them. It's not good to stack wrong on top of wrong. Something gotta mean something to you. If it doesn't, then you'll become the most dangerous person in the world. We are already robbing them. We're professionals, not savages."

Terrell asked why Lucky took the dude's diamond, so I explained it.

"Because it wasn't a sentimental moment. I wouldn't care if you took his socks but there are always exceptions to the rules. You gotta have some principles, never be too greedy. You get it?"

"Yeah."

"Cool, you got fifteen hundred dollars now, go buy yourself a watch."

After the robbery, we split the money. I took my cut and got my transmission repaired. Since the girls were working part-time, I had to make up by hustling. We called this light-weight hoeing. Things seemed to be moving but in what direction, I didn't know. Sitting in my room, I was thinking my army test was approaching and I took a moment to think about my future again.

'Robbing people can't last forever and I don't want this to be my main hustle. Taking from people who are struggling just like me is not good at all. I'm deciding at this moment never to rob individuals anymore, only franchise establishments and I'm about to stop that.'

Reno and Lucky rang my doorbell and it was time to pick up the girls. I had a new girl, Angie, who was a 6 foot, fourteen-year-old who I picked up on the Stroll. Her height made her look older and she worked well. As we dropped them off, I watched a clean, new body style, green Cadillac drive up and let two girls out. Then the car pulled up parallel to us.

"Are you Earthquake?"

"Yeah, what's up?"

"No offense, but your girls told me that you were their pimp. I'm always on the come up, but I respect a pimp. Just making sure there is no renegading (girls working without a pimp) going on. I'm Lee Lee."

"Are those your girls?" I asked, and he confirmed that they were.

Lee Lee was the first young pimp that I ever met. Like us, he was only sixteen and driving super slick.

"What else did you do besides pimp?" I asked him.

He looked at me with a cool stare and said, "All I do is pimp. I'm a bona fide player, straight "P" with no mix. I don't hustle no other way. Pimping is my only game. If you are a real pimp, you just pimp hoes."

I was too impressed. This cat was "straight like that." He was young, but he moved like the older cats. Right then I knew that my stick-up days were numbered; one way or the other, it was coming to an end.

On testing day, we prepared Lucky to take my place and off he went. In the middle of taking the exam, two trainers interrupted

Lucky and asked him to come with them. They took him into a private room and questioned his identity. Lucky insisted that he was me, reciting all my personal info, trying to convince them that they were mistaken.

The lead trainer-recruiter said with confidence, "I remember you personally, you performed the best on the test, and got a perfect score. You are Andre Hill (Reno)."

"A lot of people say that I have a neutral face and they always mistake me for someone else."

"Well, we are going to call the MPs and see what they think," the recruiter warned.

"That's not necessary. This is a small problem that can easily be taken care of. My best friend is not that smart, but we want to join the army together, so I took the test for him and now I'm taking mine," Lucky said remaining calm.

"You took the test once and can't take it again," the recruiter said.

"Maybe you can hire me to help others study and pass the test. I could work under you. I'm smart, daring and a risk taker. I am a soldier, willing to do what it takes to serve my country."

"That would have been possible, but you broke the rules and I have to disqualify you and your buddy. This is a fair warning. Don't ever come back here again or you will be arrested," the recruiter said.

Lucky hightailed it out of the hotel and called me two hours after I dropped him off, telling me to come and get him. I asked what happened and he said he would tell me when I got there. Lucky told me the whole story.

"It's ok, I'll try something less strict. Maybe auto mechanic school since their classes start in 4 months. Hopefully I'll pass the test, but I'll have to hustle until then. I can be a full fledge pimp if all else fails. Being a doctor is getting gloomy. I almost can't picture it now, but I'm not going to give up hope. I just have some decisions to make," I told Lucky. I visited my grandma, Auntie Tea, Aunt Vivian and cousins Cup, Chevy and Shady and hung out with them for a little while. After that, I sat on the front porch with Terrell (who lived nearby) and a group of my Mob folks. When we were out there, the girls always walked up and down the block capturing our attention.

A pretty girl named Linda boldly shouted out, "Hey handsome."

All eight of us replied, "Hey baby."

"Hey fellas. I was talking to the magnificent one," she responded.

"Oh, you must be talking about me," Terrell blurted out.

"No, I am talking about the piece of art, with the long hair standing next to you," she said smiling.

All the Mob cracked up as Terrell replied, "Because he got his shirt off, that makes him the man?"

"Yep, it sure does," her girlfriend butted in.

Then my buddy Diamond walked up saying, "Big June just got out of jail and he's around the corner acting like he's running things. He's arguing with Bodie from Loomis Street."

Bodie's reputation preceded him. He was Mob also, but they called themselves the Loomis Boys. Big June, a former captain in that territory, went to jail for 5 years and lost his rank. Now he was back on the scene, trying to vibe off his reputation, attempting to put together a crew so that he could restore his position.

He grouped up some of the young gang bangers who just turned Mob to follow him. We all went to see what was going on. Hearing the feedback, it was apparent that Big June was a bad Mob member, standing behind the organization while causing strife on both sides. Anytime a person tried to divide us, it was a bad sign. When we walked up, neither were backing down, even though Bodie was my age (sixteen) and Big June was about twenty-eight years old.

Big June stepped in Bodie's space and Bodie swung, slightly braising his jaw. Since I naturally fit into the role of peacemaker, everybody kept their eyes on me to see how I would react. I had a knack for diffusing situations, always fair to both sides. The young gang bangers watched me as I walked over near them and punched Big June in his chest, making it obvious who's side I had taken. They immediately turned on him, chasing Big June as he fled.

Bodie and I were good friends from that day on. He joined us as we walked back around the corner, positioning ourselves on the porch and continued girl watching. The cuties were thick on the block, still flirting. With her fresh, short finger waves, Re-Re walked up the steps and gave me a hug as Terrell grabbed her hand. She slid her hand away, slightly ignoring him.

"Earthquake, if my hair was long like yours, I would be throwing it back with my hands saying, 'Step back you baldhead hoes," Terrell said. We all laughed as we continued to shoot the breeze.

I looked down the block, and from a distance saw a tall figure coming our way. He was wearing a white, short sleeve, button down shirt, beige khakis and black shoes. Each of his steps were intentional, slow but precise, a gangsta pimp walk with a GQ style that demanded respect. This dude had a distinguished, noticeable presence. As he walked closer, the shadow of his face revealed unique features, a smooth mocha brown skin tone, thick eyebrows, a thin mustache and a perfectly aligned goatee. His hair was medium length, relaxed with thick curls.

He was carrying a large, black duffle bag, looking like he meant business. I couldn't help starring at him which made everyone else look too. We all watched, slightly cautious but not in a panic. We were all silent and my heart began to race. His big white smile lit up and I knew that face from anywhere. I yelled, "There goes my brother! Pow Wow!" He was out of jail!

He walked on the porch and hugged me, took a step back and said, "Man you're huge. You feel like a ton of bricks."

"You know that I gotta protect my folks." Everyone laughed and talked with Pow Wow. They drew to him immediately. Pow Wow went upstairs to visit with our family and then he called Prescott, who arrived thirty minutes later and they left. I didn't see Pow Wow for two days.

Prescott brought Pow Wow back to 55th Street and they hung out for a while since I was still there. Reno and Lucky stayed over since we had been working our girls closer to us on the 63rd Street Stroll. We still worked them on the Cottage Grove Stroll as well. Pow Wow told us about all his experiences in jail. He was locked up with Prescott's brother Junior, Mr. J-Hawk's oldest son. Junior was ruthless, carried two shanks and threatened highly ranked gang members. Junior was nuts, but nobody messed with him.

Pow Wow said that he also saw Creature Feature on the transportation bus that shipped prisoners to different penitentiaries. He grew his hair out long and straight. He was wearing jailhouse make-up created out of packages of Kool-Aid. His face was made up with eyeshadow, blush and lipstick. He had his white t-shirt tied in to a knot, showing his belly button and skin-tight khakis. Pow Wow said, "I kept starring at him, but he wouldn't even look at me."

I saw Phony Tony in lock up at Joliet Correctional Center, the holding spot until you are shipped off to prison. As they were doing the count, we talked for a minute. He told me that he got a two-hundred-year sentence and was accused of being a serial rapist, committing 20 home invasions and killed all the victims with his bare hands.

Shaking his head Lucky shared, "The last time that I saw him was when we did a caper in the Pill Hill neighborhood. He had rope, duct tape, eye masks and handcuffs. I asked, 'What is all that for?' and he said that it was a precaution kit. I said to myself that it looked like a kidnapping, rape kit."

"Cause when you think about it, Phony Tony was always weird," Prescott said.

Then Pow Wow had a revelation saying, "Remember when we did that burglary with him? He told us no one was home. He had staked out the joint for weeks and watched that morning and told us that the homeowner, a woman, had left earlier. We climbed through the window thinking she was gone but the woman was there, getting out of the shower, only dressed in a robe. When she saw us, she panicked and started to scream. Phony Tony grabbed her and put his hand around her mouth. I told her, 'Calm down miss, no one is going to harm you. We are going to take your merchandise and leave.' Phony Tony tied her hands with rope that he had wrapped around his waist. He placed her in a corner of the living room while Prescott and I were getting her valuables. I heard soft, faint cries and looked over at the corner where the woman was sitting on the floor. I saw that Phony Tony kept starring at her in an obsessive way. I told him to get away from her. 'We are not here for that.' He said, 'I was making sure that she didn't try anything.' Man, I told them lets go, right now. Phony Tony, Prescott and I headed for the back door carrying the merchandise that they were taking. As I did the final surveillance, I looked back at the window and noticed that it was unlocked. I am sure that I locked that window when we entered. I locked the window again, untied the woman and told her not to move for ten minutes. I made sure that both doors were locked, and we left.

As we split the money and merchandise, Phony Tony was anxious, insisting that he had something to do. It was something strange about that caper and Prescott and I decided not to hustle with Phony Tony anymore."

"Cause you probably saved that lady's life. I think he was trying to go back there that day," Prescott said.

"He sounds like a rapist and if it is true, I hope they give him the max, lock him up and throw away the key. I hate rapist the most," I said.

Pow Wow Works for A Cigarette Company

We kicked it with Pow Wow, updating him on what was happening in the streets. His parole officer set him up with a job interview at a cigarette factory and Prescott took him to the interview on that Monday morning. Pow Wow got the job and wasn't there for two weeks before he and Prescott devised a way to steal cigarettes. Prescott would meet Pow Wow at the docks in the back and load his trunk with boxes of cigarette cartons. Prescott would take off while Pow Wow went back to work.

They sold the cigarettes to the local Arab and Indian corner store owners in various neighborhoods. The merchandise already had the required state seal so it was difficult to catch them. Prescott and Pow Wow were making thousands each week and Pow Wow was back on top, looking sharp and clever as ever. Pow Wow sold his green Cadillac, Prescott gave him his red one and purchased himself a brand new white Seville.

Things were going very well. After being disqualified from entering the army, Lucky's aunt gave us a hook up and we got jobs working for the park district. I was required to cut my hair in order to meet the grooming and dress code. We were pimps at night and recreation leaders in the day time. The summer job came to an end and I was accepted into the trade school where I took a two-month course in auto parts and sales since there were no other courses available.

I interviewed for a couple of positions that were minimum wage. My teachers encouraged me, saying that I could work my way up in a few years. It wasn't just the money, selling auto parts was not something that I was even interested in, so it was not gonna work for me. I thought, *'Why should I be the low man on the totem pole making minimum wage when I can stay the high man on my own set with people working for me?'* If I didn't have a job, I wouldn't mind minimum wage, working my way up but I didn't see a future in this.

CHAPTER 15
Kentucky Fried Chicken

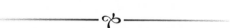

A FEW DAYS later, we saw Nik Cannon on the Strip and he told us about a job he had set up. He explained, "On Sunday, I'm not making the drop. If you come through in the morning, you'll get double the cash."

We couldn't resist. I was thinking, '*This will be my last robbery and then I'm done. After this one, I'm focusing on being a bono fide pimp.*'

Saturday night, we finalized the plan at the clubhouse. Reno got a new Great Dane mixed with boxer. A dog I called "Soup Hound." He and Lucky took a walk on the Strip with Soup Hound. After a few hours, they hadn't returned so I went looking for them. I noticed the Strip was light, not much going on. Reno and Lucky were nowhere to be found and no one had seen them.

I saw Nol man and his friend Donnie walked on the scene. We called him Nol man because he was the neighborhood syrup head (drug addict) and he knew everything that was going on around the Strip and the Stroll. He was about 5'8", slim with a short afro, brown skin and he talked and walked with a drag. Nol man appeared to be in his early forties.

He hung with his friend Donnie, who was tall and skinny with a huge afro, a keen nose and a big smile. Donnie acted and walked like an ex-pimp who got hooked on drugs. Nol man stepped to me saying, "Earthquake you know you are a real pimp." I interrupted him, asking if he saw Lucky and Reno.

"Yeah. The police came on the Strip and took everybody to jail for disorderly conduct. Reno and Lucky walked up and they grabbed them and threw them in the police Pattie wagon too."

"How? Reno had his dog."

"I know. Reno tied the dog to a pole and then they arrested them. The dog kept barking, so they locked the dog up too. You are my man. Let me get a dollar out of you," Nol man said.

I reached in my pocket and pulled out a semi-bankroll. As I handed him a dollar, Nol Man said, "Let me get another one."

"You only asked for one dollar and now you're asking me for two."

Dragging his words, he said, "Nawl, I asked you for one, Imma borrow this one, so I owe you a buck. I 'm gonna pay you back next weekend."

"You don't owe me nothing!" I gave him a fist bump and the two of them walked off.

'Dag! My plans are spoiled,' I thought. I went to the pay phone and called Cannon to let him know it was off. Cannon expressed that I had to do it tomorrow morning.

"I didn't make the drop tonight. They open at 9:00 a.m. and there will be only one manager in the store and she knows the combination to the safe. I can ride down there with you but I can't go in. You gotta find at least one person before morning. It's twenty stacks in there ($20,000). I'm sure of it. We'll never have a chance like this again."

I told him that I would try.

I called and found out that Lucky and Reno would be held until holiday court. That would be too late to do the caper. First, I took the girls to work and then went to get Terrell, but he went out of town to a funeral. So, I tried to find Diamond or Bodie on 55th but had no luck. Neither were around. I doubled back and went to the Manor looking for Smooth O or Babyface.

I learned that Smooth O had just shot a guy and he and Babyface were both arrested. Maceo had broken his foot. Time was flying and I was getting anxious. My last resort was Moe, so I went to his house and his little brother Pook said that he wasn't around. Pook volunteered saying that he would go with me but at fifteen, I told him that he was too young. It violated the code of protection. We tried to steer youngsters right.

A manor boy named Jerry walked up while I was talking to Pook. He asked why I was looking for Moe and I told him.

"Imma gangsta, a real gangsta. Take me and let's get that money!" he said boldly.

I was thinking, *'I've never known Jerry to be a gangsta but maybe he stepped up his game, a late bloomer.'* Since I only needed someone to guard the door, he should be able to handle that. I told him to roll with me until morning.

We picked the girls up from work and dropped them off. I kept my new chick Angie with me. As I explained the layout to Jerry and went over the plan multiple times, Angie listened and then asked if she could participate.

"I bet I could do it with y'all."

I thought about it and decided that she could sit in the car as a backup. Next, I went to get Cannon and he allowed me to borrow his .22 automatic that I gave to Jerry while I carried my .38 special.

We discreetly parked down the street, behind some trees, about ½ block away. At about ten minutes before they opened at 9:00 a.m., we walked up to the door. I looked in and saw four women and four guys, so I knocked. The manager announced that the store wasn't opened yet. I asked if they were hiring and she replied, "As a matter of fact, we are. You can come in and complete an application at this table," she pointed. She went back behind the counter and finished her tasks.

I looked at Jerry and said, "Let's do it now."

He paused and then said, "Wait a minute. I have to use the bathroom." Looking somewhat annoyed, I said, "Hurry up." That should have been a red flag, but I thought to myself, *'I don't need much from him.'* I walked up to the counter and flirted with the girls to stall time while Jerry was in the restroom. I asked them if that was the manager who opened the door and one girl confirmed that it was.

I gave her a smile and whispered, "I'm going to give you my number, ok?" She nodded as the other females listened. I could tell that they were all off guard. Finally, Jerry walked out of the restroom as the manager went and unlocked the front door. The store was now open to customers. Just as we rehearsed, I looked Jerry in his face and said, "Here we go! Stay on cue," as I leaped over the counter with my gun in my hand and announced, "Everybody, hands up, this is a stickup. Nobody move and nobody gets shot." I grabbed the manager by her arm and forced all seven employees to the back, inside the walk-in storage cooler.

From my peripheral vision, I saw a shadow move towards the front door, but I kept my focus on the robbery. I escorted the manager to the safe and told her to open it. After she put the first combination in, I told her to wait two minutes. Then I walked her to the front door, made her lock it and we returned to the safe. After the red and green lights stopped flashing (as Nik Cannon had informed me) I instructed her to dial the second combination.

She opened the safe and I pulled out my plastic garbage bags and filled them with cash. Then I had her open each register and I took the money, placing it in my pockets. I looked around for Jerry and my suspicion was confirmed. He must have left. As I prepared to leave I saw a squad car pulling up. I warned the manager to act normal or get shot. An officer tapped on the glass door and asked if we were open. I pretended to be working, wiping off the front counter and answered, "No, we open in one hour."

He said ok but someone reported seeing a man running out of here. I said, "No. Everything is good." As the officers were leaving, two more police cars and an unmarked detective vehicle pulled up and four more officers came to the door. They asked me if I could open the door and I replied, "Sure," as I turned to the manager, with my back to the officers, and softly reiterated, "No funny moves, don't get shot." I inconspicuously kicked the garbage bag and slid the gun under the counter.

We walked side by side to the door and she opened it as I stood on the side of her. The officer said, "We're just making sure that everything is ok."

"Thank you, officer. We really feel safe," I said graciously. The manager confirmed saying, "Yeah everything is alright." I watched her as she slowly inched her way out of the door, as the officers were walking away. Suddenly she leaped out, into the arms of the officer that was standing closest to her and shouted, "That's the robber right there."

The officer asked, "Where?" as the other police turned around, heading back towards us, she pointed at me and I pointed inside.

Confused, the officer was looking around, charging past me with his gun drawn and she reiterated, "No, him, right here and he has a gun," as she pointed at me again. About five or six officers said, "Freeze!" and then tackled me to the ground, with their knees pinning down my head and back, another one handcuffed me. They started searching the place, found my gun, the garbage bag full of money and let all the employees out of the refrigerator. One of the employees said, "There were two of them," as his teeth chattered, and he folded his arms.

I'm thinking, 'This coward Jerry ran off.' They grabbed me up and searched me. The detective said, "Hey fellas, check this out. He has a stash in all his pockets." He laughed and said, "So, you were going to swindle your buddy. Where is he?"

I was placed in the detective car and taken to the police station where I was interrogated for a couple hours, as they demanded to know who my partner was. "If you don't tell us his name we are going to charge you with Armed Robbery, Kidnapping, Endangerment with The Intent to Do Bodily harm and that's an automatic 30 years without probation. Now, tell us who he is and we can cut your sentence to 15 years."

I insisted that I was by myself, it was just me. Finally, they gave up and said, "Tell it to the judge," but they charged me as they said they would. I was placed back in lockup until preliminary court on Monday morning. I was charged with a crime that had no probation and a mandatory sentence of 6 to 30 years. Since I refused to give up Jerry, I was also charged with the additional crimes and looking at 30 years in prison.

I thought long and hard about my life. I adjusted my mind and accepted that this was my new world, the consequences for my actions. At about 4:00 a.m. the next morning, I was transported to the Cook County Jail and held for court. The judge asked the State's Attorney for my rap sheet and prior convictions. The judge looked up from his desk with surprise when the State's Attorney said, "Your Honor, he has no prior convictions."

I was given a $2,500 bail and my case was placed in one of the most hardcore courtrooms in Chicago, with the honorable Judge John Hope. After court, I was shipped upstairs to a part of the jail called The House of Corrections, where they held most of the young criminals. I was given one phone call, so I reached out to Pow Wow's girl, Sugarfoot. I told her where I was, my court date which was three months from today, and to tell everyone not to worry about me.

I had some concerns since this was my first trip to "The County." It was all new to me and I didn't know what to expect. I did know that gang life on the streets was different from jail. There is a ranking difference. You might have a leadership role in the streets but no position in jail, depending on how the heads receive you.

During the intake process, the guards asked what organization I was affiliated with. I told them "Folks" so they placed me on a Mob dominated dorm. The guard opened the large, steal door which led to a huge space filled with rows of twin beds down each wall and through the center, leaving two long walkways. It was overcrowded and some inmates slept on blankets off to the side of the room. At the front of the dorm, there was a television section with two steel benches that seated about 10 people each.

It was an old, shabby, dingy environment with high ceilings that had half broken, dim florescent lights. There were three small windows about 25 feet high, with bars and wires covering them. Even in the morning, sunlight could barely shine in. It was going to take some getting used to. As I walked in, I heard the incredible echo of inmates shouting, "On the New." I looked around and didn't see anyone I knew.

Two Mob members walked up to me and asked what I represented, and I replied, "I Be Mob, straight like that." Both dudes were big and swollen. The largest one said, "Follow us," as we walked toward the back where five guys were sitting on two beds. There was space for me at the end of one bunk and the guy who appeared to be running things told me to have a seat. He said, "Everybody must know the prayer. Recite it." I did it flawlessly. Then I said five of the laws as required.

After my successful recital, they recognized me as Folks and waiting in the cut was my homie, Brown Eyes, from 79th Street and Medusa from 63rd Street. It was against Mob law to interrupt a session, so they had to wait to greet me. They showed love by throwing up Mob signs. Brown Eyes let me know that he put his head on the chopping block for me, so even if I didn't pass, I would have been given one, based on his reference.

Next was something they called gladiator school. One of the Folks walked up to me and said, "All new comers go first." I asked what gladiator school was and Folks pointed to a guy called Bone Crusher, explaining that he led a daily exercise to keep physically fit in case of combat or battle. Bone Crusher, who looked like his name, was the Mob enforcer for the dorm. Folks grab my hat and put it on his head saying, "Man, this is a sharp hat. Imma hold on to it while you go and body punch Bone Crusher."

"I'm a lover, not a fighter," I said, hoping to antagonize him so that I could establish myself. Jail guys are no match for street dudes anyway. I was still wearing my street clothes and with my oversized jacket, you couldn't see my physique. Bone Crusher appeared to be annoyed and said, "Line him up." Anticipating the challenge, I stood up while everybody watched. He struck me in my chest with a hard blow that sounded off.

I smiled, knowing that he was in way over his head. I lunged into him with vicious blows, one after the other. Every time I hit him, he backed up a foot, until he reached the wall. When he couldn't back up any further, I hit him in his chest and he fell to his knees. I wanted to let everybody see who they were dealing with. The guards hollered, "What's going on over there?" So, we chilled. I looked at Folks wearing my hat and said, "I like my hat too." Without hesitation, he removed it from his head and handed it back to me saying, "No doubt."

I knew that anytime you get called out to see how big your nuts are, it's an opportunity to gain much respect if you rise to the occasion. One could even become an enforcer if their other qualities were intact. That person became more valuable to the Mob when they had brains and brawn, since it was a double commodity.

The Mob gave me a bunk and then we went to chow where I saw a lot of familiar faces. My man Preston Joe from 63rd shouted my name, "Earthquake, what up?" Then I saw Emmerson from 95th, Stanky Wank from 55th, Dirty Red from the Wild, Wild 100s and a few others. Seeing some of my folks gave me a sense of strength and I knew I wasn't alone.

Being a peacemaker in the streets gave me favor with both the desirables and undesirables, and that was an unforeseen benefit; a perk because my street credibility was good. It goes to show that you didn't have to be a hardcore killer for people to honor you. Showing love and being fair carries a powerful respect, a role that I've always been comfortable in and it naturally fit me. Only two days in and I regained my focus.

A few days later, I got word that the Mob General, over the entire jail, AK wanted to see me on the yard (outside grounds) the next day. AK was from 82nd Street. I knew him pretty well and he was a smooth cat. He hung out at a couple of the lounges on the Strip and the Stroll. We chopped it up quite a bit when he wasn't locked up. I didn't realize how much rank he had in jail. Since he liked me on the streets, I knew it was all love.

The rule while watching TV was that only a Mob captain could change the channels. If anyone other than a captain changed it without permission, it was an automatic violation. I turned the television station, not knowing that. This situation revealed whether I was going to be picked or chosen.

When you are picked, a leader appoints you into a position but when you are chosen, you evolve into that role. The captain spoke with favor saying, "Earthquake, you know we are not supposed to touch the TV. It's all good but be easy with that." I appreciated the warning. From then on, I knew that I was chosen.

I looked forward to seeing my homie, AK and the rest of my Folks on the yard the next day. I laid in my bunk, listening to a quartet that gathered in the back, singing a Smokey Robinson song. The echo from their voices bounced off the high ceilings and made everyone calmer. They say that music soothes the savage beast. It sounded quite good and I enjoyed the harmony. As I dozed off, a guard yelled, "Ramon Davis (Earthquake), gather your things. You're going home!"

I got my stuff, the guards escorted me out of the dorm, put the handcuffs on, we went to the holding room and finished my bond paperwork. Then on to the search room, next we headed to the identification room where my family had to pick me out of a lineup through a fiber glass one-way mirror. I finally made it to the waiting room where others lined up to collect their bond slips. It was my turn. I reached the lobby and walked through the metal detector. I was free, for the moment.

My brother, Prescott and Lucky were standing in the crowded lobby waiting for me. My first question was: "Why didn't you all leave me in jail until my court date?"

Pow Wow said, "You don't stand a chance fighting your case while locked up. You have a much better chance to make some money and hire a good attorney if you're out. A good lawyer can buy you some time and get you a shorter sentence. If the judge believes that no one cares about you, he'll lock the door and throw away the key."

Lucky updated me on the girls. "We put all the girls on double shift. They worked hard to get you out."

"You know we were still five hundred dollars short but I asked mama for it and she said no," Pow Wow butted in. "I told her, 'they're gonna kill my little brother in there. He not built for jail. They're gonna hurt him bad and he might not recover from this.' Man, I had to be real convincing. I had to do some acting and she called the next day and said, 'Come get the money and you all go and get him!"

"Cause if she wouldn't have given it to you, I was going to come and get you, but we didn't even know you were there for three days," Prescott said.

I got home and saw my mom and she immediately said, "I want my money back next week. They didn't do anything to you, did they?"

Joking with her I said, "Yeah mama, they had me washing underwear and socks and they made me braid hair too."

"Just have my money. I borrowed it off my credit card and this Sunday you are going to church with me."

Appreciating the five hundred, I said, "Ok ma, I'm going."

Lucky and I picked up Reno and then got all the girls. They hugged and kissed all over me as if I was Michael Jackson. It was good seeing them because I thought I'd never be with them again. We went to our favorite restaurant and then we dropped them off at work. My next stop was to see Nicky Blaze. Her pappy, the FBI agent was over for a visit. I pretended to be her nephew and stayed in the front room playing Nintendo with her kids. They were in her bedroom for about an hour and then he left.

I updated Nicky Blaze on everything that happened. She handed me four hundred dollars and gave me a lot of advice starting with, "There is no probation for armed robbery. You need some serious money so that you can hire a good lawyer. I got some ideas about how you can get the money." I was all ears.

Nicky Blaze got serious and in a low tone said, "I know this big-time drug dealer named Hiawatha. My friend, Shots, buys drugs from him and they meet in different places. I can easily find out when and where he's going to be. I even know they're meeting tonight. Come and ride with Shots and I so that you can see his face."

I rode along with them. We saw Hiawatha standing by a tree near a park on the Southside of the city. Nicky started in saying, "See, you can't go to jail for robbing a drug lord. He can't go to the police. The next time that Shots schedules a pickup with him, you can play stickup man and rob them both. You split the money with us and we get the dope."

After Shots dropped some money off to Hiawatha, we rode back to Nicky's place. I'm thinking, *'Doing this caper would help me out a lot but Hiawatha is a hustler like me, no way. Plus, I'm not going back on my word, no more stickups.'* I told Nicky, "No, I'm just gonna see what happens. If I get fifteen years, I have no choice but to deal with it."

My funds were limited. Some Mob buddies told me about some top-flight lawyers. One name came up several times, Attorney J. Adams who beat several complicated Mob cases. His office was located in the law district in downtown Chicago, so I scheduled an appointment. During our meeting, I explained my case. He was swamped with trial cases, so he suggested one of the associate attorneys who worked with him.

Since my case was in Judge Hope's courtroom, the associate recommended the judge's ex-state's attorney who was now in private practice. I went to see him and he took my case with the following stipulations: I gave him my bond slip and a one-thousand-dollar payment due on my trial date.

Being caught "dead to the right," I requested no delays so that I could hurry up and serve my time. The attorney did exactly as I requested. He got me two continuances and then a quick bench trial. The state's attorney was already prepared since the evidence was stacked against me.

My mom said that she wrote the judge a letter on my behalf. She also made me go to church with her. They would form a circle around me and "lay hands on me (pray)." I didn't mind because I knew that only a miracle could get me out of this trouble. I went through the motions, but I was still preparing myself for the penitentiary.

I drew closer to the Mob, learning all the laws and literature, keeping my ties good and staying focused on my pimping. I hung out with my girls more often and even took them with me when I traveled around the city. They tapped into how discipline and committed I was and it seemed to help them be more structured as well. We ran into my Mob buddy Dee Dee from 71st Street. He cut off his long hair and was headed to the army the next day.

Wow! I was going to miss seeing him around. I thought if I had only taken the army test myself things might be different. I would be preparing for the army instead the penitentiary. It's the difference between getting paid, an education and building a career verses being set back, sitting still and unable to build wealth with any trade locked up.

My trial was in a week and I still owed my lawyer four hundred dollars. I was sad but ready to do my time. The day before my trial, I stopped by Nicky Blaze's place since she had been leaving me messages. She asked me to let her hold four hundred dollars and she would give me eight hundred in the morning.

Since she always looked out for me, giving me money whenever I needed it, I reiterated that my trial was in the morning and I needed that $400 to settle the balance with my attorney. I stressed that I needed that money by 7:00 a.m. It could be the difference between getting a sentence of 30 years or 6 years. She said ok and I handed her the money. She breezed off as if she was going to handle some business.

I caught up with Lucky and Reno and discussed what would happen with my girls. Once I got to jail, I was going to tell my girls that they could ride it out or go their own way. If they chose to ride, Lucky would collect and send my trap to me in jail for as long as it lasted. We decided to pick up all the girls hang out together until morning. The girls took the night off. We all said our good-byes and then I went by Nicky Blaze's house to pick up my money.

I rang the doorbell several times but got no answer, so I knocked and even banged and still got no response. Now I didn't have the balance due to my lawyer and it was time to head to court. There was no time to waste, I had to be there. I prayed for a miracle that he would still represent me and get me six to eight years, not thirty.

When I got to the courtroom my attorney motioned for me to come to the front where the lawyers waited for their cases to be called. He said, "Your case is up next so stay close." There was a trial going on so I sat and watched. The defendants were three, seventeen and eighteen-year-old Black teenagers who had no prior convictions and were facing a rape case. They were convicted and got a sentence of fifteen to thirty years each.

Their family members were hysterical. After the verdict, the judge called for a recess. I headed to the restroom and saw Judge Hope walking toward me in the hallway. As he got closer I said, "Good morning Judge," and he hit me with his newspaper. I grabbed my arm like it hurt. He smiled and kept walking. I had a good feeling about my case after that.

Maybe he would give me six years, when I get back in the courtroom. My attorney asked if I had his money. I told him what happened, and I promised that I would pay him if it was the last thing I did on this earth. "Please represent me." He looked with a shroud face and walked to the judge's chambers. Fifteen minutes later he came out and said, "You better pay me you hear me?"

"Yes sir, I promise."

"When you had the gun pointed at them, at what position were the three bullets in the barrel?" my attorney asked.

"They were the last three bullets in the chamber. There were no bullets in the firing pin," I answered.

Then he asked again, as if he needed me to confirm, "They were away from the firing pin?"

"Yes." I didn't know what that meant but I hoped it would get me less time. My attorney walked back into the judge chambers.

When he returned, the judge announced that court was back in session. Then the clerk called my name. My lawyer and I walked up to the bench and he spoke to the judge saying: "Your Honor, I want to present the case of Mulligan vs. Spenser. The charge of Armed Robbery was reduced to a Robbery, since the bullet was not in the direct barrel of the firing pin. Therefore, the charge of Armed Robbery against defendant, Ramon Davis should be reduced to a Robbery because the bullets were not in the direct barrel of the firing pin."

Judge Hope granted the request. My attorney replied, "Your Honor, my client pleads guilty to the lesser charge of Robbery and is ready for sentencing." The judge explained my sentence in legal terms, much of it I didn't understand. I did hear the number thirteen mentioned. I thought to myself, *'I'll be out when I'm twenty-five, that's not so bad.'*

The judge looked at me and warned, "Don't get into any more trouble young man."

"Yes sir, Judge Hope," I humbly replied. He walked off the bench.

I was in shock. Then he asked, "When are you going to pay me? I want my money." He put on his suit jacket, talking as he walked, rushing to get to another courtroom.

"Wow thirteen years, man." I repeated.

"Did you understand what happened?" my lawyer asked.

"Not really."

"You got thirteen months of probation. I want my money. You know how to get in touch with me."

I sat in the empty courtroom for about five minutes. I was astonished by what just happened. It was a pure blessing because there was no way that I shouldn't have gotten jail time. I was caught red handed. I went home and surprised all my people.

When I hit 82nd Street, the first person that I saw was Nik Cannon. He asked what happened to me during the robbery, so I told him. Then he explained what Jerry told him when he got back to the car without me.

He relayed Jerry's version saying, "When Earthquake jumped over the counter, two people walked in and before I could pull my gun up, they ran out of the restaurant. I hollered, 'Earthquake, let's go!' I thought he was running out, right behind him. I thought I saw him following me. By the time I got to the car, I realized that he wasn't behind me."

"That was his story," Nik Cannon said. "We waited there for ten minutes before driving around the corner. There were police and detectives everywhere. Then we saw them walk you out of the restaurant in handcuffs and place you into a detective car, so we hurried and drove off."

He asked if I talked to Jerry. I said no but they renamed him Scary Jerry in the Manor and no one has seen him since that day. Nik Cannon asked, "You're not doing anymore robberies, right?" I let him know that I was done with that.

I went into the Corvette Lounge on 82nd Street where folks were enjoying the after work happy hour. Milton and King Fish were sitting at the bar talking to a few chicks, so I joined them. They were shocked and glad to see me.

"Good to see you," King Fish said. "We thought you had a six or eight ball (years in jail) to do."

"I've witnessed some strange things, but I don't know how you pulled that off. You gotta tell me about that," Milton said.

As we were talking, Nicky Blaze knocked on the picture glass window. When we ignored her, she hit the front door with her sword yelling, "Earthquake come out here, I know you busted my window." King Fish and Milton looked at me and Milton said, "I've never seen her act so crazy." "You better be careful going out there." King Fish said.

With no worries, I replied, "I'm not even paying her any attention." Since she kept banging on the door, I decided to go see what she had to say.

I walked out and asked, "What's up?"

While breathing hard, in a slight rage Nicky Blaze asked, "Why did you bust my window? I saw your car pull off right after it happened, and I followed you here."

I looked at her with a frown and asked, "Is that all that you can come up with? Why would I bust your window? That's super petty. You think I'm a mark, that would do something that goofy? If you thought I did that, there is no need to say anything to me. You got four hundred dollars. That's more than enough to pay for your window."

She said in a softer voice, "No, I need to talk to you. Things have been crazy, I just got out of the hospital. When I got back at about 4:00 a.m. that morning after you gave me the money, I turned the key to my front door and got dizzy. Suddenly, I felt a knot in my stomach. Cramping badly, I looked down and saw that my pants were soaked in blood and I passed out. My kids heard me fall and called 911. I began to hemorrhage and suffered a mis-carriage. They did an emergency surgery which included a process called a DNC. I didn't wake up until this afternoon. See, the hos-pital band on my wrist, proves that I was admitted."

I folded my arms as I listened to her story and then replied, "Ok, I understand."

"I'm sorry I wasn't there but that was the reason. Please don't be angry, I'm begging you. I'll get on my knees if you want me too."

As she dropped to one knee I said, "You don't have to do that, we're good. Don't worry about it." She tried to hand me four hun-dred dollars, but I told her I was straight. "I'll talk to you later," and went back into the lounge.

"You're not going to talk to her anymore are you?" Milton asked.

"Nope, I'm through with her."

CHAPTER 16
The Heartbeat of Pimping

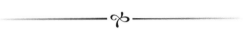

WHEN I MADE it home, I went straight to my room since no one was there. I sat on the bed, thinking about my life. *'What's my plan?'* I started with a process of elimination. First, no more capers and that meant, no more sticking up, pickpocketing, three card molly and short changing.

I thought about my options. *'I could work a low paying job for someone or somebody could work a high paying job for me. Starting at minimum wage wouldn't be a problem but it would take years to feel any progress, if at all. Is it wrong for me to find a trade that will get me out of a bad situation? I don't know but I must try.*

I see one viable option that could work for me – pimping. It's a misdemeanor so I wouldn't get a long stretch in prison, even if I got caught red handed. Plus, it comes easy to me and feels natural, like I was chosen for this. I accept it whole heartedly and I can deal with those consequences, however they come.

Now I must think about where I'm going with this. I'm seeing a vision of success. I can accumulate enough cash to buy all the essentials necessary. With enough capital, I can purchase whatever skills that I need, attorneys, accountants, etc. My journey is to build this pimping into a business and make it work for us all.

I can take the skills from every hustle that I've tried and use them for pimping, incorporating the three games into one. Using the taking game, the con game and the pimping game together will make my hustle scientific. This is a strategic move and I'll put everything into making it happen. Believing in my business is very important.

I can't keep trying to make myself into something that I'm not. I've tried the path through education, completed high school and trade school and I'm thankful for that. At this moment, I'm accepting who and what I am, and I know what I'll never be. I am now a bona fide pimp, dedicating myself to this craft.

My new focus is learning how to win, committing myself and doing what's necessary to succeed. The main key will be to concentrate more on my communication skills and ability to interpret body language. Keeping these thoughts in mind is important, so that I don't lose sight of the path I'm paving. I'll cause tremors, moving the earth but I'm ready to shake up this game.'

Married to this game plan, I stood up and left the house to pick up Reno and Lucky. I didn't have to go far because I rode up on them standing on the corner of the 82nd Street Strip. They jumped up like the Bulls had just won the championship when they saw me. After a mini celebration, I told them about the blessing that happened in court. It was a phenomenon and the days of miracles were not over yet.

I also shared my new mission and they were all in.

"My homie is back," Lucky said.

"We're about to be some real kings around here!" Reno shouted.

Still overwhelmed, I restrained myself long enough to speak calmly, "Now fellas, it's time to make it happen."

We got the girls and took them to work. After a while, I saw Angie returning from a date. While she was handing me the money a woman walked up to us and asked her, "What are you doing up here?" Not knowing who she was, I backed up as I continued to listen.

The woman was tall, thin with the same light complexion. She was an older looking version of Angie. She turned and addressed me.

"I'm Angie's mother."

"Nice to meet you Angie's mother."

She glanced back at Angie as asked again, "What are you doing out here?"

Angie answered in a sweet, innocent voice, "I don't know." Angie's mom grabbed her by the hand and said, "You're coming with me."

As they walked off, Angie looked back at me and said, "I'll be back."

At least Angie didn't mention the real reason she was out there but still, that was a dumb answer. All our girls laughed at Angie's reply. Reno and Lucky joined in and I laughed too. When she returned two hours later, I asked what happened. She told me that her mom took her home and her mom's boyfriend was there, so she said she left. I asked why she didn't stay home. Angie said, "I don't mind being out here."

I wanted to know more so I asked, "When did you start being out here?"

"About six months ago."

"Why?"

She revealed that her ex-boyfriend David brought her out there saying that this is how they could get money for weed. I didn't like girls that were spacey, not quick on her feet and hoeing for no cause. Her answers turned me off, so I passed her to Lucky. He always said if I ever got rid of her, she could be with him. I took Angie's hand and put it with his and told her, "You are with Lucky but still in the family."

My quest was to find women with a level of intelligence who understood me and my purpose. I was coming up quick. For every five women that I engaged in conversation, one of them was willing to be down with me.

As fast as I got new women, I would get rid of them. If they had too many slow days, they were gone. If they didn't follow instructions well, I'd let them go. If they were too loud, smoked, drank alcohol or responded with an attitude, they got fired. If they were late or not showing up for work, they were out of there. I had my choice of many women, so I became overly picky. If they didn't adjust to the way that I was, they didn't make the cut.

I hung around 55th Street more because there were more women in that area. I spent more time with the ladies and less time with the Mob. Our girls worked all the major Strolls across the city. I always kept at least four chicks even though I had a high turnover rate. Reno came up with a seasoned hoe named Lucy. She was a money getter and a thief who stole from her tricks.

One week, Reno asked what happened to the last three girls after I had fired them and hired new ones. I told him that they weren't smart enough for me and didn't listen effectively.

Reno replied, "Man you are turning into a hoe trainer. After you teach them the ropes, you get rid of them and then start the process over with new ones. They would be ready made hoes for other pimps. You can't make no money like that."

He had a valid point. My money was much shorter than his. With two hoes working the same hours as my five girls, he was purchasing a new Cadillac while I was buying a used Bonneville.

Reno advised, "Every time a hoe does something wrong you can't fire her, she has to get checked. Stop responding the way that you dismissed girls in the Manor. You are a pimp now, so you can't lose sight of what this is all about. You don't allow them to have any imperfections. We need to figure out what's going wrong. Let one of your girls who is not bringing in enough cash work with Lucy tonight. If she comes up short, just check her (whip) but don't get rid of her."

We took all the girls to the 43rd Street Stroll for work except Lucy and my girl Wonnie, who we dropped off on the 63rd Street Stroll. Feeling somewhat uncomfortable I told Reno, "I'm not into beating up my girls. That's why I'm trying to create a new breed of hoes, star status chicks that don't need to be checked."

He responded, "Ok, let's see what happens." Lucy did well and Reno's trap was on point but my girl Wonnie's money was short again.

Lucy reported to Reno that my girl Wonnie spent half the night with the same trick. He suggested that I put my foot down if I wanted to have a variety of girls, which required me to spread myself thin. "This is a business so treat it like one and keep your broads in check," Reno reiterated.

The next night was a repeat for Wonnie and Reno encouraged me to do something about it because at this point, she was playing with my pimping. He dropped me off on 55th Street while he and Lucky left to handle some business. Prescott and Pow Wow came through, so I hollered at Prescott about the situation. I asked what he did when his girls got out of line.

"Cause I wait until they keep doing little stuff, it accumulates, my anger builds up and then I knock all of their heads off. After that, they were straight for a while. That's my way."

I revealed that I didn't like hitting women and that wasn't my way.

Prescott suggested that I do whatever worked for me. I was determined to get it right and if I had to make some adjustments, then I was willing to do so. When the girls got off work, Wonnie was short with my money again so I told her to get out of the car. Reno and Lucy watched as I commented saying, "Your trap ain't right, again." She rolled her eyes and replied, "It was slow out here."

I pimped slapped her (using back of hand) and she fell. I snatched her by the neck, picked her up and body slammed her to the ground. Then I grabbed a water hose that was attached to the building that we were standing near and commenced to beating her with it. Reno jumped out of the car and said, "Hey Earthquake, that's enough."

"Show me that you're serious about this or don't come back!" I commanded in a stern voice.

I got back into Reno's car, he drove off and we discussed what happened. He teased me saying that both he and Lucy were scared. "We were about to run to the Stroll and get your money ourselves. You're such a violent guy," Reno jokingly said.

We waited to see what would happen. She paged me three hours later and asked me to pick her up. Wonnie handed me a nice bankroll and I dropped her off at home.

I didn't have this thing totally figured out but what Reno said about accepting their imperfections had me re-evaluating my strategy. Realizing that I was an extremist who went over and beyond in whatever I did, meant that my method of checking the girls had to be controlled.

From that point on, I slapped my broads when they got out of line knowing that this was not always the answer. I only used it when it was highly necessary and when I checked one of them, I did it in front of all my girls, making it more impactful.

I was mostly attracted to women with one style, beautiful and intelligent but this is business and only connecting with one type of chick would limit my opportunities. I also had a valuable skill set that I wasn't even using and my ability to adapt could be quite useful. As a chameleon, it was easy to accept their imperfections and guide them to use their inadequacies as an advantage.

I began responding to my girls in a smooth way that soothed them, and they reacted by allowing me to take the lead by choice, not by force. As time went on, I made them comfortable with their shortcomings. I accepted their imperfections and understood how to guide them right. My women didn't mind making mistakes because they knew that I had them covered. There was a comfort level that I gave them when I adapted to their style in this way. Teaching them how to accept their flaws and use them to their advantage made them trust me to guide them in any direction I chose.

Cigarette Sacrifice

My business was very good on the 63rd and 43rd Street Strolls so I moved with my grandma permanently to be closer to the action. Pow Wow spent fifty percent of his time on 55th with me as well. One night, when Prescott was dropping Pow Wow off, they walked straight into the dining room, while I was on the phone talking to a cutie who had potential. A strong aroma followed them and caught my attention. The scent put my nose in the path of a sweet, tangy sauce that drowned a batch of freshly fried breasts, legs and thighs, enough to interrupt any conversation. It was the unmistakable smell of Harold's Chicken.

Prescott motioned to me and pointed at the food saying, "Cause you gotta wrap up your conversation and grab a plate before Pow Wow demolishes this food."

I politely got off the phone and got a few pieces of chicken. As we sat at the dining room table eating, I asked, "What are y'all about to do?"

"I'm going to the South suburbs, to the Numbis Night Club," Prescott said.

"You riding out to Pow Wow?" I asked.

Prescott interrupted before Pow Wow could answer saying, "No, Pow Wow has go to bed so that he could be on point getting those cigarettes tomorrow."

With excitement, Pow Wow laid his bankroll on the table, laughing as he said, "Yeah, Prescott and I been killing them (doing well), selling these cartons of cigarettes all over the city and we're clocking thousands (money)."

"That's why I want you to get some rest, so that we don't blow this," Prescott said.

Pow Wow sat there counting his dough as he was fighting sleep. Looking sharp, Prescott was wearing a winter white tailor-made, double breast suit with shirt and shoes to match his brand-new Cadillac Seville. Fresh from the salon, with his auburn colored long, straight, hair styled into ocean waves, Prescott looked and sounded like a boss.

Prescott and I teased Pow Wow since he couldn't hang out.

"We get to stay up late," I said.

"Cause you got a job. We got lots of cigarettes to organize and distribute tomorrow. I won't be out too late, just call me when you get to work."

Prescott gave Pow Wow a pat on the back and calmly said, "Go to bed Pow," as he looked up from his nod, "I'll call you in the morning."

Prescott gave me a fist bump as he was headed toward the door.

He turned around and asked, "Oh yeah, how is that situation working out for you? Have you been checking your hoes?"

"Only when necessary. My adaptable style allows me to do less checking and more teaching. I'm real ambitious about my business, doing whatever it takes to make it work."

"For me, Gorilla pimping is not the answer. If I must check a broad, it's a rare occasion and I make sure to do it in front of the rest of my girls so they all know what's up." I laughed as I reminded him, "I got that from you." Prescott appeared to listen intensely and said, "Cause you killing me! You're going to be the scientist of pimping. You getting real sophisticated with your game but I love it."

The next day Pow Wow called and asked if I'd heard from Prescott because he never picked up the boxes of cigarettes. "I had our biggest batch ready and tried to call him but his girls said that he wasn't there. Man, I had to put all the cartons back."

"Maybe he went to jail. He seemed adamant about you guys getting those squares (cigarettes). He'll call you later."

Calming down a little, Pow Wow said, "Yeah you are probably right. He knew this was the biggest caper we've done on the cigarette side."

I reminded my brother to call me when he talked with him. That night, Pow Wow phoned me. "Prescott's girl called. She was concerned that he didn't pick them up for work."

"Prescott might be in jail, that's what I believe," I said.

Pow Wow said, "I think so too. He's been going out to Indiana, talking to a young white chick. The police warned him if he gets caught out there talking to her again, they're going to lock him up and throw away the key. She was a pretty little Italian girl and I think her father was a judge."

"I hope he didn't go back out there. If he did, he's probably in jail, for sure," I said.

"I'm going to call J-Hawk and see what he says."

I asked him to call and keep me updated. That night, I took everybody to their own house and went home alone. Pow Wow called and said that J-Hawk was on his way to pick him up.

J-Hawk picked Pow Wow up. His son Smooth O was in the passenger seat and one of their homies from the Manor, Slim, was sitting in the back. He got in. Everyone in the car was quiet.

"What's up, Uncle J-Hawk? Where are we going?" Pow Wow asked.

"To the borderline of Illinois and Indiana."

"Is that where Prescott is?" Pow Wow asked.

"I don't know. I got a call saying Prescott's car was out there," J-Hawk answered.

J-Hawk drove to the borderline of Indiana, got off at the first exit and headed back toward Illinois. Right before the border, J-Hawk pulled into the safety lane. They all got quiet when they saw Prescott's car about a quarter of a mile ahead. When they pulled up, no one was in the car. Then J-Hawk drove half mile down from Prescott's car and stopped. They all got out.

J-Hawk walked as they followed him along the safety lane which had a slope that went down into a ditch. They all looked over the side of the ditch and saw Prescott and his pimp friend, Skinny Kenny, stacked on top of each other, frozen stiff. Both were shot in the back of the head. Pow Wow ran to Prescott's frozen body and dropped to his knees, while Smooth O yelled with anguish. Slim was crying in shock. J-Hawk just stood there in silence.

J-Hawk called the police and an ambulance, who took the bodies to the morgue. Pow Wow cried continuously, "Whoever did this is going to pay dearly. Oh my God." It seemed like every few minutes' reality hit him, he broke down again and again, it seemed so unbelievable!

"Pow Wow, it's going to be ok. We will make it through this. God called Prescott home. Don't question it," J-Hawk said.

My brother connected with me that afternoon. I was waiting for his call, thinking that Mr. J-Hawk would get to the bottom of this. When the phone rang, I picked it up. I heard a sound from my brother that I never heard when he replied Hello. I asked if they found Prescott.

"Yeah, Prescott is dead!" he told me.

My heart felt like it stopped beating. I grabbed the dining room table to hold myself up and then asked what happened. Pow Wow told me how they found them.

I never lost someone that close to me. Prescott was my brother. Pow Wow without Prescott is incomplete. I was very sad and disturbed not knowing what happened. The next day they had a suspect, a pimp from Indiana named Red. I couldn't believe that. The police reported that he hung himself in his cell one hour after he was arrested. That was strange to me, Red? It was unbelievable because he was easy going, laid back and didn't have that kind of disposition.

Nothing about him seemed to match. I didn't see that in Red. Just thinking about it had my chest caving in. This was difficult to digest and seeing Pow Wow without Prescott kept reminding me of the whole situation. I loved Prescott with all my heart and I know that Pow Wow would have jumped in front of a bullet for him.

Pow Wow hung out with J-Hawk every day after that happened. Mr. J-Hawk was kind of quiet through it all. Everyone attended the funeral, including my mom. Prescott looked like himself, it appeared that he was sleeping. His long hair was ocean waved and he was wearing a dark red, tailor-made suit, looking handsome as ever. Most everyone from the Jeffery Manor, 82nd Street and 55th Street neighborhoods attended, and it was very crowded.

Several pimps, drug dealers, hustlers and many women from various times in his life were also in attendance. Keeping with tradition, Prescott's entire family sat in the front. His mom, Mr. J-Hawk, their son, Smooth O, and his two daughters. His other son Junior was still in the penitentiary, so they allowed him to view the body before everyone got there.

The preacher delivered a message to us young folks. The sermon was about salvation. Mr. J-Hawk walked up there next wearing dark shades that completely covered his eyes with a dark blue custom designed suit and tie, fitted around a crisp white shirt, matching handkerchief and freshly shined dark blue gators (alligator skin) shoes.

Mr. J-Hawk talked about carrying a heavy load and slipping on ice when the load is too heavy. I was trying to be strong for everyone, especially Pow Wow who couldn't stop crying. You could see that he was heartbroken and strongly affected by this. All four of Prescott's girls took it hard as well. After Mr. J-Hawk left the podium, three Manor dudes that we grew up with sang a cappella "It's So Hard to Say Goodbye," in perfect harmony and a cloud of emotion came over the place.

It put me in a trance, thinking about so many moments with him, when I was trying to prove that I had grown up. I remember when Prescott tried to chastise me and I went to blows with him, but Mr. J-Hawk made us stop. He was the one who taught me how to box. He would spend the night and we stayed up late, talking, listening to music, steppin' and playing ping pong. I miss my big brother already. I tried my hardest to hold back the sadness.

Reno, Lucky, Dirk, Mike D, Pow Wow and I were the pallbearers, so we prepared ourselves as everyone said their last goodbyes to Prescott. All the women in attendance were overwhelmed with sorrow and tears were falling like rain. We carried him out of the funeral home and placed him in the hearse. After we put Prescott to rest, Pow Wow spent much more time with J-Hawk and they went everywhere together. I believe they were a comfort for each other.

Those days were sad, and morale was low. Reno, Lucky and I were trying to get back on track. Even our girls felt the effect. Reno came up with one of Prescott's girls, bringing his total to three. A couple weeks later, Reno took his girls to New York City to check out that vibe. I spoke with him every day. He told me about the environment and how they got down on the stroll.

Lucky also came up with another girl and he was now three deep. I was eight strong and still building momentum while working my plan. We were trying to move things back to normal. Pow Wow didn't go to work much and eventually he lost his job. He began working with Mr. J-Hawk selling clothing for the boutique.

He also moved to my grandma's permanently and was trying to be a part of the action with the girls and the Mob. Everybody loved Pow Wow and he got close with my closest Mob friends: Bodie, Poochie Slim, Diamond, Terrell and Gino. Mr. J-Hawk came around more often and sometimes we all hung out together. He rode around in a sharp van that he named "The Playhouse." It was beige with soft pillow seats and a curtain that sectioned off the back area.

I always said when I got my money right I was going to get me a van. One day J-Hawk dropped my brother off while I was taking my girls to work. As I walked down the stairs of the porch, Mr. J-Hawk pulled up. I was wearing a black Persian lamb skin coat, eel skin shoes and carrying an eel skin briefcase.

He called me over to the van and asked, "Are you going to drop your girls off because you look like a businessman? Boy, you sure look pimpish."

Pow Wow nudged Mr. J-Hawk and said, "Uncle J-Hawk he's about eight deep. He must make two trips to get his girls to work and he got some broads on "layaway."

"You are going to need a new car, partner. Like a Cadillac."

"I'm saving up for one and plan to get it next month. I'm going to the dealership where Reno got his Caddy."

"I tell you what, I got the perfect Cadillac for you. What are you going to do with the old car?" he asked.

I told him that my friend wanted to buy it. "I've been stalling him until I got my new whip."

Mr. J-Hawk suggested that I tell my friend to come purchase my old car tomorrow.

"In two days, I'll bring you the new Caddy. Have your money right."

The next day, I sold my car to my Mob buddy. The following morning, Mr. J-Hawk blew the horn. I woke up, looked out the window and it was beautiful! A polished, burgundy Cadillac with a white strip down both sides.

He looked up at my window and said, "Come on down." The car salesman, Roy and J-Hawk were waiting on me. I was super excited, put on my robe and went downstairs. J-Hawk did all the talking saying, "Listen up. How much do you have?" When I told him, he said, "You are three thousand short, so you'll have to pay him in installments, five hundred dollars a week. You can handle that; you pimping. You can give it to me every week. Ok, I'm counting on you."

I agreed.

I would have accepted any cost, at that moment. I was thinking that my game was headed to the tenth power. Mr. J-Hawk handed me the keys and registration.

Roy said, "Come pick your plates up next week." As I was walking back into the house, I was thinking that I couldn't wait to show Reno when he returned and show Lucky in a few hours.

I went back in the house after gazing out of the window at my new car for a while. I was elated and couldn't wait to show Pow Wow but that made me think about Prescott. Even though the ordeal was over, it never settled in my mind. I sat in the window reflecting on the whole situation about Red. Prescott had introduced me to Red a few months earlier, at the hotel where they all had their girls working.

When I met Red, I watched his body language and his demeanor, but it didn't say "Killer." J-Hawk told me that Red was in the back seat when he robbed and murdered them. I'm thinking, if they were killed while driving, they would have swerved and crashed. If Red made them pull over and then shot them, he must have slayed Skinny Kenny first since the bullet went through the center back of his head. Prescott was shot behind his ear as if he was probably turning around.

Red must have caught them off guard. He only weighed about 185 pounds and would've had to carry them both, drag them into a ditch, stack them on top of one another, in zero-degree weather. Then he would have to drive the car about a mile away from the bodies. I questioned whether Red could have done that by himself.

It's more logical that they were executed and moved in another vehicle, driven a quarter of a mile and then dumped in the ditch. After that, the perpetrators must have pulled off, leaving Prescott's car at the first location so that when it was towed, their bodies wouldn't be found.

Why would the police suspect Red and lock him up? Then they reported that he took his own life by hanging himself one hour later, after being arrested. He didn't appear to be suicidal and that type of killer, but you really can't go by looks.

I spent a lot of time around all kinds of killers and it didn't seem reasonable that Red would commit this crime and then take his life an hour later before evidence was even presented against him. Why would he be that meticulous about the way he executed them and then hang himself?

Some killers are the politest, most laid-back people that I know. Some are soft spoken and friendly and that got me to thinking. I don't think that this crime was committed by one person. Prescott was warned by the Indiana police not to pursue the Judge's daughter. He could have paid Red to commit the crime and then doubled crossed him. The judge, the police and Red were all from Indiana. They may have hung Red so that he couldn't tell what happened. I think Red was the fall guy.

These murders could have been about something totally different. My brother said Mr. J-Hawk went straight to the dead bodies like he knew exactly where they were. Maybe Mr. J-Hawk knew what really happened. I'll ask him about it again, on a later date.

After being fully engulfed in my thoughts, I snapped out of it and immediately started thinking about my girls. I couldn't wait to show them the car. They loved it and were motivated to go to work. After I dropped them off, I drove out West to visit Ice Kat. I hadn't seen him since Prescott's funeral. We met up at the Karate Club. When I pulled up, Ice Kat came out and saw my new Caddy.

"Man, your whip is cold." Then he gave me dap. "Pimping is your style. It's you all the way."

We were kicked back at the bar enjoying orange juice and easy living's (a non-alcoholic beverage). The ladies were all around us and we were harmlessly flirting. One of the Mob Generals with the same rank as Ice Kat walked in with two guys. He came over and spoke then started a conversation with Ice Kat.

"Hey Ice, man I just talked with one of the board members about you. They were saying that you was using the chief's name to expand your operation all the way to the Rock territory. I told him you were my man, you weren't on nothing like that. I hollered at the chairman and cleared up the rumors." He hugged Ice Kat and went and sat two tables behind us.

Ice Kat recalled what happened. "Remember when the two guys was getting money off of my name, that was one of them. The chief gave him some favor, but he is still at it. We both know that the traitor always brings the news."

Being concerned, I advised Ice Kat to watch him. "He's overly friendly, compensating for something treacherous." Ice Kat explained to me that he did expand into the Rock territory because there were Rocks who were all good, just trying to eat. "I didn't gangsta my way, I negotiated and put a few of the Rocks on payroll and they have maintained their loyalty.

We are all trying to eat but the General has been trying to gangsta and take over the territory, using Mob influence outside of the Mob laws. Don't worry, I keep my friends close and enemies closer."

"Yeah you right, let's get back to partying." The steppers song "Sha-ball" by Marvin Gaye played. I grabbed this chick and we stepped while Ice Kat cheered me on.

"Get it Quake, Quake."

The floor was packed. I motioned, "Come and get some of this Ice Kat." He stood up, three suspicious looking dudes walked in the joint and headed in our direction. They pulled out their pistols and started shooting. People were shot and fell to the floor as bullets kept ringing out. Women were screaming, yelling, running and scrambling on the floor, trampling on top of each other.

I hit the floor and all I saw was darkness. Then I saw light as the crowd thinned out and people crawled off me. I saw Ice Kat face down, laying a few feet away from me as some of the crowd rushed for the door after the three shooters fled. I reached for Ice Kat's arm and shook it as I called his name, "Ice Kat, Ice." He didn't move.

I jumped up off the floor, he looked at me, I helped him up and asked if he was ok. He quickly replied, "Yeah, let's get out of here." We looked back and saw the General and his two friends plastered to the floor dead. I got in my Caddy while Ice Kat jumped in his Benz with his two homies in tow. We drove to his territory in the projects where fifteen Mob members were waiting on him.

Ice Kat got a beep from two of the Rocks that worked for him and we met up with them a few blocks away. They reported to Ice Kat that the General attempted to pay them to hit Ice Kat and get their future work from him, so they decided to eliminate the problem and knock off the General and his two goons.

"The General getting what he deserves. This been a long time coming. I wish it wouldn't have come to this, but greed is everlasting," Ice Kat commented.

I reminded him of the motto that we live by: "Always stay alert and aware of your surroundings. Stay fair and in the middle, knowing that there could be a traitor amongst you, so be mindful."

Ice Kat shook his head in agreement, "Yeah, it takes a moment to get into trouble and a lifetime to get out. I always remember."

"I love you man. Lay low for a few days," and I went home and thought about what had just happened. I couldn't take Prescott and then Ice Kat dying, that would have been too much.

That's why Ice Kat didn't go up, he was trying to expand out. You can only go so high but when you grow outward you can widen your range and there is no limit. We were both trying to spread our wings from two different spectrums. So far, we were parallel in our success even though I was on the Southside and he was holding down on the West side. We still had love for each other, we were ride or die!

I went home after that experience with Ice Kat. I fell back on the bed ready to relax when the doorbell rang. It was Peggy,

Chevy's friend who considered herself my girl. She showed a lot of interest in me from the moment I met her. Even though she had a nice body, she was very plain looking so I didn't want her on my squad. She had the heart, no sex appeal but she still contributed.

Peggy was a bartender who stole money every night and gave it to me for the cause. With that came interference in my business. I gave her a chance since she racked up money each night but there was one too many altercations. Peggy grabbed and broke my pager when I didn't answer her pages, but she immediately apologized and bought me another one. Next, she threw a brick through my car window when I wouldn't answer the door.

On the day of the pager incident, Peggy saw me driving with my girls in the car. She paged me all night. When I got home, she was waiting in the hallway. I had my girl Wonnie with me and Peggy proceeded to clown (start trouble). I warned her that if she said one more word then we were through, so she left. I noticed that Wonnie didn't say anything about Peggy, but she tried to say something about Wonnie. I thought about it. No matter what she gave me, her mind was still a square.

That led me to make a serious decision. I concluded no more square broads for me unless they had some significant role in my pimping. Peggy didn't understand me or what the pimping game was all about and for those reasons, we could never be on the same page. She couldn't fit into my lifestyle. I was committed to the game and fair to my girls. If a square chick couldn't work the streets, then she couldn't be with me.

Later that day, I called and told Peggy that it was over between us but she came over to my house anyway.

"I just want to talk to you. I would like to say what's on my mind one last time," she pleaded.

I gave her the floor and let her speak.

"So, you like hoes, nasty girls who go around screwing and sucking off random guys, huh? I know hoes, but I've never been one. I am a one-woman man."

"Excuse me, but I don't like hoes. I'm down with women of leisure."

"What's the difference?"

"Every hoe ain't a prostitute," I explained. "Hoes like sleeping with men they're attracted to while women of leisure do it for business. Hoes have sex with men whether they get paid or not and prostitutes are strictly about getting money. Personally, I strongly prefer women of leisure but when it comes to business, I don't look at hoes personally because it's not always about what I like. If a hoe is willing to use her talent for the benefit of my team and be converted into a prostitute, then I might give her a chance."

"So, you'll sleep with a hoe if she brings in enough money, right?" she asked.

"First, I'll tap into why she acts promiscuous and then teach her how to fulfil those desires in a different way. That puts her in a new arena and she transforms from a hoe to a woman of leisure," I said, giving her a little game.

"Do you only desire prostitutes?"

"I'm attracted to women that understand what I'm about. They see my destiny and want to be a part of it. That's what draws me to a chick."

Still somewhat confused she asked, "You don't care that they're having sex with all those men. That don't bother you?"

"No, I look at it like a business where she performs a job. If you are a doctor, you must be able to deal with seeing blood. That's a part of their business and anyone who can't handle it needs to choose another profession. My women must accept that I have multiple ladies and I must accept that my girls have sex with a variety of men. That's a pimp and a prostitute's genuine understanding."

With a new-found confidence Peggy stated, "When I'm at work, I get a lot of offers like that. Even my boss propositioned me, but I turned him down. If I wanted, I could do that and make money too. I would probably bring in more than your girls." I was silent and so she spoke again, "I could be on your team."

"Wait a minute, there are a few other qualities that are required, and you are missing those. Keep your night job."

"What am I missing?"

"The way that you view issues is not conducive to my business. You've got too much tunnel vision. Also, on my team, you need to have a certain amount of sex appeal and that's not your strong point. I've already ignored my last five pages so we gotta wrap this up."

Warming up to me she said, "I love you and I still want to be with you."

"See, you don't get it. I gotta go right now. We're good," as I escorted her out the door and then ran upstairs to answer my beeps.

Three in One

The beeping was one of my chicks, so I returned my girl's call. When she didn't answer, I went over to pick her up. Her mom came outside of the door and blatantly announced, "I'm not having it! As long as she's living in my house, my daughter is not coming outside anymore, so don't come back!" The mom walked back into her house and slammed the door.

I left and went to pick up another broad and for the third time, she wasn't where she was supposed to be, so I dropped her like a bad habit. Now I had just lost two girls in less than one hour and though I was still six deep, I didn't like going down in numbers. I took my broads to work and headed back toward the house.

I spotted a sexy, brown skinned, 'just right kind of chick.' She was the perfect size and had the right look. I pulled up as she walked my way, blocking the sidewalk so that she had two options to get to her destination. If she went around the back of my car, I would pass on talking to her, but if she walked in front, where I was standing with my foot on the bumper as I watched her, all systems were go. As I anticipated, she came toward me.

"Have you ever played flip a coin, heads or tails and won?" I asked.

"Yeah, why are you asking?" She stopped to answer me, smiling.

"I just did it with you and won. I knew if you walked toward the head of my car, I would win and if you had walked toward the tail of my car I would lose, but I won."

"What did you win?"

"You, of course."

"How do you know you got me?"

"Because my psycho command powers tell me so. I'm Earthquake."

"I'm Lola. How does psycho command power work?"

"It's a gravitational mechanism that draws you to me."

We both laughed. My beeper went off three times. Since it was two of my girls, I quickly asked, "Where do you live?"

"Up the street."

"Hey, get in the car so that I can take you home." She did.

"I was about to go to KFC," she told me as we drove.

"Write your number down. We'll get something to eat later." I dropped her off and went to a pay phone.

My girls let me know that the 47th Street Stroll was hot with cops. The police informed us that it was "Vice night" and we needed to be gone off the streets by midnight. So, I picked them up and took them to work on the 111th Street Stroll. After that, I rode to the 63rd Street Stroll to check my trap (money) from two of my chicks. I rotated from each work spot until the morning.

I collected my dough, dropped the girls off and met Pow Wow and Lucky at my house. When I got there, they were talking about how Pow Wow had just come up with a new hoe. The two of them had ridden together that night and their girls worked the same Stroll. Pow Wow looked over at me and said, "I want my new girl to work with some of your girls so that she can learn the ropes."

I knew Janet (his new girl) from Lon City (Avalon Park). "Doesn't she have two kids?" Pow Wow confirmed that she did and added that her mom was going to babysit. "She's starting work tomorrow."

"Man, I just lost two girls tonight," I shared with them. "Let's go to breakfast so I can get some energy."

"You'll be two more deep by the end of the week," Lucky said.

"A week, never that long," I said.

"You right, my bad, I meant a couple of days."

"No way, that's too long. I lost two girls within an hour so I'm going to bump (get) three girls before an hour."

"Quake-A-State, you are cold but you ain't that cold. Getting three hoes in an hour, I don't know about that," Pow Wow said.

"Ok, let's go and get breakfast and as soon as I get to the restaurant start counting. I'm about to call a cutie that I met yesterday, after picking her up I'll meet you at the Big Apple restaurant on 63rd & Ashland."

"If you need me to give Angie back, it would make it easier for you," Lucky offered. We all laughed.

They left, and I called Lola. She answered in a sleep filled voice.

"Hello."

"Put on your clothes, I'm about to take you to breakfast."

"Yeah, because I've been waiting to get something to eat all night. Your psycho command powers didn't tell you that I was hungry?"

"I forgot to tell you, it cuts off from 11:00 p.m. to 6:00 a.m., but it just came back on so get dressed." She giggled and said ok. I picked her up and when she got in the car I immediately said, "You know that I am a player, right?"

"I can see," she said as she looked me up and down.

When we got to the restaurant, I spotted Pow Wow and Lucky and we walked over to their booth. I politely said, "Lucky, let me sit next to my girl." He got up and sat on the opposite side, next to Pow Wow. I introduced them. Pow Wow looked at his watch and then at me and said, "It's on!"

I immediately scanned the place to determine who my prospects would be. As my eyes scouted the room, I noticed several chicks having breakfast and a few of them were looking my way. It was a younger lady with an older guy who caught my eye so I kept starring at her to capture her attention. The man must have had some alcohol or something because he drank a lot of water and I knew that it was only a matter of time before he would have to use the restroom.

When I looked up, our waitress said, "Here are your menus. I'll be back to take your orders." She was a tall glass of water who carried herself well.

The goal was to get Lola to admire and adapt to my style, that way she would cooperate with me bumping other girls. I put her in a situation where she could adjust before picturing us as a monogamous couple. I wanted her to understand that my process was about team work. I shared with her, "If you want people to be receptive to you, then compliment them. When the waitress comes back, say something nice and we'll get better service."

The waitress returned and asked to take our orders, starting with Lola.

"Your hair is very pretty. I'll have bacon and eggs scrambled well," Lola placed her order.

"Thank you so much," the waitress responded with a warm smile.

You could easily see how much more attentive she was to us after the compliment. When she returned with our food, I said, "You have a skill for serving people and you need to use it in some way that is more beneficial. When you serve me well, I serve you back. Give me the number here and page me so I can pick you up after work."

"Thank you, Earthquake," she said.

"Do you know me?"

"I know who you are."

I reached out to shake her hand and felt a slight movement, so I asked, "Are you trembling?"

"No, but I have to get to my other customers," she answered bashfully.

"Well, give me a card really quick and put your home number on the back. I'll call and make sure you're here."

She took a card from her apron and wrote her number on the back. As the waitress walked away, the older guy went to the restroom.

I excused myself from our table, got up and walked over to the young lady. I asked her what her full name was and she replied, "Rainey Nichols."

"I want you to know, can't nothing stop what is destined to happen," and walked back to my table.

"Baby your food is getting cold. Eat your breakfast," Lola said.

Lola's focus was on me. She noticed the small things, watching where I lacked, and addressed those needs while not giving much attention to how much I gained. Meanwhile, the older guy returned to his table and I walked to the pay phones near the restrooms. I dialed the restaurant number from the card that the waitress gave me. The manager answered the phone and I told him that there should be a customer named Rainey Nichols having breakfast. I kept talking, "She has a family emergency. If she is there, can you please ask her to come to the phone. She's wearing jeans with a white tank top and should be dining with an older gentleman."

The manager asked me to hold on while he checked. I watched Rainey as she hurried to the phone.

"Hello, don't be alarmed, I'm the dude that just came to your table asked you your name. I got excited looking at you. Are you surprised by this phone call?"

"Yes, I am, this is out of the norm. I could feel you looking at me as well."

"There was something attractive about the way you sat across from me."

"What's so attractive about it?"

"I can see many creations of you and me in my thoughts and time brings about a change. Starting now, nothing will be the same and there is no stopping me. I'm like a train with no brakes and I won't stop until we get there. I don't want to come off as facetious but I'm looking for something extraordinary to happen. Do you agree?"

"Yes." Holding the phone tightly she said, "Impressive, I didn't expect this."

"Well listen to me, this is what I want you to do. Give me your number right now and I'll call you in one hour. When you go back to your seat, tell the gentleman that you have to get home. Take your napkin, place it over the top of your water glass and put a straw through it. That will let me know that you are with me and rolling with my plan."

She said ok and gave me her number which I wrote on the card that the waitress gave me.

I went back to my seat and Lola went to the lady's room. I told Pow Wow and Lucky to look over there as I steered them in Rainey's direction. If she puts a napkin over her water and then puts a straw through it before they leave, then you know that I got her. On cue, Rainy did exactly what I described. I updated the fellas saying, "Now. You know that I got Lola and she helped me get the waitress and the waitress helped me get Rainey. Each of them helped me bump the other."

Lucky and Pow Wow looked at me with amazement. "See, there is one thing that they all have in common," I told them.

"Explain that Quake-A-State," Pow Wow asked me.

"Out the gate, each of them knew that I don't live my life like an ordinary man. They knew that I live my life like a king!"

Lucky looked at Pow Wow and said, "He's the extraordinary one! King Vitamin, we're having breakfast with the king." We had a good laugh and Lola returned to the table.

After leaving the restaurant, we walked to the car and I jingled my keys and asked, "You got a license?" Half surprised she said yes. I tossed her my keys and said, "You drive." Lola comfortably got in driver's seat and drove off. I watched and calculated her driving skills, just observing her style. I don't know why but I asked her, "Do you have any kids?"

"Yes, I have a baby girl." She was the first girl that I encountered who had a kid.

As I got comfortable in the passenger seat I inquired, "Where is her father?"

"In jail, and for what reason, I don't know," she answered nonchalantly. It was apparent that she liked me a lot. She had a southern girl mannerism, bottom girl potential. Lola smiled and asked, "Are you trying to get those two girls at the restaurant?"

I rested my head back on the pillow of the seat, "Yeah, I believe that they've got a space on my team but I'm concentrating on you right now. You seemed like you would make a good bottom broad."

Looking somewhat impressed she stated, "Oh, that must be your main girl. Am I right?"

"Yeah, you're right," I smiled.

"Well, I'm glad you see me as your main girl, but what does she do?"

"She helps me hold things together, caters to my wants and needs but that's also the tricky part because she can become your wildest dream or your worst nightmare. See, certain fellas need to be handled a certain way and she's capable of adjusting to that. For instance, I need a woman to talk to me in a certain way, motivate, inspire and believe in me. A good woman will provide that. She will have a genuine concern about your well-being and will always put you first. All these qualities make her a valuable woman."

"But what if more than one of your girls have the same qualities?"

"It's like fingerprints, ain't no two women alike. There might be a lot of similarities but there will always be differences."

"Well, what kind of a woman is a worst nightmare for you?"

"It might be difficult to detect at first because a selfish woman will give you what you want to get what she needs. She sees my potential and desires to rule and dictate for me. She wants to control me so that she can control everything that goes on. She wants me to believe that I need her rather than growing from my own potential. A woman's insecurities can result in her believing that I'll outgrow her. Fearing that she may be dismissed leads her to focus on making me think that I need her and no one else. You get what I'm saying?"

"I hear you loud and clear. You don't want nobody messing up your biz."

"Exactly. Your role is to enhance my business, not hinder it."

As we pulled up to her house, my pager went off. "It's The Waitress. I'll come back and pick you up later." Then I went and got The Waitress from work.

She jumped in the car and we drove off. She was much more talkative than I expected after we spent a few hours driving around the city. The Waitress made a comment stating, "You are nothing like I thought you would be, you're different."

"How did you think I was?"

"I saw you a few times when you dined in the restaurant. I was afraid of you. I don't know why, but I was."

"Is that why your hand trembled at the restaurant?"

She laughed as she slumped back in the seat and said, "Yeah."

"Let me tell you a story about a boy and a girl. The little girl was afraid of the little boy because most girls are afraid of things that they don't understand. When she was in his presence, she was fascinated by his looks and admired his style but didn't know why she was scared.

When the little girl matured into a woman and the boy into a man, she was no longer afraid because she saw where she fit in. She developed a sense of intuition and saw a man's perfections and imperfections which gave her the ability to assess where she belonged. If she didn't, there'd be no reason to be with him because there was nothing to fix. She had to feel needed."

"You can't change or fix a man, that's what I was taught."

"That's not entirely true. A woman was born to make things better. If she cares about a man and can't make him better, it would drive her crazy. Even if she stares in the mirror for 15 minutes she will change something about herself. Change things for the better is naturally what she does. So, don't be scared baby."

"I'm not scared of you now," she giggled.

"Then you must see where you fit in, right?"

"Of course, I do. I fit right in with you."

It was getting late, so I dropped her off as we wrapped up our conversation. I left her with instructions to call me every two hours.

I went to the crib, freshened up, rested for a few hours and visited Lola since her mom was at work. I got there quick since she only lived about a mile away from me. They stayed on the second floor of a two-flat brown stone building. She lived in a roomy, four-bedroom apartment with her mother, two older sisters, nine-year-old niece and her daughter. Lola occupied the room located near the front door.

I met them as they all were walking out the front door. I walked into the dining room and she guided me back toward the front, to her bedroom. It was a soft, comfortable looking space with a decorated, full size bed, matching dressers, nightstand and a chest-of- drawers. The window had brown curtains that matched the comforter set. The sun beamed in on us as I got a page from Rainey. Lola walked out of the room. I asked if I could use the telephone which was on the nightstand next to her bed and she yelled back, "Sure you can."

As I was talking to Rainey about hooking up that night, Lola walked back into the room. She was wearing a t-shirt with no bra and gray shorts which revealed her flawless golden-brown legs. I noticed how soft and sexy she was. I got off the phone and paid attention to what was in front of me. Since it was only about 3:00 p.m., I had time to vibe with her.

"Lola, it's me and you forever, right?" I asked spontaneously.

"Yes, forever!" she said with sincerity.

"Nothing or no one comes before me, right?"

"No one comes before you."

I told her to come here. Lola strolled over and sat beside me on the bed. She leaned over and we kissed. I could feel her warm, wet tongue on mine as my body temperature rose and I was truly aroused.

I quickly pulled back the comforter and pushed her down on the white cotton sheets that had to have a high thread count. I could smell the strawberry fabric softener on her bed linen. I licked around the edge of her lips with my tongue and she put her arms tightly around me as I eased her downward in a comfortable position.

I kissed her on her neck and she let out a slight moan. Lifting her t-shirt and sucking on each breast, she gripped my shoulders. My excitement rose and led me to slide her shorts and panties off at the same time because my erection was coming fast. I wanted to pleasure her in every way so, I took off my pants and shirt, exposing myself.

She looked at me in an inviting way as I laid beside her filled with desire. Lola kissed my neck and then made her way to my chest and around my tattoos as I watched. She looked up at me and then continued kissing on to my navel. I could feel her warm, wet tongue gliding across my stomach and the sensation of her nose and faint breathing traveling around my forest area. She made her way to my joy stick and licked it like a lollipop, gently going up and down on the head.

My excitement was building as she raised up and I spun her around, licking her back and slid my tongue down between her crack and then back up. My fingers ran up and down her thighs, arriving at her wet tunnel which felt like it wanted to be invaded. Lifting her torso up into a doggie style position while the sunlight beamed in on her round, brown butt cheeks, I eased the tip of my joy stick into her tunnel as I swerved my hips from side to side as if I was Elvis Presley performing live.

Then I gradually filled her up and the love came down, rolling in and out in a rhythmic motion as I watched the wetness flow. I got more and more stimulated, so I gripped her hips, pounded on her gently and consistently as she groaned louder and louder. Spinning her back around, she frantically pulled my shoulders towards her and sucked on my chest. I placed my hands on the bed to maintain my balance and then entered her again as her head fell back on the pillow. It was obvious to me that she was going to be my main girl.

She spread her legs wider as if she was opening herself up to me and I accepted the invitation, going in deep and grinding on her with a mighty force of energy. She grabbed my biceps and held on as I took her on a tour, riding harder and deeper in a rapid motion until she peaked with a scream that I had never heard before.

I continued thrusting her with passion as I considered her surrendering eyes and face filled with pleasure. I called my joystick back, halfway and then delivered short and quick stabs, plunging into her, swelling with anticipation, about to release a rush. She held on tightly as my volcano erupted into an explosion and my lava overflowed.

As I lay beside her with our bodies dripping with sweat and the sun shining directly on her bed, I asked, "Can I take a shower?"

"Yeah, come on," as she walked me towards the bathroom. A few minutes later, she came in and handed me a couple of bath towels. She went back into her bedroom, got a couple of hangers and put my clothing on them then hung them on a hook on the bathroom door.

I was thinking to myself, '*I really like Lola and the tricks are going to love her.*' I stepped in the shower confidently knowing that I had her. While in the shower, I heard the bathroom door open and then close again. It was Lola with her hair pinned up. She got into the shower with me. Her body looked amazing. She grabbed the soap and washed my back as I reciprocated, just looking at her small curves.

She turned around, placed her arms around my neck and asked me, "Do you want me to fix you something to eat? We've got chicken, steak and some barbeque ribs."

Before I could reply she kissed me tenderly on my lips. "What kind of cereal do you have?"

She giggled and then named them: "We got Fruit Loops, Frosted Flakes and Captain Crunch." I chose Captain Crunch as she washed my body all over. We got out of the shower and got dressed.

She reappeared with my bowl of cereal and I sat on her bed with my legs crossed happily eating. I started talking about working, explaining the process and giving her instructions. She seemed eager and was very receptive, only asking a few questions. I could tell that she had thoroughbred qualities, strong but soft.

Shortly after, I went to check on my other two new girls. The Waitress had been calling every two hours like I told her and that let me know that she was receptive and down with my program. I was six deep with three prospects and through this process, I learned many lessons trying to successfully juggle many women. It didn't take long for me to realize that quality retention is more important than having a high number of girls.

I was eager to know how far I could stretch myself. Many women were drawn to me during this time and since I already had a full plate, I introduced several girls to my crew and Mob buddies. This was a process that we called tagging. It was an impromptu ceremony where I took a girl who wanted to be with me by the hand and joined it with one of my most compatible homies.

My focus was on Lola and everything else was secondary. Getting The Waitress and Rainey ready for work was next on my list. For the next couple of weeks, they were all working out amazingly. Money was flowing, and I was making my Cadillac payments to Mr. J-Hawk on time, every week as we agreed. That gave me time to kick it with Uncle J-Hawk. He became one of my favorite people to hang-out with.

Late one night, I got a few hotel rooms because sometimes the girls would get a little slack and couldn't go home when they stayed out too late. When I got there to pick up my girls, Lola wasn't there. I asked everyone if they saw her, with slight apprehension. I inquired about the police, asking if they were hot on the Stroll that night. Then Rainey confirmed, "Yeah, they were hot when we first got out here but it was smooth after that." I dropped everyone off and then went home to wait for Lola's call.

That afternoon, DeLana, Lola's sister called wanting to know her whereabouts. Trying to figure it out, I contacted the local police stations and there wasn't a record of her being in lockup. We agreed the first to hear from her should notify the other. At about 1:00 p.m. that afternoon, DeLana found out that the police took Lola to the Cook County Jail and gave her a State Disorderly Charge for loitering. She would be released after her finger prints cleared.

DeLana gave me a heads up saying, "My mom been babysitting her daughter and getting suspicious about Lola leaving with you and being gone every night until morning."

Relieved that Lola was ok, I said, "I'll call you back when I pick her up and we're headed that way."

My doorbell rang and I answered it. To my surprise, it was Reno. He had just returned from New York City. "What's up homie, how was the Big Apple?"

"It was cool. I gave them a little bit of that Chicago flavor. Ya dig, but I'm back now."

"I have to pick up my main girl when she calls. Wanna ride?"

"How deep are you?"

I told him that I was nine deep as I jacked my slacks.

Acting as if he was disappointed he said, "I thought you would be at least twenty deep."

"You just want me to draw up and disappear, huh?" Just then, the phone rang and it was Lola asking me to pick her up from 31st and California Ave.

When I arrived, she jumped in the back seat and started telling me what happened.

Anxious to share her experience, she explained, "They took me and five other hookers to jail as soon as you pulled off, but the officers promised to give us a break next time."

I was pleased when she mentioned "next time" because that let me know that she was still playing main girl position well. As she calmed down, I introduced her to Reno, letting her know that he was a member of our family.

On the ride home, I watched her movement. It was very subtle, but she was eager to go back out there. Lola was kind of tough, it didn't shake her at all. I looked in the back seat and spoke, "You know DeLana called, she was worried about you." Lola smiled as she pinned her hair up and asked, "What did you tell her?"

Nothing much, we were trying to figure this thing out together. When we got there, DeLana came outside, introducing herself to Reno. She was stuck on him immediately, giving him the eyes, choosing him. Reno was cool. I told Lola that I would pick her up for work later and we pulled off. I looked at Reno inquiring, "What's up with you and DeLana? She's meddling, choosing you."

"She ok."

"She's just ok?"

"She's just one hamburger away from being fat. Yeah, she's super thick. It might work, we'll see," he replied.

You're Busted

That night, I went to get Lola and Reno followed me over there so he could holler at DeLana. They invited us in and we sat in the living room talking while Lola walked to her room to finish getting dressed for work. Lola yelled, "My mom just left for work, late. She was slowing around so much that I thought she would never leave."

DeLana agreed and said, "She was acting all strange like inspector Gadget," as she turned her head towards Reno smiling.

"I hope those police don't mess with me tonight because it's going to be a lot of money out there. Take me on the 45th Street Stroll. I have a couple of tricks meeting me there and I need to make up for last night," Lola said in a raspy voice.

While Reno was shooting the breeze with DeLana, I was thinking to myself, *'Lola is most definitely acting like a bottom girl now.'*

Suddenly we heard a noise coming from the closet. The door swung open and Lola's mother jumped out. She was extremely expressive and in a serious rage.

"I knew something shady was going. You whore! You nasty, disgusting whore. You weren't raised like this. You have gone to the gutter. You and DeLana. Both of you are stupid, dumb girls."

As she kept yelling at her daughters, Reno eased out of his chair and slowly walked toward the door, keeping his eye on their mom. Without drawing attention to myself, I attempted to discreetly follow Reno as he was making his way out of there. Their mom shouted, "Look at them running. Just like rats, they scatter when the lights come on." Then she called out, "Don't leave now Earthquake."

I looked down the stairs and saw Reno motioning me to come on while Lola's mom was saying, "Come back and talk to me." I turned and walked to the dining room and sat down. Lola's mom looked in my eyes and said, "You pimping my daughter, you are a low life." She went on ranting for about twenty minutes. I sat there in a humble stance, listening to her intensely. She asked, "What do you have to say for yourself?"

"I believe in what I'm doing, Ma'am," I answered honestly.

"Don't you know that what you are doing is wrong?"

"Many times, we start off wrong but some good can come out of it. My family has been making something out of nothing for several generations. I'm taking the backroad because the main road is unavailable. There are possibilities in everything that we do, specifically if you are dedicated to it," I explained.

"Not with my daughter working the streets, prostituting."

"She has a choice."

Their mom sat down across the table saying, "She wouldn't be doing this if it wasn't for you."

"Ms. C, she is presented with all kinds of choices every day and she has to decide. Lola can walk away from me right now and she would still be faced with life changing decisions about drugs, church, guns, jobs, stealing, school or whoring. It's about what she is attracted too."

"Well you should be teaching her something educational."

"How can I teach her what I don't know? I am teaching her what I know and she seems to be comfortable with it. Meaning you no disrespect, what did you teach her and why isn't she drawn to that?"

"Because she is influenced by you," her mom answered.

"Exactly, but why isn't she influenced by you?"

With disappointment in her voice she said, "Because she's smelling her herself and thinks she know what she's doing. Why aren't you in school trying to make something of yourself? This is nonsense."

"Everybody is not built for school and even when you get through college, you are not promised to be a millionaire, have a job or money. You could wind up broke, in the same place, facing the same challenges. When I graduated from high school, this is where I landed."

Lola's mom directed her next statement to her daughter. "He is a user, making money off women instead of getting a job and earning his own keep."

With a calm rebuttal, I said, "In business, we all are being used and there is nothing wrong with it, no matter what your job is, whether you work at Burger King or as a teacher. You might not like it, but this is my business."

She talked to her daughter directly. "Do you see this Lola? This man is all about himself. He doesn't care about you."

"I don't mean no disrespect. How can you say what's in my heart? Some people might believe that you're a bad parent because you allowed all your unwed daughters to become teenage mothers. Can people say what's in your heart?"

She appeared to be very annoyed and defensive saying, "When her father died, I did the best I could. People try to blame me for their actions and that's wrong. You can lead a horse to water, but you can't make her drink."

Accepting what she said I replied, "I totally understand your point because I can't make her drink either."

Ms. C cut her eyes over at me and then turned back to Lola, "God says your body is a temple. It's sacred and no man that loves you will allow you to be sinful with other men."

I looked over at her and asked, "Sacred? Why do people pick and choose what is sacred? Yes, God says your body is a temple and you should not allow anything unclean in your temple. I learned in bible study that our bodies are temples, but we put a lot of things in them that God says not to. Men are not supposed to enter a woman outside of marriage. That's number one. Secondly, we also allow scavengers into our temples by eating pork, shrimp, lobster, crab, catfish and oysters when they were put on this earth to digest waste, grime, corpses and feces. You are digesting the filth of the earth and it stays inside of you indefinitely, much longer than a man. Is one sin better than the other?"

Ms. C replied, "Yes, it is much worse to sleep with men for money."

"Is God a respecter of sin?" I asked.

With hostility, she quickly replied, "I don't know about that but I do know that Lola needs to listen to me. Look girl, this man got a bunch of women and you deserve better than that. Why would you share a man when you can get a good, monogamous man, go to college and get a good job. You can build a family of your own, not working in a harem of women."

"She can do that, find a man good for her, go to college and be a virgin again. It's about whatever she chooses to adapt to. But we're not doing that over here. I'm looking for a woman that is good for me. Lola is my main girl and she has to want to help me hold it together."

I started thinking as I watched her mom's frustrated behavior. Ms. C was showing vulnerability. By questioning me, she gave me a chance to answer and plant seeds of doubt about what she was saying to Lola. Subconsciously, she was also defeating herself because this allowed her mom to be more tolerant of the situation. I knew that this was a bad idea if she wanted to gain control of her daughter. If I kept answering questions, soon the things that didn't make sense to her would start to seem reasonable.

Ms. C continued on, "Don't buy into this nonsense! He is a manipulator who only cares about himself. Why would he put his woman out in the dangerous streets, sleeping with all kinds of dirty men who have been with all kinds of filthy women?"

Giving her some additional knowledge about the streets I said, "Men who purchase services from prostitutes are known to be 'cleaner' then men who don't because the Johns use condoms and prostitutes use extra protection every single time they engage in any sexual act. The tricks don't trust the hookers and the hookers definitely don't trust the tricks, plus, most girls get checkups every three months."

Before she could respond, I continued addressing her statement saying, "All the pimps are familiar with the girls and the girls know most of the tricks while the police patrol the area all night long. Danger is kept to a minimum and each day I learn more and more ways to help my business operate safely. However, girls on college campuses are being raped, date raped, assaulted and even murdered. On top of that, a high percentage of college students catch STDs from promiscuous behavior all the time. Where in America can you go and there is no crime? Not trying to compare prostitution and college, but there are risk factors in everything. Ms. C, I am being honest with you, I know you don't approve of me but this is just who I am."

In a more relaxed voice, Lola's mom said, "Yeah, you both are just two seventeen-year-old misguided fools," as she got up from her chair and walked to her bedroom yelling back at Lola, "tell Earthquake goodbye."

Lola escorted me to the door she whispered, "Do you want me to come with you?"

"No, stay here and call me tomorrow," I kissed her on the forehead and left.

Reno was heading up the stairs as I was walking down. "Man, what took you so long? You've been up there for over an hour. I thought she might be holding you hostage for the cops." We both laughed.

We drove to pick up the girls for work. I thought about that incident and wondered how I could avoid it in the future. The next day, Lola called and told me that her mom was still ranting about what happened. She paid it no mind and would be ready for work at 7:00 p.m. I told her to meet me a few blocks away, to avoid any future run ins with her mom.

I was with my crew when Lola walked up. She had her sister DeLana with her. She had a sad look on her face and said, "Earthquake, I'm not able to be with you anymore."

"I thought it was me and you forever?"

"I know but my mom is really tripping. She woke up this morning and told me that I am not allowed to eat from the dishware. Then she handed me all plastic utensils and separate linen that I couldn't wash with the rest of their belongings. She had a list of instructions which stated that I needed to sanitize the bathroom because she wanted to make sure that none of them caught a disease from me. To make matters worse, my little niece had some Kool-Aid and I tasted it. She started crying saying to my mom, 'Lola drunk some of my Kool-Aid. I don't want it because she got the cooties.' Can you imagine that? She said, that I've got the cooties. They made me feel so dirty."

I stood there just looking at her. "I respect whatever decision you make. I'll just part with you now," as I kissed her on the jaw and walked away.

I was kind of crushed because I had high hopes for Lola. The next day, I went to pick up Rainey and ran some errands. I went to make my car payment to J-Hawk at his boutique and took her next door to his beauty salon so that she could get her hair done.

J-Hawk was the savviest person that I knew. I told him all about the incident with Lola. As we were talking, Rainey stepped inside and asked me if she could borrow three dollars. I asked when was she going to pay me back? She answered, "Tomorrow when I see my mom." I gave her the three dollars and she went back over to the salon.

J-Hawk continuously laughed and then asked, "Is that one of your girls and did she just borrow three dollars from you?"

"Yeah."

J-Hawk laughed uncontrollably as I continued to tell him about Lola but he stopped me in the middle of my conversation and said, "Let me tell you partner, you can't draw all of the water from the well. When you got hoes, everybody is against you, including the parents, other pimps, tricks, police and especially the renegade broads."

Giving me more game, he continued, "Your women are not focused on other people's messages right now, they can only hear you. But when folks get in their ear, they'll see everything you do. I'm not telling you to make a deal with them or give them half, but you must give something back. It's only human nature to want to see reward and progression. If you do that, your game will be super tight. And another thing, you will never be in control of your pimping if your girls are under their parents' roof. You have to get them out of their mama's house."

I thought about what he was saying. "You're right. I've already lost some girls like that. I'll start working on my plan today." I had to add to my game plan. J-Hawk gave me a lot to think about.

Two weeks later, Lola called me and told me that she wanted to come home. I asked if she was happy at her mom's. She poured the deepest part of her loyalty out to me, "No, I promised I won't leave again."

"What about your mom?"

"My mom has been tripping ever since that day. Every time I leave the house she thinks that I'm going to see my pimp any way. Plus, I miss you and I love you."

"Are you ready to go to work tonight?"

She answered like a soldier ready for battle. "Yep! What time are you picking me up? At 7:00 p.m.?"

I could tell by her voice that she was eager as a race horse coming out of the gate. I said, "Ok, I got my main girl back, right?" I gave her the run down on what was going on.

I blew my horn and waited down stairs. She walked out of her building looking fine as ever, tossing her hips like she do. When she got in the car, her mom was walking toward my car fast, holding Lola's daughter in her arms. In a frustrated voice, she told Lola, "Since you're going to work with your pimp, take your daughter with you."

Ms. C walked to the driver's door and held the baby up to my window as if she was my responsibility. I got out the car and took Lola's daughter by the hand and Ms. C reiterated, "Take her with you."

"Ok Ms. C but wouldn't it be better if she was with someone she knew, like her grandmother? I've got a babysitter, but maybe we could pay you to babysit. I was going to give the babysitter two hundred dollars a week," I told her calmly. "Why don't I give it to you?"

"Give her back. Just because you are ruining your lives, you are not going to take her to the gutter with you. Now give me that two hundred dollars." I turned slightly away so that I didn't come off like a "big willy" and got two hundred dollars from my pocket.

I confirmed that it was for the week and she said, "Ok, as long as I get my two hundred dollars each week, I don't have anything more to say about what you dummies do."

I got back in my car, drove off and we had a good night. That morning after I dropped the broads off at the hotels, I was driving the Strolls to check out the day work flow.

The Enforcer

As I drove down 63rd Street, I decided to visit my steppin' buddy, General. Known to be of one of the coldest steppers in Chicago, he was also trying to be a pimp. On top of that, he styled hair at his house so there were always ladies around him. There were two sisters, Lena and Venus, visiting him when I got there.

Lena chose me right away. She was 5'5" with a medium skin tone, solid build, with thick legs like a track runner and a perfect size 36 cup. Lena had a radiant smile that lit up the room, but she didn't have a whore's sex appeal. She presented herself as one of the top thieves in the city. Being a pimp and all, I wasn't looking for a good girl but a booster ain't no square chick. That was good to hear since I was trying to come up with different ways to make my girls feel more appreciated. By frequently supplying them with new clothes and things of that nature, it might make a difference with my new defensive strategy.

Not only that, she was known to be a brawler who knew how to keep law and order. Lena could also be useful as an enforcer that kept lightweight action off me, whenever one of my girls needed to be checked. She really wasn't hoe material, but those qualities made her an asset, so I accepted her.

Lena had an apartment that she shared with her two kids a few blocks from my grandma. That made it convenient for me. Within the next few weeks, she stole me a huge wardrobe. I was frequently at the tailor's being fitted for a suit but, I had so many designer outfits that I never wore the same thing twice. I passed a whole lot of clothes to my crew.

It also helped J-Hawk because I fenced the clothes to him and only charged a third of each price tag. Early on, I learned to keep the money in the family and that took our game to another level. At the same time, everybody was converted into pimps. Most of all, my women were sharp from head to toe in designer clothes when they went to work. Lena played her role well and was a great contributor to the team.

The whole crew was looking grandiose and it upped my game. Even my hookers got recognition. They were known as the best dressed girls on the Strolls and that attracted more females than I could handle. Trying to keep up with all twelve of my women had my hands full. Pimping was definitely a 24-hour a day job. Money was flowing, and I was clocking around fifteen hundred dollars each night, excluding expenses.

Some nights we just rode the Strolls checking out the action and counting our traps. On this occasion, I went down the 63rd Street Stroll to check my money and saw a few of my girls working hard. I noticed that one of my broads, Amelia, was missing. I thought that maybe she was on a date. She had been with me for about nine months and her trap was always decent, but it started to get light. Anyone could have a bad night but when her money changed, her disposition seemed to change. That led me to assess the situation.

Amelia

I met Amelia at a location called Ogden Park on 63rd Street in the Englewood neighborhood where we often hung out. I walked up on her having a conversation with Poochie Slim. She was telling him how pretty his eyes were. Poochie-Slim had long curled eyelashes with eyebrows that were naturally arched, and the girls seemed to love it. He was my homie with the freshest mouth piece and it always carried him two steps above his finances. He looked the part and had some notoriety and that drew chicks in.

Some girls came along for the ride since they wanted to be a part of the excitement. Those ladies enjoyed hanging around our crew and were willing to work in order to check things out. They were inquisitive and just wanted to see what the lifestyle was like, kind of like groupies. I didn't particularly care for those kinds of girls, but I knew how to adapt to them. Amelia was one of those types of broads.

She focused on me after Poochie-Slim gave a brief introduction. I didn't mean to come in and shake things up, but she never took her attention off our conversation. Poochie-Slim got bored with that so he started working his number on other fly hotties in the park. Amelia was kind of slutty, but I gave her a pass since she was cute and there was something about her that I liked. Even though I didn't see longevity, for the time being, she had a place on my team.

Stashers

Until this moment, she had been working out fine but it was time for me to figure out what was really going wrong. I noticed her movement had changed. Her posture was stiff and straight up, kind of robotic like, when normally she would be more relaxed. After I observed this change, I investigated further and watched her carefully. When she was uncomfortable, she moved like that, especially when something was on her mind. I read her body language much more than her words, but Amelia's verbal communication was also important.

For several days, Amelia's money was the shortest of all my girls, so I set her up to work the Stroll with Lola. My bottom broad came back with three hundred dollars and Amelia only had sixty.

I asked Lola, "How were the tricks flowing?" Softly chewing her gum, convincingly she said, "The night was good, the tricks were out there."

I tried to figure out why Amelia's money was so short. My tactic was to give her something in order to get something. This was the perfect time to do what J-Hawk advised and give back to the well. I put my offensive plan into action and informed Amelia that, on my team, whether she made a lot of money or her trap was short, I treated everybody the same and gave her a reward for her effort.

I took the second part of J-Hawk's advice. In order to get them out of their parents' house, I got hotel rooms for my girls, some double and a few singles. I gave Amelia a single and I stayed with her two nights in a row.

After showering her with some extra special outfits and five hundred dollars, I laid back to see if the plan would work. Over the next few days, Amelia's trap increased.

"Your money has been right on point, what did you do different?"

"I just worked twice as hard and tried to make up for being short last week."

It was a good gesture, but I wanted to know more. If there were underlying or surface problems, immediately, I planned to get to the bottom of it and 'nip it in the bud'. After work that night, I dropped everyone off and went back to Amelia's room. The next step in my offensive plan was to be alone with her and talk.

When I walked in the hotel, I kissed Amelia on her forehead, she turned away and said, "When I got with you, I didn't care whether you liked me or not, I just wanted to be down with y'all but now it's different."

She kept talking as I was thinking, *'That's nice, she's got a good script and I'm not the only one with game.'* She tried to use reverse psychology saying, "Don't kiss me unless you really mean it."

I turned her head toward me, gave her a big, forceful kiss, and then asked, "What is it that you really want from me?"

"I just want you, but if you are not into me, please don't stay another night. Either way, I'm still gonna get your money." She walked toward the door as if she was going to let me out.

I stood in the same spot, as if her tactic didn't faze me and kicked some game right back at her.

"Let me explain things. I'm drawn to you because you are attracted to some part of me and I appreciate your comfort. Man, there's a radiance that flows from you. I have to admit, it's amazing. You just got a natural way of captivating my heart and it's refreshing. I mean, your spirit is just so gentle. You know how to move me like no other. And the most viable thing that I love about you is your honesty. It is undeniable, and I need that in my life. Straight like that. You made my day and I feel lucky right now, like I'm about to win something good. What you think?"

Amelia took her gold hoop earrings out of her ear and sat them on the nightstand as she walked toward me and replied, "You are a winner, that's what you do."

"But I can't win until you step into your rightful place. Are you ready for that?" I expressed enticingly.

As I leaned back on the wall, next to the window, she took a step closer, looked up at me and hesitated, "You making me blush, and a few other things."

I could tell that she was feeling sexual as she batted her eyes. That was her sign for being in the mood for love. I stroked the back of her neck softly and in a light, seductive voice, "I'm feeling the same way." Reacting as if I was trying to maintain my composure, in a mackish voice, I said, "I can't let this magnitude of your presence overwhelm my thought process. Then I would be out of control, so I have to remain tamed until you answer this question."

I knew that she was a slick broad, trying to determine whether I was real or not. Amelia was looking quite content as I continued by putting on my game (sincere) face and asked, "I need to know where you're at. Are you trying to be a part of my program, on my order or on your own?"

She threw her hands up, as if she was surrendering and said, "Well I'm trying to be down with you like Burger King and have it your way."

"Did I really win the prize?" I asked with a smile.

"Yes, you got me!" she answered quickly.

I looked at her and asked, "How did I get so lucky?"

"I'm seeing that you're not like most pimps."

Carrying the conversation over to the bed, I sat down and asked, "Why do you say that?" Amelia sat next to me.

"Can I be honest with you?"

I gave her a pleasant smile and answered, "Yeah!"

"They said that pimps don't give hoes money or anything, but you proved them wrong. I think that you are misunderstood."

Pretending to be somewhat puzzled I blurted out, "Where did you get that from?"

"A couple of old hoes on 63rd Street was trying to put us up on game."

I was thinking to myself it was a good thing that J-Hawk schooled me on this.

"Do they have men?"

"One of them is a renegade who used to have a pimp but not anymore. Her friend has a pimp and they all get high off dope (heroin)."

"How old are they?"

"They're old, at least twenty-seven or twenty-eight."

"What's her man's name?"

"You know him, the pimp Reggie Steel."

That caught my attention, thinking back, I revealed, "I remember when I used to look up to him, he was a good li'l pimp."

I immediately told Amelia, "Those are cows and you are a calf. They don't mix. If they get high and have looser men, that's on them. They're trying to drag everybody else down with them. Baby, watch the company that you keep because birds of a feather, flock together. Owls don't fly with eagles."

"Well, I was thinking we are all hookers, women of leisure, right?"

"Let me give you some game, if they use dope, they're not hookers, they are dope fiends and they'll do anything to get some dope."

"That's the company they keep. They are all dope fiends now so don't call Reggie Steel a pimp. Him and those hoes are a disgrace to the pimp game. When Reggie Steel got high off weed and alcohol that was one thing, but then he started substance abuse, that's another." I continued my explanation.

"He used to be sharp. What happened to him?"

"He really fell off," I told her. "He's no longer a real pimp. The drugs took over and he lost his pimp status because the drugs are in control. He switched roles and became the hoe while the narcotic became his pimp. You see, Reggie allowed the drugs to control him, then he became his best hoe. The pimp game should have always been his number one priority. When a pimp is more loyal to dope then the dope becomes his pimp. Reggie became vulnerable since drugs took him out of his game plan. Had he still been making the right moves while using drugs, then he would have been a pimp that uses drug. There is a distinct difference between a pimp that uses drugs and a dope fiend. Acceptance is the key but a lot of times the pimp doesn't want to face that he lost his way and is now a dope fiend, like my man Reggie Steel."

She slowly looked up and confessed, "I stashed some money, but I gave it back. I put it with the money you gave me and handed it over to you in my trap. I'll never do it again, I'm sorry. I'm telling you now to let you know that I am with you all the way."

I grabbed her by her chin, kissed her on it and said, "You have this pure, baby-fied, honest way about yourself that I never seen."

At the same time, I was thinking, she listened to the old hoes which made it obvious that she allowed them to plant seeds. I knew that she was drawn to negativity and I adapted to that expeditiously. I took her weakness, used it to my advantage and kept my defensive plan in effect. By gaining her confidence, I took a bad situation and made it work for me.

I knew that if one girl stashed, there had to be a few more. I inquired, "How many of my girls are stashing (keeping money)?"

"I think two of them."

I told Amelia that I was going to need her to talk to them. "That's your job, your new assignment. Make sure that no one is stashing." I knew that giving Amelia the task would weed them out and work in my favor. Once I gave her the responsibility, she would find out who they were. Giving her the job would also show her worth. At the same time, she would realize that her value on my team increased.

"This is your new assignment. First, make sure my girls don't converse with old cows. Then, make sure that you identify all stashers and let me know who they are. This is your responsibility; can you handle it?"

"Yes, anybody stashing or holding out I'll find out and tell you, I promise," she said confidently.

However, it was a rule that I didn't promote wrong doing but to catch foxes you need traps. I'm thinking to myself, *'Once she does, I'll eliminate all of them as a strategy move in my defensive plan.'* After getting what I needed from Amelia, I tucked her in, gave her a kiss and went home to rest for a few hours.

CHAPTER 17
A Day in the Life of Earthquake

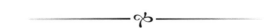

THAT MORNING WAS the first day of June. As an early riser, at the age eighteen, I was always the last to go to bed and the first to wake up. My grandma's house became our fortress. A lot of my crew hung out and often spent nights. Grandma and Auntie Tea got up around the same time I did. They didn't mind the extra company but my Auntie Vivian, who owned the building and lived in the first-floor unit was ok with the guys being there, but she had a rule that the girls couldn't spend nights, so we kept that to a minimum.

I got up stretching and yawning and let out a human roar. My first thought was on what to wear, as I stepped out of bed onto the warm floor, heated by the sun rays beaming through the curtains. I walked back to the enclosed porch that we made into a walk-in closet. Since Lena kept me laced with the finest gear money could buy, and there were so many clothes, Reno and I built some racks to hang and store all my garments. We also covered the floor with plastic and had clothing folded and neatly arranged. There were piles and racks everywhere.

All the fellas would go into the walk-in closet and choose the gear they wanted from the racks. I enjoyed watching my crew look clever every single day. I selected my outfit and walked past.

Lucky, Diamond, Poochie Slim, Bodie and Pow Wow were all laid out asleep on the furniture and on the floor.

My Auntie Tea didn't let Down's Syndrome stop her from making her money. Every day we each paid her five dollars to iron our clothes. She was the best. She'd iron everything by the time each one of us got out of the shower. That included ironing socks, t-shirts and even underwear. It was funny, but we loved it.

I wore my baby blue colored, French cut shirt, gray linen pants and dark gray, snake skin sandal shoes, topped off with a straw

Borsalino hat with a baby blue band around it. Always with jewelry, I wore a couple of gold rope chains and two newly purchased pinky and finger cluster diamond rings, feeling and smelling like a million bucks. I carried my gray snake skinned briefcase that held my personal items that would be needed in the day and headed out the door.

The shorties on the block stopped playing and ran toward my porch as soon as they saw me open the door. My daily routine was to look out for them. I always gave them chores so that they could earn some money. I popped my trunk so that they could get the shimmy towels and wipe down mine and Pow Wow's Cadillacs along with Lucky's Oldsmobile.

I sent two other li'l homies to the store to get groceries for my grandma while other shorties picked up paper, litter and glass to earn their keep and maintain cleanliness in the hood. Two others did the weekly run to the cleaners to pick up and drop off my clothes. I also treated them all to breakfast at McDonald's. That morning routine usually cost me two hundred dollars before I even left the neighborhood.

At about noon, I went to pick up all four of my second shift girls who worked the mornings from 5:00 a.m. to 12:00 p.m. We stopped by A & H on 63rd & King Drive and got a carryout order of lunch before going to the hotel where six of my girls were staying.

The other two girls were already asleep since they worked the first shift at night from 7:00 p.m. to 4:00 a.m. I dropped the first two off at their room and chatted with them for a few minutes. My broad Amelia, pulled me to the side and advised me to keep my eyes on the two stashers and that she would share the details later.

Afterwards, I went to hang with the second two when my chick Wonnie announced that she was going to visit her girlfriend who lived a few blocks away, leaving me and The Waitress alone. The Waitress took a shower while I relaxed.

When she finished bathing, she asked, "Will you take a nap with me since we are alone."

I sat there as the air conditioner blew a cool breeze in my direction. I got up from the arm chair, walked over to the bed and softly said, "Let me tuck you in." She reached under my shirt and grabbed my chest muscles, so I made my pecks jump as she looked up and smiled with a look of anticipation. With sparkles in her eyes she directed her attention to the clock on the table as I thought, *'Well, I guess Wonnie won't be back for a while, why not have a little fun.'*

I tossed my Borsalino on the night stand, took my clothes off and since she wasn't my main girl, I reached for a condom out of my pants pocket. I got under the cover with her and we went at it full speed. Twenty minutes into wild sex, Wonnie came back, walking in on us so I turned my attention from The Waitress to her. In true player style, I immediately signaled her to come and join us. I didn't know of any other options, so I figured that was the only thing to do.

Wonnie took off her clothes and got in bed beside me and I got on top of her after giving The Waitress a soft kiss on her lips. Starting off slow and roughly picking up momentum with each stroke, I hit her harder and harder which made her legs flap like wings. Then I slowed down and came off it, drove in like a ball tossed into a catcher's mitt. As I sucked on Wonnie's left breast, she moaned with pleasure. I looked over at The Waitress who watched eagerly, as she waited for her treasure.

I stood up at the end of the bed, positioned both in front of me, in doggy style on their knees; I broke off each one of them with ease, thrusting upon them twenty strokes a piece. I fondled the other, put The Waitress on top and said, "Enjoy yourself, make it good to the last drop." She straddled me like she was riding a bull. She climaxed and I heard a splash, like in a pool. Then I jumped on Wonnie and rode her slowly until she palmed my butt, shoving me into her boldly, as she oozed out an orgasm, like she adored me.

They both laid on my biceps as if they were pillows. I kissed each one on the cheek. My pager went off and it was Lena advising me that she had a new selection of clothing for my girls and a load for me to sell. I jumped in the shower and headed to her house. It was about 3:00 p.m. when we met up. After handling the clothing business, I informed her that I had an assignment for her. "I want you to hit the 45th Street Stroll and watch two of my girls. I just need to know how many dates they turn tonight."

I stopped by the second hotel where my night workers were relaxing. It was their turn to get first choice at the clothing selection, so I presented them with the items and they proceeded to try them on. There was a black, super soft, lamb skin, sleeveless V-neck, hot pants, body suit designed by Versace that fit my girl like a glove, matched with some strappy, six inch stilettos that were sensational.

"You looking like you can make a little change," I commented.

"A little change? We're raising the bar out there. We got all the hoes trying to find out where we shop. They want to dress like us. When we told them that our man buys our clothes, some of them have been asking about you ever since," she responded eagerly.

Keeping the look going, my next chick came out in a Louis Vuitton halter, short set with Louis Vuitton thigh high boots, looking like new money. I hollered out, "You're wearing that tonight! We are gonna make the pimps work hard to have their girls compete with us."

As my girl was walking out of the bathroom to model the next outfit and the other was going to change, they smacked hands, high-fiving and said with confidence, "That's going to be next to impossible, because we are the baddest chicks on the Stroll." I jacked my slacks and chuckled.

The next change was into a Yves Saint Laurent, satin, cherry red color, spaghetti strap, slip dress that hit her mid-thigh perfectly as she walked in gorgeous silver color, high heel pumps by Gucci. I revealed, "Every time I look at y'all, I see how I can take this pimping to another level." My chick agreed saying, "Yeah, you might have too. We be so sharp that the tricks think we are the police, because our dress code is so different than what they're used to."

My other broad butted in and said, "From the new tricks that know this style, we've been getting a whole new clientele. Some of the Johns told us that we look like the girls on the North side. I think we should go North."

"We were not only going north, but we are going around the country," I announced.

They seemed to be happy hookers and that's a good thing! I enjoyed watching them try on the Jordache, Gloria Vanderbilt, and Sassoon jeans. My girls looked irresistible in well-crafted shoes that had them walking like they were worth millions and it heightened their sex appeal, as they exuded more confidence.

Their new style also increased my money from fifteen hundred to more than two thousand per day. I learned that the better the quality, the more tricks are willing to spend.

After my two-hour modeling presentation, I headed to J-Hawk's boutique to sell him the garments. This was another extension of keeping the money generating in the family and within our community. J-Hawk had several independent consultants that purchased clothing from him at wholesale prices and then sold them off-site.

One of the sales consultants was there when I arrived. Her name was Shalina, a 40-year-old, afro-centric looking Israelite woman who was kind, soft spoken and intelligent with some knowledge of street game. She had a light skin complexion with a few freckles on her cheeks which accented her pleasant smile. Shalina was a good friend of J-Hawk's and someone who I had come to adore, like you would an aunt.

I greeted Shalina and J-Hawk and headed to the back carrying all the clothes from designers like Jones of New York, Burberry, Ellen Tracy, Ralph Lauren, Calvin Klein and Guess. While J-Hawk was assessing the value, I tapped him on the shoulder and handed him cash as I announced, "Here's my last car payment Uncle J-Hawk, I'm paying you off early and now I'm clear."

J-Hawk laughed the unique sound that he made when he was amused. He handed the bankroll right back to me to pay for the clothing order. I made him a deal that he didn't see coming. He selected certain items and took them in the front for Shalina to examine. J-Hawk sold a bundle of items to her and tripled his money. It was a win-win situation for everyone and we all were happy.

J-Hawk said to Shalina, "Earthquake is a true player. He's going down in history with this pimping. Watch what I tell you."

She laughed and said, "Don't say that about him. He's a nice young man."

"Nice? There's nothing nice about him. He's the coldest pimp I know and I've been all over the country with this. He's the real deal!"

I was wondering why he was saying this. I'm going to stack all my money and when I turn twenty-five years old, I'm buying a franchise and retire early from pimping. So, there is no way that I'm going down in history.

"I don't see that in him. He's gentle and sweet," Shalina said.

J-Hawk came back with the comment, "He's clever like your husband. That's why you're number three out of his four wives. Your husband talks super slick. He's got too much game. I remember when he talked to me for four hours about being an Israelite." J-Hawk looked over at me and confessed, "I'm telling you partner, he had convinced me to close down my shop and go to Israel with him. He told me to meet him on 87th Street where he would be waiting on a private transportation bus that would take us to the airport. I went home, changed into my dashiki gear, packed two suitcases and headed to the meeting spot. As I drove down 87th Street, passing the Godfather Lounge, I saw my folks out there and I thought to myself, *'J-Hawk, what in the world are you doing? Man, you ain't going to no Israel. You better turn around and carry your narrow butt back home.'* See, that man can talk."

We all laughed. He pointed at her and continued in an analytical way, "I know why you are an Israelite."

Shalina focused her attention on me and said, "Tell J-Hawk that is not what you want to do."

In a bashful voice, I uttered, "Well, I kind of do. This works for me."

Trying to understand my position she stated, "See you are being influenced into that life. Your friends and peers must be coercing you."

"Not even in the least," I said, reassuring her.

"I'm curious, why are you doing that, when you know that it's wrong?"

"I don't know why. It just came to me. It might not be right but there are opportunities, even in wrong."

"You are just callow."

"Well, no."

Not sure if I understood she asked, "Do you know what that word means?"

"Yes."

"How do you know what it means?"

"I heard it in a song. It means that I am young, right?"

J-Hawk was standing against the wall with his arms folded, just observing.

Shalina continued analyzing me and requested to know, "Were you abused as a child?"

Somewhat tickled, seeing that she was trying to find a rational excuse for me, I responded, "No, you don't have to be hit with a ton of bricks to learn something. It just comes to you like, rain or puberty. You just wake up and it's there."

"Most people learn from experience. They go through things, get hurt and make mistakes. That's how I learn," she said.

"Yeah, that's true but there is more than one way to look at any situation and you don't have to get knock down or abused to get it. People learn from many different perceptions. You might not see it developing, like maturity, desire, wisdom, the cold or a breeze; you feel it but you don't see it coming," I explained.

"Yeah but that's not a good business for you to pursue," she said as she prepared her wardrobe rack to be transported to her van.

I grabbed her bag and replied, "It's a good business for me because sex sells all kinds of ways, all over the world. Everybody buys some form of it; ladies and men from many walks of life, you name it and they're buying sex."

"Women are not known for buying sex."

I replied, "They buy a different source of sex. Men favor prostitution and pornography while women enjoy erotic books and romantic movies. Men go by sight while women operate off emotions and they can easily be touched by words. Women use all their senses when they partake in sexual material. Their emotions, mind, feelings, soul and spirit are all involved while men only go by sight, making it is much more intense for women."

With a happy-go-lucky smirk, J-Hawk held the door open and said to Shalina, "Now you see what I'm talking about?" as we loaded out her items. She looked at him and conceded, "Yeah, he definitely has something special, but I think he'll find another path along his journey."

I chopped it up with J-Hawk for a few more minutes. He stated, "Man, that was cold what you said about women and sex. How do you know all of that?"

"Uncle J-Hawk, I had this old chick name Nicky Blaze and she had a bunch of exotic books and movies. Nicky Blaze was addicted to Harlequin Romance books and movies always fantasizing about what was in them." I looked at my watch and said, "Uncle J-Hawk, I gotta go."

Next, I stopped and picked up Lola so we could kick it since we still had a couple hours before work. We stopped at 31 Flavors and got a large chocolate fudge sundae and headed to my house where all the fellas were chilling out front. I announced, "Here comes the queen!" All the crew stood up, moved to the side and greeted her as Lola and I stepped onto the porch. She smiled and spoke to them.

They all wanted a girl like Lola; she was the little sister to my folks. She sat there feeding me spoons full of ice cream while we listened in on the crew talking about pimping and hoeing. Reno playfully asked Lola, "Where's DeLana at? You know she's going to work for me next week."

"Be down like you live. Congratulations, you'll have a good girl," Lola answered still feeding me ice-cream.

The crew were talking about bouncing to a party in Rock territory where a lot of Mob would be attending. We always went fifty deep (members attending) in case problems broke out. I decided to go because I hadn't seen a lot of the folks in a while since I had been extra busy with my pimping. After hanging out for a while, Reno, Lucky, Pow Wow, Lola and I left to pick up the girls and dropped everybody off at work.

Lucky and I met Poochie-Slim and Terrell back at the house and we all got dressed. Looking real spiffy, we packed up our cars with Mob folks and went to the party. It was like a mini reunion as folks from all over the city were there. I even saw my elementary school, best friend, Wayne and his buddies. Even though they weren't Mob, they partied with us. The place was turned up with wall to wall chicks and the night was going real smooth.

The Mob rallied around me as if we were in a crowded elevator and treated me like royalty. It was similar to having my own personal bodyguards on duty and next to impossible for the girls to get near me. I had to signal my guys to let the girls get close. After three years of pimping, I was coming into my notoriety, quickly being recognized as one of Chicago's finest pimps and it was all love. Until that moment, I hadn't realized how much my pimp status grew. I was usually known for my steppin' at these parties but this time was different.

There were twelve folks standing near me as I pranced around, jacking my slacks, coming off clever but friendly. At the same time, I was kicking game at the folks. They wanted to know about pimping, so I showed them, as a variety of girls kept maneuvering their way over, passing me their phone numbers. Some who couldn't get close enough, threw folded pieces of paper with their info on it to me. Poochie-Slim said, "All these hoes are just choosing you man. You could be twenty deep by the end of the week."

"Earthquake catch so fast that he's trying to miss," Lucky added.

In my player stance, wearing a tailor-made burgundy and white, short sleeve walking suit with a matching baseball cap and lizard skin shoes, I slid my foot over, frolicking from left to right. "Out of all things in life, I've learned many lessons. When juggling a lot of women, let me tell you what I know 'fo sho'," as I popped my collar. "I came to the realization quickly that quality retention is much more important than having a high number of broads. Quality is always better than quantity so whatever little bit you have, see the value in it and make it work for you, chief. In that order! Straight like that!"

They stood back and marveled, threw up forks (gang signs) and gave me Mob handshakes. As we engaged in player behavior, Lucky spotted Terrell and alerted us. "Look at Terrell, he's the coldest pimp in the house." We all watched him as he hollered at a chick (talked to a girl), easily getting her number. Terrell pimp walked back over to the circle and in a slick voice said, "Y'all see how I get chose. I ain't faking, I'm bout this pimping, I'm Earthquaking." We all showed him love. It was the first of many times, over many years that I heard my style defined as "Earthquaking."

It was fun to kick it with the fellas, but business was on my mind. It was time to get back to my pimping. At the end of the party, we rode out. I got the girls to their hotels, picked up the second shift took them to work and dropped Rainey off at her parents for a visit. The plan was to get her for work later that day.

The Next Day

I finally got home at about 6:00 a.m. and went to bed. Exactly two hours later, the phone rang. It was one of Pow Wow's girls. She was upset as she shouted, "Pow Wow and Thurston had a car accident on the 94 Expressway. He fell asleep and crashed into a pole near the exit ramp around 87th Street. The ambulance took him to South Chicago Hospital on 93rd & Kingston. I don't know his condition but please hurry."

"We are headed there now," I told her.

I woke the fellas up and we rushed out. Poochie Slim, Lucky and I arrived at the emergency room and Pow Wow's girl spotted us. She walked up to me and asked if I was Earthquake and I confirmed.

"What's your name?" I asked.

"I'm Tonya."

"I never met you. How long have y'all been together?"

"About four hours."

"Where did y'all meet?" I asked, confused.

"Right here. They wheeled him in, while I was waiting on my brother, who broke his arm. The paramedics parked him a few feet away. He told me to come here and we started talking," she explained.

"While he was laying on the stretcher?"

"Yes. He's kind of sexy and very nice. He asked if I had a guy and I said no so he asked me to be his woman. He told me that he needed me now more than ever, so I couldn't leave him in this condition. He's my man now," she replied.

I was thinking to myself, *'Man, she's nuts but I've heard of stranger things. This takes the cake. Then again, we are talking about Pow Wow.'*

Eager to get to my brother I said, "Tonya, where is Pow Wow?" She took a long, intoxicating breath, blinked her eyes and cleared her throat. Before she could answer, the nurse walked up with an update saying that Pow Wow had been admitted and was being transferred to room 403. Tonya said that she was going to check on her brother and to tell Pow Wow she'd would be there soon.

In a hurry to see what condition he was in, we proceeded to the elevator. When we got to his room, Pow Wow was lying in bed with a neck brace on, a shoulder strap on the left side, and a fracture nose guard and bandage. He appeared to be drowsy like they gave him some morphine. He saw us and pulled his body up on the right side and smiled. His first words were, "Quake-A-State, did you meet my new broad downstairs? She's going to be down for me, watch."

I held my tongue but was thinking, 'Are you kidding? *This chick is a fly by night.*' Acting as if I agreed with his prediction I said, "Yeah Pow, she's good to go." Changing the subject, I asked, "When will you be released?"

With enthusiasm, he answered, "Maybe later today or tomorrow so take my broad Janet to work with your girls tonight." I shook my head yes and confirmed that I would.

We left and I went to pick up second shift, including Amelia who was on rotation that week. When we got to her room she revealed, "Those two broads that were stashing are still doing it, baby. They were planting seeds, trying to corrupt me but this is what I told them. Our man treats us far too good for that, no dice. I'm not doing that."

I stood up from my chair and walk toward the door. In a cold-hearted voice, I told her, "Let me handle them." I left Amelia's room and went over to Lena's at 3:00 p.m. She anxiously awaited my arrival and immediately started spilling the beans.

"Yeah, the first one turned eight dates and the other one turned at least nine that I saw. I left a few times and when I returned, that's the count that I'm sure they both have."

I told Lena to, "Gear up, it's time for you to handle your business." Lena changed into a jogging suit, gym shoes and braided her hair into two French braids going down each side of her head.

I told her that I would seal the deal with a kiss which would be her signal to get at her a little bit (give a beat down).

Lena sat in the car while I walked in to talk to the first stasher. She was up, dressed in a blue jean Jordache vest and above the knee skirt and appeared to be in a good mood as she wrapped up her phone conversation. I made myself comfortable, laying across the bed and started, "Hey baby, how was work last night?" She sat on the edge of the bed and pulled her skirt down towards her knees.

"It was slow, but I'm gonna try to make up for it tonight," she answered immediately.

Her tugging on her clothes let me know that she was hiding something. I commented, "Man, you only made seventy dollars last night. How many dates did you turn?"

With a straight face, looking directly into my eyes, without blinking she said, "Daddy, I only turned two dates." Her eyes let me know that she was uncomfortable, and her verbal response let me know that she was lying. She never called me daddy.

I sat up on the bed and said in a soft voice, "You got a chance to come clean with me. How much did you really make?"

Her voice rattled as she said, "I gave it to you. That was it."

I paused, creating an uncomfortable silence as I observed her. She had simple body language that spoke out, making subtle jerky gestures which reiterated that she was lying. I took a mental note of this movement to identify that behavior in the future.

Then I addressed her as the liar that she was. I stood up and walked over to the window and said, "Let me explain something. You can't be beneath my umbrella under false pretense. When you make a commitment, you must abide by the rules. You can't be with me and be a renegade at the same time, you gotta get down on your own."

Somewhat sarcastic, she said, "I ain't trying to be funny but how can I steal money that I made?"

I looked at her sideways and said, "Yeah you made the money but under Earthquake's name. You can't have my protection, my clothes, my support, my housing, my food, my transportation and all my other resources and then be a renegade. If you want to ride

solo, then get out there on your own. You can't be no fake product, carrying my name, like you down for me when you really are a
perpetrating thief. We need to part ways, sweetie!"

I motioned for Lena to come in as she pleaded her case. "I'm
telling you, that's all that I made. Why do you have me on a tight
rope like this? I told you I'll make it up tonight."

I opened the door for Lena and walked back over to the thief,
giving her a kiss with extra tongue so that Lena could be more
irritated.

"How many dates did you see her turn?" I asked Lena.

In a low, aggressive tone she reaffirmed, "nine." Lena described most of the cars that she got in and out of. I moved out of
the way and Lena fired a powerful right hook to her jaw, knocking
her into the dresser. As the stasher ducked, Lena hit her with four
consecutive upper cuts and the stasher fell to the ground. With
her body balled up, she covered her face as she squealed like a pig
and screamed. I tapped Lena on the shoulder and said, "That's
enough." Lena stopped and walked out as easily as she came in.

I calmly announced, "Like I said, we gotta part ways. I don't
want you around my broads or my business. Leave this hotel room
within 2 hours." Without turning around, I walked out, and went on
my way to handle the second stasher.

As I walked into her room, she was hanging up the hotel phone,
so I assumed that the first stasher just warned her.   I asked the
same question and she fessed up saying, "I turned eight dates, but
I got robbed. I didn't want to tell you because I didn't want you to
get mad at me."

Looking up at the ceiling, I suggested, "You wouldn't happen to
be stashing on me, would you?" Trying to be helpful she said, "Not
me but I could tell you who is doing it. It's Amelia, she is the one
who tried to get me to keep money. She is the one that is stashing."

She continued fabricating. "See, that's why I'm glad you came
early because I was going to tell you before work!"

I smiled at her while thinking, '*The traitor is always the one
who brings the news.*' I walked to the window and gave Lena
the signal. She knocked, and I let her in. I turned to look at the
stasher, Lena punched her in the jaw, she fell-down as she kicked

her feet out. Lena grabbed her by her feet and punched her in the face, as she twirled like a spinning top. I tapped Lena and she got up, walked out of the room and went to the car.

I told the stasher, "This is the end of the road for us. I don't want you around my girls or my business. When your buddy leaves, you can leave too." As she laid on the floor, she tried to grab my hand but I pulled away, jacked my slacks and walked out the door.

I took Lena home and let her know that she did an awesome job. Then I gave her a juicy tongue kiss and said goodbye. My next stop was to head home to change and pick up Rainey and the rest of the girls. As I drove toward Rainey's parents, the block was lined with police cars and ambulances all around. There was yellow tape around her apartment building. Curious to know, I pulled over, parked and walked toward the crowd.

Some of the people out there knew me and proceeded to tell me what happened. Rainey's step father raped her and she killed him. He allegedly had been doing that to her for a while. Rainey took a knife and stabbed him to death and her mom went hysterical. So, they took her mom to the hospital and Rainey to jail. Breathing deeply, I held my chest, like I was having pains, then gathered my composure, looked at my watch and took off to get the rest of my girls. I dropped them off but didn't talk about what happened. I decided to wait until I found out for sure what went down.

Police Brutality

I got a page from Lucky and pulled over to call him back. I told him what just happened. He shared that he had some more bad news and wanted me to meet him in front of the Criss Cross Lounge which was about five miles away. The folks were standing outside when I arrived. Lucky broke the news.

"Ralph is dead."

My heart felt like it dropped for the second time.

"What happened?" I asked.

"They were in the South Deering neighborhood, near the Jeffrey Manor and Ralph got shot in the arm by a Hispanic gang.

Everyone thought that he would be ok, but he got hit in a main artery and bled to death within hours."

I told them that we were going to the Manor. As we were getting into our cars a detective car pulled up and blocked me in. They threw me up against the car and tightened the handcuffs on my wrists saying, "You're going to jail, pimp!"

"Why?" I asked the officers. One of the detectives said, "For pimping. We just locked one of your girls up and she is going to testify against you in the morning. We saw her give you money after she turned a trick."

I heard them but it didn't really register, my mind was still on Ralph and Rainey.

"Don't worry Quake, we got you," Lucky hollered, as I slung my keys toward him. The cops put me into their car and skidded off. They warned me saying, "Your buddies better be careful because they're next!"

When we arrived at the police station, an officer yelled out, "Is that Earthquake right there?" One of the detectives replied, "Yeah this is the pimp," as the others stopped to look up. I didn't realize that the police were aware of who I was. I knew law enforcement knowing me was not a good thing; sometimes it's not so good to be popular.

The detectives handled me with animosity and every move was with force. They held my arms up to my shoulders while my hands were still cuffed behind my back, making it painful. Then they pushed me into a holding room, cuffed my right arm to the wall as tight as possible so that the steel dug into my skin like fire. Left alone for about five minutes, I discreetly stuck my driver's license into my shoe.

A detective returned, charged me with pimping, asked for all my information and I lied about everything, including my real name. Then the officer took me to a cell and shoved me in. There was a stench in the air and a spirit of violence around the room while I was suffocating with emotional hurt, trying to breathe. I felt a need to create some space so I could breathe, but there seemed to be no room for oxygen.

As I sat on the cold, hard, steel bench, I wondered which of my girls got caught up. It could only be between two of them, but I didn't worry about it too much since I would know who she was in the morning.

As the minutes rolled by, I was immersed with thoughts of Ralph and Rainey, trying to figure out how we could get even with the Hispanic dudes that killed my childhood homie. I was also pondering about how Rainey could have been getting molested and I didn't know. I was thinking, *'In the future, I'm going to start talking to my girls about their background so that I can understand them better and help them deal with these kinds of issues, possibly avoiding these kinds of outcomes.'*

Remaining in thought, the police guard addressed me saying, "Hey pimp, you want your baloney sandwich?" Still in deep meditation, not really paying attention, I shook my head, no.

Suddenly, he hit the bars with his billy club, and in an authoritative voice said, "Answer me when I'm talking to you."

"I don't want nothing to eat," I murmured.

He got frazzled and screamed, "The next time I say something to you and you don't answer, I'm going to make you eat this billy club."

His partner came over to back him up. At that point, I accepted that I was the bad guy. In a pleasant voice, I answered, "Ok chief."

With fury, he stormed back to my cell and said, "You trying to be funny pimp? I'll come in there and mop you all over that cell, now try me!" Still focused on my people, not paying him no mind, he opened the cell in a rage, like I stole his mama's purse.

The officer rushed over and hit me continuously with his flashlight, aiming for my torso, as I blocked his blows with my arms. After a few seconds, his partner came in and grabbed him out the cell, as I was thinking, *'He's worse than me. We both gangstas! Two wrongs don't make it right. That's one angry, dirty, treacherous cop.'*

The jail cell was a reminder of the brutal punishment of injustice. I imagined all the people who encountered brutality here. The short, wide-waisted Caucasian officer showed signs that life had left its mark on him. He was a very irate man and I was just the person for him to take out his frustrations. This particular officer had a short fuse and he was fixated on doing me harm. He attempted to find any little reason to justify his behavior, the worst kind of person to have in any organization. He was simply a bad member. This officer used his police badge as a pass to dehumanize people. He appeared to be the kind of guy who got bullied in school and now was trying to pay all those bullies back. All the girls must have laughed and rejected him. He used his job to release his pain and unleash his wrath at will. I felt sorry for him as I observed his bogus behavior.

Misdemeanor Court

That morning, the officers got all the arrestees lined up in the courtroom for mild and petty misdemeanor charges like loitering, simple theft, prostitution, soliciting, disorderly conduct, pimping, etc. They had one line for women and another for men positioned so we could see each other. I saw one of my hookers in the female lineup, it was Bambi. I also spotted Lucky, Reno and Lola sitting in the courtroom.

I met Bambi about eight months ago, on the south side, standing in front of a lounge. She was a cute, brown-skinned chick who had been working out well; but this was the real test. I had my game plan together just in case they convinced her to testify against me. I couldn't imagine her doing that, but you can never tell. It's better to be safe than sorry.

I didn't trust those detectives and I didn't know what they told her. There was one male State's Attorney handling everyone's case. When the clerk called our names, they made us take an honest oath, asking us to swear to tell the truth, the whole truth and nothing but the truth. After doing so, Bambi and I stood there looking at the Judge.

"Is this your pimp and did you give him some money?" the State's Attorney asked Bambi.

Looking paranoid, with fear she hesitated and said, "No," in a faint tone.

The State's Attorney warned her saying, "If you lie, that's Contempt of Court and you're going to jail. Now speak up! The officers clearly said that you gave him some money, right?"

The Judge interrupted and asked, "Are the officers in court?"

The State's Attorney said, "No your honor, but I have a signed statement from them."

"Ok, continue," the Judge replied.

He repeated the question and then Bambi asked the State's Attorney, "If I get caught in a lie, I'm going to jail? Am I going to be locked up?"

"Yeah, you will be locked up," the Judge confirmed.

"I don't want to go to jail," Bambi said nervously.

"Just tell the truth," the State's Attorney instructed.

With no expression, I looked at Bambi out of the corner of my eye and saw her staring at me. She said, "Well, I didn't give him no money tonight."

Eager to get a conviction, the State's Attorney asked, "Well what night did you give him some money?"

Since Bambi was slow at the draw, I butted in, gripping the conversation saying, "That's my girlfriend and we give each other money all the time but I didn't know that she was prostituting."

Pleading my stance, I continued, "I saw her getting out of a car with a man and I was puzzled until she told me that was her uncle. I really trusted her. Now I don't know what to believe." Then I looked over at Bambi and asked, "Are you prostituting?" A few folks in the courtroom laughed as the Judge chuckled, hit his gavel on the desk and threw the case out.

Bambi was weak, certainly not ride or die so I knew that it was over between us. She didn't handle pressure very well and there wouldn't be a second time, especially since the police now knew that she was with me. She had to go! After we left court, Bambi ran up to me and tried to give me a hug saying, "I'm glad this is over. It was horrible in jail."

I looked her up and down and confirmed, "Yeah it's over. I'm about to take you home."

She asked if we were going to the hotel and I responded, "Yeah, so that you can get your stuff." As we walked outside, Lucky and Reno pulled up in his car and Lola drove behind them in my Caddy. Then we all headed to the hotel. When we got there, I told Bambi, "Pack your things you gotta go! You're not cut out for this. Listen, I'm going to the other rooms and when I get back, be packed and ready to go."

When I returned, Bambi was sitting on the bed with her two big, green duffle bags on the floor next to her, crying in an affectionate way so I sat beside her as she moped. Bambi asked, "How do you know I'm not cut out for this?" I stood up, walked behind her, reached into my pocket and threw some change on the floor. Then I asked her, "What was that?" She answered without hesitating, "That was some money falling on the ground."

I moved my bankroll around in my pocket. Showing her alertness, she blurted out, "That's money also. I know the sound of fresh bills." Inquisitively I said, "Tell me this, you recognized the sound of money. Can you also identify my voice when I'm pleased or disappointed?" Bambi answered, "Yes! I can tell that you're not happy with me right now."

I walked in front of her and said, "See, that was easy for you to tap into. Reading a person's voice is a sixth sense we all have. Some people don't see this tactic as special, so they often overlook it but once we become aware, we can use it properly. For instance, I know your voice and it told me something. Even your body language spoke, and I can't ignore that. You do understand, right?" I Extended my hand out as she reached and held the palm, softly kissing the back of it and apologized while I slowly pulled her off the bed. Her humility took the harsh feeling away from my resistance. Bambi put her arms around my neck and hugged me tight. I gave her a goodbye smooch on the lips and said, "Let's go."

I took Lola with us so that she could drive. I liked keeping my broads around each other to stay abreast of what was going on and knowledgeable about these types of circumstances. It wasn't healthy for them to be with me by themselves all the time because they could start to get possessive. There wasn't much conversation in the car but I did tell Bambi that I would keep in touch.

After dropping Bambi off, I gave Lola an overview of what happened in court so that she could remain alert and then took her back to the hotel. Wanting to be inconspicuous, I used the phone to call Rainey's house and spoke with her sister saying, "Hey, this is Earthquake. What's going on with Rainey?"

Sounding like she was drowning in sorrow, her voice quivered as she said, "Well, Rainey is probably going to use a self-defense plea."

Her sister revealed that her court date was in two months. I asked what happened.

"Our step-father was an alcoholic and he used to molest Rainey. He stopped for a few years, but he tried to touch her that day. They started wrestling and she ran to the kitchen and got a knife. He ran up and slapped her while trying to take the weapon. Rainey said that she was afraid and started stabbing him until he fell to the ground. I really don't want to talk about it anymore."

Feeling a sense of despair, I said "No pressure, I understand, ok!" She said goodbye.

I went home and Pow Wow opened the door, glad to see me. I asked him where his nose guard and arm sling were and in narcissistic fashion he replied, "Man, I ain't wearing that, I'm on the come up. I only wear it at night when I'm going to bed."

Poochie Slim, Bodie, Diamond, Lucky, Reno and the rest of the crew were in the house. We also had extra Mob members visiting after what happened and they were having a meeting. Still consumed with thoughts of Ralph, I immediately asked what the 411 was on his murder and they updated me with all the details. Pow Wow reassured me saying, "We handled that business with Ralph."

My brother broke away from the mob meeting, got serious and said, "Quake-A-State, this is how it went down. The Latin Mob and the Latin Rocks were warring in South Deering, right outside of the Manor and Ralph got caught in the crossfire. He was at the wrong place at the wrong time, visiting a chick. The Latin Rock who shot Ralph in the arm, struck a main artery and no one knew that he had internal bleeding. That trigger man got gunned down by the Latin Mob during the shootout. I talked to his little broad and she told me that they took him to the hospital and he died because he bled to death before they could give him some medical attention."

Pow Wow shoved his pistol down in his pants as he kept telling me what they did about it. "When we went over to the hood, we got up with the Latin Mob and they told us where the Latin Rocks ran a few of their dope spots. So, we drove over to a couple of the spots, shot the places up, ran them out of their own joints and then robbed them. We took all their dope, weed and the cocaine. With the assistance of the Latin Mob, we are taking over all of the Latin Rocks' dope spots and we're going to control that area."

I vacated the conversation to straighten myself out. I had to wash the smut off from being locked up all night. While in the shower, I thought about another valuable lesson. Nearly getting busted in a pimping case was a close call! I knew that I had to school my broads on how to react in case they got caught up with the police or found themselves in court. I also decided that I would educate myself on the laws around entrapment so that I would be able to counter it and teach my girls to do the same.

After my shower, I kicked it with Pow Wow and the rest of the crew. They were all jaw jacking (talking), finishing up the meeting about Ralph. The new plan was for the crew to extort the independent drugs dealers in key parts of the city and then establish their own drug cartel with the profit. Pow Wow was leading the effort and even my immediate crew was lending an ear. If they decided to get down on this, at least he had ten of the most dangerous dudes from the hood on his side. Even though they were all Mob members, this was a separate act, solely of their own doing.

I was unfazed by my brother's ruthless conversation. I had moved on while Pow Wow reverted to that kind of behavior after Prescott died. I noticed that he had been hanging with the Mob a lot more, even though he and Prescott were angled towards straight pimping. I walked out of the door and remained focused on building my kingdom. My purpose was to have an empire by the age of 25 and my plan was in full effect. I needed something to pick me up after those two tragedies, so I went outside for some fresh air.

Hitting the porch and feeling the warm breeze, as the wind glided me down the stairs, a pie face cutie came into view. She was walking up the block with those heavy thighs, stomping the pavement like thunder. As she got closer, the caramel skin on her oriental face delighted my vision. It was pleasant to witness a perfect waist on an athletic body with breasts that stood at attention and it was banging. You could have bottled her up and sold it!

She stopped at my porch as if she knew exactly where she fit and introduced herself saying, "My name is Geisha."

Pow Wow and the crew walked out of the door and he yelled out, "You talking to that li'l gangsta chick? Yesterday, she was helping Re-Re and her sister fight some other broads around the corner. I was trying to holla at her, but she started talking slick."

I looked up on the porch, used my right hand to block the sun out of my eyes as I directed my attention toward Pow Wow and then answered for Geisha saying, "She's supposed to talk slick. You slick, Pow."

He lit a cigarette, leaned on the porch and asked, "Quake-a-State, why do all the rough chicks like you when your thing is about being smooth?"

"Because Kemosabe (brother), I'm the earth and she is the water, the land absorbs the sea, that's why she takes to me. That's how it's meant to be. Straight like that! In that order!" I replied.

I noticed that all the Mob congregated on the porch, listening. They all got the spirit of pimping in them as they jacked their slacks and joked about being just like me. Pow Wow gave up an innocent laugh saying, "My li'l brother is super clever." Pow Wow failed to realize that some rough girls need to be complimented with a smooth touch. *'I've gotta teach him how to adapt, but for now, let me turn my attention back to this thoroughbred.'*

Geisha 's eyes blinked slowly and transitioned as they shifted, showing a high level of sexual desire. Then her pupils went from large to small and remained little which is a true sign of evilness. It was apparent that she could be adventurous, daring but most of all, ruthless. Her personality traits also revealed the ability to be smooth, cooperative and somewhat comforting, even though she had a tough exterior.

I invited her to ride with me. "Come on, we're going to get a bite to eat." We jumped into my Caddy, and went to Home Run Inn Pizza, got an order to go and rode back to my spot where the house was clear. Pow Wow and the fellas were gone.

As soon as we walked through the door, my Auntie Tea asked, "Who is that Buckwheat (her nickname for me)?"

"This is Geisha."

Auntie Tea gave her a warm, friendly hug and said, "Hey Geisha."

"Hey Aunt Tea," she replied.

"I'm alright."

Geisha looked at me and said, "I didn't ask her how she was doing yet."

"She reads minds and she knew that you were going to ask." Geisha laughed. I gave my grandma and Auntie Tea some pizza and took Geisha into my room.

We sat the pizza on the dresser and Geisha tore the box apart like it was an enemy. I commented, "You're a wild child that needs to be tamed."

"Everybody says that, but nobody can tame me," she said with a little sass.

I got a slice and sat on the bed while I watched her, giving her the most concentrated stare.

"You know, some people are meant to be together but if one person becomes resistant to the process, they'll wind up rolling in many circles until they end up by themselves. Do you know what I mean?"

Not trying to rock the boat, she shot back a careful but fly response. "I understand how it goes. I know how to be down so whatever you got, give it to me."

Showing my strength as I laid down the law I responded, "You're gonna give me your loyalty, without a doubt. If you're not ready for that, you can eat this pizza and walk out that door because I am most definitely about my pimping."

Geisha seemed deeply receptive, which confirmed her not wanting to be left behind as she sat beside me and purred up against my chest like a Persian cat making friends with a new master. Even with that, I could tell that she was a mean, finicky, over protective chick who would be good for my team because I also saw loyalty in her.

I really didn't have to convince Geisha to be down with prostitution. It wasn't a hard sale because she was cut from that cloth. Since Geisha had hustling in her blood, she gravitated toward my pimping with ease and saw exactly where she fit in. I set her up to work with Lola for a few days and Geisha was on her own after that. Out the gate, she was a money maker who liked to work.

While I was fresh and still learning the game, Slick Rick was a boss pimp in Chicago, one that I looked up to and admired. He was an older, more experienced cat who drove a brand new, fully loaded, silver Cadillac. His girls worked on the 82nd Street Stroll at Cottage Grove Avenue. One day, surprisingly, I saw him on my block, visiting with his relatives across the street.

Geisha and I were standing outside, and Slick Rick came over to chop it up with me. He was sharp and everything about him said 'big pimping.' Slick Rick was dressed to the "T" with a tailor-made, silver colored, walking suit that matched his car. His long hair was relaxed, styled in a feather cut and was blowing in the wind. He stood there glorifying pimping to a young player like me and I enjoyed conversing with him; talking slick talk.

Geisha and I went into my house and kicked it for a minute when Lena dropped by and handed me some new outfits for my ladies. There was a sexy green short set that I gave to Geisha. She said with eagerness, "I have the perfect wig that matches. Earthquake, I'm about to run home for a minute, grab the wig and I'll be right back before work." She lived about a mile away, in a 3-Flat building with her Grandma and three of her siblings. They occupied the first floor while two of her older siblings lived in the two units above. Feeling charged up about my business, I told Geisha to hurry back so that we could get an early start.

Geisha, who had become one of my most prized chicks, didn't show up for work that day or the next. Four days later, she called and said, "I'm in the Big Apple with Ricky."

"Who is Ricky?" I asked.

"You call him Slick Rick." Her voice was sugarcoated with attitude.

"Oh, ok. That's cool. Have fun in New York. I'll talk to you later" …. click.

I hung up the phone thinking, *Man, I just got peeled*, as I stood there slayed with disbelief. Consoling my ego, I told myself, *'You're still nine deep so it's not a big thang.'* It taught me to tighten up my game. I contemplated on where I made my mistakes. Was it me, or was it her? I concluded that maybe he offered more excitement, taking her to NYC. I didn't think about it too long, just kept it moving.

Work Rape Is Robbery

Later that night, the unthinkable occurred. Jewel paged me from her hotel room during working hours. When I got there, she was sitting in a chair hyperventilating and frightened. I waited for her to calm down a bit before asking any questions.

"Tell me what happened?"

Jewell told just how it went down. "I got raped and robbed! He paid the fee and everything was going as planned. He took me to a location not far from the Stroll and parked against the back of a building wall, on the passenger side, so that I couldn't get out of the car. He inquired about the price asking, 'How much?' I asked him what he wanted from the two services offered, head, frontal sex, or both. He replied, 'Sex,' so I jagged him off and then put the rubber on his penis. He got on top of me and performed his duty."

I asked Jewell if she checked his pockets when his pants were down, and she said, "No."

"After he took care of his business, what did you do next?"

"I tried to get out of the car, but the car door was too close to the wall," she told me.

Still shaking, I comforted her as she gave me more details.

"He got aggressive and said, 'give me back my money and I want yours too. I answered, 'No. That's out. No dice.' He pulled out a knife, and threatened me saying, 'Give me those ends. Don't let me have to slice your throat.' So, I just gave him all the money. He started the car and kept the knife pointed towards my neck as he backed away from the wall. Then he told me to get out. The trick hit the corner fast and sped away."

As we sat there, in a soft empathetic tone I explained, "Listen to me Jewell, you have to decipher the difference between sex for money and rape. Remember that one is consensual and one is nonconsensual and the way that you react will make all the difference. You must separate yourself from the emotional barrier that exist. When you are selling sex, it is not sacred, it is a commodity, it is business, so you don't take it personal. Do you understand?"

She looked at me as she loosened up and replied, "I think so."

"Acceptance is the key. Just recognize that you were robbed and keep it moving. When you fall, get up quick!"

She reluctantly agreed but said, "Yeah, I really didn't look at it like rape but that knife scared me."

I assured her that I would come up with a plan that would be conducive for everybody.

My Anti Robbery Plan

That morning, I called an emergency meeting. "Everyone, listen up. We are going to talk about turning a date." I went right in on the subject. "When y'all turn a date and the trick refuses to pay after you've already had sex, you have to consider it robbery." I instilled in them not to look at this situation like society views a traditional rape.

I continually reminded them, "When you are turning a date, it is strictly business and you are agreeing to have sex for money so don't ever be upset about a trick taking your sex. But, be upset that the trick is stealing a service that you are selling which makes it different from a man forcing a woman to have sex. Let me explain the difference: Y'all must value your sex as a commodity and there is a price on it. Make no mistake about it, just like selling a diamond ring, if someone steals it then you are owed the value of what was stolen. It's robbery!

Now, let me give y'all some guidance on not letting bad experiences overrule your lives. I want you all to focus on the art of taking, selling, and giving. Like oil and water, they don't mix. If someone robs you, then they have taken from you. If someone is selling, then there is always a price to pay. If someone gives, then that is a gift to you and those situations should not be tangled."

All my broads were very open and expressed full confidence in me. They seemed to be very receptive to my teachings. Even though it was delivered in a meeting, I structured it as a personal message to each of my girls as if it was directed strictly for her. Somehow, I think it brought us closer together. I took a mental note of that as I carried on.

After the meeting, I had regular conversations with my broads. I would ask each girl a variety of questions and they shared their backgrounds and experiences. For those who went through any kind of abuse, we discussed in detail how they reacted to it. I guided them away from holding negative perceptions and reacting in ways that were counter-productive. I helped them restore optimistic thinking, conducive to understanding and reacting in productive ways. I talked about the difference between an act being bad or good and how to effectively process both to make them work for them.

This incident helped me to put things in perspective and strategize ways to keep my girls safe. I created a drill and developed a solid training process that each of my girls had to follow. The tactics used were:

1. Always use their pagers during work hours
2. Identify the trick's license plate by paging it to me before accepting the ride
3. Decide upon one of the approved locations to turn the date
4. Before entering the car, look in the back seat to make sure that he is alone
5. Before entering the car, check the door locks to ensure they're working properly
6. Check under the seats and glove compartment for weapons
7. Give pre-arranged signals in plain view of the trick, making him believe that someone is watching while you are getting into his car
8. Check the trick's pockets (affectionately searching him) and look at the driver door to see if there are any weapons
9. Always keep a trick's hands in view at all times during the date
10. Always... always, make sure that you have two stashes for your money; a decoy stash in your bra in case you get robbed, and the true stash hidden in a secure place

Next, I gathered the main crew along with Pow Wow's ten deadly killers and told them what was going down. They were angry and anxious to eliminate this problem, like dynamite ready to explode. Me delivering the message was a lot smoother than any of them doing it but they had my back 100%. Besides, it was my broad that got robbed. I got dressed in my all black, wearing a tailor-made suit, snake skin shoes and a custom made beaver hat with a burgundy band.

I immediately delivered a stomp down message, in person, with the entire crew in tow, AK 47s and Glocks blazing as I walked the 45th Street Stroll. It was a breezy summer night and the block was jumping. I pulled my Caddy up to the middle of the street. All eighteen Mobsters packed in four cars drove behind me. Jewell was the only girl with us and she sat in my back seat watching. We invaded the streets as we all vacated our cars in unified formation, looking like we were going to war.

Similar to a grand Marshall leading a parade, they trailed behind me like a brigade. I swung my tech 9 (mini machinegun) in the air as if it was a baton, slowly cruising the block ready to do harm, lynch mob style if you tripped the alarm.

Everyone on the Stroll was quiet and they all stared as I made my announcement. The message was heard loud and clear. I snatched everyone's attention and laid down my rules. As the crew followed, we struck terror in all the spectators, looking intensely at everybody like they were the perpetrators. This was one of those rare moments that you hardly ever see twice.

I let it be known to all pimps, hoes, tricks and stickup men, through the underground grapevine, real gangsta style saying, "There is a zero tolerance for anybody to lay a finger on Earthquake's broads. Death will come upon any person who wrongfully sneezes too close to any of Earthquake's hoes. All tricks need to remain respectful and considerate of the process adhering to the guidelines to enjoy the services. Everyone better remember, announcement comes before judgement!"

Sitting up as if shockwaves aligned her body, Jewell watched me make the announcement as she sat on the crush velvet back seat of my car. By that time, I had it looking cold (good); A tricked out, burgundy, Cadillac Fleetwood, with the custom-made grill nose, white stripes down each side with Trues and Vogue rims and tires. It's not what you do, it's how you do it that matters. I wanted her to be totally comfortable as I took charge.

When I got back in the car, she smiled, with a jolt of motivation and said, "Baby, I'm ready to go back to work." I knew it was good to comfort your broads, but you must give them confidence when it's needed. Before I could answer, Ice Mike, a pimp who also had girls on the Stroll, cautiously walked up to my car door.

"Earthquake, playa, it's your world, you ain't got no problems around here," he said in a friendly tone.

The police also heard on the streets that I made claim to that Stroll, which meant that it was mine. It was official, I was now large and in charge!

A few days later, I dropped my broads off on the Stroll for work. As I was leaving, a detective car followed me and pulled me over about two blocks away. They told me to get into their car. While sitting there, the detective got on their radio and announced to other officers that they had me waiting. About 5 minutes later, two more detective cars pulled up next to us and I noticed that the sergeant was rolling with them. The detective ordered me: "Go sit in the backseat of the sergeant's car."

When I got in the sergeant's car, he turned around from the passenger seat and said, "Listen, I heard you're getting all the respect around here but let me tell you one thing. This is my district and I run this. You listening?"

"Yes sir," I replied.

"I'm gonna tell you what's gonna happen and what's not gonna happen. You hear me?" He was strikingly direct and shrewd.

"Yes sir, Sergeant Bill."

"When I tell you that there is no working tonight, you better make sure that no girls are working. When I say pull them off the Stroll, you better make it happen. I don't want any fighting and keep the stealing from those Johns down to a minimum."

"Yes sir."

"If you do that, we gonna be alright," he assured me. Pulling his glasses down his nose he asked, "You understand me, don't you?"

"Yes sir, it's understood," I said very calmly.

"Ok, be careful out here."

"Yes sir, likewise," I replied.

I got out of the squad car and headed toward my vehicle. The lead detective called me over again and suggested, "Why don't you buy me a cup of coffee?"

"Sure." I got into the back seat of the detective car and dropped a $100 bill.

I got out and headed toward my car again and he told me, "Thanks, I appreciate that." I motioned my hand in a downward wave, indicating that it was no problem.

"Make sure my broads stay safe," I requested.

"Sure, that's what we do, serve and protect," he answered.

"In that order!" I replied.

A few days went by and the crew and I planned to meet at Ogden Park where we hung out on occasion. While I got dressed, three surprising page messages came in from Geisha. I ignored them and continued to get ready. The phone rang.

"My time your dime, you rap."

"Hey, I took a bus back to Chicago. I realized I don't want to be without you. I missed you so much," Geisha said in complete surrender.

I felt vindicated and in an egotistical voice, I asked her, "Whatcha tellin' me for?" and hung up the phone. We continued to get ready as the rest of the crew pulled up to my house.

We drove and got our cars washed and waxed so that we could floss. Then we trailed each other and cruised through the park, flexing and socializing. Apparently, she saw us or got word that we were rolling through the park, because I saw Geisha with the Mob Chief's nephew, Li'l Muke. He was her buddy. They walked over. I spoke in a nonchalant voice, "Hey, what's cracking?" I took no real notice of Geisha and quickly deviated from the conversation as I continued to enjoy myself, spreading love in the most vivacious way, giving off good vibes with everybody.

A few hours later, it was time to take my girls to work so I said my goodbyes and we headed out. Geisha met me as I opened my car door and said, "Please, can I go with you?" In a two-second, thoughtful silence followed by a cold, clear stare, I said, "Don't embarrass yourself," then Poochie Slim, Geno and I jumped in my Caddy and pulled off.

I dropped my fellas off to ride with Bodie and then took my broads to work. I looked up and there she was; Geisha was standing on the Stroll. After all my hoes got out, she approached my car and bogusly jumped in. Before I could object, she handed me four hundred dollars being cautiously tender saying, "Here, this is just for you to listen." I took the money then let her talk.

Geisha 's movements were soft and her voice was remorseful like she was giving an altar confession. She then expressed, "I wish there was a rewind button that I could push, but I can't." While her oriental, piercing eyes swelled with sorrow, she gently explained, "Baby have you ever made a mistake before?"

I looked at my watch like she was running out of time and answered, "Yeah, but not on the disrespectful side."

I was thinking, '*She better say something more clever than that or she about to get kicked out my car in a minute.*'

"Sometime the grass seems greener on the other side."

I replied, "My grandma once told me, 'It will probably be a higher water bill on that other side.' See, you got lost with no cause."

"Yeah, I'm lost but that's the only time you should look for something or put an effort into finding it. So, now I've found my heart and its hurting. I've been tossing and turning, can't even sleep or think clearly. Please don't do this, don't give up on me. Take me back!" she cried. In a softer voice, a tear rolling down her cheek, "I'll do anything you want. This will never ever happen again, I swear!"

I thought, '*That spill deserves an encore.*' I immediately said, "You have to work triple shifts, then I'll think about taking you back. I also have rules that must be met. I've been listening to everything you said. So, I expect you to stand on what you say. Show me that you believe that a lost cause is worth fighting for.

You do that by turning this incident into something monumental and everlasting. Proving this is the foundation of a new beginning, that your willingness to sacrifice is worth more than money, then you'll turn this situation from a lost cause into a great legacy."

As I turned and looked at her, with my mouth twisted to the side a smirk on my face I told her, "This is your only chance because next time you ain't coming back! Now, get out."

With new life, eager to prove her worth, Geisha got out of the car looking relieved. I picked her up the next afternoon and she had a huge bank roll for me. I took her to the hotel so she could shower, eat and rest, to be ready for work that night.

CHAPTER 18
Teaching My Hoes the Tricks of the Trade

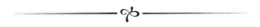

I WENT TO the hotel and Geisha was on her job, in the room, turning a date. I knew that the white paper in the window indicated that she was working and everything was ok. Geisha was taking a long time, so I looked in the window and saw her performing oral sex. It should never take 15 minutes to handle that job. I realized that I had to teach all my girls how to perform better than that. When Geisha was done, I went to the room and she handed me six hundred dollars.

She was so happy to see me and acted silly, like a good girl in love. I played it cool while she gave me a rundown on how her triple shifts went, after she finished brushing her teeth and gargling. As I stood there looking at the television, Geisha seductively eased her way into my arms and kissed me with a happy smooch.

Feeling the taste of minty mouthwash from her kiss I said, "Your lips have an innocence that only a school girl wears, silly lady."

Interlocking her fingers in mine she stated, "Everything feels right when you are where you're supposed to be. I want to be all that you need. It might sound silly, but I mean it!"

With a conning smile, as I stood in a thoughtful silence, thinking to myself, *'look at Geisha trying to show some appreciation since I'm letting her off the hook.'*

She put her arms around my shoulders and, with a riveting stare, said, "I'm glad you forgive me, in your own way. I want to be important to you because I love you beyond suspicion or doubt. My life is in your hands."

I listened but was still thinking, *'Wow, a guard dog acting like a house pet. Good game Geisha, I love the way you're working this.'* "I know, long as you honor me while you are on my squad, I'll never let you down, if you listen," I said with a smile.

I learned that some rough chicks are twice as likely to cover up their vicious side. They portray themselves as loving and friendly. I analyzed those characteristics in Geisha. She couldn't have gotten with me if she was mean and nasty and she learned that fast. So, she immediately switched gears and presented herself as warm and cooperative.

Even with all her rough and toughness, I used my adaptation skills to bring out the innocence that existed. I saw it, but most people were not allowed to experience that side of her. They only saw the hardened expressions she projected. I knew how to make her feel special and not like a beast and she naturally showed her ability to be lovable and soft.

As we continued to talk, I let her have the floor. Geisha told me about her experience in New York City. "Slick Rick wasn't what I thought he would be. It brought me to the realization of how much I love you."

She even talked about work so I asked, "How was the dating situation tonight?"

She answered while undressing, "There were no problems out of the ordinary during my shifts."

Slightly pinching her jaw, I explained, "I need to talk to all of you all. You took approximately fifteen minutes to give him head and that is unacceptable. I have a new strategic plan starting now and you will be taught first."

I wanted to create a trick proof plan that would guarantee satisfaction, that she would be able to execute swiftly, letting Geisha know time was money.

Oral Sex

First, get manicures and maintain soft but strong hands. Always have coffee, hot chocolate or other hot items that will allow you to keep your hands warm before performing oral sex. At the tip of the penis head, use gentle upward strokes, with a slight squeeze, keeping your focus behind the head of the penis, where a man's arousal feeling is located.

Mimic a downward motion, as you move your head up and down, while you're moving your mouth from side to side, so that your mouth lands on the side of your hand, rather than directly on his penis. Keep your back towards the trick, to block his ability to see what you're doing.

Frontal Sex

Always insert the trick's penis in, rather than allowing him to do it. Put your legs up high, in a "v" shape angle, and hold them tight while your ankles and feet are close together. Between the butt cheeks, keep that area oily, so that it's slippery, allowing you to stop the trick from penetrating you. Usually, he thinks he is inside of you, when most of the time, he is not. If you keep your legs high and never allow the trick to press down on you, then he can only go so far in and he usually won't know how far, or how deep he is inside of you.

Anal Sex

Follow the same flow that you execute during frontal sex, except that you tighten your butt cheeks, and avoid laying down on your front side. Because this is a more difficult act to perform an illusion, this service should rarely be offered in our business. In all 3 cases, you jag the trick off first, since that gets him aroused, so that he is ready to explode.

Any sexual performance that takes more than 3 minutes demonstrates that you are not at peak performance. Each of these skills must be perfected for you to be at the top of your game. The tricks should almost always be satisfied, and many will become regular customers.

Some of the tactics that hoes in the business use include knowing how to please a trick within 3 minutes. I taught each girl skills that allowed them to be great at their job. Most men get aroused very quickly, and they can have an orgasm much faster when a woman uses specific tactics that create the illusion of sex, rather than a full fledge sexual experience.

Here Comes St. Luke

Geisha had been with me for about two weeks without calling her mom. We were so focused and caught up in the business that she forgot to check in. My little cousin Shady from down stairs, Reno, Geisha and I were hanging out at the house while I was getting ready to leave. The doorbell rang and Reno said, "I got it," opened the apartment door and yelled down, "Who is it?" A deep voice answered.

"This is Detective Roberts. Is Earthquake and Geisha there?" Then a woman cut in. "This is St. Luke, Geisha 's mama, open the door!" This was an unexpected visit.

Reno looked down at the window glass opening of the outside door and told them. "They're not here. I'll tell him you stopped by."

That wasn't the right answer for St. Luke, so she kept knocking on the door, insisting that we were there. "You better produce my child. I know they're up there. I see his car right here."

Geisha softly whispered, "That's my mom and her detective friend."

Backing her away from the door I told Geisha, "We will talk to her tomorrow but not right now." I signaled to Reno, "Tell them we're not here."

I couldn't have a situation at the house. This battle had to be avoided and dealt with another day, cause right now it needed to go away. I didn't want any problems, especially centered around a girl when my aunt warned us not to have women staying over. We already had my crew basically living there and mobsters hanging out all times of the day and night. Without my Aunt Vivian saying it, I knew we had one foot in the door and one foot out. This could result in me being homeless. In pure caution, we stood there, hoping St. Luke would go away.

We heard a thundering crash of glass. St. Luke had reached into her purse, pulled out a black jack broke the window, unlocked the door and let herself into the building. She ran upstairs and banged on the apartment door with Detective Roberts following her. Reno told us to hide in the basement. Quick but quietly, Geisha and I went down the back stairs. Reno ignored her pounding, but St. Luke kept knocking and he finally let them in.

My grandma and Aunt Tea were in their bedroom with the door shut and didn't come out. Cousin Shady was frightened by the commotion. We could hear her screaming from downstairs in the basement and footsteps trampling around the dining room table while St. Luke followed her. "Where is my daughter?" Shady's words sounded like they were caught in her throat. She kept saying in a panicky voice, "I don't know. I haven't seen her. She isn't here. Leave me alone!"

The detective was dressed in a bullet proof vest with his gun visible. He flashed his badge like a thunderbolt in Reno's face. Thinking quick on his feet, he told Detective Roberts. "Man, get off me. Show me a warrant and if you don't have one, this is illegal so get up out of here! You don't have one. Just like I figured, get out!" With that, I heard the ruckus die down followed by slow walking, leaving the building.

We ran back upstairs and I promptly got a number and called a window repair company. "I need a window fixed on a hallway, apartment door!"

"Tomorrow," he said. "We're closing up now, but we can get to you in the morning at 7:00 a.m." This couldn't wait this was an emergency. "Man, I'll pay you triple the cost if you come now, to clean up the mess and repair the window before my Aunt Vivian gets home."

"Hmmmm... I'm on my way. What's the address?"

It was a forty-minute process for the repairman to arrive and install the new window. After cleaning up that mess, I took Geisha to a new Stroll on the Westside to work incognito and changed her hotel room until I could speak with her mother. The next afternoon, I picked up a new shipment of clothing from Lena for J-Hawk and Geisha rode with me to his boutique.

When we pulled up I said, "Wait in the car and keep the music down." I walked in and greeted J-Hawk as I tossed the garment bag on the floor.

"Hey Uncle J-Hawk, here's the merch. There are some Versace and Bally gear included in this package. You're going to do good with this."

He walked toward the picture window as the sun's glare met his eyes and noticed Geisha sitting in my car. "You're going to do good with that."

"Uncle J, she is one of my girls and I gotta call her mom today." The mask of concern grew on his face. He squinted his eyes while folding his arms as he took a deep breath.

"Ok Earthquake. What kind of mom does she have?"

I told him everything. Then I asked, "Do you know a lady name St. Luke?"

He thought about it for a moment and repeated her name in a slight whisper.

"Yeah partner, she's a known hustler, booster, check writer. An old school broad. Yeah, you should call St. Luke. She understands how the game goes." He tossed me a dime so that I could use the pay phone.

I looked out the door and said, "Geisha come in here. We're about to call your mom. Dial her number. By the way, this is my Uncle J-Hawk." She greeted him and continued to dial.

"Hey mom. What's happening?"

"Why you haven't call me?" St. Luke asked.

"I been with my dude ma," she responded in a childlike voice.

"You better check in if you're not going to be at your grandma house. I don't care who you with. I know who Earthquake is. Don't play with me. Now let me talk to him." She handed me the phone.

My tone casually emerged like a soft flute. "Hello, this is Earthquake. How you doing, St. Luke?"

Her voice roared like a big title wave. "I'm fine now. Make sure my daughter checks in with me. I need to know she's good. I'm gonna find out one way or the other. Communication is always easier or I'll have to use more than words to make my point. I don't like to be played with, so I had to show you I meant business."

Displaying no hard feelings in my conversation. "I understand St. Luke. Here's my number. Whenever you need to talk to us, we're here."

She calmed down. "Ok, I'm at my new house having some work done. Stop by so I can see my daughter. Can you do that?"

"Ok, give me the address and we're there."

After hanging up, J-Hawk asked, "What did she say Earthquake?"

"She wants us to stop by her house so that she can see Geisha. She probably wants to see who I am too. Let's go Geisha."

"After you drop your girls off at work, come back through here," J-Hawk instructed.

"Will do."

We rode to see Geisha 's mom. There were workers installing carpet and drywall in her three-bedroom brick house. You could smell the stench from the molded carpet being pulled up and the aroma of fresh paint.

St. Luke walked out of the master bedroom. I had my mental pen ready. When I saw her, I was a little surprised. Her mother was the first female that I saw wearing a man's suit. She was a masculine woman who stood about 5.8' with cold black skin, looking like an older version of Geisha.

She walked up to me and said, "You Earthquake? You look a lot younger than I expected. How old are you?"

Straightening my posture. "I'm old! Money is making me look too young; but seriously, I'm 18."

She chuckled and guided me to her bedroom while Geisha went into the kitchen and let us get familiar with each other. St. Luke sat down on her bed with stacks of one hundred dollar bills sitting in rows beside her. It looked to be about five thousand dollars. With every word she spoke, I observed her body language.

"Geisha can be naive at times, you know."

"Well St. Luke, compared to someone like you, maybe. but I see a thoroughbred, someone growing beyond measure and our potential together makes us one powerful entity. Whatever we do, we make it an education, learning how to identify a problem, treating it like a lesson and finding a solution to solve it. She's the star on my team."

St. Luke looked up at me, counting her money. "You know, I've been a gangsta, a hustler. I've even been to the penitentiary four times. I did it all. Her father is a hustler, sold dope and we've been in the streets our whole lives. But with all that said, Geisha still my daughter and I want to make sure you look after her."

"I get it St. Luke, I know. I work really hard at what I do. Imma handle her with care. I take everything I do seriously and I make it mean something; just like you. Look how careful you're counting your money. You handle it with such precision. That lets me know how well you treat the things that mean something to you. There appears to be a deep concern about whatever you do. I'm the same way and Geisha means everything to me as well."

St. Luke excused herself and walked outside to pay her construction crew, leaving me alone with her five thousand dollars. I walked into the kitchen and told Geisha, "Your mama left me in the room with her dough. It's about five G's on the bed."

"She's testing you. That's her test," she said laughing.

"I got six thousand in my socks. Plus, I don't steal money no way. I'm not a thief. That's chump change."

I walked back into the bedroom and waited. A few minutes later, St. Luke came in and continued counting her cheddar. I could see the wisdom from the wrinkles in her face. It let me know that she knew the game. I respected her after our conversation. We fell in love with each other's style and I admired her like a mother figure and she treated me like a son.

With everything that I said to St. Luke, I was practicing handling her with precision and care and I believe she recognized how I did it. She let me know she trusted me to handle problems and saw that I was developing impressive habits. I was unchained from the wrath of her fury. She granted me permission and I was out of her clinches. St. Luke released Geisha to me.

I pulled up to the house and Pow Wow was standing on the porch. He said, "What happened? Why do you still have Geisha? That's not your style. You usually avoid problems."

"Yeah, I do but when you are confronted with an issue you straighten it out. I met up with her mother, St. Luke and watched her movements like I always do. Then I handled the problem delicately."

"How?" he asked.

"Just like you're handling that cigarette, with care. First, I identified the problem instead of running. Next, I showed my concern about it. Then, I worked on a solution that was satisfactory to St. Luke and to my business. The bottom line is that I made it mean something to me."

"So, when you identify problems with your girls do you handle them the same way?"

I shared some intricate details. "I have many solutions for dealing with these situations but here's one. When I have a girl, I watch how she handles my possessions. If she loves me, then she'll handle them like it means something. If she doesn't, then she'll handle them without thought or consideration."

I carefully took his cigarette out his mouth making sure he paid attention. "Also, I look at how she handles other people's property. If she's rough, careless and shows no regard, then that's how she'll handle me. If she's jealous-hearted, I can tell that as well. She'll try to ramble through my possessions and control what I do, and that behavior tells me whether to keep her close or at a distance.

It's all in a day's work. Gotta stay on top of it 24 - 7. Now, if your girls are rolling, I'll drop them off at work but come now because I got to get to Uncle J-Hawk's." I dashed to the car and up the road to drop everybody off and headed to the boutique.

CHAPTER 19

Doony and God

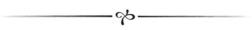

"EARTHQUAKE, RIGHT ON time," J-Hawk said. I walked through the door while he was conversing with the notorious Doony. "You know Doony don't you?"

Intrigued I said, "Yeah, he's one of the original OGs (original gangstas) who lived in Jeffrey Manor." I extended my hand with the admiration of a rookie meeting an all-star. "Doony, this is my li'l nephew, Earthquake. He family!"

With a speedy dialect, he said, "Yeah, I know about Earthquake, he's a bad li'l playa. If he's family with you, then he my man too."

Giving me a quick history lesson, J-Hawk added, "You know Doony used to be the golden glove, champion boxer and one of the Rock's main fifteen (board members). He was also the Chief's personal enforcer." Standing 5'8", solid built like a bullterrier, I knew that he had a huge power of eliminating people (hitman). His reputation preceded him.

They continued their conversation. I listened closely. It was an interesting topic about God. Doony said, "I remember this one situation. I went to bed early that Sunday night with dude on my mind. It had been weeks and I couldn't catch up with him. At about 12:00 o'clock AM, the Almighty woke me up in the middle of the night with my stomach growling and said, 'You hungry. Go get some McDonalds.'

I jumped right up thinking, '*I have a taste for a Big Mac*,' hurried and drove to McDonalds, entered the drive thru and look who I see. He was standing twenty feet away, right under the street light smoking a cigarette as if he were waiting patiently. The Almighty brought him straight to me. I got my food, drove a half of a block, got out of the car, walked back around to the opposite side and blew his brains out. The almighty brought him straight to me!"

"Man, that dude was always polite. What did he do against the Chief?" J-Hawk asked.

"He robbed the family of a guy that was paying dues and under the Chief's protection. That dude barged into their house and tied them up at gun point. Even though the mom and dad were cooperating, he put his 9-millimeter gun in the two-year-old baby's mouth and told the dad if he didn't give him $100,000 he would blow the baby's brains out. The dad gave that dude the money and then word got back to the Chief. The Chief told that dude to return the money and he ignored the order."

Wow! Listening to the conversation left me trying to grasp the understanding. *'Did he just say the Almighty brought dude right to him? That the Almighty led him to kill someone?'* My wheels were turning trying to figure this one out. Normally, I comprehended quite well. I never thought about God leading someone to kill a person to this extent. How could he believe that the Almighty led someone to their death? *'Let me try to make sense of this.'*

Doony appeared to be normal but two wrongs don't make a 'right.' He's a nice guy but that conversation was a little farfetched. He killed many people. Does he really believe that God sanctions what he's doing?

Then I thought back to when Lucky, Reno, the girls and I were talking about becoming soldiers and their duties. When soldiers kill their enemies in the military they earn medals and get praised. Before they go to war, soldiers pray that God delivers their enemies to them. They believe that God is on their side. So, I guess there is no difference.

They're all soldiers fighting for different armies. People pray that their enemies fall into their hands all the time. Come to think about it, even the President of the United States orders people killed in the name of God. Wars are fought using the name of God and we all pray that we be victorious over our enemies. We have no consideration for the victims left in the aftermath.

There is some rationale in Doony's belief. One is celebrated for taking human life if people believe that the reason and purpose are justified. Who am I to judge that? We all need soldiers on our teams. I now understand Doony because I'm a solider for a different cause. So, I wouldn't kill the instinct, just redirect it. I like Doony and respect that he stands on his beliefs because I'm most definitely standing on mine.

"Hey Uncle J-Hawk, Doony, I'm about to leave."

"You wanna go and get something to eat with us?" J-Hawk asked.

"Naw, next time. I've got to head out."

I left J-Hawk's boutique, my routine gliding through the night with ease. After work, Wonnie was aimed to please. She stole two gold rope chains from a trick who fell asleep at the hotel. What an extra treat.

"Here, put this on. They'll fit perfectly with the rest of the jewelry draping from your neck," Wonnie said.

I was so pleased that I started to take her home with me, but something told me to drop her off at the hotel. I didn't want to turn a good thing into something bad, so I went home alone. Getting caught with a chick could lead to an eviction.

Walking into the house, there was an empty quiet in the air. A room filled with no presence of gangsta buddies or pimp partner but when I looked in the living room on the couch and loveseat, I saw two half pint bodies. It was Pow Wow's girl, Janet's children. That curiously led me to creep to my brother's room in silence, hoping not to wake anyone up. I could hear a slight snore from Pow Wow while Janet lay curled up beside him.

I tip toed back towards the kitchen thinking he better not get caught. Smelling the leftover aroma from Sunday's dinner, I opened the refrigerator and got a chicken leg and bit into it as I walked back to my room. I could see the dawn of sunlight peeping into the curtains. It was 6:00 a.m. I undressed and took a shower. The water ran down my face, warm and tantalizing while I thought about my new gold ropes. *'I'm gonna look so cold. My jewelry is phenomenal.'*

After my shower, I laid down. Suddenly, I heard the creaking sound of a door opening. It was coming from the kitchen. I could hear footsteps coming my way. I shut my eyes and settled into a soft, sleep position. I could see the shadow of my Aunt Vivian standing and looking in my room like she was doing a body count.

Then she proceeded toward the living room where the toddlers were. I was thinking that Pow Wow was in over his head. Good thing I didn't bring Wonnie home with me. We both would be in hot water. I could hear her opening his door, just standing there while Pow Wow and Janet laid there, dead to the world.

Aunt Vivian made her way back past me toward the kitchen door. I continued to act like I was in the most peaceful sleep. She cruised by like a prison guard walking the deck with sounds of footsteps that meant business. I still hoped for the best even though it didn't look good for Pow Wow. I comfortably drifted off to sleep.

I woke up to a sunny afternoon. The day turned into a beautiful, warm and breezy evening, a good night for work. The girls were sucking the last summer day up like a hot toddy, staying sun bound until it was show time. It was lights, camera, action and all was good. They were dressed to cause intoxication, making the Stroll look like Hollywood as I let them out of the car.

They strutted their stuff so smooth, like sweet wine, making the tricks drunk with lust, treating them to the sweetest hangover. These are the nights you hope for; a pimp's paradise with everything on the upswing. I laid back and kicked it with my crew 'till it was time to pick my ladies up.

The next morning, we pulled up to Geisha 's house. Engulfed into Rap music, I turned it down, trying to be discreet and let her out. The girls waved bye while we dropped her off so that she could check in and hang out with her family until work. Me and the rest of the girls went to the hotel where I stayed there mingling with them. I switched from room to room to keep tension down and shared equal time with all my broads until 6:30 p.m. and then headed home.

I trotted up the front stairs kind of sweaty. *'I must get fresh for tonight. I've been out all day long and I'm feeling sticky.'* The door was locked! I couldn't get in. I knocked; my Aunt Tea answered looking down the stairs like she was identifying me in a police line-up. "Hey nephew." I knew something was wrong she didn't call me Buckwheat.

"Open the door Auntie," I said.

"Sorry Buckwheat. I can't open the door for you. The boss said y'all kicked out. I can't let you in Buckwheat. Sorry, naah. Ma, Buckwheat at the door."

I heard my Aunt Tea whisper through the door. "My nephew got kicked out cause of those prostitutes." Naah! A bit of reality sunk in. My grandma came to the door, pushed the frame of her glasses to her nose to see more clearly. "Your Aunt Vivian said that you all can't live here anymore and we can't open the door. If we do, she's going to kick us out too."

"Gram I need my clothes."

Gram looked at me with sympathy in her heart and said, "They on the back porch that y'all made to a closet. I also packed some underwear and personal toiletries in one of your briefcases. You can go around and get them because I can only open the back door."

I took a few items, loaded them in the trunk of my car, then headed back to make my last stand, ringing my Aunt Vivian's doorbell. I could hear her coming as I gathered my composure. She opened the door and I could see her pupils from the light in the hallway. They instantly went small which let me know she was extremely irritated.

"What is it?" she asked.

My throat suddenly went dry. I swallowed and said, "Why are you putting me out?"

"Because y'all had girls spending the night."

My words went soft. "I didn't have any girls spending the night Auntie."

Her conversation was rigid as she released the final blow. "I don't play favoritism. If your brother gotta go then you do too," and she slammed the door. Reality just slapped me in the face.

Out of all the things I went through, getting kicked out was the worst. My heart was filled with remorse and I was bombarded with anxious emotion. This had been a safety net, a household filled with camaraderie, family and fun. The way I see it now, it was just memories.

'What am I going to do? I walked down the stairs. *I have to come up with a game plan.'* As I stood there, Geisha came running

down the street at top speed. She said hysterically, "The police are after me and I ran all the way from my grandma's house. Let's go!"

I was still thinking about what had just happened but asked, "Why are the police chasing you?"

Geisha caught her breath. "I got into an argument with the dude down the street. He slapped me and we started fighting. I flew and got my mom's gun and was chasing and shooting at that punk. He ran into his house and I shot a bunch of times through the windows and doors, trying to kill that fool. I put my mom's gun back and took off when I heard the police sirens."

I could hear what she was saying but wasn't really listening. I was paralyzed in thought; only partially snapping out of it as Geisha stared at me like there was no time to spare. I guided my attention towards her. "Ok, go sit in the car and duck down." She frantically looked around and got into the Caddy. "What are we gonna do?" My mind was racing one hundred miles a minute.

Before I could answer, Pow Wow pulled up in his tight, new Cadillac yelling out the window, sounding all grandiose. "Quake-A-State, what's up?"

Drawn out of the rude awakening that just hit me, I answered, "You!"

"How you like my new whip? It's cold, huh? I got a new spot on Jeffery Avenue and I also got a dope spot. I'm getting money," as he flashed his bank roll. "You can chill at my spot if you want to Quake-A-State."

I knew I didn't want to be in the mist of his dope selling and gang bandit activity. "Where are Janet and Tanya?"

Seeming unfazed about the whole ordeal, he said, "At the spot. You coming?"

I shook my head and said, "No thanks, I'll pass. You know we just got kicked out, right?"

"Yeah, I know. That's why I'm telling you about my cribs. Alright then, I'm out of here." He backed his car up, all the way down the one-way block.

My mind was noisy. '*I need to think. Maybe my mom might let her stay there until the coast is clear. This is a start.*' I didn't want my broads to know I'd been kicked out. Plus, I didn't want Geisha around my girls while the police were after her. "Geisha this is what we're going to do. We're going by my mom's to freshen up, then we'll go from there."

Geisha sat up in her seat while I drove. "Do you think she'll mind?"

In the back of my thoughts, I really didn't know. "Don't nothing beat a failure but a try." We arrived at my mom's place and I rang the bell. She opened the door and greeted us by saying, "Y'all just got kicked out, huh?"

"Yeah, we did. Can Geisha and I take a shower?"

"Yes, sure you can," my mom said.

Geisha went to take her shower first. While in there, my mom crashed her words down on me, pointing her finger. Her face got stern and voice vastly changed. "Geisha a pretty girl and she seemed to be friendly, but she can't stay here. You can stay but she's gotta go."

What buzzard luck. My selfish conscious was working on me. I analyzed my options. *Without Geisha, I'm eight deep. If I let her go, I can stay and at least I'd have a foundation again. Naw, that's the coward's way out.* "That's ok. I don't want to stay," I said to my mom.

I was way out of my comfort zone trying to find complacency but eager to know the unknown. I must break from the cracks and spread like lava to make a new oasis. Now is the time. *'I gotta see what I'm made of. This is either gonna make me or break me.'* I realized, *'I can't set up a Kingdom in my mama's house. I must build my own foundation and set my own rules. If I'm a pimp, I gotta be a real pimp.'*

"What are you gonna do?" my mom asked.

I witnessed the evolution of my vision unfolding before my eyes. I understood what rolling with the punches meant. "I gonna go."

With a bit of concern, she asked, "Where you going?"

I gave her a boyish smile so she wouldn't be apprehensive. "I'll be alright." When Geisha got out of the shower, it was my turn. Afterwards, I said, "Let's go."

Geisha had a worried look on her face. I saw the fuel of despair begin to emerge. I said, "You look nervous. Embrace your fear. Be scared."

"I am scared."

Deep down inside, I was scared too, but I put my hands on her shoulder. "Listen Baby, fear paralyzes and weakens potential. It prevents you from stretching yourself and we can never reach our goals like that."

I felt the burden being lifted. "We gotta move forward even though you're scared. Use your adrenaline to drive your aggression to forge ahead. You will either fight or take flight and this is a time to fight. That's called courage and that's the only way you can show it. The cure to fear is always courage!"

In complete confidentiality, I said, "My Aunt Vivian put me out tonight and I'm only telling you."

She grabbed my hand and asked, "So, what's the plan?"

"I'm taking you to the Westside to work until I figure things out." We left my mom's and I dropped her off then I called St. Luke.

"Everything's quiet on this end but hide Geisha out for a couple of days, until this police hunt dies down," she told me. I agreed because Geisha being sent to juvenile detention was not in my plans.

We hung up and I met with Lucky at one of my girl's hotel rooms, giving him the rundown.

"My friend Vamp could probably offer you a place to stay. Let's take her over there," Lucky said.

I'm thinking, '*This could be worth trying. It might come in handy as a good crash spot.*' "Let's go over there, Luck." We pulled up to a red brick house with steep stairs leading to the front door. It seemed like a nice roomy place. Lucky knocked. With a friendly greeting, Vamp invited us in. He was a cool mild-mannered guy. Lucky introduced me.

"Yeah, I know Earthquake from the Mob, back in the day. You need to stay for a couple of days?" Vamp asked.

I casually viewed the surroundings. The living room was full of plastic covered white furniture while the dining room was empty but smelled like a gym locker. Then I saw five Mob dudes laid out on the floor. They looked like a band of gypsy thieves hiding out in a flophouse. They all appeared to be fugitives. Too many hard legs for one Geisha. I'd have to stay with her every night, like a guard dog. Naw, that wasn't gonna work. I said, "I'll let you know," gave him a few dollars for his hospitality and broke camp.

We stayed faithful to our work routine while hunting for refuge. Lucky said, "Call me Daddy because I talked to my brother and he said Geisha can stay with him and his wife for a few dollars."

After work, we took her over there. I knew his wife and he were cool. She was slightly older, average looking, with not much sex appeal and I was concerned that someone like Geisha could definitely get under her skin. I noticed Mick's throat kept jumping and he couldn't stop staring at Geisha.

A few minutes later Mick and his wife went into their bedroom. When they came out, he gave me back my money.

"What happened? Why can't she stay?"

Mick's wife cut in the conversation. "I'm sorry. This isn't going to work out but we wish y'all the best." There was no need to try and convince them. It would be like forcing a square peg in a round hole. I took Geisha back to the hotel.

The next night, we moved discreetly and kept our steps quiet, cautious but unafraid. I sent Geisha to work with the rest of my hookers. When I picked them up, Geisha wasn't out there. I didn't worry since that was normal for her. She always made it back to the hotel.

For the time being, my sense of humor was active. Occasionally, I came up with games for us to enjoy. I hung out with six of my broads in Lola's room. We played a game we called "The Grand Prize." We used the hotel room garbage can as a basket and placed it 12 feet away from the starting line. We folded up pairs of socks into balls. Then each girl took turns shooting the sock-balls into the basket. The girl who shot the most baskets would win.

The winner got a free day with me and could choose what we did. "Ok girls, line up and give it your best shot." The competition was hot and they were shooting baskets like Magic Johnson vs. Larry Bird. They shot basket after basket, getting it in. All of them were on point and you couldn't tell who was going to win.

Finally, my girl Natalie won; jumping up like she'd just scored the winning point in the NBA Championship. "I won, I won!" Usually, she was soft and quiet, but she was a beast when competing in this game.

I looked down at my watch and noticed a few hours had passed. The room was still filled with their high energy. "Ok pussycats, settle down and meow to sleep. I gotta roll out."

Sarcastically disguised in a playful voice, Amelia said, "I want a rematch."

Shooting wise cracks with facts I said, "The economy is growing. What's a playa to do? I'm on the come up and it's showing. Got more pimping to do." Impressed by my own wittiness, I chuckled as I walked out the door and went to check on Geisha.

Geisha still wasn't back so I lounged on her bed and waited in the dark. Fifteen minutes later, she walked in. With an involuntary reflex, she jumped, startled by my presence. Immediately, I knew something was wrong, reached over and turned on the lamp sitting on the nightstand. Geisha sat my money on the round table but didn't look my way. Her cream-colored jacket and blouse were covered in blood.

She appeared to be disturbed, agitated and swirling with confusion. I asked, "What happened?" I could hear the anxiety beneath her words.

"Well, I was with my older brother." I observed her every move while my mind shifted in fourth gear raced a million miles a minute.

"Why were you with your brother when you were supposed to be at work?"

She struggled with her answer and recited her spill. "I was working but my brother was hanging out by at the El station (elevator train) near the Stroll. He asked me to help him rob this guy who he scoped-out. He wanted me to distract the guy while he came from behind. My brother pointed his knife at the guy's stomach and told him, 'This is a stickup, give me your money.' The guy resisted and tried to take the knife from my brother. As they struggled, the knife fell.

The guy picked up a bottle and cracked it on the sidewalk so that he could use it as a weapon. I grabbed the knife while my brother struggled to avoid being cut with the bottle. We stabbed him about 50 times."

I could feel the tremble of my anger about to explode. "Did y'all kill him?"

She buried her face in her right hand and shook her head, "I don't know, he was just lying there with his eyes open."

I couldn't believe she put herself in that position.

After Geisha shared the lingering confession, I punched her up side her head and she fell to the ground. I said, "You shouldn't be out there killing nobody, especially while you're at work. Your focus should've been on making money, not murdering people." I knocked her down again and threatened her. "Long as you're with me, don't ever let me catch you around your brother."

I picked her up off the floor, grabbed the collar on her shirt and slung her into the bathroom. "Take a shower." She cried as she turned to grab a towel. I swiftly kicked her in the butt, to let her know she was on my doo-doo list. "Your brother used your skills to a disadvantage, in a way that could've ruined your life. You committed to use your skills for our advantage, to help me build a Kingdom. Either you are with me or against me. When you do something like that for someone else, I don't care who it is, you're showing you are against me."

She paused, looked me straight in the eyes and her fear seemed to pass in an instance. In a strong voice, "I'll never be against you!"

She took a shower, balled the soiled clothes and put them in a plastic bag. I asked, "Where's the knife?"

She reached into her purse and pulled it out. "Here it is, but can I keep it for protection?"

I opened a towel and she laid it in there. I cut my eyes at her with a hardened expression, "What do you think?" Then I walked in the bathroom and washed the knife off with soap and hot water, placed it in a separate plastic bag and secured it with a knot.

"I'm sorry," Geisha apologized again.

I stood up from my chair as I grabbed the plastic bags and placed the clothes under the bed. "When you take somebody's life, you can't ever give it back and there's no apology that can make up for that. You're jeopardizing your freedom and you can destroy my business at the same time. You're supposed to be selling a service, not robbing and killing people for what's theirs. Your only enforcement should be to protect what's ours. You got that?"

"Yes sir."

Before I walked out the door I warned her, "Don't touch that bag," and then took the knife with me. I drove three miles away and subtly disposed of it in a sewer.

I went back to Geisha 's room and got the plastic bag of clothes. My mind was swarming with thoughts of being a prisoner of the game. I was committed to serving and protecting all my hookers. I had to remind myself that this was the hustle I chose, and these rules came with the territory.

As I lurked through the streets of Chicago's Southside during the wee hours of the morning, right before the crack of dawn, I was faced with a variety of problems. I had to handle situations, no matter what they were. Since Geisha didn't commit an act against me, it was easier to deal with. I couldn't correct her behavior, but I could help her redirect her actions.

I dropped the bloody clothes off in a dumpster in the opposite direction and went back to the hotel where I was now staying.

CHAPTER 20
Stroll Control

AFTER THE GEISHA incident, I was in my room thinking to myself I needed to expand and this was a better time than any to move around. There was a knock on the door. It was The Waitress.

"What are you doing?"

"I was waiting on a goddess to come in and here you are," kicking a dose of flattery at her. The Waitress gave a little giggle, then glanced at the ceiling like I was only saying that to be nice.

I scooted over in a gesture for her to sit on the bed next to me. I looked at her with intimacy but spoke with conviction.

"These might be nice words, but I say what I mean and I mean what I say, so don't ignore it; and don't doubt yourself. I told you everything about you is how it's supposed to be. You didn't get here by accident. From your sweetness to your weakness, you have great communication and cooperation skills and a knack for dealing with people. That's the birth of building anything. You're my innovator and you keep us balanced. That's your role here. Everybody tells you things that they don't tell others, even tricks.

By the way, you remember those Strolls on the Northside, further than where you all work now; where you said they were clocking dough (making money)? You know, the places that the tricks were telling you about?"

"Yeah, on Lincoln Ave and there's a few more but the tricks said those girls got it locked down."

"Don't worry, there's room for everybody, by choice or by force," I smiled. "We need to venture out in every direction throughout Chicago to build and make my brand recognized. You with me?"

"You know I am," she smiled.

"Now, go get Geisha."

She stayed sitting on the bed. In a whinny voice, "Ok, but can I have some first?" Before I answered, she jumped on me like a hungry savage that hadn't seen a meal in days. The Waitress crashed down on me while I gave her quivers with shockwaves of passion, loosing herself in the heat of the moment, until she completely fulfilled her desires.

Afterwards, she happily delivered my message. Geisha walked in the room still sleepy eyed. "You want me?"

Wiping the sweat from my forehead, "Yeah! We're going deeper on the Northside, to new territory. Be cool but get into your role. That's our Stroll now."

Her eyes bulged with excitement and a twisted sound of joy floated from her lips. "I'm gonna make sure that Stroll is ours! Whatever you tell me to do, I'm going to do just that."

I scooted to the edge of the bed where my feet hit the floor. "Listen up Geisha, I'm sending you to all the new Strolls to establish our existence. You know how we get down in new territory. You gotta gain control in all the highly competitive locations. If you show any weakness, those girls will run you all off a Stroll as quickly as you got there. I'm reminding you to redirect your energy for business purposes only. This will allow you the perfect time to release your gangsta. Don't cause no static, let it come to you but don't run from it. Don't let nobody handle your role. If you see anybody messing with your wife-in-laws (my hookers) you step in, understand?"

She gave me a soldier salute. "Aye, aye captain. What time we leaving?"

"At 7:00 p.m. Tell all the other broads to come to my room now. Wake them up if they're asleep."

Geisha bent down and kissed my lips and left charged up. She was more excited than a sissy with a bag of dicks. That just tickled me to death. Geisha was a born gangsta goon girl. There were rapid knocks on the door. I jumped up. "Who is it?" The girls fumbled with the door. I let them in. "Alright girls, this gonna to be quick. At least six of you are going to a new Stroll. Geisha will weed out all trouble makers so we can take over new locations.

One thing that I know about Geisha, if a girl goes for bad, she will step into her role. Geisha will challenge any woman that thinks they're tougher than her. Let her handle the rough stuff. Being a goon gangsta is a smart attribute if used in a positive way. To be wise is to know when to cut it off."

I reiterated, "Continue to have each other's backs. If a woman threatens one of you, get at them. Any pimp who gets into hoe business must deal with me. Y'all are my number one priority. Meeting over girl scouts!"

The Lincoln Avenue Stroll

At 7:00 p.m. sharp, me and six of my hoes headed to the new location on the Northside. Once we hit the Stroll, I could see it was very lucrative but highly competitive. Those hoes were looking good, like they were walking the red carpet at a premiere. Then my hoes got out of my Caddy looking gorgeous, like they just stepped out of a Vogue Magazine ad. They were shooting fire on ice, ready to burn it down. My girls blazed up while the rest of those hookers melted down.

The hoes out there mean-mugged my broads. Geisha stepped up first and viciously stared back. Then all my girls followed suit. Immediately, I knew my presence had been felt. I hollered out to my girls so that every prostitute out there could hear, "Any pimps or hoes that ask who your man is, be sure to tell them loud and clear, 'Earthquake!'"

The pimps were swarming down on them like they were the police. I knew that pimps usually challenge a business until you establish a strong reputation. There was one girl on the Stroll named "Cut-em-up Sand," a gangsta broad with a reputation for beating girls down and cutting them up. She went for bad. Within a few days, the hoes provoked Cut-em-up Sand to get rid of my broads because they didn't want any new girls on the set affecting their money.

My girls started making money immediately. Cut-em-up Sand approached my girls and told them to move down to the next block. Geisha looked the 5'9" stallion-built girl straight in the eyes and a direct threat burst from her mouth, "Make me!" They locked in positions and stared at each other for about 10 seconds. Geisha looked her up and down and tore into her like a pit bull.

Geisha landed the first punch, hitting her directly in the jaw, immediately followed by another punch to the face. Cut-em-up Sand faded back and regained her composure. She lunged at Geisha, throwing left and right hay makers, hitting Geisha in the head. Pow-pow! Geisha threw a left punch to the eye and then a right upper cut, which landed hard on Cut-em-up Sand's jaw.

It was a grueling street fight. Cut-em-up Sand pulled out a switch blade and Geisha grabbed her hand as they fell to the ground. The knife fell on the ground. Geisha landed on top. As Cut-em-up Sand reached for the knife, Geisha grabbed her 6-inch spiked, stiletto shoe off her foot and hit her in the head multiples times. There were gashes in her head that bled. Geisha kicked the knife 2 feet away.

Cut-em-up Sand's pimp pulled up, jumped out the car and ran up to the fight. He grabbed Geisha off his girl. As Geisha tried to get at Cut-em-up Sand, her pimp busted Geisha in the mouth with his fist. He was wearing 2 diamond rings and Geisha 's mouth was bleeding badly. She hollered out, "I'm telling my man about this."

"Go get your man. Say something else and I'll beat you down," the pimp replied.

Geisha called me and told me what happened. I picked her up and took her to the hospital and she got 2 stiches. I let her rest for a day. My other girls worked that stroll, telling them to call if they saw Cut-em-up Sand or her pimp.

Geisha went back to work on the stroll the next day. Business grew as time passed and no one had seen that pimp or his broad for weeks. We continued to enjoy control of the stroll, when one of my girls spotted Cut-em-up Sand a few blocks down. Lucky and I drove to that location with bad intentions and saw her. I lingered knowing that her man would surface at some point. We cruised the area until I spotted him. The description that Geisha gave of the pimp and his girl matched perfectly. The pimp drove onto a side street and was standing outside his car with his passenger. I pulled up directly behind his car, got out and walked towards him while Lucky stood against my car, with his arms folded, watching my back.

"Hey what's up, I'm Geisha 's man," I told him.

He smirked as if he just ate a sour lemon. "What's up?" he asked.

"You hit my broad in the mouth. What was that all about? You know, I don't believe what no hoe says. Ain't no meat too thin that it don't have two sides to it. Just pimp to pimp, what's the deal?"

He tugged on the front of his pants while raising his shoulders and tilted his head, over-exaggerating his pimp style. "Well, you know, you dig, your broad was out of pocket you know. Your hooker was out of line, all in a pimp's business. Hoes need to stay out of pimp business."

I'm thinking, '*This mark sound awful slick. Why is this fool talking so aggressive? I guess he feels brave since his homie laid back with a stone face, like he got his back.*'

Two inches taller than me, he stood 6 feet, with a solid build at about 200 lbs. He was talking with his face in a frown and his lip turned in a defiant snare, gesturing his hands while pointing his finger like he was checking me. I couldn't hear him anymore because of his rude conduct. His demeanor was very hostile, as if I hit his broad. I looked at his body language and it was saying, "So what chump?"

I got mad because his conversation became unacceptable. I hauled off and busted him in the mouth. I knocked him to the ground, releasing my wrath through every swing, plunging blows disfiguring his face. His homie just looked, saw how I was annihilating him and he didn't want none. His dude just stood there watching while his broads were screaming and hollering saying, "Don't kill him."

"The next time you put your hands on one of my girls, I'm going to kill you." The anger rushed down in satisfaction – I felt redeemed.

He laid there more dead than alive. Cut-Em-Up Sand ran to the payphone on the corner screaming and she called 911. Lucky and I jumped in my car and left. "Man Quake, you beat that mark half to death!"

I was still breathing heavy when I said, "The pimp got what he got for not knowing how to use his pimp status. He got hit in the mouth for hitting Geisha, but he got beat to a pulp for not knowing when to turn off his aggression. His tone, posture and stance could have made a difference. He should have humbled himself. It's not what you do, it's how you do it, even when you do something wrong."

We didn't see that pimp or his hoe for a while. We enjoyed taking over that Stroll. That wasn't good enough – we spread our wings.

CHAPTER 21
Venturing Out Around the Country

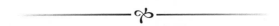

THE SEASON WAS about to change, autumn seemed to be a good time to sightsee. My crew and I roamed around the country, attending popular events and exposing my pimping style. I always traveled with at least six girls who worked the events. My crew and I visited Detroit, New York City, New Orleans, Las Vegas and Miami to name a few.

We were in and out of the Chi, back and forth from different cities for seven months and our reputation was solid. By now, spring was in full effect and we were headed into the month of May. The Kentucky Derby was coming up in a week and we all planned on kicking it there. Giving that town the smooth taste of pimping, even J-Hawk was rolling with us and we were all excited.

Having so many girls led me to purchase another vehicle right before the trip. This time I bought a Cadillac Seville and had it customized by a Mexican owned detail shop that most of the high rollers used. The caddy was triple black with beige stripes around the doors, so I had them add a Gucci canvas top and wheel kit on the back. The interior of my car was designed with the Gucci logo embroidered on the beige leather seats; real pimpish looking!

Now my newest car was on point. I saw J-Hawk with a briefcase that he kept with him all the time. He got in his car, opened it up and plugged a cord from the briefcase into the lighter. He picked up the receiver and made a call. That was the first time I saw a briefcase phone and I had to have one. That made me upgrade my game. I purchased two of them for both of my Cadillacs on the day before the trip.

Next, I got more bling so I could be even flashier so when they saw me, it would be like a flash flood going to the Derby so impressive. I hooked up with J-Hawk since he designed jewelry part-time.

We went to his wholesale jeweler who was located on Jewelers Row in downtown Chicago. I bought three more rings and a big gold medallion with clustered rubies and diamonds in the center of it, to add to my collection.

After jewelry shopping with Uncle J-Hawk, I told him I'd stop by later to pick up my suit. I called Reno and headed out to meet him at the carwash to get my burgundy caddy cleaned. While we were getting our vehicles detailed for the Derby, he suggested that I ask his mom to rent her house since she was never there. She spent most of her time at her fiancée's place. We stopped over and I talked with his mom. We agreed that I would pay the mortgage and all the bills and she would completely turn the house over to me.

I was thinking I'd have to get my weight up since I just spent about 30 stacks ($30,000). This trip most definitely was about being on the come up. The countdown was on, only one day to go!

I went to the hotel and chose three of my girls: Geisha, Wonnie and Amelia. We packed all our things and headed to the house. It was a nice change. It was a 3 bedroom, 3-bath house, with a full attic. The blue suede couch and matching love seat sat in the living room next to an oversize red colored recliner. An oval shaped oil lamp hung from behind the couch. The custom made red and blue drapes set the room off. The glass table with 6 black chairs graced the kitchen. There were 2 rooms in the basement with a bar and 2 let out couches. Upstairs, there were 3 bedrooms. I occupied the master bedroom which had a king size waterbed. Reno had converted the attic into a loft space where we did most of our hanging out when we were kids. I thought to myself, '*The house is cozy and I could get used to this, very familiar with a being back-home kind of feeling.*' The girls automatically started cleaning but there wasn't much to do since Reno's mom, Jean, always kept a super clean house.

For the Derby trip, I decided to leave Geisha, Wonnie and Amelia in Chicago this time. I wanted them at the new house so they could settle in and have the place arranged to suit their comfort level when we got back. I really didn't need Geisha in Kentucky since we were familiar with Louisville. It was a soft town and at times, Geisha didn't know how to control her aggression. Everyone seemed content for the most part, except Geisha – she was acting pretentious.

"Make sure y'all bring me a souvenir back since I must house sit," Geisha said with false kindness, faking a giggle.

Detecting some underlying resentment, "Yeah Geisha. I'm going to give you a gift before I leave; a flashlight so you can find some happiness in your deep, dark frustration until I return." She twisted her lips while cutting her eyes, trying to be inconspicuous.

Geisha was secretly being closed minded about me leaving without her. I was aware that she was upset, overcompensating with jokes and sheltering her disappointment because she couldn't go. I knew she loved traveling with me but I always left one of my strongest money makers in town so that my trap would be right. That was Geisha's position this round.

I went back to J-Hawk's boutique to see if Mathew put the finishing touches on my Gucci suit to match my car.

I walked in. "Hey nephew, Mathew's almost done." I followed Uncle J-Hawk to the back to wait on my suit. The area was set up like a lounge with magazines and old photo albums sitting on a coffee table. I took a seat and looked through some old photos of J-Hawk.

Impressed, I said, "Uncle J, you're dressed extra clever, looking cold." Flipping through the book, there was this one picture where he handed this guy a big trophy. I looked up at him with curiosity, "Hey uncle J-Hawk, who's this you're giving a trophy too?"

"I don't know that Willie."

"Then why are you handing him a trophy?" He walked toward me and looked down at the photo.

"See partner, I was hosting the Players Ball that year. We had already selected who was going to win. We chose Monkey D. He was a bad pimp back then. That year, only one player could win the Player of The Year title. There were a lot of good pimps, but it came down to Monkey D or King Richard. I thought both were sharp but we picked Monkey D. I was in the dressing room about to go on stage to announce the winner and this guy knocked on the door and walked in.

He said, 'Hey J-Hawk. I always admired you. How you doing?' I thanked him and told him I was alright. The guy said, 'I need you to choose me tonight. My name is Virgil. I'm a player from

317

the West Coast.' This guy was wearing a white, sequin jacket and walking with a blue rhinestone cane. I said, 'We already picked a winner partner. Go enjoy the show. Maybe next year!'

The guy reached into his pocket pulled out a bankroll. He said, 'J-Hawk, if you call my name I'll give you $5,000; $2,500 now and the rest afterwards.' 'Partner, you do look kind of familiar. Where you from?' 'California.' 'Yeah partner, you sharp. How many girls do you have with you?' 'I have four.' 'Go get them and bring them up front. I'm about to call your name. Make sure you meet me in the back to give me my money after I call your name.'

When I walked on stage, I saw Monkey D jacking his slacks, acting like I was about to call his name. I grabbed the mic. 'Ladies and Gentlemen, it's star time at the player's ball. The baddest player from the Himalayas, the coldest mack in the house, it is my pleasure to present you with the Player of The Year Title. The most valuable pimp is Virgil! Virgil! Virgil! Come and get your trophy.' When he walked on the stage, I handed him the trophy and the photographer snapped the picture."

I held my breath, trying to hold back my laugh, "But Uncle J-Hawk was he really a player? Did you know him from the West Coast?"

"Naw, I didn't know that dude from a gas station attendant."

I'm thinking, Uncle J-Hawk *is the real deal* as we both cracked up. Uncle J-Hawk selling game all day, every day.

I got my Gucci suit and went back to the house to prepare to leave. J-Hawk, Reno, Lucky, Pow Wow, Diamond, Poochie Slim, Maceo and Bodie all had their girls loaded in their Cadillacs. Lucky rode with me and his girl Ada drove his vehicle. Lola drove my burgundy caddy with five of my girls. We loaded up in a caravan like modern day pioneers of the pimp game and rode out at about 5:00 a.m.

No matter where I traveled, my business was always my pleasure and I kept it on my mind while my crew and I cruised into Kentucky. As soon as we hit the crowded hotel lobby, players from all over greeted us. We got a lot of attention while checking into the hotel and that drew all kind of folks to introduce themselves and ask us who we were. The hottest music out was rap and those artists were the newest and the biggest thing going. As one of the platinum selling rappers checked in, they invited us to come to their suite and kick it.

While my pimp buddies had a ball getting their props and accolades, admired for being players from Chicago, I spent my time establishing a rapport and networking with key prominent people. We kicked it with beautiful women, pimps and other players from all over the country. We also chopped it up with entertainers and celebrities. The rappers really made their presence known. They were all over that eloquent, five-star hotel with plenty of women and weed smoking.

The first thing that I did when we got to our rooms was set my hoes up for work. I had them registered in double rooms. I went to Lola's room first and had a mini-meeting with all of them. "Lola, you know the briefcase phone is in the car. Use it when necessary. I'll be expecting your calls with my traps every 4 hours. Reach me on my other phone. Remember, there is absolutely no dating in this hotel. Go get 2 work rooms at the motel that I pointed out on our way here and use them."

We got dressed, went to the Derby and watched a few races. It was a multicultural event with people from all walks of life. While the horse races were making money, it wasn't the climax of my trip. My hookers made it lucrative for me because they were shaking and 'quaking' money. We left the Derby and bounced to a couple of strip clubs to check out some new prospects. Right away, I had my sight on 3 white girls who kept trying to choose me and I wasn't planning on leaving Kentucky without them.

We made ourselves comfortable at a table toward the back of the half-crowded joint. Since only pimps and tricks frequented the clubs, our clever style of dress made it apparent who we were. My eyes spoke to them from across the room. Their curiosity drove them my way.

The blue-eyed girl walked up first. She was a southern blonde with a thicker than usual butt, full lips and a pretty face.

"Were you saying something?" she asked.

"Must we keep speaking at a distance?" I replied.

"No, that's why I came this way. I'm Becky. What's your name?" she smiled.

Her two friends walked over and stood a few feet away.

"I'm Earthquake. I still feel like I'm talking across the room. Invite your friends to join us; I want to touch all y'all with my conversation."

I thought my sight was on hyped and everything was just right. I looked at her like I'm the downest dude in the world, but I like you. My vision was at its most magnetic pull. My adrenaline glances were working all in full. "What's your names?"

The brunette was short and slender with nice legs.

"I'm Samantha." The red head girl had a pretty smile with keen facial features and a voluptuous chest. "I'm Ginger, nice to meet you Earthquake. Where are y'all from?"

Speaking for the group. "We're from Chicago." My pimp buddies were like kids in a candy store, circulating and handling business.

With a slight nudge, Samantha told Becky, "Go on stage, it's your turn."

"Don't be so pushy. Stop telling me what to do and being so bossy all the time," Becky said.

I observed her and said, "From my experience, most people that are bossy are really just confused. They're usually trying to make up for something."

"I'm supposed to be bossy, I'm a boss!" Samantha said sarcastically.

Awakening my inner teacher, I gently said, "There is a difference between a boss and being bossy. A boss is a problem solver for the betterment of a business, making sacrifices for a cause. Being bossy is attempting to dictate a situation for the benefit of ones' self with no cause. Don't get them confused!"

"Wow, I thought bosses told people what to do. I guess we learn something new every day." I sensed that I uncovered who she was, the naked exposure just beneath her words.

I touched her hand and said, "I hope my message touched you and that it meant something. I know you sexy ladies hear a thousand lines in here, but I hope you felt this one."

They stood there spellbound. I handed each of them my card and told them to call me. "I'm leaving in two days. Stop by the hotel."

"What hotel are you in?" Samantha asked, and I told her.

J-Hawk walked over. "Let's go partner. Are they coming with you?"

Joking, I said, "Yeah, they'll be with me when I leave. They're moving to Chicago." I hugged and kissed each of them and then we left.

We headed back to the hotel to get ready for the highlight of the trip, the famous night club, Joe's Palmer's Room. This was the spot where all the players and celebrities hung out. We got dressed in our finest attire. I was Gucci down, wearing a black and beige tailored suit. We left our rooms and walked to the 3 elevators. While standing there waiting, we heard loud thundering sounds. J-Hawk stiffened as a wave of curiosity hit him. "You hear that partner?" As we all looked around the elevators opened.

About a dozen shot gun cocking Sheriffs rushed off the 3 elevators like a swat team. Another dozen detectives, cops and deputies charged through the stairway door. A terrifying sound came pouring out of an angry mob of law enforcers. "Freeze! Get on the ground, face down!" We all hit the floor faster than a speeding bullet. They jammed the barrels of the loaded assault weapons in our faces.

"Don't look up until I tell you to," the Chief said.

This felt like a KKK lynching about to go down. J-Hawk said, "Excuse me Chief, but can he get that cocked-loaded gun away from my head?"

They all just stood there like they were ready for target practice with sitting ducks.

Poochie-Slim was face down on the ground lying next to me. He was a hothead and I could feel the resistance in his body language. I saw him begin to raise so I looked him in his eyes and pushed reality in his face with a stern stare as I whispered, "Stay down. Don't be resistant."

The Sheriff asked, J-Hawk, "Are you their manager because there's no destructive behavior in these parts Billy Bob?! I don't know what you do on the East Coast but you ain't doing it here. You're disturbing the peaceful citizens of Kentucky."

As we wallowed in humiliation, J-Hawk inched his head up. "Mr. Gentleman, we're not from the East Coast. We're from Chicago, Chief."

He looked dumb founded and stuttered, "You're not the rap group that's here from New York City?"

J-Hawk stood up, dusted his pants off and said, "They been gone for a couple of hours."

"Chief, I think they were on the 4th floor," one of the officers said.

The Chief un-cocked his gun, not seeming to be apologetic at all when he spoke.

"Sorry buddy, it's all in a day's work. Sometimes you make those mistakes. Ok fellas, we're done here." They crammed back on the elevators, went through the stairwell and left.

"Those guns could have gone off," J-Hawk said.

I patted J-Hawk on the shoulder. "Uncle J, I'm used to it. When you're young, black and got swagger, this what you get, no matter what city you're in." We all agreed as everybody untightened and brushed the ground off our clothes.

J-Hawk looked at me. His voice was smooth but engaging with a southern twang to it. "Does anything faze you?"

"Nope."

He frowned and dropped his lip on one side when something was unpleasant or disgusting.

Pow Wow said, "These crackers ain't got nothing to do but mess with us. Those sheriffs probably knew that the rappers left and just harassed us anyway. They're just a bunch of thug honkies with badges and guns."

"People have their own belief factors and are not open-mind-ed. In fact, they grow up with hatred and stereotypes. The hardest thing to break is a tradition," I said.

Diamond reeked with aggravation in his voice, and said, "How do you deal with something like that when they're steadily harass-ing you?"

J-Hawk stood there quiet with his lip turned up — which meant that he was impressed — while I answered the question.

"You must work on their conscious first and then the heart. It's the only way to bring about change since your mentality creates your reality. The most difficult part is making them understand it. The way you think is the way you act. Old habits are hard to break when you're taught that way."

I kept my eye on J-Hawk and noticed how calm he was about the situation but Poochie Slim's face was balled up – eroded with tension. I didn't even care. I was ready to snap.

The aftermath of the mistreatment weighed on him. I gently tugged his tie as I raised the noose up, adjusted it into a straight position and calmly said, "You can't win when there are loaded shotguns pointed at your head. You have nothing to counter that so if you jump up, try to fight or talk trash, they could blow your head off and you certainly can't win like that."

I kept rationalizing, trying to keep Poochie-Slim from remaining paralyzed under these circumstances. "They got the law on their side, their account of what happened and they have weapons pointed at you and all your homies. You don't have anything but hopefully the smarts to know how to choose your battles. You can lose the fight but win the war if you give yourself an equal amount of ammunition. Don't fight when there is no way to win. Use that energy to generate a plan to be effective. Then you have a weapon to fight with."

"Man, when I get angry I don't be thinking like that. I don't like nobody treating me like a hoe," Poochie-Slim said.

"I understand but listen to me Poochie. You must subside your anger by reminding yourself to look at the situation in a logical way. If you jump and let your emotions get the best of you then you'll sabotage yourself. If you wait and strategize a plan to be successful so that you don't live under those conditions, you will win.

That's why I'm creating a life so that I don't have to deal with this. Why would you allow yourself to go to jail for hitting a cop or resisting arrest? Most likely they'll trump up more charges and you could wind up in jail for 10 more years while the officers go on with their lives. I gotta think smart and use the situation to fuel myself into doing something about it. You don't want to go to jail and have a record because they can use it against you. That's written permission to harass you."

We went to our gala affair and didn't think about what happened. Like the disrespect from our previous encounter, it just seemed to evaporate. The atmosphere was hot but carried a cool vibe. Pow Wow and the rest of the crew had a ball. It was still business with me and I was on the come up. I invited the 3 chicks from the strip club and they came after their work shift. I spent most of the night with them talking about my operation.

My phone vibrated so I excused myself and walked out of the loud club to answer it. It was Lola, so I immediately called her back.

"Hello Lola. You just called me?"

"We need to turn our money in. Where are you?"

"I'm at Joe's Palmer Room. Bring it up here. I have 3 prospects, so make sure you hand me my traps in front of them. I'm bringing them outside to meet you all."

I walked back into the club and said, "Hey y'all, come outside and meet my broads. They'll be pulling up in two minutes."

Lola pulled up and all my girls got out of my caddy dressed to the nines. Each of my six girls handed me a large trap. After that, I introduced everybody. I told the 3 white girls, "This is my showcase and I don't leave home without them." Everyone was pleasingly polite.

"Girl, I love Kentucky. My girlfriend Sally is from Kentucky," The Waitress began.

"I love Chicago. I visited once," Becky responded.

"Y'all welcome to come to breakfast with us," Lola invited.

"Oh, that would be nice. We can do that, right ladies?" Ginger asked.

Becky and Samantha happily accepted the invitation.

I intervened, saying "Go back to the hotel so that y'all can rest up. I see you later." The prospects seemed opened like a can of tuna. Walking back into the club, I noticed J-Hawk leaning against the wall. He watched me the whole time.

Kentucky Girls

I gave the 3 Kentucky girls a sense of what my expectations were. Before making our exit from Joe's, I said to them, "I leave in the morning so if you want to be with me, don't meet me there, beat me there."

Becky looked up with shiny eyes and said, "This is where I am, but Chicago is where I wanna be."

"I received that. Words are the start and the finish of most things. If that's what you say, then make it happen. What the world has to offer is right at your fingertips. Once again, we are speaking at a distance. Reach out and touch me. Straight like that!" I said.

My pimp buddies and I went back to the hotel and prepared for an early checkout. That morning at around 10:00 a.m. we loaded up and headed out. I rode with J-Hawk while Poochie-Slim and Lucky drove my car. During the drive, J-Hawk asked, "What happened to the Kentucky broads? Why didn't you call them this morning before we left?"

Feeling bold and streaked with confidence, "See Uncle J-Hawk, I'm waiting for them to call me. I told the girls to 'beat' me to Chicago."

J-Hawk looked in disbelief. "You must don't like white girls. When they respond to you, react right then and there. You should've went and got them."

I took a moment to understand who I was talking to. This wasn't one of my pimp buddies. He's the Godfather and his thoughts didn't appear to show confidence in me. That certainly wasn't reassuring.

Unsure whether I made some mistakes, I wanted him to know what I'd gained. Fishing for a positive reaction. "Well, my trap was $10,000 in two days. I may not have come up with the Kentucky broads but I can't miss what I never had. What's meant to be will be. Besides, soon as we get back, we're going to Boston, Connecticut and Philly in a few days."

"Yeah, fast money is good but long money is better." He seemed unenthused and his conversation was dry as if there was something heavy on his mind.

J-Hawk's thoughts may have hypothetically led him to his conclusions. That may be the reason he was checking me out so close at Joe's Palmer's Room. Perhaps I went about things the wrong way. Uncle J-Hawk was unpleased with every conversation that I initiated, and a wave of thoughts took over my conscious. My mind retreated away from any further questions as I turned my attention back to the road. J-Hawk relaxed his head, adjusted the seat, turned on some Tyrone Davis and fell asleep.

A few hours later, I woke J-Hawk up and told him that we were almost home. My phone rang. Samantha said, "We're on 22nd & Cermak in Chicago. Becky's car overheated, and men are stopping to assist us. A tow truck just pulled over and the driver said he can tow our car to his shop and repair it." With my confidence reestablished, I sat up in my seat and pointed at the phone.

Now Uncle J-Hawk was wide awake listening to my conversation. "Let him do that and give me the address so I can pick y'all up."

J-Hawk tightened his lips up like I'd just hit a homerun. He reached his left hand over and gave me a fist pound. "Partner, you surprised me this time."

Reeking with self-assurance I said, "I knew that I had it in the bag. Shouldn't second guess me, Uncle J-Hawk."

"Boy, you got a cold style partner but I gotta have one of those whiteys."

"Uncle J, which one do you want? I'm always willing to share with you."

"I want the one with big tits and red hair. I'm coming out of retirement for this."

"That's Ginger. Ok, I'll see what I can do." We drove to the tow shop to pick them up.

Before we got there, J-Hawk got serious again.

"Now about you traveling out of town. You, your money, and what you do…. let it all speak for itself. Don't you come to it. Let it come to you. You can send your hookers out of town, but don't you go. When you send them, it's just like you're there. You don't gotta be in all those different places, so stop running around and having fun. Remember, this is business! You don't wanna be like your pimp buddies, because they're just playing. They're in it for the fun and then business but you are in it for the business, then the fun.

While we were in Kentucky, you stayed on your business and they focused on fun. They were so caught in the moments, enjoying themselves that they weren't observant. You walked outside to handle money and not one of them watched your back. Kentucky might not be hardcore, but you never underestimate nobody or no place. There are snakes everywhere.

When you're conducting business out of town, you have to be aware of a few things. If you take your hoes across state lines with the intention to pimp and the police catch you, they can charge you with 'White slavery,' which carries a minimum of an automatic 7 years in the Fed joint. So, if you decide to go out of town, make sure that you travel separate from your hoes and reside in separate hotels because if they can show a paper trail that you brought the hoes across state lines for the purpose of pimping prostitutes, then you'll have a federal case, so be really careful."

I sucked in every word like a sponge and immediately strategized how I could minimize these risks. I had to create a whole new set of rules for out of town travel if I didn't want to get caught up. From that point on when I traveled, we'd never leave at the same time. If I flew, then my hoes would drive and vice versa.

I had to implement a plan for my broads to exchange the bills at different currency exchanges the next morning after work and then secure the funds in a hiding place until they dropped it off at my hotel. That put distance between the time that they earned the money and it got to me. All funds changed hands at least 3 times before it hit my pockets. I never dropped my hoes off or picked them up on the Strolls. My out of town plan was in place in case I made the decision to travel. Also, I decided whenever J-Hawk gave me advice, I'd thoroughly analyze and follow it.

When we got to the mechanic shop, the tow driver had already repaired Becky's busted radiator hose. They followed us to J-Hawk's boutique. I explained to Ginger that my house was crowded so she'd be staying at J-Hawk's apartment.

"It's nice and you'll like it. I'll bring Samantha and Becky over after they get situated. J-Hawk, choose Ginger some nice outfits for work and I'll call Lena so she can meet me at the house with some gear for Becky and Samantha."

"That's fine with me," Ginger said as she pranced over to get the flower printed, rust-color sun dress that J-Hawk handed her.

"Ladies, you're going to be working with the all-star team. Welcome to the big league. Y'all moving up in the world." I announced.

They looked up and Becky made eye contact with me. She smiled, appearing to be enthused with the rapid pace that we were flowing in. Samantha said, "We can keep up. The good news is that we're ready to give these lonely city boys some southern hospitality."

"Ginger, I'm gonna let J-Hawk finish accommodating you while we roll over to the house. We all family. It's one love. Uncle J-Hawk, I'll be back to pick y'all up for work later," I said.

I already gave Geisha the heads up that we were coming home with the girls so that they could prepare our arrival. My broads trotted out of the house and helped Becky and Samantha with their bags and introduced themselves.

Geisha grabbed their bags and took them to their quarters, downstairs in the basement, next to her room. It was set up like a living room with two sofas that let out into beds. While Geisha was occupied with them, I checked on Amelia and Wonnie who went upstairs to their rooms.

I went upstairs to the living room where Amelia and Wonnie were standing; they were happy to see me. Amelia licked her lips as she appeared silently excited. Her body language exposed her inner need for attention. She looked me in my eyes and gave me a sexy smile. She slowly bit her bottom lip.

Wonnie slowly came into view with her coffee black skin and beautiful white smile. She kept staring at me without a blink. I noticed that her pupils were smaller than usual. She gave me a hug and went upstairs to her room. Sensing that something was wrong, I followed her.

As she stood there, I walked up close, gently grabbed Wonnie's face and looked into her eyes.

"Why are your eyes so revealing?"

She faded back as if posing for a picture, somewhat conceited and said, "What do you see? Do you see rose petals, do they twinkle like stars or are they so lovely that you just have to admit it?"

"No, they look like two little angry black beans. Now tell me what's wrong."

"Last night on the Stroll, a black guy with a foreign accent wearing a dashiki looked as if he were lost. He asked me to help him find a hotel room and to hail a cab. He said that he would pay me handsomely for my assistance. He pulled out a bankroll and handed me $20 just for talking with him so I helped him find a hotel and flagged down a cab.

He told me his name, said that he was Nigerian and that he had a business meeting in the morning. He asked if I had a man because he didn't want any trouble. I told him I got a pimp but he's not around. He showered me with compliments, telling me that I was a pretty, young lady that reminded him of the girls in his country. We took a cab to the local hotel that we dated in and he checked in while he had the cab driver wait.

He explained that he needed to go downtown but offered to give me $300 if I stayed in the room and I agreed. Then he said that he would give me an extra $200 if I was nice to him right now. I agreed to stay and be nice to him. He counted out $500 and placed it in an envelope, licking and sealing it closed. Then he placed it back in his side pocket. He suggested that he keep it for me and I said, 'No, let me keep it. I'll still stay.'

He said, 'Ok, I'll tell you what. Let's put it between the box spring and mattress.' I watched him as he placed the envelope under there. We turned a date. He said, 'I'll be back in less than two hours. Wait for me now.' I said ok and watched through the window as he got into the cab. I got the envelope from under the mattress and opened it up. It had paper cut into the shape of bills. I got hoodwinked.

Five minutes later he called the hotel room and asked me to be his woman. I said, 'Yeah, come on back.' I was trying my best to get another shot at him. I wanted to get that bankroll."

I chuckled. "You mean the slick got out slicked?" That brought a little laughter out of her. "Now listen, don't ever let anybody show you money, put it away and then hand it back to you. What he did was have two envelopes. One was sealed and the other he showed you. He predicted that you would suggest that you keep the envelope so he switched when he placed it back into his pocket and pulled out the dummy envelope and put it between the mattress so you could feel like you had control of the $500. That's called the flam bucket. I'm curious to meet him. I'm going to ride down the Stroll tonight. He might still be around."

I told J-Hawk that I would meet him back at the boutique and dropped Wonnie off last, after taking her by the pool hall on the Stroll where all the hustlers hung out. I figured if he was still around, that's where he would be. She looked through the window and spotted him.

I walked up to the Nigerian imposter. "Hey, the girl outside the pool hall asked me to come and get you. Do you know her?"

He looked at the window and nodded with lust in his eyes, "Yeah, that's the pretty black girl I was with yesterday."

"Well, that's my hoe."

Coping a plea, he said, "Man I didn't know she had a pimp. I don't disrespect nobody's game. I apologize. She didn't tell me that she had a player. All I know is that she's a hustler. I ain't no player. I'm just chasing money and looking for a hustling broad. She's cute and I was trying to come up."

I had to laugh. It was funny, but I told him, "Right church, wrong preacher. You turned a date with my broad. I ain't gonna charge you the $500 but Imma need $100 out of you." I stood in my stance, looking like I could tear into him at any given minute. If he gave me any problems, I was going to drive my fist through his face. He was in my hood and stood no chance.

"That ain't a problem homie. Here you go." He handed me a $100 bill.

I gave him a pass because game recognizes game! I walked outside and kissed Wonnie on the lips. "Get to work." Then I drove back to J-Hawk's. My whole crew was there kicking it with the godfather, talking pimp talk while playing Backgammon.

Lola called. "Hey, I'm just calling to let you know that everything is working out. The new girls are doing well."

"So, what are you saying? They're selling like vanilla wafers?"

"Yeah they are but you know most people like chocolate chip cookies." We both laughed.

"After work, bring all the girls to the new house so I can get my traps."

That morning all the traps were good so they went to the hotel while I chilled.

Later that day, when Geisha changed her clothes, I noticed that her stomach was bloated. I asked was she on her period and she said, "No. I'm a month late and I might be pregnant."

"We're not having babies right now."

"Earthquake, my friend took some pills called Humphrey 11 which she got at Walgreens and they made her period come."

"Cool, let's go get them right now." We headed to the store.

"Here Geisha, take these 11 pills. If you double the dose, your period may come faster."

Nothing happened. The next day, I gave her 6 more and still nothing. That night, before taking all my other hoes to work, I gave her 4 more. Suddenly, her stomach started to cramp so I told her to stay home.

Two hours later, when I got back, she was cramping really bad and her period came down so heavy that her pads were soiled every 5 minutes. The pain made her retreat to the bathroom. She stiffened and grabbed her stomach as if the excruciating agony invaded her uterus. I assisted her as she clinched my arm like it was a rail to keep her from falling.

Her arms slipped through my hands while I gripped her by the elbows. Her legs were wobbling so much they looked like spaghetti strings. Her voice fell faint as it quivered. "Earthquake," as she slumped to the ground. She was bleeding so bad her face turned pale; got so weak that she passed out. I put her in the tub under the running shower and turned the water to the coldest temperature, then placed wet towels on her forehead.

This was a terrifying situation. I thought if she didn't wake in 3 minutes, I'd have to call 911. I put my hand under her nose to see if she was breathing but couldn't tell. I checked her pulse and didn't feel anything. A few seconds later, she woke up lethargic. I told her not to get up. By now, the tub was full of blood. I let the water run directly on her until the blood cleared and it took 30 minutes. Then I carried her to the bed and she fell asleep.

I woke her up periodically throughout the night and told her to rest for the next few days. She went back to work after the bleeding stopped. In the pimp game, when a prostitute gets pregnant the pimp takes responsibility for the baby, regardless if it's a trick's baby or not, it's still his. That made me realize that I had to be much more careful.

It drove me to be more adamant about protection. I enforced new rules that required the girls to not only use condoms, but birth control pills and sponges at all times. I knew I didn't want no trick babies. I was building a business, not a family.   I was deeply affected by this.

The Northside Hit – Bodie

I had to much work to do and business was booming! I was eleven deep and everything was running smoothly.   I had two broads on travel rotation, who worked the major events and clubs across the country. My girls continued to work the four corners of Chi-town: Eastside, Westside, Southside and then there is the Northside, where business was still hot. I mean really on fire with the high-end, executive clientele.   One Stroll was in Vicky-Lous territory and I established a rapport with the members.

Pow Wow was rolling with me when I abruptly turned down a side street right off the Stroll and one of the hoes that belong to a Vicky-Lous pimp jumped in the back seat. She handed me some money and got out the car. Then I rolled down further and another one of their hoes got in and slid me some ends. Pow Wow looked at me with surprise. "Did you just bump two Vicky-Lous broads?"

"No, I'm not trying to go there."

"Why not? If they choose you then you need to accept them."

"Naw, I'm just conducting business.   Don't wanna come through like a gangsta. Imma stay light on the Vicky-Lous pimps."

"It's fair game when another pimp's hoe chooses you."

"Yeah, but I don't allow them to be with me because it could create more problems than money. I do allow them to pay me a choosing fee."

"Quake-A-State, that's called back door money." Pow Wow laughed and said, "I get it. Their hoes are paying you a portion of their trap, hoping you will accept them."

"Yeah, their quest is to leave their pimps and be with me. I'm just skimming off the top. That's all. It's an additional source of income without causing static."

Pow Wow paused for a second appearing to be in deep thought pondering the logic of my strategy. "How long are you going to let them pay?"

"Until they figure out that I'm not going to let them be with me. Remember, you always advised me to never be greedy. You'd say, 'Don't be a greedy pig. It's alright to stay high on the hog but being a pig can get you slaughtered.' Well, I'm still taking your advice. I try to keep from crossing the line; another day, another play."

We cruised through the area where we set up our date location, at an old, vacant factory mill. As we rode through, I saw my li'l homie, looked over at my brother and quickly said, "Pow Wow take your hat off. We wanna remain discreet about being Mob."

He walked toward us. "What up Al? This is my brother Pow Wow. In case I'm not around, you can holla at him about our hookers."

Al stuck his arm through the driver door window and extended it across me to shake Pow Wow's hand. "What up Pow Wow?"

"What up li'l homie?"

Al was one of the main Vicky-Lous holding down the Stroll and he was cool with me. He stood about 5'8" with a slender build, dark brown skin tone, full eyes, a pug nose and a mole on his left cheek. He wore a low haircut, and always had a toothpick in his mouth. He walked with his feet turned inward. We called it pigeon toed. The Vicky-Lous looked out for my girls and made sure that they were safe. I would hit Al off with some ends for him and his crew.

I decided to spread the love and turned my crew on to this location so they could increase their money flow and for a while things were gravy. One day, Bodie and I rode together to drop off our girls and then stopped into a local store in the area. "Bodie, either take your hat off or turn it straight while we're in Vicky-Lous territory."

Calm but sitting there without concern he said, "I don't turn my hat for nobody, I don't care what the circumstances are. I'm gangsta and that's all to it."

"Look Bodie, they're Vicky-Lous who respect me and they're looking at us like businessmen, not like gangstas, so let's keep it that way and not pose a threat."

That seemed to brew a bitter taste in his mouth. He casted a frown on his face while getting out the car and said, "I told you, this is how I roll."

We went into the store and I spoke to 4 Vicky-Lous that I knew but they didn't speak back. Seeing that hat turned to the right surely altered their behavior. We left the store and got in the car.

"Yo Bodie, clearly they noticed your cap turned to the right, indicating that we're Mob. Man, you revealed yourself as a gangsta, not a businessman. That wasn't too smart. I got a feeling that we're gonna have some problems. You embraced your pride at the wrong time. Bodie, I think this gonna be bad for us. You're too head strong, stubborn, close-minded and never compromise about anything. Being a gangsta and being smart go together. That's why you separate your food dishes when you eat."

"Earthquake, what does that mean?"

"Man, you wouldn't even understand."

"Well, I got this Twinkie and it's separated. You want half?"

"No. You eat too many sweets. They're bad for you."

He took a bite, looked over at me and said, "Everything that I do is bad. Imma bad boy. You know I don't offer nobody nothing, so you gotta know you're 100 (tight) with me."

Trying not to let it get the best of me I said, "I know. Remember when you asked me to pick up your girl and take her to work when I dropped mine off? I asked you for $2 and you made her get out of the car, gave her $2 and made her ride all the way to the Northside when I was just kidding."

"Yeah!"

"Man, you're my homie, a true gangsta and that's cool, but make it work *for* you, not *against* you."

Everything was quiet for a few days, but something was lurking. A 5-star, elite Chief of the Vicky-Lous had just been released from prison and found out about Mob gangstas running a pimp business in their territory. At about 3:00 a.m. that morning the

Vicky-Lous stopped our girls on the street and told Lola to call me. She handed him the phone and he said, "Hey, this Slick Joe. I need to meet with you fellas and talk."

"Yeah, we could do that."

"Cool Earthquake, we can meet at about 3:00 a.m. tomorrow."

I heard him but wasn't listening. "Ok Chief, see you then. Let me speak to my girl."

Lola got back on the line. "Baby doll, tomorrow at 3:00 a.m. if they ask y'all where we are, tell them that we just left." I agreed to meet him but ignored his request.

Our girls kept working and a few nights later, Slick Joe made The Waitress call this time with the same message. I disregarded his request a second time, hoping the problem would go away. A couple more nights passed and Lola called right before quitting time. It was 5:00 a.m. and the sound of terror poured from her voice as she said, "The Vicky-Lous just took our money." That got my attention. I paused and asked what happened.

Her irate tone seemed to identify the uneasy position that she was left in. She said, "The Vicky-Lous were in cars, circling the Stroll and then they got aggressive. They strong armed us and took all our money. Geisha fought back and 3 of them held her down and took her ends too. There was a big brawl out here because we wouldn't give up our traps and now he's standing here, asking to talk to you." She sounded overly anxious but undefeated. "You need to get up here fast!"

"Yep, give him the phone," I said.

The Chief got on the line and said, "Listen up, this Slick Joe, we be Vicky-Lous and this our set, you dig?"

I extended my communication like a gentleman. "I understand that."

"You can't be on Vicky-Lous set and not pay. I don't know how y'all do it but this how we get down. We be Vicky-Lous on this set and these are the rules. Like I said, you need to come down and holla at me. We don't mind your girls working, but y'all gotta pay a fee every Sunday."

I stayed as accommodating as possible. "Ok man, I'll be down there."

'The Chief trying to tax me unlawfully, against the laws of the street. I ain't got no competing business with the Vicky-Lous organization. The pimps on the set are Vicky-Lous but they run their business independent of the Vicky-Lous operation. I don't owe him nothing,' I thought to myself. I knew that Bodie's hat situation would catch up with us. He left the door open and now the Chief was trying to capitalize on this situation.

Now there was no turning back. Whether we paid or not, it could only turn out one way. I called my crew and let them know what happened. The Vicky-Lous had just taxed us. My pimp buddies were boiling, ready to swarm down like a group of locusts prepared to do damage and tear up everything in sight. We all met up and rolled to the Northside, pulled up to the meeting place, on the side of a gas station and our hookers loaded into our cars. The girls were upset and all talking at once.

"Where are they?" Pow Wow asked.

Lola's revenge settled in her attitude like a shield of armor as she pointed them out.

"There they go, right there," as 7 dudes were walking toward our cars.

The Chief said, "Hey dudes, I'm Slick Joe, talking on behalf of the Vicky-Lous."

Slick Joe was 5'll" with a muscular build, the kind that you see on a dude who was just released from the penitentiary. His eyes were slightly slanted, with thick eyebrows, a thin mustache and skin tone that was paper bag brown. He wore his sandy brown hair relaxed and hanging below his shoulders. His name fit him. He looked kind of slick.

"We need to holla at y'all," Slick Joe said.

That statement ignited my homie Diamond's rage in a fraction of a second. "Holla at us? Man, you better give me my ends." He took his 9-millimeter pistol from behind his waist and busted Slick Joe up side his head. He fell to the ground like an elephant hit with a tranquilizer. I grabbed him in his collar and pulled him up toward me, where his face met the barrel of my .38-special.

"Lower those ends, right now." Slick Joe handed me all his money.

The rest of my crew gave the Vicky-Lous a hardcore pistol whipping, took all their loot and left them penniless. We had them face down on the ground pleading, "Don't shoot us."

"I'm warning y'all. If you ever rob our broads again or cause any trouble, we'll be back and it most definitely won't be nice," Lucky said.

"I should blow y'all heads off right now," Bodie said.

All our hookers stared in a silent cheer of hip-hip hooray. We jumped in our cars and pulled off.

The next evening, we all dropped our girls off for work in the same location. This was the test to determine if it was gonna be peace or war. At 12:00 midnight, Amelia called. "They just robbed us again."

"Alright, we're on our way. Meet us by the old factory mill."

Slick Joe seemed like a tax collector and this was a bad omen that just wouldn't go away. I assembled the crew and we rode to the Northside. We pulled up on our girls and Poochie-Slim asked, "Where are the Vicky-Lous?"

"I think they're on the next block. They've been prowling around and it's a bunch of them," Wonnie said.

"Go on Broadway and keep working until we come get y'all," I instructed.

We hit the corner and there they stood, congregating, about 20 Vicky-Lous waiting on our arrival. There were only 8 of us but I was ready to get down. Overwhelmed by the turbulent conflict, I carelessly leaped out of the car and my crew followed my lead.

We headed towards them but Pow Wow hollered with rationale. "Quake-A-State, it's too many, come back."

I walked back to my car while they were yelling, "Vicky-Lous. Every time your girls work, we gonna rob them." They were drunk with courage, taunting us since we were outnumbered. We drove down the block, got with our girls and told them, "Everybody continue to work down here."

Forty-eight hours slipped by. This night was quiet and tame. The wind felt noticeably easy on my skin under the full moon. All the pimps drove while the girls were sightseeing out the windows, taking our time and enjoying the music as we moved at a slow pace. Finally, we arrived at their destination, the hoe Stroll. At 1:00 a.m., Wonnie called and said, "They robbed us again. I'm tired of these marks."

"Where are they?" I asked.

"They got the nerve to be staking out the old factory mill, where our security spot is set up. That's where they're hiding, waiting for us to come back so they can rob us again."

"Don't go back to Vicky-Lous hood. Go and work on Lincoln for 2-hours, then everybody catch a cab home. That place doesn't exist anymore."

We went full throttle with the whole crew this time. Seven cars deep with two homies riding in each trunk. We had heavy artillery on us. It turned into an institution of war, all about policing our business. Suddenly, we spotted them at the old factory mill. The levy was about to bust. We drove right toward them and they stopped in their tracks.

We quickly popped our trunks and everybody started shooting. There were loud, thundering sounds of heavy gun fire as they were shooting at us and we were blazing back with vengeance. Shots rained out like a hail storm. It was a war zone, lit up like Independence Day and a haze of smoke trailed the barrage of bullets. You could smell the gunpowder lingering in the air.

Our ammunition over powered them. The Vicky-Lous hit the ground, slithering away like snakes in the grass, fleeing for cover but we kept on firing. We hit 3 of them and luckily, my folks had no causalities. We loaded into our cars and headed back to the Southside.

My pimp and Mob homies met me at the new house. It was – a familiar atmosphere. I said, "Listen up, we have to let go of that area because the existence of pride is unmatched with peace." I glanced over at Bodie as I continued, "It gets between rational thinking and reckless behavior. It creates enemies and I don't think that's a healthy future for anybody."

"Man," I just concluded. "I'm real disgusted about the whole situation and how ugly and out of control it got."

Reno and his girls stayed the night. They seemed to really enjoy our company. After everybody got ready for bed, he and his girls slept in the upstairs loft space. After settling his 3 broads in, he came downstairs to my room to talk about the future.

"I been working my girl Barbie in this joint in Cicero west of Chicago. You should put some of your girls in that club. They turn lots of dates in there. It's a hoe joint," Reno told me.

"I might check it out but you know I got my biz together. Things are good in the streets. This particular incident was just about being in the right place with the wrong person."

"Well man, maybe this is a good time to expand. You can be inside the joint and on the Stroll. Anyway, why didn't Bodie just turn his hat neutral?"

I told Reno point blank. "Bodie acted like a goon gangsta, unable to turn it if off. There's a difference between a goon and a true gangsta. A goon is a goon all the time but a true gangsta knows when to turn it off. A goon is a hood, a thug with no self-control, operating off pride. He makes every situation a gun fight, while a gangsta knows how to handle business in civil way."

"Man, I agree with you."

"Yeah Reno, Bodie was foolish and didn't follow protocol."

"That's what you were trying to say earlier, huh?"

"Pretty much. I tried to talk him off the ledge but he's hard-headed. He's cool with me and I love him like a brother, but he's destructive and you can't make money like that."

Reno sat up in the chair and took his shoes off. "That's why you should come to the club. It's some bad hoes working there too so I know it'll be a come up for you."

"Yeah, I'll think about it. Let's get some sleep for now."

Later that day, Deanna, a childhood friend from the Jeffrey Manor who now lived in that neighborhood, called and said that the Vicky-Lous put a hit out on me. "The word in the street is that the Mob came through and kicked off a shootout. Three Vicky-Lous got shot. I'm just letting you know."

"Thanks Deanna I'm straight. They better look out for me."

A few hours later I got a similar call from Money, a pimp that I associated with. "Earthquake, stay off that Stroll because there's a hit out on you."

"I appreciate your call. You my man. If you need something, let me know."

We moved our businesses to another Northside neighborhood and kissed that lucrative territory goodbye. Those were the challenges, the life of a player. Sometimes you have to give up something in order to get something. That's the way the universe works. My homie wasn't willing to give up his pride, not even for his own well-being and it had a ripple effect on us all.

I learned to be more careful with the people that I conducted business with. That was a lesson J-Hawk taught me. Moving forward, I learned to make sure that my business associates were on the same accord and had the same understanding.

CHAPTER 22

A Pimp Gets Murdered

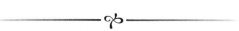

AFTER THE SHOWDOWN with the Vicky-Lous, we assessed the situation. We were deeply affected by the gun fight. It restricted our movement on the Northside. We moved to Lincoln Ave. and worked on the Broadway Stroll. We always had security for the girls but Geisha didn't need it. She was super rough, a trick's worst nightmare and I felt sorry for any John who tried to mess with her because she was always thinking of a way to get you.

A few days later, on a breezy night, Bodie called.

"What up Bodie, gangsta goon?"

"Man, I just got an emergency page from Lois. She said that a pimp was holding her hostage in a hotel room up north."

"Did she say where?"

"No, check with your girls and see who she got in a car with last."

Geisha was the first to respond to my page and I told her what just went down.

"That happened to me the other day. I bet it's the same goofball who took me to a hotel," Geisha said.

She told me about a renegade pimp on the Northside who cruised the Strolls. He watched her as she worked in Vicky-Lous territory. He also spotted her while my hookers were working on Broadway Ave.

This pimp rolled up on Geisha posing as a trick, acting as if he wanted to date. She followed procedure, checking the situation then got into his car. She directed him to go to the hotel they had been working out of. He objected and drove in the opposite direction.

"Where is your man?" he asked her. "I need to talk to him because I'm charging you for reckless eyeballing me. Break yourself hoe (give me all your money)."

"I can't do that. I didn't know that you were a pimp."

"You knew I was a pimp. You've been seeing me out here. I've rolled up on you before and you were meddling me then. I know your man got chased off the Stroll in Vicky-Lous territory so you need to get with me. Then you can work anywhere, wherever you want."

It seemed he heard about our situation with the Vicky-Lous and was now trying to benefit from it.

"You gonna make that call to him when we get to my hotel," he told Geisha.

"Ok."

With her own fiendish plan in mind, Geisha gave him a pleasant smile and thought to herself, '*I'm gonna take his jewelry.*' She evaluated the two gold, hambone chains and baguette diamond ring that he wore. Just like a black widow spider, he was being lured into her trap. They got to the hotel and entered his room. His hoe was there.

He told his girl to go to work, leaving Geisha and him alone. Geisha was acting very sensual, as if she was digging his style, trying to catch him off guard.

"I always wanted you," the pimp told her.

"I know. I used to see you out there."

He loosened up and let his guard down. He grabbed her by the waist. Her eyes sparkled as she lightly floated into him, ready to strike. She kept her arms at her sides, kissing and licking his neck, putting a sensual touch on each move while slowly reaching for the mace hidden in her sleeve.

As his hands invaded her chest, she rubbed his penis and he got aroused, unzipped his pants and took them off. With a slight edge of worry, not fully trusting the situation, he walked to the bathroom and placed his belongings in there. When he did that, Geisha instinctively knew that it would be difficult to rob him unless she knocked him out. She felt that it would be too time consuming so in a split second, she ran out the room and down the street. Then she caught a date and went back to the Stroll. She didn't mention it to me until now.

"Do you remember what hotel and which room?" I asked.

"Yes."

"We're on our way."

I called and gave Bodie the update as I raced to pick him up. I sensed the rage lurking between his words. He was furious. We stayed strapped, mine was a pearl handle, .38-special and Bodie carried his Glock. We picked up Geisha and she led us straight there.

"That's the room with #9 on the door," she pointed out.

We pulled in the hotel lot and sat for 15 minutes watching with eagle eyes and the appetite of buzzards. Bodie wrestled with being patient, eager to save his broad from danger and protect her from harm. Finally, the pimp's hoe walked out of the room.

"That was the same hoe that was in the room the other day," Geisha informed us.

Bodie and I discreetly left the parking lot and drove a half block down, around the corner. We popped the trunk and grabbed our bandanas and gloves and left Geisha in the car. We walked back to the hotel. I tapped on the door, he opened it and we stormed in with pistols in our hands.

"Don't move," I commanded. I checked the room as Bodie held his Glock to his head. I looked under the mattress and pulled out his .25 Derringer gun. I handed it to Bodie who concealed it in his waist and slung the pimp to the bed, letting him know any resistance could be fatal.

I held my gun up to his head and Bodie snatched the cords from the radio and television and threw them to me. "Tie that punk up."

We took the pimp's money and jewelry. We slapped the goofball around as Bodie's girl was sitting in the corner with no blouse on, crouched over keeping herself from being exposed. She showed relief after being released from the pimp's clutches with a grim smile. The heavy burden of fear evaporated from her face.

"Did he rob you?" Bodie asked.

"No, but he was about to," she said, with resentment directed at her captor.

It felt like we were rescuing her from a human trafficking situation. It was different than pimping because it's kidnapping, drugging and forcing prostitution on victims against their will.

"Put your blouse on and come slap this fool."

The pimp was face down on the bed with his hands tied behind his back and his legs roped together with the cords. She smashed him upside his head with an ashtray.

"Come on man, please, we good. I didn't know that she was your broad. Y'all got my jewelry, so go on and leave," he hollered.

The poor pimp didn't realize that he was messing with the mind of a goon gangsta. Bodie told his girl where we were parked and said, "Go to the car right now."

Bodie was merciless when he said, "It didn't have to be my broad, you 'mark.' You're a robber and a rapist."

"Come on Bodie, let's go," I said.

"Naw, I'm tired of these bums playing with my money. This trick won't play with nobody else's loot so if you don't want to see him take his last breath, go to the car. I'll die for mine. I told you what would happen to anybody who messed with my broad."

Bodie and I pulled our bandanas over our faces. The pimp's fear overflowed his sorrow with a pleading voice that cracked as he begged, "Come on homie." He squirmed on the bed, struggling for pity. "Please. She was coming at me. Please, just be cool."

With shook pockets and only a spoonful of life, I just looked as Bodie put a pillow over the pimp's head. I walked out and a few seconds later I heard four muffled shots, boom – boom – boom - boom.

I continued my path, imagining his life flashing before his eyes. I looked back and saw Bodie calmly trotting up behind me. I shook my head.

"Man Bodie, you didn't have to kill the chump. You're ignorant."

"It's ok. That's why I'm Bodie and you're Earthquake," he winked.

I realized that some lessons aren't learned right away and some aren't learned at all. I became aware that the actions of others could have a devastating impact on my future. In this kind of situation, there was no turning back so I'd have to be ready to face the consequences. I had to remind myself that there was a time to be around them and a time not to be. I was a pimp and he was a goon and timing was everything!

When I got back to the house, Reno was there. He and 3 of his girls spent the night and never left. They moved in permanently while his other two broads remained at the hotel. He and his girls stayed in the loft space. It was great to have my pimp buddy in the house with me. Our girls got along well so we kicked it like family.

"I heard that y'all got Lois back," Reno said.

Not trying to put him in a catch-22 situation, I remained as evasive as possible. My answer was like pulling teeth, for his own good.

"Hum, yeah, we did."

My reply was short and I could tell that Reno sensed the urgency to change the conversation. "So, what's up with the club? Are you going to bring your girls?" Halfheartedly, I was thinking I'm ok on the streets, but it could be worth exploring.

"Yeah Reno, give me a few days. Who owns the club anyway?" I asked.

"An old school Italian dude named Gus who don't allow black men to enter his club, even if they got girls working. The money is good and there are no police issues or robberies to worry about."

My wheels were spinning. I could expand in the clubs and stay on the Strolls. Since the Kentucky girls had experience, maybe I'd try them out first.

I called Becky to my room.

"Starting tomorrow, you are going to work at a club in Cicero."

"Can we do it when we come back? I have some issues with my mom that need to be addressed. Also, I want to take Ginger back home. Can Samantha ride with me? We'll be back in a few days," she said.

"Ok, that's fine. When are y'all leaving?"

"Later this afternoon."

"Why don't you get a few hours of rest before hitting the road."

When Becky woke up, she drove to J-Hawk's place to pick up Ginger. That gave me a chance to strengthen my game and solidify my stance with Samantha. I looked at my watch and knew that we'd have at least 45 minutes, so I called her to my room. As soon as she walked in, our lips touched and her mouth parted as passion overtook any conversation. We were caught in the moment. I felt her tongue twirling around mine and slowly reciprocated.

She sharply inhaled as I bent down and sucked on her right breast. Buried in her bosom, Samantha's hands gently stroked my hair, then, caressed my arms and held on to my biceps as she guided my body upward to accommodate me the same way. She frantically kissed my chest while I slid my lips to her left ear lobe and gently blew in it. Then my mouth greeted her neck and tenderly traveled to her breast where my tongue rapidly gyrated her nipples.

I could feel the intense emotions getting the best of her as I stuffed her left tit in my mouth and pulled back as my tongue danced on her breasts. Her body vibrated with the sound of a pleasurable hum and created a sweet melody that aroused an erection in me. We hit the waterbed like a falling lumber jack.

My hands moved between her thighs. I took the index finger and circled around her clitoris, then put the middle one in her vagina as she panted with a loud moan. I felt her body tense up as my penis saluted her. She spread her legs and said, "Make love to me." I put on a condom and saddled up, took the head of my penis, rubbed it up against her cunt and teased it. "Stick it in before I come." I obliged her and deliberately stroked her as I drove in deep.

I needed to invade the sanity of the Kentucky girl's soul. A loud sound emerged from Samantha as she screamed, "I'm coming. Oh my God, I'm coming." I shot off my final rocket and we fell off the bed onto the floor and just laid there. She looked at me.

"I really don't want to ride back with Becky. I wish I could stay."

"It's not where you're going, it's where you're at. Even when you're there and I'm here, we're still together. Your body might be in Kentucky but your heart will be with me, right?"

She gave me a peck on my lips and said in total delight, "That's true."

I touched her chin, gazed into her eyes and studied her pupils as I watched them expand into serenity, which is a true sign of endearment.

"Is that really true?" she asked.

"Yes, it is. I'm really feeling you."

I traced the tip of her hair with a soft touch. My tender side showed as I adapted to her aggressive style. "Truth and honesty will always be recognized as attractive and those qualities I need. It's the strongest characteristic that a person could have and the safest."

"I'll always make sure that I stay honest with you."

"Then you'll always be with me. Now go and get ready for your trip."

As she left the room I thought, *'They're most definitely coming home. Hum, I'm going to give them $500. That should get them there and back.'* After the Kentucky girls packed up and left, I rode over to J-Hawk's to find out what happened with him and Ginger.

When I walked in he asked, "Did you let all of them go back to Kentucky?"

"Yeah, I did."

"You shouldn't have let Samantha go. At least you would still have one. You act as if you don't care whether they return or not."

"Uncle J-Hawk, I'm not worried about them coming back. I got more than enough girls. If they return they do and if they don't, oh well. I've got new prospects every day. You let Ginger go, what happened with her?"

"Her mom fell down the stairs and broke her hip. She went back to help her."

"Both my girls had to take care of biz also. I'm still 9 deep."

My pager went off; it was an unknown number. I grabbed my briefcase and called back. "Hello, who this be?"

"Hey Earthquake, baby! Come get me. This Rainey."

"What's up baby, hey. Where are you?"

"I just got home 15 minutes ago. Come and get me."

"Give me about an hour. I'm going to the hotel to get you a room and check you in. Have your things packed and I'll be there."

"See Uncle J-Hawk, I told you. I ain't worried about hoes running off. My broad was just released from jail."

At that moment, Bruno flew through the door as if he just escaped from Alcatraz. He was sweaty and in a panic. I looked at him and asked, "Bruno, what's the problem?"

"I need to use the phone."

"Tell me what's going on," J-Hawk demanded as his face scowled with concern.

"I'm trying to get to my car. It's 3 blocks away from here."

"Why don't you just go and get it?" J-Hawk asked.

"Y'all know that I'm a gangsta. I've been crushing dudes my whole life and taking their money. I'm known as a bully. Earthquake you know how I use to roll."

Bruno was about 6'3", a massive 250 lbs. with a dark complexion with long relaxed hair.

"Let me tell you what just happened to me. I was at this broad's house and she had been feeling me, you know. She invited me to her bedroom. While I was standing next to her bed, she asked if I was thirsty and I said yes. Old girl said have a seat on the bed while she went to get me a 7-Up. Her toddler walked in the room. The baby was about 2-3 years old, wearing little twig braids in her hair and a smelly diaper with the aroma of fried doo-doo. I said, 'What's up li'l dookie?' 'My name ain't dookie.' 'What's your name?' I told her, 'Jack the Ripper. I'm about to rip your mama apart now get out of here stank butt.' The baby hobbled on out of the room. Old girl walked back in with a pop and sat next to me. I rubbed on her thighs. She said, 'Uh Bruno, not now. Let's wait.' I've been waiting to long for this. Come on girl, let me sneak some.

She spanked my hand and said, 'Ok, give me a minute. Let me check on my mama.' She went into the kitchen and then the bathroom, right, and the baby trotted back in and said, 'Booty head.' I gave her a little thump on her neck and she ran out of the room again. A few minutes later, old girl stepped back in wearing a short, black mini skirt and I knew I was about to do some damage. She shut the door. We were kissing and rubbing all over each other. I wasn't playing no games.

The baby pushed the door open. She pointed at me and said, 'a-ooh' here comes the big-bad-wolf.' The doorbell rang. I asked who the big-bad-wolf was and she said, 'Ooh. That's what she calls her father.' Can you hide in the closet until he leaves? He's not going to stay long.' I told her, 'Hide in the closet? He better hide from me. He must not know who I am. I'm Bruno Valentine, the biggest gangsta on the Southside. When he see me, he's liable to run.

The doorbell rang again followed by repetitive knocks. Her mom went to answer the door. Old girl said, 'I don't want any trouble. Can you please just hide in the closet?' 'Naw baby, I can't do that. I don't hide from nobody. I'll snap that fool's neck if he says anything to me.' Old girl said, 'Ok, you might know him. His name is Doony.' I jump up from the bed and asked 'Doony? Which closet do you want me to get in?'

Old girl said, 'Get in the long closet.' I flew in there and rambled all the way to the back, behind some coats and hangers. I could hear them arguing like cats and dogs. He was yelling at old girl. 'What happened to that money I gave you?' I heard him walk in the room while the mother was saying, 'I ain't having that today Doony.' I could barely see through the shutters in the closet door.

They were standing there while the baby had her arm around his leg, pointing at the closet saying, 'Him in there.' My heart was pounding but he ignored her. The baby walked up to the closet door and repeated herself. 'Him in there.' Doony stopped arguing and turned toward the closet. He said, 'Who's in there?' The baby said, 'Booty head.' 'Whoever's in there, you got 5 seconds to come out.' He started to count. Before he could get to 3, I rushed out, scrambling through the hangers and clothes and spoke, 'How you doing Mr. Doony?'

Aren't you that comedian dude, Bruno?' 'Yes sir Mr. Doony.' 'Why are you hiding in a closet?' 'Well, she told me to get in there.' You know that Doony ain't nothing but 5'8". He looked up at me and said, 'Get out of here right now!' Old girl said 'You don't have to go nowhere. You can stay. Sit down.' The mother said, 'I'm not going to have that out of y'all today.' Man, I tapped the mother on the shoulder. Excuse me Ma'am, where is the fastest way out?

The mother looked at me and said, 'The front door baby.' I started walking out the room and old girl yelled, 'Don't leave.' Doony looked at me then said, 'As a matter fact, run out the door and off the porch. I mean now and don't stop running.' I could hear him walking behind me, heading toward the door. I ran off the porch. He said, 'And don't stop running.' I ran past my car and off the block. I didn't stop running until I got up here.

Now I'm hanging around, just waiting. Old girl's been paging me but I'm not going to call her back until I think he's gone. I came up here to use the phone godfather (J-Hawk). If he's gone, I can go back around there and get my car. It's in the front of old girl's house. Now y'all know I'm a gangsta but man, I respect Doony. He's a hitman and a serious killer."

J-Hawk and I were cracking up.

In the mist of chuckling, J-Hawk said, "I know one thing, Doony wasn't gonna kill you about no woman but you'll live a long time if you keep respecting old heads."

Since I was about to head out I said, "Come on Bruno, let me take you to your car. Uncle J-Hawk, I'm going to check on my girls and get Rainey a room. I'll get back with you later."

I dropped Bruno off at his car. I was still tickled from his incident. After leaving the hotel, my next stop was Rainey.

Connecting with Her Emotionally

I pulled up and blew my horn. She walked out, looking so good. Every curve was where it was supposed to be. Her skin glowed and her smile was bright. She looked more mature, sexier than ever. I stepped out of the car. Rainey tightly hugged my neck while she repeatedly kissed me all over my face. We walked in the house, gathered her things and took them to her hotel room.

My fingers gently outlined her curvy hips as I cuffed her butt cheeks with the palms of my hands. She whispered, "I missed you. I love you." Her body was rejuvenating, almost irresistible. I kissed her on the forehead, looked in her eyes and then tenderly on her lips. Her mouth was soft and wet with the sweet smell of cinnamon. Our tongues engaged in a welcome home celebration as her breasts perked up in my hand.

There was something innocent and naïve about her; somewhat happy but with a raw sense of gloominess, in search of a change of pace. That drew me closer to her, seeking to identify her emotional struggles. I pulled Rainey close and she laid in my arms as I caressed her back and shoulders. "I thought you might have gotten too deep in your pimping and forgot about me."

"What are you trying to do, find subliminal messages in my conversation? You're here with me, aren't you?"

"Yeah, I am. The only good thing about going away is coming back to you," she smiled. "I miss you."

"Why do you miss me?"

"Because it doesn't feel good when a hoe knows she is not a part of the equation. I was unable to do all the things that you had me do for you."

"Like what?"

"Like this," as she got on her knees, opened my zipper and slid her tongue from my navel to my penis. She sucked it deep, with pleasing intentions, like never before.

With her thumbs, she peeled the back rim of her jeans down over those voluptuous butt cheeks. Our hunger surged while we took off all our clothes. We became magnetized as she leaped into my arms and wrapped her legs around me. I carried her over to the bed, gently laying her down then entered her. From the point of impact, our souls clinched together. Pleasure was creeping up on us quickly, soaking the sheets as she held back her screams.

I reminded her, "Let yourself go." I sunk down into her, pounding and hitting it intensely. She swung her body forcefully. We clashed with such conviction as she moaned louder. Rainy threw her legs wider and allowed me to go deep as it tingled my penis.

Feeling the warmth and wetness, I continuously humped my back in a rhythmic motion as I held her firmly, creating a safe place while constantly penetrating her. Rainey raised off the bed. Her stomach tightened up like a drum as she squirted away and reached her final destination. It sounded like an enjoyable symphony. I thought, *'The incarceration seemed to enhance her beauty but hid the abuse.'*

"That was refreshing," Rainey said, as we laid there coming down off a natural high.

Taking advantage of that moment, she scooted closer to me and said, "Some nights I couldn't sleep and all I thought about was you. It felt like I was running but was going nowhere and I couldn't stop moving."

I thought to myself, *'That's what I considered a treadmill life, going nowhere fast.'* I was curious but uneasy about the incident she had with her step-father. I needed to be careful because saying the wrong words could jeopardize everything, so I kept quiet as a church mouse. I didn't want to seem overly anxious, like she was being harassed. My phone rang again, and Rainey said, "I want to thank you for turning off your pimping. That really made me feel special."

"You know, I wear my pimping like a banner so you should feel privileged."

She gave a little laugh and then her mood shifted as if something compelling took over her thoughts. She clung to me like there was nobody in the world but us. "Are you ever ashamed of what you do?"

"No, I always told myself, I accept the good and the bad in what I do. You see, most people want the comfort but never the consequences. I am willing to accept it all; the good, the bad and the beautiful."

"Do you ever get lost in the bad?"

"No, I embrace the challenges and learn from them." I kept the conversation at a slow trot while she laid in my arms. Her deep, sad eyes were overtaken by the untold memories. I'd seen that look on more than one occasion and didn't want to tear the scab off an unhealed wound. She confided in me. "I think some people hurt people deliberately."

I nodded my head in agreement. "Yeah, they do. Hurt people, hurt other people, but we gotta learn how to cope without allowing it to cause us to hate or self-destruct. It takes a great deal of courage to look at ourselves and grow from it." A tear drop fell from her eye and I whispered, "You know you can talk to me about anything," as I wiped her face. She sniffled. Her lips curled at the ends with the bottom one poked out, almost childlike.

"It's a lot of stuff on my mind."

"I'm sorry about the incident that happened to you. Do you feel like talking about it?"

"Yeah, I want to."

"Ok, what really happened? Start from the beginning."

In a soft, low voice she began, "Well, my step-father came into my life when I was about 7 years old and married my mother when I was 9. He was always nice to me. When my mother told me no, he would allow me to do certain things. When she said that I couldn't have candy, he would sneak and give it to me. If I asked him for money, he would give it to me and tell me not to tell my mom. He always asked for a kiss when he gave me things.

I'd kiss him on the lips and didn't think nothing of it. I thought it all was normal. When I turned 12, some neighborhood boys liked me. They sometimes carried my book bag home from school. My step-father got so mad and said the boys were getting fresh with me. He would make me come in the house and stay. He threatened to whoop me if he caught me around them. One day, he asked if I was having sex with them.

Another time, I was walking home from school in the same direction as those boys. My mom was at work. My step-father walked off the porch, grabbed me by my arm and walked me into the house. He pulled his belt from his waist and told me to take off my clothes, so I did. He said, 'Let me check you and make sure that those boys haven't messed with you.' He stuck his finger in my vagina and said, 'Yeah they have. You've been doing it. I'm gonna tell your mother.' I pleaded with him, 'Don't tell my mother. I haven't done anything.' He said, 'I'm gonna tear your hide up and you're not going outside.'

He put me over his knees and slapped my naked butt and said, 'I'm not gonna whoop you this time but I'm gonna be checking you. I won't tell your mother. Long as you don't mess around with those boys because I'll know.' He gave me a few dollars and said, 'Give me a kiss.' I gave him a kiss and felt like he'd done me a favor. I put my clothes back on, somewhat embarrassed since I had hair on my private area and my breast were getting big. I had just started my menstrual cycle too.

A short time later, I came home from school and he had been drinking. He accused me of being with those boys again. 'Take your clothes off. You're getting a whooping.' He stuck his finger in me and said, 'Ok you've been good.' He gave me some money while I was naked and said, 'Give me a kiss before you put on your clothes.' I gave him a kiss (always on the lips) and then got dressed. He asked me if I wanted some beer. I said yeah, and he handed me the can. I took 2 swallows and then he said, 'Don't tell your mother,' and I never told her.

Another time when my mom wasn't home, he had 2 cans of beer and asked me if I wanted to drink. I said yes, and he gave me a can. This time when I drank it, I spit it out. It was pee. He laughed and said, 'That was a joke. Don't tell your mother.' I went in the bathroom and brushed my teeth. He walked up to the door and said that he was sorry, handed me some money and told me to come into my room. When I walked in, he told me to take off my clothes so that he could check me to make sure that no boys had done anything.

He stuck 3 fingers in and asked me if it hurt. I was scared and I felt dirty and useless at that moment. I didn't say anything. He threw me on the bed, spread my legs, got on top of me and stuck his penis in. It stung and it was painful but I felt numb. I knew what he did was wrong, but I was too embarrassed to tell anybody. From that moment, I hated him. He warned me, 'Don't you tell your mom because you're going to go to the juvenile detention center for bad girls.'

He did it a few more times and each time I got more defiant and resistant. When I turned 14 years old, he tried it again but he struggled with me. I knew it was wrong and I wasn't going to let it happen again. He tried to pin me up against the kitchen cabinet. I bent his finger back and he slapped me. We didn't get along after that. Two years passed and he tried to do it again. The day that you dropped me off, he had been drinking.

He grabbed my face and tried to kiss me but I maneuvered away. I punched him in his back and we started fighting. I ran to the kitchen and got a knife out of the holder on the counter. He slapped and punched me again and I took a step back. Then I warned him, 'Hit me again and I'm gonna stab you."

The tension seemed to wrap around her chest, tight fitted, almost suffocating her. I positioned myself very still and waited for the smoke to clear before she continued.

"He lunged towards me again and I stabbed him in his chest."

It was like she was giving an acceptance speech that made peace with the whole situation. I could feel the fibers of her soul as her sadness penetrated my senses. It was an unfamiliar space that was on a different scale. At that moment, it started raining outside and we could hear the drops pinging against the window. The world seemed to feel her pain as well. Rainey pulled so close to me that I could hear her heart beat. I've had a couple of girls who experienced situations that left them in deep, dark places but I've never had to take myself this low to understand their pain with this type of calamity that affects your mind.

There seemed to be no safe method to what I was about to say, but I had to know what I was dealing with. My attempt was to infiltrate the mysteries of a hurt heart. Her spirit could wind up being colder than a winter wind, leading her emotions down a dead-end street. Here goes nothing. I raised up, looked her straight in the eyes as if I was transferring positive energy and said, "I just had a notion of what we're dealing with. This is reality. The world has a way of schooling us and sometimes it's not pretty, even shameful and unfair. It's called life. Making peace with yourself determines your destiny so whatever happens now is a choice. Rainey, listen close, allow these words to be nourishing. You're beautiful, smart, intelligent and a die-hard soldier. What you did was protect yourself and that's no mistake. Don't let this situation mean more to you than you mean to yourself."

Her eyes went tender and a pleasant smile came upon her face.

"Wow, you believe in me more than I believe in myself. So, if you are saying these things about me, then they must be true. I can get through this for sure. The only question is, will it be with you? Where do you think that we'll be in 2 years?"

"Somewhere greater than this. It's only been 1½ years and look at where we are," I said a little snazzy, poetic rhyme to cheer her up. "We're about to change the game and you're a part of the plan so take my hand, as the sun shines upon your hair cause baby this I swear. Flowers will bloom when we enter a room, with our style and flare there's no doubt, roses will sprout and blossom up everywhere."

Her morale appeared to be on an upward float as the conversation about her past faded away. "Earthquake, you really make a girl feel safe, a force to be reckoned with but I know you've gotta turn your pimping back on."

She giggled, perked up and said, "You should be a poet."

"Tomorrow, you're going to be a happy hooker, back at work so relax tonight, ok."

She looked at me as if she was ready for whatever. "I don't mind. I'll go tonight if you want me too."

"Naw, rest up." I felt like I'd patched an open wound that hadn't healed but I made the best out of it.

She pouted. "I hate to be shut out. I'm going to try not to let my imagination run wild or my emotions get in the way of us."

"Rainey, sometimes the imagination and emotions can be a tricky accommodation so, use them wisely my dear."

Before I got dressed, I pinched her on her jaw as she playfully bit at my wrist. I could see it. She fought not to let the past interfere with the present as I walked out of the door. I left her at the hotel for the night. One thing that I learned is to understand where Rainey came from, to be sensitive to her needs. Every woman's mode is different. I had to recognize how each of them were shaped in order to adapt to their behavior. Every time I connected to their pain, they responded to my style. When I made a woman feel her importance to me, she wanted to prove that she was who I believed she was. This strategy in my pimping seemed to accelerate to a higher level.

The next night, the summer stars were back out and the warm city breeze was no disappointment. It was the perfect night for hoeing. I was 10 deep and Rainey was rearing to get back to work. Lola used my second Caddy to get herself and 5 of my girls to work while I dropped off the rest of them. My phone rang as I pulled up to the Stroll to let Rainey out.

"Hello, this is Samantha. We're at a gas station in Illinois, about 2 hours away."

"Ok, that's cool."

"We'll call you when we get closer."

I went back to the house within the hour and Samantha called again. I wondered why Becky didn't ask to speak to me. Come to think of it, I hadn't talked to her during their whole trip. That was strange. Maybe I was overthinking it, but things felt oddly peaceful. I heard the revved-up engine with Curtis Blow playing and saw the headlights as they pulled into the driveway.

I opened the door and walked outside as they unloaded the car and noticed a few extra bags. Then I saw something moving in the backseat, so I focused in, thinking, "What is that?"

Becky reached into the car and pulled out a kid. I walked up to her and said, "Where did y'all get this little chocolate, curly head baby?" She looked dumb founded as she explained her far-fetched story.

"Oh! When we made it to Kentucky, my mom complained that my baby daddy kept coming over asking for his child and inquired about where I was. When I got home, he came over uninvited and clowned so bad that my mom called the police. He was talking crazy to the officers and they locked him up. My mother told me to take my baby with me so I had no choice. Earthquake, this is Elijah. Elijah say hi."

His big shiny eyes looked up at me. With a short wave from his tiny hand, he said, "Hi."

I was thinking, '*What type of pimping is this? Does she think we're going to be an interracial family? No wonder Becky didn't call me. She knew I wouldn't have let them come back.*' I looked down at the little fella and said, "What's up shorty?"

My mind went into an exasperated momentum. I had to think of something quick. Oh yeah, *let me call Ms. C (Lola's mom) right now.* I got her on the phone and said, "Ms. C I have another toddler for you. Can I bring him over?"

"Sure. How old is he?"

"About 2 or 3."

"Does he wear pampers?"

"No."

"Bring him over."

My next thought was, *'They gonna bring a baby here, both of them are going to Cicero immediately.'* I said, "Dig, listen up. Tonight, y'all going to work in a club so get everything that you need for the joint and the Stroll."

We arrived at Ms. C's and I introduced Becky and Samantha to her. "This is Ms. C. She babysits for us. She has Lola's daughter and Pow Wow's girl, Janet's two kids. Both Poochie-Slim and Diamond have broads with little sons that are here also." Business was so good for Ms. C that she rented the garden apartment in her building and converted it to a day care. She even hired her granddaughter as an assistant teacher. "They're open 24-hours a day so this is where Elijah will be. You can visit him whenever you like."

I paid Ms. C $200, the overnight rate for the week, and we headed to the Dreamland in Cicero. When we got there, the girls went in and were hired on the spot. Eagerly, they came out and said, "We told the owner that our man was outside waiting to confirm if we could work." I told the girls to go back in.

"What time do they close?"

"They close at 4:30 a.m.," Samantha answered.

"Ok, I'll be back." I drove south to the house and Reno was home. "Yo Reno, I took the Kentucky girls to the Dreamland and they got hired."

"Earthquake, you're about to get a taste of club money now."

The Dreamland

Reno and I kicked it until it was time for the girls to get off work, so we headed that way, in separate cars. There were a few pimps waiting outside when we arrived. Reno's 3 girls got into his car while Samantha and Becky got into mine. They both handed me my trap. Becky made $300 and Samantha had $250. They gave me the rundown on how the set up was. It was a pretty good night.

Becky said, "I counted 20 rooms in the back of the club. It's a little bit different from Kentucky. They're hoeing like crazy. They have 10 small rooms with chairs and a timer on the door. The lights come on promptly in 10 minutes, costing $75. Their 10 larger rooms have cot beds with mattresses on the floor. The cost is $150 for 20 minutes. The house takes 50%. Tricks pay the house first, then they can tip the girls directly. After working the week, the owner shares his portion of the backroom money with the girls on Saturdays, giving them another 10%."

"Well, sound nice. You can't beat that with a baseball bat."

Becky tapped my shoulder. "The owner asked if you wanted to bring more girls to his joint."

I didn't realize how lucrative the club business could be. I was strapped to the conversation like a parachute on a jumper. It glided into my forethought, broadening my ideas. "Yeah, tell him that I'm bringing 4 more girls tomorrow." I can measure the action and determine which one is more lucrative. Within 3 hours, Geisha got fired from the joint. That was no surprise, I was just testing the waters with my roughest chick.

When I drove up, she was standing outside in front of the place and got in the Caddy. A guy in his early sixties walked out of the club and waved at my car. He was average height with blue eyes, straight, short brown hair, neatly tapered around the sides and back. This slender white guy stepped up to my Caddy and said, "Are you Earthquake?"

"Yes sir."

"I'm George, the manager." He looked in the car. "You have 5 thoroughbreds but this one (he pointed at Geisha) is a wild horse."

"I understand George. I'll have to tighten the reins on her."

"Can you bring another one tomorrow because everybody seems to like your girls? They got good manners and that shows that they have a seasoned pimp." he asked.

I'm thinking, 'Who is this white guy to tell me this?' He sounded like he knew a thing or two. George thumped his nose like a player. "Yeah Earthquake, I used to be a pimp back in the day. I even got a black wife and 3 black kids. I know the game." It was something about him that I liked.

"Hey George, you have any problems, here's my number. Let me know."

We shook hands then I pulled off. Geisha quickly adjusted her attitude, purposely trying not to annoy me. She sucked up, gripping for leniency, pleading her case. "Earthquake, they were all on my neck, crowding my space, I couldn't even breathe. That's why I don't like clubs." While her eyes were focused straight ahead, she glimpsed at me from the corner of her eyes to see my response. I stayed silent, not letting her know what I was thinking. Besides, I knew she was all about territory and conquering the land. The club environment wasn't for that type of hooker. I understood her place but thought I'd give it a try, just to make sure.

I didn't get upset about her being territorial. It wasn't necessary for me to try and change her, taking a warrior and making her into a princess, so I kept her exactly the way she was. Riding from the club, Geisha said, "When I was standing in front of the Dreamland, 10 cars stopped. They were trying to turn a date with me. You should let me work in Cicero. I bet there's money over here on Cicero Ave. but there aren't any hoes. The hookers are 2 blocks down, on the South side of the same street in Chicago."

"Ok let's see, you might be right. I'll be back at 4:30 a.m." I swung over to the curb and she got out.

I got back to Dreamland at 4:00 a.m. and parked in the club's lot. Geisha called.

"I just saw you drive past. Come and get me."

"Where are you?"

"Down the street on the Chicago side of Cicero Ave."

"Ok, walk down here."

"I can't. The Cicero police just let me go. There's no prostituting on the streets in that town. You can't even walk like you're a hoe. I had to screw two white officers in a back room of the police station to get out of jail. I don't ever want to get locked up in that city again."

I rode down the street and scooped her up.

It all clicked. I thought, *'I get it. All the strip joints out here are tied in with the police. There is still an advantage since the girls are on the inside, there are no law enforcement problems and there is heightened security.'* All my broads came over to the car when they got off work and we drove to the hotel to meet Lola and the girls that she picked up. Everybody's traps, both in the club and on the Strolls, were about even. Not bad for a Wednesday.

The next night, I sent The Waitress to the club and created a 2-week travel rotation for my 14 hoes. They switched up, working the club, Strolls and traveling out of town. Geisha was the only exception. She continued to work the Strolls. As I got more familiar with Cicero, I ventured into the other two strip joints and my broads worked there as well. All the clubs had similar setups, but the Dreamland was the money maker, so I used the other 2 establishments to break in new girls and fly by night hoes that I had no real interest in being with.

Money and Static

My regime was in full flow. Becky drove the girls who worked at Dreamland and Lola dropped all the hoes off on the Strolls. That left me time to police my business. I got to relax on 1 or 2 occasions but most nights I was up and at 'em. With my girls out of the car, it wasn't obvious that I was pimping hard. Lola called. "Earthquake, I took Amelia and Natalie to the 111th Street Stroll and Rainey and Geisha to 45th. Me and the rest of the girls are up north on Lincoln Ave."

"How is it going up there?"

"Well, it's vice night so we're ducking and dodging, but we're cool."

"Ok, be careful."

Right after that, Rainey called, "Sergeant Bill told us we gotta go."

"Where is Geisha?"

"Right here."

"I'm on my way to get y'all." I pulled up on 45th and Geisha got in the car. "Where is Rainey?"

"She went on a date." We drove around until she returned. We picked her up and headed to the 111th Street Stroll.

Rainey said, "Can we stop and get some juice?" I pulled over to the gas station and she got out of the back seat. When she went inside, Geisha said, "I'm about to get me some gum," as she sashayed out of the car. As Geisha and Rainey walked towards the Caddy, Rainey ran and jumped in the front seat before Geisha could think about it. Geisha looked stunned and calmly got in the back. I glanced over at Rainey as if she'd lost her mind.

I thought about the change in her behavior and how she'd been conducting herself lately. I noticed she was more defensive even the way she stood. At first only one leg bowed back, now she curved both.

"Hey Rainey, you know we don't do that girl," Geisha said.

Rainey carried a grim smile on her face, slightly taunting her. "Hey Geisha, you move your meat, you lose your seat," as she chuckled.

"It won't be so funny if I snatched you out the front seat and slung you in the back," Geisha said.

Rainey went from 1 to 100 just that fast, turned completely around in the seat and said, "I wish you would try it!"

I intervened as if I was judge and jury, "If y'all don't stop, I'm going to bust both of you in the mouth then throw you out of the car. Now put that in your peace pipes and smoke it!"

Rainey murmured under her breath as I drove off. There was a bitter silence in the air and you could feel the tension. It took me back to Rainey's situation with her step-father. It appeared that she released her pain in a violent way. I wasn't sure and tried to be understanding. She also had a peculiar scent, the kind of scent when you have been free basing.

I think her mom should've had the big girl 'stranger danger' talk with her when she was a small child. Rainey was just innocent, inexperienced and uninformed. Without that situation happening, she probably wouldn't have these issues. There was a loud yell. Rainey rapidly patted the back of her head to relieve the sizzling heat from her burning hair. I smelled the gritty scent as smoke lingered in the air. I looked trying to see were the hair caught on fire and saw a lighter in Geisha 's hand.

I reached back there, took the lighter out of Geisha 's hand and threw it out the window. She sat there like a little bad demon. I said, "Both of you must want to get choked out. We're about to go to the house before we head to the 111th Stroll."

Rainey was crying, "Earthquake look what she did to my hair. She burned it. Can I fight Geisha? Please, can I?"

"No, I'm gonna beat both of y'all."

"Please let me fighter her. I'm begging you."

Geisha seconded that notion, "Yeah, let us fight please."

"Ok, I'm about to take you to the house and let y'all fight. Afterwards, there should be no hard feelings and if I see any at all, I'm going to shave your heads and send you back to work!"

They cheered but I couldn't let Geisha get away with that. I had to put her at a disadvantage. We arrived at the house, I went in the basement, move the furniture back, got my mini bat out the laundry room and said, "Stay in the center girls. Before you fight, I'm telling you, y'all got five minutes. When I say go, fight!"

They both took off their clothes and were ready. I walked by Geisha, grabbed her right hand and banged it twice with the mini-bat. She hollered. I said, "Go." Rainey exploded into Geisha like a tornado, while Geisha threw one hand upper-cuts as Rainey was gaining momentum, they locked together and slung each other to the floor. Geisha started using both of her hands and threw Rainey off her and got on top. She flipped Geisha around as they stood to their feet, slugging it out. Geisha threw Rainey down.

I couldn't break it up with Geisha on top but if Rainey broke free, I could because it would look like she held her own. I stopped it when Rainey got loose and took the last swing. "That's enough!" They both were breathing hard. "Now, kiss and make up. If you don't, I'm about to shave your heads."

"I'm sorry," Geisha said.

"Me too," Rainey said.

I made them hug and kiss each other on the jaw. "Now, go take a hoe bath so I can get y'all back to work."

I kept my eye locked on Rainey as the days went by. While policing my hookers, I pulled up on her. She handed me $30. I'm thinking, 'It's a good thing I was cruising down the Stroll to see if I saw anything unusual.' The sweat was beading off Rainey's nose and forehead, but it was 69 degrees, the middle of September. I said, "What's going on out here? Why is your money so short?"

"It slow baby. They're not biting too much tonight. The tricks are all cheap. I might leave and go on Cottage Grove. Is that ok?"

"Why don't you stay with your wife-n-laws?"

"Because, I have a couple of regulars over there so I'll let a trick take me. It's slow but it's about to flow."

"Ok, handle your business."

That morning, Rainey didn't call or show up. I was convinced she was out of pocket. All bad seeds must go. That next day she called. "Hey, I'm at the room."

Before she could tell another clumsy lie, I said, "Beneath all that baggage, I would find a nice girl but, I don't have time to shovel her out. I have to many other diamond mines to dig. Gather your things. You're outta here!" I went to the hotel and fired two more girls for lack of performance as well.

While still at the hotel, St. Luke called.

"Hey Saint."

"Listen, the police are still looking for Geisha. They have a warrant for her arrest for that shooting last year. The police must've found out that she's back around. Now my Detective friend is going to help with this. Geisha 's birthday is at the end of October, so next month she will be 17.

If she goes in now, she won't be printed. Most likely she'll be released because my daughter is a minor. If Geisha waits until after her birthday, they'll fingerprint her and give her a huge bond. Then she'll have a record. Let her clear it up now so it will be off her record."

"Ok, you want me to let Geisha go to Juvenile?"

"Yes, it's for her own good."

Suddenly I felt a heavy weight on my shoulder. I was as dizzy as getting hit with a roundhouse kick that I didn't see coming.

"Bring Geisha here in the morning so I can take her to the police station tomorrow."

After conducting my business, I went straight home and called Geisha to my room. "Geisha, I talked to your mom. She asked me to bring you to her tomorrow."

"I know, we just talked. My mom said that I'll be out in a couple of days, no longer than a week and I'm good with that."

"I'll take you to her tomorrow morning."

The next day, I took Geisha to her mother and dropped her off. About 5 hours later, St. Luke called. "They're holding her until next month. She goes to court on her birthday, then it will be all over."

"A whole month, I guess."

"You can go see her. I'll let you use my son's name. Here's his info but it's going to work out fine. You will get her back but it's better this way, ok?"

"I trust what you tell me St. Luke. You're right. It's going to be all good."

I was back down to 10 broads. That night after everybody went to work, I was meeting the crew on 55th Street at one of our local spots. It was called the ET Lounge and we used it as our headquarters. As I was getting out of the car, I saw a fine white chick. She unfolded right before my eyes. A white cloud of joy floated straight into my path. Her light golden complexion matched the autumn leaves, it was like a scene you wouldn't believe.

It was about 67 degrees, the air lukewarm with the wind slightly blowing. The stars were out and the avenue was calm. The night was just right when I got out of the car. No one seemed to be walking in my direction but her. I stood still as if I ruled the world, with my hands on my waist while I waited for her to enter my space. I stared as if I was possessing her and she looked with a gaze that shouted for my attention. She fell into a hypnotic daze. Her eyes sparkled in a trance and there wasn't much left to say.

This appeared to be a moment meant to happen, a long time coming. She approached, and I said, "Hello White Cloud."

She lifted her eyes, "Hi, my name is Chrissy, but I do like White Cloud."

"Do you know what time it is?" I asked pointing at her watch. "It's 10:30."

Shaking my head, "No it's time for you to get with me. I don't know where you came from, but this is where you supposed to be. You feel me?"

She stumbled over her words. "And your name is?"

"Earthquake is my name."

"I never met an Earthquake so charming. They normally do considerable damage to a city, right?"

I went straight in for the kill.

"Yeah, but I shake up minds. You call it charming, I call it protection. That's what I do for you and all my girls." I read her eyes and her body language told me she was all in. Chrissy's face lit up with an expression of a child opening a gift on Christmas morning.

"What brings you this way?" I asked, curiously.

"I'm headed to a friend's house to spend the night. We used to live near here a few years ago but I haven't seen her for a while so I'm going to pay her a visit."

That was funny. She gave me a spill (rhetoric). Chrissy appeared to think fast and with her good looks, she had all the qualifications.

"Why should you visit your friend when you can be with me?"

She batted her eyes which let me know she was attracted to me. I extended my hand. Chrissy reached, held on and we walked back to the car.

"Let's get something to eat. What do you like?"

"I'm not choosey."

That was a great sign, indicating that she was open-minded.

"Let's get Chinese food and then I'll get you a room at the hotel where some of my girls are."

"That's fine."

We got our carry-out, went to the hotel and ate. Her eating habits revealed she was kind but stubborn. She opened her mouth wider than necessary with each spoonful which let me know that she would overextend herself. Experience taught me that women who ate with a tight mouth, barely getting their food in, were stingy. She used her fingers to scoop the food on the fork when she ate. That meant White Cloud didn't mind getting her hands dirty.

"Hey White Cloud, what's your story? Now, why were you really going over your girlfriend's house?"

"Well, when my mother died 4 years ago, my 54-year-old dad married a 26-year-old piece of white trash and she thinks she's me and my little brother's mom. She treats me like I'm Cinderella, trying to make me do all the housework and cook while she does nothing but boss my dad around. She's out of control. Now that slut is trying to turn my father against me."

I analyzed her situation.

"I see what the problem is. You're coming into your womanhood. It's difficult for 2 women to live in the same house when they become territorial. Her job is to comfort your father while your quest is to get attention from him and that appears to be a conflict of interest. Now the script has changed. Your prince charming has come to your rescue. The book closes and you finish with me, a happy ending!" I clapped my hands, "Bravo!"

She laughed, "Earthquake what's your story?"

"I'm 11 deep and bigger than life and you're my new supporting actress. Can you play the part?"

"Of course, I'm ready right now but how does your story end?"

"It doesn't, it keeps going. Tell me what you want out of life?"

"I don't ask for much, just being here is enough. That suits me fine."

I could tell she was ready to prove herself right then.

"White Cloud come sit on the bed next to me."

She got out the chair, moving as if she was walking on air, then sat on the bed, leaned in and we kissed. She melted in my warm, comforting embrace like she was dreaming but her body signaled that she wanted more. I heard her body language loud and clear as I pulled back. "White Cloud, I noticed the fact that you're fast on your feet. Most people who have those qualities are salesmen, con artists or thieves. Which one are you?"

"Whichever one you want me to be."

I put my first 3 fingers up and said, "All 3."

She nodded her head and said, "Ok, I will. Now answer this, how did you get so fast on your feet?" then relaxed and resumed her position in my arms.

"Well, when I was young, where I come from we use to signify (tease) on each other. So, when someone cracked a joke about you, the kids ranked how fast and strong you came back. If the response wasn't good, you were considered a goofball and became the butt of all jokes. Kids are cruel, huh?"

She laughed, as I studied her. One thing for sure, I didn't have to intellectually paint a beautiful picture for some reason. My attributes and lifestyle presented me in a way that she was already receptive to. An hour later, I sealed the deal.

Afterwards, White Cloud and I went to Lena's house for her wardrobe makeover. Lena compiled all the fall gear in size 7. The vibrant colors included brown, orange, and dark green leather jackets, turtle necks, wool pants and those 6-inch wedge heals which really did the trick.   After putting all the garments and shoes in 2 duffle bags, right before we walked out of the door White Cloud said, "Nice meeting you Lena."

I looked at White Cloud, "This is my enforcer. If you're bad, you will see her again."

Lena gave her a cold stare momentarily and nodded her head goodbye. We rode to the house, went to my room and placed most of her clothes in my chest-of- drawers.

I told her the whole lay out of my operation and gave the good news. "White Cloud, you will be sleeping in my room for a little while." All new girls got 5 days straight to be with me. When my other broads arrived home, everybody appeared to like her. That next morning, I took her to J-Hawk's beauty shop which was next door to the boutique, to get her hair colored golden blonde. I walked back into the boutique. "Hey J-Hawk, how do you like my new whitey?"

"Boy, she sweeter than bear meat. How many girls you got now?"

My smile told the story. "I got 12 working, 6 white and 6 black."

"Earthquake you got a dozen eggs. Reno and Lucky just left. They just bought themselves mink coats. My guy Rafael is selling them wholesale. I told him that you wanted a few. Winter is creeping up fast you and your girls will be needing them."

"Ok Uncle J-Hawk, I want 7 coats. One for me and 6 for my star players, who've been with me the longest. That will motivate them and the new hoes too. Then I'll come back for 6 more. Tell him I'll be back tomorrow before my broads go to work."

"Ok partner, he wants $3,000 for each one."

I patted my pocket, "Let him know I'll have $19,000 for the 7. If he doesn't want it, just call before 3:00 p.m. tomorrow."

White Cloud walked into the boutique looking hotter than fish grease. The blonde hair enhanced her look so much more. On the third day, we went by the Strolls to check everything out so she would know the do's and don'ts. We went back to the house, picked up some money then called Lola. When she answered, I said, "Go get Wonnie, Amelia, The Waitress and Jewel. Meet me up at J-Hawk's right now."

When I got there, Rafael had a variety of minks displayed in all sizes. I selected one. "Here White Cloud, try this on." She twirled around as if she knew it would be hers someday. My girls walked in all bright eyed and bushy tailed. Everyone spoke to J-Hawk and started trying on minks. My broads were shocked. You could smell the rich, fresh new scent and feel the arrogance filled the room with their heads held high. They sashayed with sophistication, caressing their coats with such endearment.

My hoes were so charged up. They were happy hookers ready to go to work. I paid the guy and we left. After that, you couldn't pull White Cloud away from me with a crowbar. She was in for life. That fourth day, it was time. I took White Cloud to work. I said, "You're going to the Lincoln Ave. Stroll. I gave all the instruction you need. You must take it from here. When you get to $450, call me and I'll pick you up." The time was 9:30 p.m. when I pulled off.

It wasn't long, about 11:45 p.m., my phone rang.

"Hello."

"Hi, this is White Cloud. Are you coming to get me or do you want me to keep working?"

"How much money you got?"

"I have $450 like you told me, so I called."

"I'm on my way." One thing, I'm not greedy. I was satisfied. She was off to a great start. She fit right in with the team.

Fall season was coming in, the weather was changing and most nights were comfortable and beautiful. It was the last of the Indian summer and Jack Frost was on his way. This was my favorite time of year, not too cold and not too hot. Besides, it was the 25th day of October and Geisha was being released today.

That morning, I headed down to juvenile court where I met St. Luke. I was anxious but stayed cool as St. Luke and I waited for the court clerk to call Geisha 's case. When they did, she walked up to the bench and stood in front of the Judge. He read the transcript and said, "Time considered severed. I'm dismissing this off your record. Anything after this remember, you're an adult and you will go to jail. Now behave yourself," as he hit his gavel.

Geisha came out a few minute later, hugged her mom as she peeped over at me. "Hey mom, I'm glad to see you, so let's go." We talked with St. Luke for a few minutes and then jetted out. We got in the car, drove off and stopped a mile down. "What do you want for your birthday?"

"For a start," she kissed me forcefully. That let me know I was still her king.

"Happy birthday baby." I touched her chin softly, guiding her face back in my view. "Wait a minute, I got something for you." I got out of the car, opened the trunk, pulled out the mink and handed it to her as I got back in. "I bought my star players a coat and I didn't forget about you."

"Thank you, baby. I love my coat," as she reached over and put her arms around me, squeezing my neck.

After that, we went to the house and I introduced her to White Cloud. Geisha looked at her from head to toe, sizing her up. "Hey, I know you heard about me. I'm his tough girl."

"I guess, he has a lot of girls. It's hard to keep up with them," she grunted, "but nice meeting you anyway. Welcome home."

All the other broads ran up to Geisha and hugged her. They were talking all at once, giving her the run down on who, what and where. There was something good about hoes getting along and not interrupting the flow. Pimping is always a group effort rather than an individual try. Anybody thinking it could work on its own would be sadly mistaken.

Geisha resumed her position back at work that evening after we had a rendezvous. She remained the lone-wolf of the team. Geisha knew I had high expectations from her, a nice bankroll, the kind of trap that every pimp dreams of. Seeing as she was fresh back on the Stroll, I gave her a slight bit more attention and kept my reins tight. Lola dropped Geisha and two others off on 111th Stroll and all 3 of them went to 45th Street.

At about 12:00 midnight I breezed through the 111th Street Stroll unexpectedly. From a distance, I saw Geisha with another broad and it looked like a car was trailing them. The vehicle was accompanied by 2 of the most notorious pimps on that Stroll. They had hoes out there working. I thought to myself, *'Let me interrupt this shake down.'* I pulled up beside the pimp's car as I did a peek-a-boo cockblock. By the looks on their faces, something diabolical was in the mist.

I pulled next to the car, and said, "Dag fellas, thought y'all was the police the way y'all pulled up on my girl."

The other hoe with Geisha caught a quick date, got in a trick's car and pulled off. One of the pimps' sort of reluctantly said, "We was just checking making sure the other hoe was with you. She's been drifting around like a renegade for a couple of weeks. We weren't sure she was with you. So, we rode down on her. We know most of your girls but didn't think that one was with you."

It was evident by the frown on my face she wasn't with me.

"That's not one of mine. Did the hoe claim to be with me?"

One of them said in a disturbed voice, "Naw, Geisha said she was her wife-in-law."

Furiously, I said, "Get in the car Geisha!"

As soon as she sat down, I gave her a hard slap right in front of them to keep vengeance off their minds.

One of them said, "Earthquake, we respect you man but if Geisha wasn't with you, we'd deal with her in the worst way. But you our main man," then they pulled off.

I looked at Geisha, "You know that those fellas are a hoes worst nightmare? Did that juvenile place damage your brain? Don't ever do that again. Who is that hoe anyway?"

Geisha held her jaw with her eye's tight as her voice quivered.

"She just a little young renegade chick trying to make a few dollars. I used to see her every now and then, that's all."

"Go back to work."

Later, I met up with my pimp buddies at the ET Lounge. Afterwards we went to have breakfast at this new restaurant right on the 111th Street Stroll. There were a few lounges located around there so they had a nice crowd of hungry drinkers. Lucky, Pow Wow, Reno, Poochie Slim, Bodie, Diamond, Terrell and two of his young homies went inside. The restaurant was lit up like a theater, white table clothes, black chairs, real formal.

We chose a table close to where a group of women were sitting. I sensed some attention coming our way, barely noticing the conversation the guys were having. I was too busy reading a girl's eyes as she looked my way.

"What are you doing?" Lucky asked.

"I am communicating with her through her eyes. Luck, look at how her eyes are blinking. Her pupils are big which means she's gentle and since they're blinking a lot, she's attracted to me."

There was a long pause as he faded from the conversation and then asked, "Earthquake what are you? A modern-day Swami?"

Everybody started laughing. I gave him a little smirk while maintaining my focus on the girl. I said, "Let me teach y'all something about the pimp game that nobody else knows." They all focused on my words with pure concentration.

"Ok witchdoctor, give it to us," Reno yelled out.

Everybody at our table had their attention on me.

"You can tell a lot about a person by what they say. I've learned that the power is in the tongue in many ways. It causes a variety of eating habits and is responsible for several functions. It's a link to your emotions that carries signals and barriers. For instance, when a person is stressed out they eat more. When a woman has her menstrual cycle with cramps, the brain tells her tongue to crave chocolate. The tongue plays a significant role in certain personality traits. When a person grows old, they begin to chew cautiously, the tongue becomes stronger because it's used more to push food because the teeth are weaker. Even Gram's personality traits were reflective of the soft foods she ate. I watched her eat and then she explained that she ate soft foods because it was easier for her to chew and swallow. I watched other older people and noticed that they also ate slower, becoming more careful which makes their lives slow down.

Now, for young people, the teeth are strong but the tongue is more careless and if not careful, one can bite it or their cheek or lips while chewing. They move swiftly and live their lives fast, usually reacting before thinking. Of the twelve women that I observed, seven had these characteristics. These seven were impulsive but smart.

I'm gonna give y'all a bonus tip since everybody's enjoying this. The powers in the tongue when you kiss a woman, the tongue can tell the brain to release certain endorphins that can attract a woman to you. The tongue can release pleasure to the body like no other part of the body. It can also release pain like no part; especially words."

Lucky said to the waitress who was taking our order, as he pointed to me. "This pimp Wizard, an idiot savant. He's retarded when it comes to academics, but he's a genius when it comes to reading people's body language, including your driving, eating and even your eyeballs. Then he can do an assessment and tell you everything about you. Now, bring me a sheet so he can't watch me while I eat."

I looked over at Luck, poked him in the chest and said, "This pimp Bozo. He always clowning." We all laughed and enjoyed the moment.

"My little homie right here has a gang of cute little chicks," Terrell said.

I looked at him. He was about 16 years old, a nice looking young dude.

"Is that right shorty? You got all the girls chasing you?"

"Yeah, I got a way with women, you know. Imma be a bona fide pimp like you," he told me.

I smiled. "Little homie listen, just because you're a good cook don't mean you can open a restaurant. You gotta know about the business aspect and be capable of running it fluently. There's an art to knowing how to treat your employees and be able to adequately handle problems with customers. You have to conduct routine inspections to ensure that your product is always clean. You gotta earn a street permit, provide security for your staff and deal with a lot of legal mumbo-jumbo. You must be a one-man team and a team player at the same time.

Because you have a way with women don't mean you can do what I do, li'l shorty. It's a 24-7 job. It's like love. You know when you see it and if you get close, you should sense little cues to pick up on her body language.

See, I have a mental check list. One look at a broad and I can determine if she has a place with me. Speed is important. You only have a matter of seconds to get with a chick, so you should know when it fits or when it doesn't. Next, you gotta be quick on your feet and strategize an approach. Lastly, you better give her a reason to say yes. You must be able to check all these columns to be effective.

Then know your limit. Don't get bigger than you can control. Get too big and you lose control. Remember, every time you add a hoe there comes a problem now you must create a solution."

I was schooling shorty but also refreshing my game.

"My dude doesn't ever be faking. This here is what I call Earthquaking!" Terrell said.

"Your pimping is magnificent and you make it look easy," the shorty said.

"Hard work makes everything look easy. You gotta be up for the challenge and be ready to deal with the consequences."

After the fun and games, we all got into our cars and left. Lucky rode with me. Before we could get off the Stroll, the police pulled behind me like they were stalking us. We knew the routine. The cops approached the car.

"Get out Earthquake," and we did.

"Hands behind your back," as they cuffed me and Lucky like we were two common criminals. The second officer got into the driver's seat of my vehicle. The first officer put us in their squad car while his partner followed us to the police station in my Caddy.

"You guys are going to jail. The Sergeant gave a command to lock up every pimp that we see," he said.

"Officer, you know me. I just came from having breakfast."

"We know, but two lowlife pimps rope tied the hands of a young girl to the back bumper of their Cadillac and dragged her a block, horrifically burning off one side of her butt, half of her arm and a part of her face, leaving a blood trail 15ft long. She's in intensive care and may not live. We know you didn't do it, but these are the orders."

When we arrived in front of the police station, the 2nd officer got out of my Caddy and pressed the alarm on the key ring to lock the doors. He walked over to the squad car while the 1st officer pulled us out of the back seat. The 2nd officer twirled my keys in his hand, possessing them as if he was the owner. He looked baffled and patronize me with his words. "I work hard every day, sometimes overtime to serve and protect scum like you and I don't even have a Cadillac like this. You don't even have a real job. Got all those girls working for you. Pimping ain't even legal. Do you know that?"

I thought to myself, '*I can't help that you ain't got no swagga,*' as I blurted out respectfully, "Yes sir. I know," always keeping my temper intact. The officers put Lucky and me in the same cell. There were a few other pimps locked up as well and the word in the streets was that the police had a lead on who did it.

We were released that afternoon. The story spread like wildfire and became national news, making it hard times for a pimp. The Strolls were hot as cayenne pepper even though they had a suspect in custody, so I stayed away for a few days. He was one of those notorious pimps who approached Geisha. She better be glad they respected me, it could have been her too.

A few days passed and Halloween had finally come. The Waitress had her day off, so we got sharp to go to an Earth, Wind, and Fire concert. After I scooped her up, we headed to their hotel to meet up with Luck, Poochie-Slim and a couple of their girls.

On the drive, The Waitress was so hyped that she wiggled in her seat. I smelled the fragrance of her perfume. It was so pleasant that I complimented her. "You must've taken a bath."

"Stop playing. You know I did," she said sarcastically.

"For real though, you smell really nice."

Her mouth stretched, forcing her teeth to show from being flattered. "You really think I smell good?"

"Yep!"

We were ready to have a good time when I saw a glare through my rearview mirror as I tilted my head back to get a better view. It was those familiar flashing lights of a police car pulling me over. Here come the cops again.

"This is becoming an everyday routine," I said. We pulled over. The White officers cuffed both of us put us in the back seat.

"You Earthquake huh? We're going to take you and your girl for a ride you maggot." The officer tailed the other one.

The Waitress looked over at me, "Baby, where are they taking us?"

I could see a slight panic in her eyes. To keep her from worrying, I stayed calm and said, "I guess they don't have nothing better to do." As we suspiciously began detouring down back roads, I started hoping this wasn't a murder plot. The officer started making racial comments. We drove up to a graveyard. The other officer trailed him to the end of the graveyard then got back in the car and went around to the front.

"Get out," he demanded as he took the cuffs off us. "If you want to get out of here, your car is on the other side of this graveyard. To get to it, you have to go through to the other side then jump the fence or else."

The Waitress experienced the bitter taste of brutality. Her attitude began to be of a defiant nature. The fear engaged in her eyes was like watching a horror movie but I wasn't surprised by their behavior.

"All right whore, let's go," the officer said.

Her caramel skin turned peach red and her voice went up 10 octaves screeching into a high pitch.

"I'm not going in there."

"What's the big deal you scared of rats? There are more scarier things out there than a rodent."

I'm thinking, 'Ok Earthquake, now you have to see what The Waitress is made of.'

"This come with your lifestyle. This is where your kind end up," the officer said.

She looked at me. "Is this some kind of Halloween joke? Tell me it is." The Waitress pulled her collar up around her neck hunching her shoulders. I shook my head in a way to let her know, 'Don't be in denial this come with the game.' The graveyard wasn't the fear it was what was waiting for us in the graveyard.

"Your keys are in the front seat so walk across and get your car but you have to jump that fence. Now go ahead," the officer instructed.

I'm thinking, 'I'd rather take a chance on the graveyard then with them.'

"Come on Waitress, let's get this over with."

Her teeth chattered. I definitely wasn't planning on going to jail tonight and it being Halloween didn't make it any better.

The Police hollered, "Watch out for the Ghost and Goblins. They might get you or some white sheets could catch you," as they got back in their car watching.

Her hand tightened around mine. There was a chill in the air with a drizzle that slapped us in the face as the wind whispered how mighty it could be. The fog was heavy and every sound made us quiver. The ground was soft and muddy as her stiletto heels stuck in the dirt with every step that she took. It was almost a tumbling act. We made our way through thousands of grave sites, through the dark, foggy night. I wasn't sure if the officers were going to shoot us, as we walked, or if there was other danger that awaited us.

"Oh my God," clinching my neck as she rode the back of my shoes. "What is that?" The Waitress screamed out.

"That's a possum." We began to move at a slow trot. A rat ran across our path, I could feel her collapsing on my shoulders as she screamed, distracting me. Barely stopping in my tracks, I tilted over as my feet hung 3 inches from a ditch. Catching my balance, I swung my body back from the hole we almost fell 6 feet under into an empty grave, reserved for some poor soul. I stopped.

She looked startled, "Who is that?"

"A skunk."

The Waitress leaped in my arm as I carried her the rest of the way with her head buried in my neck. There was a repulsive smell of death that stuck in your nose. Everything that moved seemed like something frightening. I repeatedly said, "Just be cool, everything is going to be alright. I won't let nothing happen to you," I promised while trampling over tombstones.

I felt a deep sorrow for humanity and began to feel no fear. I looked at my corruption and their corruption too. Seeing all the atrocity made me think, 'How much worse could it get?' I was walking amongst the dead. My car was in view as we made our way through the dark, rainy, foggy night. The Waitress laid in the comfort of my chest. I said, "You can look up now, we're at the gate." She gave a sigh of relief. Her eyes drew upward looking at the 6-foot iron fence. "I'm going to lift you up and then I'll climb over then help you down, so believe me, I'll make sure you don't fall, ok?"

"Alright."

We climbed up and I said, "Now jump," as we leaped together then went to the car. The keys where on the front seat. There was a relief of tension afterwards. It was the longest 20-minute walk I had experienced.

"Why would they do that?" The Waitress asked.

"Let me explain. There are good and bad cops just like there are good and bad pimps. Don't accept what they said as true. How can they judge us and say how awful we are? The accuser is always the worse. Two wrongs never make it right. That's just like the pot calling the kettle black when they should be leading by example. We're in the trenches, a fight that we can't see."

"Earthquake, sweetie what do you mean by that?"

"Good question. They try to hide racism and justify their wrongdoings but sometimes you should lose the battle to win the war. Baby, that's why you must reflect me and do what I do, remain courteous and always polite. You see, that's why I'm teaching you how to take what we know and make it work for us. Instead of getting upset, we use that energy to remain on point."

I glanced over at her, "Don't allow them to shake a branch off your tree. Don't get bitter, be better." As my thoughts jumped down to my heart, it was so genuine that I was inspired by my own message and she was tingling with light as if her mind had been hit with a spark.

"Yeah, I know. That's what Pow Wow called Earthquaking," she said.

I smirked at her and said, "Now dust yourself off, we have a concert to rock."

Her courageous performance solidified her place on my team. She said, "Thank God we're out of the woods. That just made me horny. Can I have some before we get there?"

"Didn't you have enough excitement for one day?"

"Baby I was just kidding."

There was a slight pause. "You know I had to throw that out there. But for real, I'm going to need you to slow my heart rate back down. Feel my chest."

The chill from the cold heightened her nipples while she extended her breast in my direction. The idea almost sounded attractive as I reached over, squeezing her left tit.

We laughed while the fear parted from the inner thoughts of our escapade. "Oh yeah, tonight is my night baby, so everything is fleet (good)." Trying to sooth her of any unanswered questions from those barbaric accusations, I attempted to prove the good outweighed the bad by showing her an amazing time.

The concert was off the chain. Earth, Wind and Fire did their thang. We met up with Lucky, Poochie-Slim and their girls, receiving red carpet treatment from the world. The music was loud like it descended from above while The Waitress remained illuminated, falling deeper in love. There were five thousand people rocking as one and the feeling of togetherness was so much fun.

We left the concert while inhaling the remains of a beautiful night. As we flossed on our way home she said, "Wow, those love songs had all the ladies on 10. Baby, it even had you grooving. And you can't tell me it didn't."

I was checking where she was going with that statement, so I put the icing on the cake. "Yeah, I'm charged up."

Without hesitation she said, "Let me see," as she reached her hand down my zipper, dipping her head as she performed oral sex on me while I was driving. I enjoyed the moment while exhaling all the highlights of the bad situations that occurred.

For the next 30 days, it felt like an uncharted war between me and the police. They wrote me bogus moving violation tickets every day and conjured up disorderly conduct charges to arrest me at least once a week. It got so bad that I put a lawyer on a $3,000 retainer because my show had to go on.

Every time they tried to jumble me up, I loosened the strings and made my way through it. It never stagnated me in any type of way. I was still out and about, combing the city like I do and we landed on 87th Street at the Godfather Lounge this night. I was kicking it with J-Hawk, Lucky, Reno, Poochie Slim, Bodie and Pow Wow. We were galloping and having a good time. At about 4:00 a.m. White Cloud hit (called) my phone.

"Where are you?"

"Earthquake, I'm in the cab. This trick held me up, he didn't pay me all your money after we dated. I just left his house."

"White Cloud, ride up here to the Godfather's Lounge."

J-Hawk and the crew asked what was going on.

"I'm waiting for my girl to get here. She just got robbed by some trick that I'm about to go treat."

"I'm going with you partner," J-Hawk said.

"We all are," the crew said.

Ten minutes later, White Cloud jumped out of a taxi. We all congregated around her while she told what happened. She handed me my $400 trap and said, "This trick who I regularly date, took me to his house. He had been drinking and while we were dating he told me if I stayed 20 extra minutes he would give me an additional $200. We continued for 10 more minutes and I stayed approximately 20-minutes longer. When I asked him for your money, he was drunk and wouldn't get up. He told me he would give it to me in the morning if I stay. I got tired of waiting so while he laid there knocked out, I left leaving the door unlocked."

"Do you remember how to get back there?"

"Yes, I think so."

White Cloud led us straight to his apartment. We went through the locked iron gate as someone walked out. When we got to the court way building, someone else was coming out so we went in and headed to the 3rd floor. I twisted the knob, it opened so we strolled in. White Cloud pointed to his room. We circled him as he laid there in a comatose sleep in the one-bedroom apartment.

"Be cool," J-Hawk said, "let me handle this, fellas. Nobody makes a move without me saying so. What's his name White Cloud?"

"Willie."

He tapped him on the shoulder and said, "Hey Willie, wake up."

Still in a groggy daze, Willie looked up and then closed his eyes; he appeared to think this was a bad dream. He was laid out under a white sheet, naked and pissy drunk.

J-Hawk tapped him on his shoulder again. "Willie get up."

He opened his eyes and looked around. J-Hawk said, "Willie, do you know this young lady?"

He shook his head no. J-Hawk slapped him, Willie's eyes bucked and he said, "Yes."

Then J-Hawk said, "Willie, did you rape this woman?"

Willie's eyes adjusted to the bright light, "No."

J-Hawk slapped Willie while Reno and I impulsively leaped toward him but J-Hawk stopped us. "Did you have sex with her and didn't pay? Don't lie."

Willie looked discombobulated and said, "Yes."

He slapped Willie again as we tore into him. J-Hawk stopped us again and said, "Now Willie, where is this young lady's money?"

He pointed to his pants that were under his recliner chair. I got his wallet out and took the 2 crisp one hundred-dollar bills from it and gave the wallet to J-Hawk. He set the wallet on the night stand. Then he looked at Willie and said, "Now Willie, we're going to need $300 more for this inconvenience so where's the rest?"

Pow Wow and Bodie started pacing the floor going back and forth to the window saying, "Let us blast that chump."

"That's all I got," Willie whimpered.

"Please let us throw him out the window!" I said.

"I'm trying to save you. Can you get your hands on $300? If you don't, it could be bad for you. Willie, I'm trying to help you," J-Hawk said.

"That's all the money I got."

J-Hawk gave him a direct threat. "Okay, don't you ever do that again. You hear me?"

"Alright."

"The police just pulled up, me and Bodie got pistols on us so were about to get out of here," Pow Wow said.

Pow Wow and Bodie headed for the door. A few seconds later J-Hawk, Poochie-Slim and I left. Then White Cloud, Lucky and Reno trailed a few feet behind us. As J-Hawk pulled out of the parking space, I peeped through the side view mirror and saw that 2 police officers stopped Lucky, Reno, and White Cloud.

"Uncle J hold up. The cops are talking to my broad and them. Wait right here while I check out what's happening."

"Naw, partner, we'll meet you back at the shop."

I slid into the mix and directed my question to Reno. "What's the problem?"

"Someone called the police saying that a home invasion was taking place on the 3rd floor."

Two more squad cars pulled up and 2 of the 4 officers went upstairs after being updated on situation. They returned saying that a tenant said that he was robbed.

"Naw, he raped my friend White Cloud and now he's trying to cover up," Reno quickly responded.

One of the cops said, "Ok, you guys follow us to the police station and we're gonna get to the bottom of this."

As we drove off, I noticed the cop escorting Willie out of his building. Once everybody arrived at the station, they separated White Cloud from us. The 3 detectives entered the interview room. They identified themselves and then the black male detective asked, "What happened over there on East 68th Street?"

Reno took the floor. His voice was brass but dramatic, pleading the case. "Willie raped White Cloud and she called me to come and pick her up."

"Where do you know her from?" the detective asked.

"Off my grandmother's block," Reno said.

"Do you fellas have anything to add to this?"

"Naw. I take the fifth," Lucky replied. He shot a look over at me. It felt like I was dangling from a noose. I was trying to make sure that they couldn't use anything that was said against me, so I bit my tongue.

Instantly I told him, "No." Thinking to myself, '*I hope White Cloud doesn't allow them to trick her into giving me a case.*'

The black female detective sat on the edge of the desk and directed her attention to Reno. "Wow, that's an expensive leather coat the girl has on. She's dressed so nice to be only 16 years old."

The white detective officer stood in the corner just observing us. Reno continued, "Well, I let her borrow my mom's coat, blouse and shoes. She told me that she was going on a date."

The female interrupted and abruptly asked, "Are you her pimp?"

Reno lifted his head in shock, like a deer caught in headlights. "No, why would you say that? I was trying to help somebody and y'all are making me into the villain."

The white officer said, "Who's the older guy that was with you? Was that her pimp?"

"No, that was Mr. Johnson. I think he owns a funeral parlor or used to. He just be on my grandmothers block all the time giving people lifts if they need a ride or something."

The black officer said to Reno, "So, she's with you? You're her pimp, right? Plus, Willie said that you're her pimp and you robbed him. Admit it or all 3 of you are going to jail for pimping and robbery."

There was a brief silence. The female officer stood up and said, "You're all under arrest." She read us our rights and then the detectives left the room. Reno's face turned flush and sweat beaded up on his forehead. He gave me these considerable options. "Earthquake, that's your girl. It doesn't make sense for all of us to go to jail. If we all are locked up, who's going to bail us out? It's more logical for one person to take the case." Reno turned his eyes toward the floor, then slowly looked up at me, "Since it's your girl, this should be on you."

My thoughts were, '*If I don't tell, that would be putting a lot of stress on Reno.*' To ease the pressure, I said, "Reno, don't worry. I'm gonna say she's with me. I'll take my own medicine, chief."

Reno had a momentary sigh of relief. Then he took another too close for comfort breath and finally closed his mouth. The detectives walked back in the room. I said without hesitation, "White Cloud is with me."

The white detective said, "So you're her pimp? She already told us. You had her working, huh?"

"No, I just know her, that's it."

"Let's go. You're under arrest for robbery and pimping. How old are you?"

"I'm eighteen."

"Ok, let's go and get you finger printed."

Reno and Lucky were charged with disorderly conduct while I got pimping and robbery. Still thinking, '*The detectives* probably used the tactic telling White Cloud I confessed that she was my hoe, but I know she's smarter than that.' It was all in her hands. I'd never tell on myself.

They allowed me one call. I got in touch with my lawyer to be at court in the morning. I could see Reno and Lucky in the cells next to me. They were released that morning. I had to appear in front of the judge. So, they drove me to 51st Street court house located on the South side. I was hoping I wouldn't have that same judge that I appeared in front of with my ex-girl Bambi.

While passing time in my cell, in came a decoy officer playing the role of a criminal. He was dressed real slick like a hustler. He was personable and talkative. "I'm Snooky, what's the scoop?"

I shouted something smooth back, "What's up dude? I'm Boss Chicken."

Snooky laid on the hard steel bench and said, "Man, I'm furious. The police locked me up. They found some merchandise, but it wasn't even on me. I stole it but they didn't catch me. Dirty cops. What you in for?"

He must have learned that in training 101. His slick look didn't match his conversation. That was a dead giveaway. Even his posture was uncoordinated. His face reeked with street inexperience. It was obvious that he was planted in my cell.

White Cloud most definitely didn't rat me out. If she did, they wouldn't be sniffing for a confession. Since everybody was playing games, I said, "You know chicken put a wedge between black people. They accused me of stealing a piece of white meat and they locked me up." Then I turned towards the wall and acted as if I was sleep. Not even 15 minute later, they let him out.

Twenty-two hours later, at 6:30 a.m., the officer announced, "It's time for court. Let's go."

They had about 15 of us chained together and officers escorted us to the sheriff bus. Since I had an attorney present, I was first to be called to the bench. My lawyer said a few words and the case was dismissed. I asked my attorney, "What happened?"

"They made a deal with the complainant. The young lady, Chrissy (White Cloud), told Willie she would drop the rape charge if he dropped the robbery against you."

"What about the pimping case?"

"There wasn't one because she never said you were her pimp. You're in the clear. Her parents had her sent to juvenile for theft. She stole some money from them and ran away."

"I forgot. She did tell me she stole money from her parents."

A haze of regret sunk deep inside me for White Cloud. There was no means to an end until I knew she would be ok. It was good that I was out, but it didn't scratch that itch of satisfaction. I gave my lawyer another $3000 retainer fee for any further incidents. It was time for me to get incognito.

CHAPTER 23
Meet Joann

I PURCHASED A brand new, custom designed, Cadillac while still holding it down. I had to make another come up. I met Joann while we were standing in line at a grocery store and she chose me right away. I introduced myself and initiated a conversation.

"If a man doesn't like you then he doesn't like ice cream." She laughed. She told me her name and said that she lived up the street with her mother and sister. Joann graduated from high school and was simply living day to day, with no job and no real plan.

I offered to take her groceries home and asked her if she wanted to ride with me after that. Joann said yes; we dropped off her groceries then she rode with me. I took her to dinner and she was talkative. I found her easy to talk to so we sat and conversed for hours. I led the conversation based on her eating habits. You can learn a lot from a woman's cooking habits and even more when you take her out to eat.

When a woman cooks and piles food on your plate, the more she gives you the greater her concern is for you. The less she puts on your plate, the less of herself she will give to you. If she prepares a plate for you both but she has more food, then she wants to control you in all situations. My experience taught me some very remarkable facts. I took Joann to dinner. I watched the way she ate her food, how she expressed herself and learned a lot from observing her.

I learned that a person's eating habits tell a lot about them. For instance, if a woman only orders a salad at dinner, most of the time she is pretentious, a person who doesn't reveal her true self. A woman who mixes portions of food together, is usually sociable, open-minded and flexible. A woman who separates each dish on her plate — the spaghetti can't touch the kale, etc. — usually has very distinct ways of viewing situations and her perception is the only one that counts, making her closed-minded and a prisoner of poor perception. A woman who is indecisive when ordering food usually doesn't know what she wants out of life. A woman who enjoys a large variety of foods usually won't have any sexual restrictions. A woman who is uncomfortable eating in front of others usually has insecurity issues. A woman who drops food often is usually careless. A woman who "sneak eats" usually has a food addiction. A woman who licks her fingers during a meal usually doesn't enjoy wasting time with undesirable things. A woman who hates to eat alone almost always has a dude in her life. There are always exceptions to these rules, but generally this is a guide that worked well for me.

I made observations about Joann. She had macaroni with greens, sweet potatoes, baked chicken, cornbread and lemonade. She placed a bite of each dish on her folk, and as she chewed, she would take a bite of cornbread, mixing her food. After taking a few bites, Joann would have a sip of lemonade, which cued me in that she was probably very sociable. I asked her if she had a job, and she replied, "no." Then I asked if she ever had a job, and she replied, "yes."

"Once I had a park district job through my high school at South Shore High. It was through a summer job program. I was a recreation leader."

"I used to be a recreation leader also," I told her and we both laughed.

"Are you for real?"

"Yeah."

"I can't imagine you with that kind of job."

"It's true, I sure did," I assured.

"What was that like? Tell me all about it!"

"Well, my childhood friend Lucky had an aunt who was connected with the high school youth work program and she got us summer jobs as recreation leaders. It was the first job I ever had. We were high school students, but Lucky and I were both hustlers who dressed real slick. The training manual said to wear red and blue, so I dressed in my most clever gear and walked into the orientation. I wore a red, pure silk shirt with fancy buckles on the two front pockets and sleeves, with red linen dress slacks and red snake skinned shoes. My hair was freshly styled with ocean waves that hit my shoulders."

"I bet you were too cute," Joann commented. Then she asked the waitress for her third refill on lemonade. That let me know that Joann probably had addictive behavior.

I told her that the park district supervisor asked me to come to his office after orientation. He was an older, clean cut guy who ran things with an iron fist.

"What kind of job do you think this is?" he asked.

"What do you mean?"

"You are working with children. You'll be taking them swimming and to the park, not the disco or a bar." He went into his file cabinet, pulled out a red t-shirt with the park district logo on it and threw it at me. "You have to wear this with jeans and white gym shoes."

"Ok."

"When you come here Monday morning, I expect you to be dressed accordingly and cut that hair off," he told me. Joann laughed, as I continued my story.

"Over the weekend I got Reno to cut my hair short, with a part on the side. Reno laughed at my haircut, but I did what I had to do to look cool and conservative at the same time, you dig?"

Joann laughed. "Man, I guess you had to thug it out."

"Yeah, because I was still hustling at night. I was pimping, selling weed, and robbing and then working with kids during the day."

"Wow, you're a real Jamaican." We both laughed as Joann licked her fingers, letting me know that she didn't like wasting time. So, I knew that she was feeling me.

I explained that I'd get a few hours of sleep each night before I headed into work. I halfway watched the kids since I was asleep most of the time. I brought a lot of candy bars to work. The kids each had big lunches packed by their moms. The kids would see me eating Snickers and M&Ms and would ask to trade their sandwiches for candy, and I obliged them. I traded the best candy for the best lunches. The kids would line-up ready to trade. This allowed me to eat turkey and ham sandwiches and for them to eat Kit Kats, Baby Ruths, Sour Grapes and Banana Splits.

Joann looked up from her plate and asked the waitress to bring her a slice of chocolate cake. There she was, eating dessert while I was still eating my curry chicken. I asked Joann if she liked curry chicken and she said that she never tasted it. While she was eating cake, I put the chicken up to her lips and she took a bite. She gave me the stink face. I asked her if she liked it and she told me not really. I gave her another bite and she ate it, which let me know that she probably had no sexual hang-ups.

"What happened next?" she asked, wanting me to continue the story.

"The recreation worker said, 'you're not right, you are stealing the kids' nutrition."

"How am I stealing the kids' nutrition?"

"You are eating their lunches and giving them candy, and I'm appalled," the worker said.

"They wanted candy. I didn't see anything wrong with that because I didn't look at it from that perspective."

Lucky's older cousin Chris also worked there and we all rode the bus together. I'd enter the back of the bus and ask people for transfers so that I could ride for free while everyone else entered the front door of the bus and paid.

"Why are you always trying not to pay? You are supposed to pay just like everyone else," Chris said.

"I'm a hustler and everything that I do is about hustling and making things happen. I can use my money for something else. Why should I pay to get on the bus when I can get on the back and ride for free?"

"It's not fair, you're not supposed to do that."

I thought to myself, 'Ok, they can keep on paying and I'm gonna use my money to buy more candy and get more lunches.'

"You were on the grind, huh baby?" Joann asked.

"Without a doubt!"

Joann dropped food in her lap as she said, "Tell me more." That let me know that she was careless.

"During play time in the field house, I wore my dark shades. The boys would be throwing the balls real hard, kicking and hitting each other. They were all over the place while I'm just sitting in a chair up against the wall, knocked out asleep. Balls were flying everywhere, hitting the walls 'boom – boom.'

Lucky walked into the field house. Lucky said to himself, 'man, look at Quake, he is so cool.' Lucky enjoyed telling this story. He saw a ball flying towards my face and thought, Quake better look out, but I didn't move, and the ball just hit the wall – Pow! I pulled my shades down to the tip of my nose and looked around, and then pulled them back up. Lucky said to himself, 'either he is the coolest dude in the world or he's asleep.' He said that he walked over and just stood in front of me for a few seconds, and then said, 'just like I figured, he's asleep." Joann started laughing uncontrollably. "Lucky called my name, 'Quake!' I said, 'what's up Luck?' He said, 'man, you're sleeping on the job and these kids are running around like crazy people.' I said, 'hey kids, everybody get together, lineup and get right.'

On one occasion, I almost caused a lawsuit. The kids were slapping each other's necks and one boy had the nerve to slap my neck. All the kids laughed. I was a good sport about it but it stung badly. I knew that the time would come for me to get him back. He kept a towel around his neck so that I couldn't get him. So, I just waited. His towel fell and I slapped his neck. He cringed up and let out a loud scream, "OUCH!" Everybody started laughing. He kept on whimpering, so I said, 'Stop crying.' I looked at the back of his neck and saw four big, swollen, finger welts. I put cold water and ice on his neck, trying to get the swelling down. I told him that I would bring him his favorite candy bars tomorrow. I said, 'Stop crying, don't be a baby, and don't tell your mama.' He said, 'I'm not a baby.' I said, 'what do you want tomorrow?' He said, 'Snickers, M&Ms, Pay Day, Twix and a Kit Kat.' I said, 'ok, I'll bring it tomorrow."

Joann asked, "Did you make it through the whole program?"

"Yeah, and they offered me the job the following year."

"Did you work the following year?"

"No. I was on to bigger and better things."

Joann finished every bite of her food, letting me know that she wasn't wasteful. Like clockwork, she was very sociable and open-minded. From the start, she had an affectionate way with me and I really enjoyed it. Joann also had an insecurity about herself that I found appealing. She made comments that I responded to, reaffirming that I liked her style. Even though she was very beautiful, she didn't act as if she knew it, and that made me more attracted to her.

"How many boyfriends have you had?" I asked.

"About six."

"What happened?"

"Nothing really."

"Do you sell sex?"

"No, I'm not a hooker."

"Ok, so you give it away for free. Do you back up against the wall and say, don't give me nothing for it, I'm giving it away?"

"No, I'm gonna get something for it."

"Ok, that's better," I said as I grabbed her hand and the waitress appeared and removed the dishes.

Joann seemed to be intrigued by me. "If you had a man would you help and stick by him no matter what?"

"Yes, I'd do anything to help him."

I told her all about my business and she was down with me from the start. I grabbed her hand and appeared to be reading her palm.

"You are a friendly person, very sociable. You are a team player and you play your position well. You are a determined person who gets what you want. You are sweet and very kind. You think about your man first. You are mild tempered and you know how to handle a problem. Sexually, you are not afraid to try new things."

She placed her hands between her thighs as she rocked back and forth. "Oh, my goodness, that is so me! How did you know all of that? You got a gift. You must be psychic."

"No, I'm not really psychic. It's call telepathy. You are me and I am you. We are one," I told her.

She confessed, "This is so true because I really feel connected to you. It's kind of strange, but it's the best feeling I ever had."

Like most women, Joann would conform to the situation if I presented it the right way. So, I explained that I had 12 other women and that she would be number 13. "Baby you have to show me loyalty and then you could easily move up in rank."

With the sweet taste of rising to the top on her mind she said, "I know I'm going to be your main girl. I already see it."

I looked deeply into her eyes and said, "I believe in you baby. If you can see it, you can make it happen." I saw that she could only focus on what she wanted. From that day, Joann was with me and became my hooker.

Joann was very enthused about my operation and the training process. She strived to be good at every aspect of her job and even better in her relationship with me. She mastered the 10 rules and seemed to be cut out for this – a real natural. Joann catered to me, always thinking about my comfort and ensuring that my needs were met. When I told her that my goal was to have 15 hoes, she went on a mission to make sure that it happened. I took her everywhere with me. She was so into me and I really liked that. She was my buddy, my friend and I enjoyed having her around. I kept her around Lola so that she could learn the ropes.

Joann didn't have any hang-ups when it came to other hoes. She would be open, even scoped out other women and assisted me with hooking up with them. Joann never showed any jealousy or resentment for the other women and I liked that about her. She fully and completely accepted who I was and how I got down. She was a team player, she knew her position and played it well. She was a star!

A few weeks later, Pow Wow got word that one of his gangsta goons saw White Cloud at a bus stop heading to see me. He gave me a call and I told him to hold on to her until I got back with him. I contemplated about going to get her because of what the judge told me.

I went to J-Hawk and told him my dilemma.

"Uncle J, the judge warned me not to come before his court again with a pimp case, especially regarding White Cloud. She won't be 17-years-old for another two months."

"Well partner, you only have until January to wait."

"But that's a long time to have a girl in limbo."

A long silence followed.

"Listen nephew, she can do one of two things. I can't tell you what to do. I know she can either buy you a Rolls-Royce or send you to the penitentiary. That's up to you. By the way, you know that the apartment where Ginger stayed, on South Shore? She was one of my ex-girls who's not with me, so I was thinking about giving it up. You want to transfer it over so you can put your girl White Cloud over there? You know it's fully furnished. I'll sell you everything."

"Yeah, I'll take it."

"Give me $2,500 and it's yours."

"Ok, but it's not going to be for White Cloud but my new girl, Joann. I'll put a few of my broads that ain't up to peak performance there too. That will save me on hotel fees and balance out the money. If I decide to go and get her, White Cloud will be living at the house." I pulled out $2,500 and gave it to him on the spot. He dropped those keys on me and I proceeded as planned.

I thought about it for 4 days before I decided to pick her up and put her back on the team. The depth of my pimping was kept to a minimum because her potential was limited on the streets until her 17th birthday. My plan was to have her keep a low-key profile. I took her to 63rd & Halsted Street, under the El (elevator train) station where a vendor sold fake identification cards so that she could get one and work at Dreamland.

This night, I took White Cloud to the Dreamland myself. She was cable, ready, and charged up. My girls had already prepped White Cloud for her debut of being a private dancer hoe. Just so happen when I pulled up, the owner was getting out of the car. He was an Italian with dark hair, dark eyebrows, standing about 5'10". He appeared to be around 65 years old, like a seasoned businessman.

He looked over and asked, "You're Earthquake?"

"Yes. You must be Gus."

"Yeah, I am."

"I brought one of the stars from my team to work."

Gus looked at White Cloud. "Yes, she sure is a star. Is she coming inside to work tonight?"

I shook my head, "Yeah, if you allow her to."

Gus motioned his hand to White Cloud, to come on. "Ok go. I'll see you later. You know what to do from here."

Things seemed to be working out pretty good at the Dreamland with White Cloud. I stayed under the radar and kept everything on rotation. I had 2 months to wait until White Cloud turned 17. Her birthday was January 8th. Stepping into the month of December started out cold. Old man winter was surely present, but wintertime was the best season of all. Surely it was going to be a white Christmas.

All the girls worked harder, jumping in and out of cars more frequently to keep themselves warm. Many of the Strolls were located on main streets, near motels, restaurants and gas stations. The hoes usually stayed close to one of those locations so they could duck in and out of the freezing temperatures. The girls kept hot cocoa to knock the chill off and keep their hands warm when they provided oral sex service.

My teachings were second only to mother nature. If you wanted your broads to learn fast, let mother nature do the teaching. The hurtling winds motivated the girls to learn the ropes without any instruction. Instinctively they thought fast and automatically knew what to say to a trick, convincing him to turn a date. They hustled hard to stay out of the hawk. After experiencing mother nature, my girls were swift and quick at the game. The winter was cold, but it had its perks.

The Kentucky girls weren't used to driving in the harsh weather, dancing with the brutal temperatures or competing with the Chicago blizzards. As time passed, 25 inches of snow accumulated, salt trucks pushed it into 15 feet high mountains, temperatures dropped to fatal degrees and the wind chill factor fell well below -3. Becky wasn't skilled enough to drive in these drastic conditions. I drove 6 of them to work, Lola and the remainder of my girls hit the Stroll.

When we arrived at Dreamland, the lights on the signage were out and there were only 2 cars in the parking lot. I knocked on the door and the manager George answered.

"Are y'all opening?"

He invited my girls in.

"I'm going to call Gus and let him know your girls are here. Don't go anywhere." So, I went and sat in the car and waited. A few minutes later, he reported that Gus was on his way.

When Gus got there, he invited me in, then we walked to his office at the back of the club. We started talking.

"You brought your girls to work in this weather?"

"Yes Gus, the day you lay off is the day it may pay off."

"You're a shrewd businessman," he laughed.

"It takes one, to know one." We hit it off right away and stayed in his office talking.

"I never let a black man in my office," Gus confided. I was the first black to be in his establishment without getting kicked out. I stayed for about 4 hours and then we left.

I went back the next day; the temperature was still brutal. George opened the club and told me to wait again. When Gus arrived, we went back to his office and talked 4 more hours. He told me his whole life story about how he came over here and couldn't speak English. He mentioned how he drove a cab, ran numbers and bootleg.

He insinuated that he was part of the family. It was all quite interesting.

"Do you have any more girls?" he asked.

"My brother and my crew got girls," I said.

"You can tell them their girls can work but no black men are allowed in my club. If anything, ever goes wrong, your crew would have to get the rundown from you."

Gus walked over to George and the barmaids and said, "Anytime Earthquake comes here, let him in. He's welcomed. He's family."

Gus introduced me to the other two strip club owners and several police officers in Cicero. He told them that I was family and those connections made a difference. After that, I had favor and influence all over that town.

The flexibility that I had on my new-found pavement made it enjoyable to take my hoes to work. A part of my world now included Cicero and Dreamland became a main stomping ground. I explored the foundation to build on a true pimp's game. For me, the harsh weather was on my side and it helped to reinforce my position at the clubs. Even winter is beautiful when your game is together. Like I said, "The day I layoff is the day it may have paid off." That's why I get down like a mailman, through rain, sleet or snow I always deliver.

As the temperature rose into the 20's, I had Becky drive the hoes to Dreamland. That gave me more time to check out the action on the Strolls. Sometimes we had breakfast after the hoes got off work on 63rd Street, in a 24-hour restaurant that the pimps and hoes frequented. The night was brisk, the stars were out, and my mind was famished with thoughts of a good, homemade meal. Lucky and two of his girls met us there. Six of my hoes and I walked in the restaurant.

To my surprise, look who was sitting there. One of the pimps that I most admired when I was coming up. "Slick Rick, my man, where have you been? Long time no see, my most valuable pimp buddy."

It was obvious he was overwhelmed when he saw me and he sounded more sarcastic than he probably intended to. He snarled as he looked me up and down and said, "What up dude?" Slick Rick sloped down in a pimp lean in the booth at his table. He slighted me while attempting to make himself look like a giant, acting mackish, trying to over play his status in front of my girls.

Slick Rick didn't even get up to embrace me. He sat there in his little coyote coat, choking the collar around his neck to keep the cold from making him shiver. Every time a customer entered, the mighty wind gushed through the door with a whistling echo as mother nature demonstrated her power. Each time, the wind seemed to part and rush directly toward him as he sat two tables from the entrance, trying to knock the chill off him.

I had on my full-length maxi mink coat with the matching hat and jewelry that sparkled as if pimping was in full effect. My diamonds lit the room like a crystal chandelier; like glistening snow on a mountain. I stood there ready to greet him as a brother, but he ignored the gesture and sat there in a negative posture. I was thinking, '*I wondered why he was mad when he was the first pimp* that took a girl from me. He had Geisha all the way in NYC a week after I first got her.' I was not looking for any retribution for Geisha choosing him. There were no hard feelings. It really was a valuable lesson and I took my hat off to him.

Slick Rick allowed his tongue to slip right from under him, but he probably wanted to say that anyway.

"Man, you ain't pimping that hard. You're selling dope."

I was momentarily insulted. I wanted to rapidly reciprocate but I held my composure as he looked around as if he hoped no one was watching. I was knocked down but not out by the impact of his words. When I shifted my eyes towards him trying to understand his strife, I fired back but in a subtle way.

"Let me come down from this altitude. When you try to come up this high you lose oxygen. The brain can't function when you elevate to this level. You can't see beyond the stars. You never reached this dimension of the game I'm going to drop you down in some water to break your fall and then put you back on dry land so that you won't think it's a mirage. Now waitress, please give this hard-working man some breakfast for his stomach while I give him nutrition for his mind. It's a new mack in town. Grab your plate, I'm about to make it shake. So, pass him his eggs and steak cause both meals are on Earthquake."

I walked over to the counter where Lucky and the girls were. Rick said, "Man, you ain't fooling nobody. You ain't pimping like that. Walking around like you Fluky or Fontaine. You know you're riding on dope money."

"Hey, y'all sit down for a second. Let me handle this," I said, as Lucky shot me a look. My girls and Lucky sat there ear hustling (eavesdropping). I walked back over to Slick Rick and leaned towards him as if I was exposing some vital information and said just listen. "It's harder for a person to accept that a person could climb higher than you. It's a new era and things are different, the game changed. I've got girls on the streets, in the clubs and on travel rotation so I'm able to get more money at this particular time.

Y'all probably only had girls on the streets and getting more problems than money. I got more angles. My style is perhaps more organized and structured. Not taking anything away from you, you're still one of the coldest pimps ever. I'm just more advanced. These opportunities were not offered to you at that time. I learned from my mistakes and the way y'all did it. I had a better plan, not that I'm a better pimp."

Slick Rick said, "So, you the downest in the game, huh? You got your hoes under control?"

I gave him a slight smile, but I could see whatever he thought he still believed in his head.

"Naw, I don't.   There's one thing the pimp manual doesn't teach you. They say the key is to control a woman's mind but that key only last so long. That key only takes you to one level. But the one thing they left out was that 'Favor' last forever. That's what I know. I just wanted to share that with you."

"What's wrong with Slick Rick? He trippin'," Lucky said looking at me.

"Lucky, it's the beginning to an end for him. You can be so truthful to some people, they swear it's a lie. They can't believe you can take something so small and make it great. But now he has a debt to pay," I explained as we got our food and vacated the premises.

The snow continued to fall heavy as we headed into January and the winter was cold but smooth. White Cloud made 17-years-old and on her birthday, I told her we were going to celebrate.

"I'm taking you out and we're celebrating."

"Can Lola and Wonnie come with us?" she asked.

"Yeah, sure White Cloud." She put on her pretty, royal blue silk dress accented with gold shingles around the neck. Her golden blonde shoulder length hair made her look stunning.

Reno, Lucky and I got sharp. They both had 2 hookers each with them when we headed to the Flukie's Lounge. It was located on Cottage Grove on the 82nd Stroll, our old stomping ground. We were surrounded by the elite of the streets who checked out a powerful demonstration of our rise from young hustlers to bona fide players. It felt good living the results of being loyal to the mack game. We set the hoes up with champagne then Reno, Lucky and I went outside and stood in the front of the lounge.

"I remember when we couldn't get in the Flukie's Lounge," I said to Lucky and Reno.

"Now the shorties want to be like the 3 kings," Reno said.

"This proves if you see it, you can make it happen. Now let's go back inside. Y'all know I hate to be cold," I said. We stayed until about 2:00 a.m.

While we were riding down the hoe Stroll on Cottage Grove, White Cloud said, "Thank for showing me such a good time. I feel free as a bird." She looked out the window, watching the hookers at work and abruptly said, "Pull over. Let me out. I want to go to work baby." I locked the door as she grabbed for the handle. "Let me go. I want to do something for you. I'll do anything for you Earthquake. I mean it."

"Naw White Cloud, this your day off. Save that energy for tomorrow and work double. Just enjoy the night with no working."

"Ok," as she sang along to 'Lady Marmalade' by Patti LaBelle as it played on the car radio. That's my favorite song you know for some reason," she said laying her head on my shoulder.

"It's because you can relate to that song, that's all."

"I guess I'm a little tipsy."

"I know."

When we arrived home, she went into the kitchen, sat at the table and ate a piece cake. She fell asleep at the table and I picked her up and carried her to her room. The next day, I put my 17-year-old hooker back in rotation without any fear.

As the weeks passed in a steady flow, a warm spell descended in the month of March. You could feel that spring was knocking at the door, but the winter was not about to let us forget that easy. Winter was still manifesting a chilled performance and bringing us encores every now and then. Hanging around was a sheet of snow even though the frigid temperatures had passed. Later that month, the rosebuds sprouted as the April showers washed away the residue.

Now that the weather changed, it was the perfect time to switch things up by busting out with a new car. I traded my Gucci Cadillac for a custom designed silver, Seville with a bubble gum colored canvas top and two belts down both sides of the trunk, Peter Pan stripes on the doors and in the back-window my name "Earthquake" circled in dollar signs, with Trues and Vogues rims and tires. So much for staying inconspicuous, but this was my style and that's how I rolled. I went to the house and White Cloud was standing in the doorway talking on the phone. When she saw the car, her face lit up and lip synced, "I love it," as I walked to my room.

It was Good Friday and White Cloud had called her father who invited her to Easter dinner. They spoke for a while and then she came in and sat on the bed. "Earthquake can I go see my father on Easter? He wants me to have dinner with them."

I was thinking it wasn't a good idea based on what she told me happened the last time she was home. "White Cloud, didn't you tell me that you and your stepmom got into an altercation and then you stole all of their money and left the house?"

"Yeah, but that was a while ago and I want to see my dad and my little brother."

Who was I to deny her dinner with her family on Easter?

"Ok, I'll drive you over there." Her eyes were filled with joy from the instant gratification.

"Thank you." She flung the door open and had a little bouncy sway in her walk.

On April 11, 1982, Easter Sunday, White Cloud woke me about noon. "Hey, I'm about to get ready. Are you still taking me?"

"Yeah, get dressed."

As I showered, Reno and all the girls were making dinner. Lucky and his 3 broads arrived and joined in. The scent of home-made turkey and dressing tickled my nose and the sound of familiar voices filled the air as I came down stairs. I shouted, "What up Luck butter? I see you are down here with chef '4-RD'," as Reno acted in the manner of a head chef.

I pointed my finger in Reno's direction and said to Lucky, "Come on and ride with me. We'll leave 'Greedy Gertrude' here so that he can orchestrate these rookie cooks."

Reno's girl Barbie yelled, "Hey White Cloud, taste my spaghetti sauce before you go. It's my great, great grandmama's special recipe, it goes back to slavery." She extended the spoon full of spaghetti and White Cloud tasted it and in a southern accent said, "Ooh-wee master, this sauce is good."   We all laughed.

I told White Cloud, "Be careful with that hole in your mouth or you'll get sauce on that white cashmere turtleneck." With the sweater, she was wearing a tan leather jacket and matching boots with Jordache jeans, looking really lady like.   Say goodbye and let's roll. The three of us jumped in my Caddy and headed to the Northside. We pulled up on the block a few feet from her parents' home, dropped her off and Lucky and I headed back to the house.

When I got there, the remainder of my hookers were there for dinner. Lola bought a feast that included honey baked ham, greens and cornbread, potato salad, an apple pie and a German chocolate cake that her mom, Ms. C cooked.   It was a good thing to because there were 24 mouths to feed. We played music, laughed and entertained each other.   It was a family affair and everybody was all through the house, talking loud and being carefree. At 7:00 p.m. it was time for everybody to go to work. I announced, "All good things must come to an end. It's time to work that food off." We settled into our work routine. White Cloud hadn't called but I didn't think about it too much.

Two weeks went by and I hadn't heard from White Cloud. All the hoes asked about her, even Reno's girls. Then I got a collect call from the Cook County jail. I accepted the charges.

"Hello."

"Hi, this is Susie. I'm calling for White Cloud. She wanted me to let you know that she's in the Cook County jail."

"Why is she locked up?"

"On Easter when she visited her parents she got into a bad fight with her stepmom. The police were called, and she pressed charges against White Cloud for Assault and Grand Theft. The police arrested her because there was a warrant on her for the Grand Theft."

Susie was talking real fast, trying to report all the details before running out of time. "Now, she's in solitary confinement and they have her in a straitjacket because she was fighting the guards. They've been shooting her up with some type of medication called Thorazine or Methadone, supposedly to keep her calm but I'm worried about her. She said she will call you when she gets out the hole."

I took in everything that Susie relayed but I wasn't surprised. I'd told White Cloud that it was a bad idea to go home that soon. "Okay Susie, thanks."

I thought, *'At least I know where she's at.'* That night, I hooked-up with Lucky, Poochie-Slim and Reno at our unofficial headquarters, the ET Lounge on 55th Street. I updated the fellas on what happened to White Cloud.

"Man, I like White Cloud. She's a smart little whitey," Lucky said.

"No doubt Luck but those are the breaks. When one door closes, another always seems to open."

"Dag man, you shouldn't have let her go if you had any inkling of a doubt."

"Yes, I should've. I teach them this game so I'm not doing one thing and telling them another. They can see I'm true which allows them to observe my discipline. My pimping didn't influence her to choose my point of view, so I allowed her to make up her mind. That way she wouldn't thirst for her own decision making and go against what I say. When I teach my hoes, they honor me and that nurtures likeability. Whether her choice is good or bad, she will always be open to me and that's what I call favor. I know that when a runaway child runs wild, they always come back home. Now, on the other hand if I took control of the situation and said no to her, that negative thought would continue to grow and sooner or later it could turn into resentment rather than resilience. I knew this could bite me in the butt but that's real pimping and there ain't no negotiating with that."

"Yeah, Earthquake I see your point. You got to accept the bitter with the sweet. It's all about top hats and caps."

He got quiet long enough for me to focus on what he just said. "Lucky, what does that mean?"

"I don't know, it just sounds good." We laughed. "On a serious note, when you teach someone, you do have a great deal of influence on them and that's real."

Speaking of influence triggered thoughts about how I'd guide Joann. Since she had bottom broad (top hoe) potential,

I connected Joann with Lola before work so she could learn the ropes. As the night went on, something strange happened at work.

Joann called and said Lola left a few hours early and returned to pick them up. I found that strange because she had never left the Stroll without contacting me. Early that morning, after collecting my traps, I went to the hotel unexpectedly. Lola wasn't there. Ironically, she'd been staying at her sister Jada's house a lot. Jada lived right down the street from the hotel, so I went over there and knocked on the door. Nobody answered but my Caddy that Lola had been driving was parked out front.

I was thinking, *'Something's not adding up. I need to figure out what's going on so I can nip this in the bud.'* The next day, Lola arrived at the hotel to pick up the hookers. I said, "I need to see you after work."

She looked drained. Her eyes stayed steady, but her pupils shrank and that wasn't a good sign. Lola replied, "Ok."

"As a matter of fact, tomorrow I'll drop everybody off on the Stroll."

The next day, I went and picked up the hoes but allowed Lola to drive. I grabbed her by the chin and noticed that her face was cold and her nose sweaty. She pulled away from the curb and merged in sequence with the traffic. Lola started crying uncontrollably. She appeared to be filled with frustration, looking like a walking time bomb. I didn't say anything as we drove on the expressway.

The weather was thundering relentlessly on this rainy night. I sat there as I pondered, looking for logic and equations to arrive in my mind about her. But more unexplainable, we hardly noticed the unimaginable. My thoughts drifted into a sudden oblivion after considering the circumstances; a car was speeding down the wrong side of the highway and was headed straight toward us.

With a quick reaction, Lola skillfully swerved in a split second and avoided a head-on collision. It gave a thrust of terror that could have swept us into the stormy state of non-existence. This image pounded in my head. Even though the car was one second from killing us, Lola was helplessly caught up in some unknown force. A merciless grip had her clogged with despair. Her soul poured out sobs from the core of her guilt as she wept. The near accident didn't seem to faze her. She kept crying and I knew there was a huge problem.

The incident happened so fast that there was a delayed reaction from everyone. This was a goat roping situation for us all. When we got to the Stroll, the girls took a minute to gain their bearings. I knew Lola was plagued with torment, but she had just saved our lives at the same time. I watched her walk away, knowing it could have been a disaster.

After work that morning, Reno's girl Simone disappeared. Reno, Lucky, Pow Wow and I went over to Lola's sister, Jada's apartment since they had been hanging out. We assumed that Lola was there because my Caddy was parked outside. I tossed the spare keys to Pow Wow and said, "I'm gonna need you to drive the car back. Wait while Reno and I go check these broads." As we climbed the stairs you could hear the creaking sound of each step. Reno glanced over, signaling me to knock on the door.

There was low chattering in the apartment which floated to our ears as we stood there. Reno gave a hard knock and the talking stopped. We continued to knock for about ten minutes. I yelled out, "Lola open the door we know y'all in there."

"Simone, open the door! Now!" Reno said.

Frustration settled in his voice as his anger swelled and became intense. He scowled and his nostrils flared like an angry bull ready to charge. Reno planted his fist in his hand and said, "If you don't open up, I'm going to kill you when I see you!"

I got tired of talking so I jacked my leg up and plunged my foot through the door, kicking the deadbolt lock straight off as the chain snapped. Simone and Lola were sitting in the middle of the floor, both hunched over with a pipe in one hand and a lit torch in the other, fighting to get their last inhale as they smoked cocaine. I lunged towards Lola while she quickly took her final pull.

I kicked the pipe out of her hand like it was a stick of dynamite that had just been lit and the glass shattered everywhere. I cocked my hand back into a fist as I prepared to daze her. As she surrendered, laying her head back in acceptance, I caught myself. There wasn't a punch or a kick that I could deliver that would erase the plight of where she was in her life. I had already traveled that road with Tamar and Rainey. There was a crack, the pavement split, and we were heading in two different directions.

Reno grabbed Simone by the neck, choking her as he dragged her over to the window. He said, "Didn't I tell you I was gonna kill you if you didn't let me in? Imma show you what I do when hoes get out of pocket."

Reno opened the window with one hand while holding Simone by the neck with the other. He crashed her head through the window screen. Simone gagged while attempting to plead for her life as her body slid further out the window. You could hear the screen hit the concrete as it dropped from the 3rd floor. "I'll kill you before I let you kill yourself."

I could hear Pow Wow's voice as he hollered up, "Throw that hoe out the window." Reno held her out the window for about 30 seconds before he pulled Simone back. She held on to him tightly by the waist. He plied her off his body and slapped her to the floor as she begged.

"Please Reno, I'm sorry. Please."

"You're fired hoe." As he walked away, she grabbed him by cuff of his pants. He jerked his leg and kept walking. I caught up with him and we left the hoes there, high and dry.

I went downstairs and said, "Pow Wow, drive my Caddy to the house."

He walked over to my Seville and said, "You know I just crashed my El Dorado. I'll tell you what, if you let me drive the burgundy caddy I could pick up your other girls on the Stroll and take them to work."

Convincingly, his face showed such compassion with the right voice pitch, but I knew his selfishness would rise to the surface sooner than later. "Ok Pow Wow, you can take Lola's place dropping the hoes off at work but keep your gangsta goons out of the car man." Without hesitation, he jumped in the burgundy caddy.

It wasn't five days before Pow Wow had an accident, smashing the front and back ends of my burgundy whip (car). I had it towed to the 'Esses' (Hispanic dudes) body repair shop. To floss it up, they installed a newer front end. After the repair, we heard a loud click on the left side of the front end when the car was in motion.

Since my caddy was three years old and the front end was new, we concluded that caused the issue. I parked my burgundy Cadillac across the street from J-Hawk's shop until I figured out what to do with that front-end noise. The car made me think about Lola. Since I was about to pick up Becky and take her to see her son at Lola's mom's house, my mind grasped thoughts of what I could have done different with her.

Having more than 12 hoes created an unforeseen problem. I was spreading myself too thin. I became so laid back with Lola that she had too much idle time, which allowed her to get into trouble. My plan was to erase their negative moments alone by replenishing positive time with me, so I gave serious thought to lowering my numbers. To do this, I decided on the process of elimination. Any broad that I considered dead weight would be cut first.

I decided to hire my buddy Derrick from Jeffery Manor to drive my girls to work on occasion so that I could have extra time with them on their off days. Meanwhile, rumors quickly spread about Lola and Reno's girl Simone getting high. I hadn't seen Lola in a week when I took Becky to Lola's mother, so that she could visit with her son.

"Hey Ms. C, I haven't seen Lola in a while. Have you?" I asked.

She folded her arms as she tilted her head somewhat agitated.

"That child and her sister Jada have been hanging around with some undesirables. They stopped by here yesterday before heading to Milwaukee. I think they're both using drugs. The company they were keeping didn't look right. I must say, the way that she was looking and acting, she was better off being with you."

I paused with a stretched silence as I thought to myself, '*Lola broke the rules and didn't follow protocol.*' I had to remind myself this was her mom, so I kept quiet for a few seconds longer and then said, "Well Ms. C, Lola is one of the most reachable people I know. She's a smart girl. Whatever she's doing will fade away fast."

I hoped my positive perception was giving Ms. C faith in her daughters. "This situation takes me back to our first conversation about people having choices."

She took a deep breath and lifted her eyes with sincerity as she spoke with a mother's worry, "I understand what you were saying. I just have to give this one to God."

After leaving Ms. C, I made sure all my hoes were off to work then met up with Lucky and Reno at our familiar spot, The Criss Cross Lounge. They were standing outside when I pulled up.

"You know Simone came back today and she's at work right now. You seen Lola?" Reno asked. While they anticipated my answer, I tried not to appear as if I was wrestling with the loss.

I brazed my thumb across my nose and gave a gentle snort, "I'm not taking her back. Lola is not Lola. She's a different person now and it would be a waste of time, kind of like trying to resurrect a dead horse."

Lucky said with his arm clinching my neck. "The pimping must go on grasshopper. Now, get on stage and act like never before."

I grabbed his shoulder and said, "I lost 2 broads but that don't stop the show. It's natural for me to jump back into pimp mode which means I'm always looking for new talent."

"Like a replacement?" Lucky asked.

"Naw, not really. I want someone that will create a new experience. I'm searching for supplements, not substitutes. There's nothing better than a pimp checking loot from his new prostitutes."

Between their laughs, Reno suggested we go gambling.

"Let's go to the gambling spot on 63rd Street. I wanna win those fools' money. I beat them for $1,500 last week. Pow Wow, Bodie and Poochie-Slim just left and are headed that way," Reno said.

There were all kinds of hustlers from the slickest of the slick, pimps, players, high-rollers, gamblers and shot callers usually at the joint. In addition to the three crap tables on the 2nd floor, the owners also ran an after-hour spot downstairs. When all the clubs closed, this was the place to be when you wanted to continue drinking and socializing. There was a $20 admission fee so that usually kept the peons away.

We walked in and captured everyone's attention. The smell of smoke and bourbon filled the space. The loud overtones of voices spread in the air of winners while the grief of losers was quick to be silenced. Two of the Mob buddies came over and gave me dap. I hadn't seen them since I got out of the county jail for that armed robbery case. Reno and Lucky went straight to claim their seats at the gambling tables while I mingled and kicked it with an entourage.

The owner called me over to the king's table.

"Earthquake, come have a drink with me."

The crowd parted to let me through and I pimp walked over. Beautiful Bobby said, "Earthquake, you gotta front row seat baby," as he gave up his spot to accommodate me. The waitress mixed a drink for me (non-alcoholic) while the hustlers drank champagne. I had dice in one hand and sipped on an easy living in the other.

The king's table was high stakes, no bets under $250 but everybody crowded around trying to come up. Just to be sociable, I joined the game after one of the ballers hollered, "What they hit for? Try your luck Earthquake." I took the dice, shook them and rolled them fast. Within 15 minutes, I lost $2,500 and instantly got an unmistakably bad taste in my mouth. It was difficult for me to accept. It took me straight back to a memory of 3 Card Molly, trying to get something for nothing.

Putting my faith in dice was the worst con game of all, a revolving door to ultimately lose. Something felt real uncomfortable about this. It affected me in a place that I didn't want to be touched. My gambling career was over before it ever started. I told the fellas goodbye and headed home.

CHAPTER 24
No Macking, Just Me

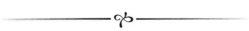

WHEN I WALKED through the door, Reno's girl Barbie was parlaying (sitting) on the couch, talking on the phone with Maya about her next steps. Barbie whispered to me, "Maya left Lucifer and she's staying in a hotel in the South Loop." She interrupted my thoughts with that news and I said, "Let me speak to her." Barbie covered the receiver with her hand and said, "She's a money maker," as she handed me the phone.

"I'm Earthquake," I said, introducing myself.

"I know who you are." After talking for a few minutes, I suggested, "It would be nicer if we spoke in person." Maya accepted and extended an invitation for me to visit but alerted me, "I'm not interested in being with a new man."

I heard her but wasn't listening; too focused on finance because I bought a new car, lost two star broads and $2,500.

I headed over there, processing information about when I first saw her at the Dreamland. She was one of Lucifer's girls and he kept a tight rein on all his broads. Lucifer was a pretty boy pimp from the Northside and very few players tested him. He had a cool but manly demeanor. He resembled the recording artist, Prince, sporting ruffled shirts with all his suits. He had big brown eyes with flawless skin. The girls said he was so pretty that he looked like he wore makeup. Lucifer had his hair styled long with thick curls on the top, like Prince in that new movie Purple Rain.

Maya was gorgeous! She stood about 5'6" and had fair skin with a golden tan. She had Italian features, long thick black hair colored blonde, perfectly arched eyebrows, straight teeth, a contagious smile and a curvaceous body.

On my drive to the South Loop, I was thinking that this was going to be a piece of cake. On my menu, I anticipated taking her to breakfast, reading her body language and quickly wrapping things up. She'd be my new girl in no time. When I arrived at the hotel, I walked in her room with confidence and said, "C'mon let's go to breakfast."

With a surprising counter move she said, "No thanks, I already ate." I stood by the bed with my hands in my pockets and observed her as we talked. I moved in closer to see Maya's features better, so I could diagnose her. She didn't flinch and showed little expression, making it more challenging and indicating it would take longer than expected. I gave myself three days to come up with her (make her my girl).

My overcrowded thoughts lead me to redirect my game plan. I didn't want to have any preconceived notions so, I sized her up for what I observed. I knew that she was a prostitute who made money and had just left her pimp. Therefore, selling her dreams with slick conversation was not gonna work because she was already a money maker. So, I laid back, just being myself so that she could realize my imperfections and see where she fit in.

I started off sharing my dislikes and revealing my shortcomings, pushing out answers before questions. "I sleep with my socks on, always claim the left side of the bed, brush my teeth for 15 minutes each morning and I don't use curse words."

She listened, looking straight at me with no expression but gave a little chuckle. I kept reminding myself, no clever conversation!

Even though the response was flat, Maya appeared to be getting more comfortable. She turned on the television and sat on the bed. I asked, "Do you like Kung Fu movies?" I caught a slight sparkle in her smile.

"Yes, I like Bruce Lee. I love the action."

"Yeah, the action is gripping but I love the discipline."

"Why do you love the discipline?" she asked.

"Because the student always stays focused until they reach their goal. What are your goals?"

She stared off in a wonder. "I'm thinking about getting me an apartment on the Southside, maybe in Hyde Park. That's one of my plans."

With an encouraging posture, I complimented her strategy. "That's a good idea."

"I'm thinking about which choice I'll make first, whether to get an apartment or a car. I'll probably get a car first so that I can get around and then look for an apartment. It's better that way because I'll have to furnish it."

"I believe whichever way you choose, it will work."

"I think I'm gonna be alone, without a man for a while," Maya sighed.

Embracing her independent side, I agreed. "That's good, it gives you a chance to get yourself together." I reminded myself again, no slick talk! I was being a 'girlfriend' to her at that moment, lending a listening ear, just letting her share her dreams and being supportive of it all. She talked for two hours and I listened attentively.

She went on and on about her work, parents, growing up as an only child, being a straight "A" student, on the honor roll, and lead cheerleader in high school. After the 4th hour, it was time for me to go. "Maya, I'll come back tomorrow if you want me too."

Her eye pupils got small, a signal that she was disappointed that I was leaving. She said, "Yeah, please do. I enjoyed talking to you."

"Likewise, I'll see you tomorrow."

The next morning, I visited Maya again. Fresh out the shower, she answered the door in her thick, white terrycloth robe, with her tooth brush hanging from her mouth. With very little excitement she said, "Man, I got something to tell you." I kicked off my shoes and flopped on the bed. Maya grabbed her pants off the chair, pulled out a bankroll, put it in the top dresser drawer and hung her pants in the closet.

I thought to myself, *'Right now she possesses the money, but I need to get that trap from her before it starts to possess her.'* She put the toothbrush in the bathroom and sat across from me, folded her legs and in an even tone said, "I found a car and I'm going to purchase it on Monday."

I smiled at her and said, "That's nice, would you like for me to go with you?"

With a half-smile, "Yeah, you could. It's red, the same color as my car that's with Lucifer."

I stopped her in her tracks and gently asked, "Why don't you get the vehicle that you owned?"

Maya sat there a few seconds before speaking with no emotion, "Nope, I just don't want to go through the drama." The minimum amount of excitement that she had seemed to vanish. "Lucifer is always about drama."

"Then how in the world did you get with him in the first place?" I asked.

She gave me a look as if she didn't remember. Then it snapped into view. "Oh yeah, I met him at a friend's party. I was attracted to him because he reminded me of my favorite recording artist, Prince." I laughed as she kept talking. "We dated for a few months while I worked at a bank as a revenue specialist, counting money and processing checks. Shortly after dating him, I was accused of stealing and got fired. My manager explained they'd received a call from a customer who claimed that I accepted a check that wasn't processed through the bank and was cashed by me personally."

Maya turned down the corners of her mouth with little emotion and said, "After I lost my job, Lucifer started telling me about making money in this lifestyle and I was game for it. He was my pimp. After I worked as a prostitute for 6 months, Lucifer revealed that he called my job and got me fired so that I'd be with him."

I shook my head and was appalled, thinking to myself, he's a one-dimensional pimp, using trickery and manipulation but I guess I've heard of worse.

Maya yawned, and I knew she was tired, so I left the hotel after a few hours and told her to get some rest. I was thinking that I had one more day to adapt to her style because I hadn't quite caught it yet and her bankroll was getting way too big.

Early Sunday morning, still dressed in my blue tailor-made slacks with a matching baseball style cap, silk burnt orange shirt and blue alligator shoes from the night before, I went by her room. Maya was fresh out of the shower, dressed in a silky black bathrobe. She had her pants in her hand, took money from her pocket and placed it in the drawer again. I thought, *That bankroll is out of control. The longer she holds on to it, the more difficult my challenge will be to get it. I must do something fast.'* It felt like trying to unlock a door with the wrong key.

"What's your favorite breakfast restaurant?" I asked. The only change in expression was that her eyebrows slightly lifted.

"The Golden Griddle, on the Northside. They make the best homemade waffles served with a special maple syrup."

"Get dressed so that we can head to The Golden Griddle." I was thinking now it's time for some real progress to take place. While we were walking to the car, I asked, "You want to drive?"

"Yes, are you going to let me drive your car?"

"Yeah, it's just a car."

I handed her the keys and we took off. I immediately observed her driving habits. My experience taught me some very remarkable facts. I learned that a person's driving habits tells a lot about them. If I don't learn from her eating habits, I most definitely will know from her driving.

When a woman adjusts the seats, checks her mirrors and slowly pulls out of the parking space, it lets me know that she is cautious about making decisions. A woman who allows drivers to proceed or pass in front of her, says to me that she is considerate. When a woman drives fast and reckless, that demonstrates that she lives her life fast and reckless. If a woman drives at a moderate speed and obeys the traffic signs, that lets me know that she follows the rules. When a woman drives slow and careful, I know that she lives her life slow and careful.

A woman who drives over potholes, and does nothing to avoid them, shows that she is susceptible to problems. If a woman tries to avoid potholes, it illustrates to me she tries to avoid problems. When a woman is driving on a crowded freeway and has to get off because she can't stand the slow traffic, that indicates to me that she has no patience, is very one sided and runs from problems. When a woman is driving on a crowded freeway and she accepts her place in the flow of traffic, that lets me know that she is patient and doesn't run from problems. A woman who displays symptoms of road rage, demonstrates that she is aggressive and controlling, always trying to guide what others do.

If a woman can't judge a parallel parking space effectively, that lets me know that she has poor judgement and if she can, she has good judgement. If a woman can read a map effectively or follow directions well, that tells me that she has a fluent mind. If a woman has a dirty or junky car, that indicates to me that she is not a good housekeeper. If a woman drives in her lane without drifting and maintains an appropriate distance to the car ahead of her, that lets me know she is very receptive and open to feedback and if she does not, that lets me know that she is not. There are always exceptions to these rules, but generally this is a guide that worked well for me.

Maya was a careful driver. She adjusted the seats, checked her mirrors and slowly pulled out of the parking space. That let me know that she was cautious and observant, always watching her surroundings. She allowed drivers to proceed in front of her, which told me that she was considerate. She drove moderately fast, honoring all traffic signs, which indicated that she followed the rules. When she drove near potholes, she tried her best to avoid them, demonstrating that she tried to avoid problems. When she entered the crowded freeway, she was patient and displayed no sign of road rage.

I asked if she wanted to exit the freeway and drive on the streets in order to avoid the traffic, but she said, no. That let me know that she wasn't controlling and didn't run from situations. Upon exiting the freeway, we saw a police officer standing on the corner and she immediately slowed down to obey authority. Only two types of people react in that way, criminals and people who respect authority. When we pulled into the parking lot, I watched how carefully she parallel parked, which told me that she had good judgement. With that, I learned all I needed to know in order to adapt to her style. Now I no longer had to wonder about my anticipation and expectations.

The Golden Griddle had an old-school diner style with red and white table cloths and a dozen booths that sat in front of big picture windows. The restaurant was moving at a fast pace, but the waitress immediately escorted us to a booth. She was friendly, efficient, and quickly took our order. Maya ordered homemade waffles with the special maple syrup that they call Griddle sauce. I ordered an omelet with turkey sausage. The waitress put in our orders and returned a few minutes later to ask Maya, "Would you like the regular syrup because we're out of Griddle sauce?" She replied, "No thank you, I'll cancel the order and just have orange juice." Her reaction let me know that Maya wanted what she wanted, the way she wanted it and nothing less. I knew I could close in the gap now. If she chooses me, she was choosing whole heartedly.

Since Maya wasn't having breakfast, I hurried and ate my food and we headed back to the hotel. Everything was clear now. I took control and drove while she led the conversation with small talk. She said, "Let me tell you about some of my favorite television shows. I enjoy old school comedy like, *Sanford & Son, Happy Days, Laverne & Shirley and I Love Lucy*." She laughed as she talked about the funnier episodes. Soon after, we arrived at her hotel room.

I asked her for the key and opened the door. At this point, I felt like the janitor of the game. I possessed all the keys and unlocked her mind. That confirmed what I told my homies that I do. "Maya, get comfortable." She went into the bathroom and changed into a black satin robe while I took off my shoes and cap and relaxed on the bed. She laid beside me and her pupils enlarged, signaling a lustful crave. I received her unspoken words and that led me to brush her forehead with my mouth as the scent of honey rose from the lotion she wore. Her eyes smiled, and she surrendered her body to me.

I intentionally slid my tongue across her eyelids, down to her nose and then softly on her lips. She inhaled deeply as my hands traveled gently across her chest. I stroked her breasts and journeyed to her navel, moving back up to her chest again. Her skin was warm and moist creating, immoral suggestions from the flesh. She panted, clenching her teeth with a groan. She murmured as our tongues countered each other with pleasure. My touch caressed her entire body as I floated the robe off and removed her black silk panties.

I got out of my clothes, back in bed and continued caressing her. Maya started to reciprocate, wrapping her hand around my penis sliding it up and down as it throbbed. She rubbed me with intensity and deep yearning. She pulled me into her, attempting to please that urge of full contentment as we started making love. I stroked her with long, deliberate motions that I could feel impacting her body as it quivered.

With every movement that her body made, I adapted and greeted it with a counter rotation, staying in sequence with her. She held on to me tighter as I moved deeper inside of her, in sync with every move. Feeling her intensity as it rose, I could feel her ecstasy about to explode!

After our passionate love making session, I looked over at her and Maya smiled the most intense, beautiful, sensual smile. I rolled over her, went into the top drawer, took the bankroll out, walked around the bed, got my pants and put the money in my pocket. I no longer had to consider my position. Then I went and took a shower and when I got out I said, "Take your shower and get dressed. You are moving out of here!" She smiled and said, "Ok."

Maya packed up all her things after her shower and we headed to my main house. I introduced her to all the hoes and she fell into her role. She adapted to my style very quickly and was receptive in every way. Maya went upstairs to kick it with Reno's girl, Barbie.

I went into my room, Reno entered.

"Earfy, you came up with Maya huh?"

"Yeah, but her style was different. She was being truthful and blunt it wasn't a distraction to me, but it could be to a man who couldn't learn her demeanor."

Reno sat on the bed and asked, "Whaddabout her demeanor?"

"Well, her being so pretty and honest boosted my ambition but it could wound another man's ego if he misinterpreted how she expressed herself.

I had to learn what her expressions meant. That stemmed from having a knack for learning a person's communication style. You taught me that when we were in grammar school – to watch everyone's body language which includes facial expressions, tonality, word patterns, word usage, hand gestures, body language and delivery. You used it to signify, but I used it for pimping."

I laid back on the bed with my arms folded behind my head in teaching mode. "See Reno, her behavior was transmitted to me through driving. At certain times, I use this as a very important tool because there are situations where I misjudge styles of expression. You remember Felicia I had a couple of years ago?"

"Yeah, she was cute. What happened to her?"

My ego died down fast.

"Felicia was communicating in an unusual, happy go-lucky-manner so I thought that everything was ok, especially since we had sex that day. To my surprise, she left me and I didn't see it coming. I started analyzing individual behavior and noticed that the standard meaning of an expression wasn't necessarily true for everyone. Every grin is not a smile and every giggle is not a laugh. In each situation, I learned when it was typical and when a gesture meant something different. With Felicia, a giggle was not a laugh.

I saw Felicia a few months later and asked what happen. She said, 'Well, you are always dressed in the very best. You wear tailor-made suits and alligator shoes and I wanted to look good like you, so I asked you to take me shopping. You gave me $30 and sent me into the local K-mart store.' That was hard for her to swallow. 'I worked hard for two weeks straight and thought that you would take me to a nice boutique.'

I said, 'But I thought you were cool with that because you seemed happy, you were even giggling.' Her voice went faint. She said, 'True, but I giggle when I am upset.' An instant chain of events happened in my mind. I learned two lessons that day – to study a person's reactions and behaviors, analyzing them more intensely to predict future conduct and you can't draw all the water from the well. I'm conscious of both, not planning on making either one of those mistakes again."

"Now that's why you're cold. You learned it from me, so called janitor."

"Yeah, you're right but I took it to the next level. See Reno, Imma tell you the essentials of the game. Don't no man want a lock that every key can open but every man wants a master key that can open any lock. You gotta elevate to graduate, buddy. I'm no longer the janitor, I'm the locksmith." We both cracked up.

Maya settled into the main house. She became Susie-homemaker, often making dinner on her days off. I often found my way back to the house for a home cooked meal.

On her off day, I went to the house but Maya wasn't there, so I waited in the room, laid in the bed and turned on the television. She returned 15 minutes later and handed me $200. Then bent over and her moist lips hit my face. I laid there realizing I'm feeling good about Maya. She's constantly thinking about the business, often making extra contributions.

It was a treat for her to walk to the store when she needed a few items.

"Maya, I noticed every time you return with the groceries, you have an extra $200. Are you flagging down cars?"

She stared with no emotion. We both laughed.

"Can you come down stairs in the kitchen, so I can answer your question? Please with sugar on top?"

Acting sleepy, I stretched, "Ok." Her eyes lit up with a dance giving off beautiful energy with no expression. I trampled behind her down the stairs.

I sat at the table and looked in the grocery bag while she explained.

"Every time I walk outside, men stop me and I respond to at least one of them. When they ask where I'm going, I say, 'To the store to get some food.' Usually, the man offers to buy my groceries if I talk to him so I would say ok and get into his car. Then I explained I need money to pay bills because my husband doesn't work. I would ask him if he had $200 and usually he'd say yes. If he had less, I'd consider dating him for at least $100. Once he gave me the money, I would tell him to pull over in a discreet area and give him a little something, something (sex, oral sex). Afterwards, when he asked me for my contact info, we exchanged numbers. Usually he asked if I lived in the neighborhood and I'd say yes, 'my husband is a pimp.' He would say, "Do you live in that house on 99th street?"

Maya shrugged her shoulders and continued to cook. The fried grease popped with a sizzle that captured my attention. I watched the crispy legs and thighs as the skin formulated into a brown crust. I got hungrier by the second. She poured the macaroni in some boiling water and kept talking.

"Yeah, let me tell you this one guy said. 'Is Earthquake your pimp?' I said yes. He said, 'Aw man, please don't tell him that I turned a date with you. He knows my sons.' I said, 'Ok, bye!" Maya and I both laughed as she cradled and stirred a bowl of cheddar cheese. After she finished cooking, we enjoyed a nice quiet dinner and watched re-run episodes of Sanford & Son.

Now that Maya had experienced my softer side, I needed to show her my business ethics, to tighten up any bolts that were loose. Early the next morning, she rode with me as I did a special run, picking up two of my lower ranking hoes from work. They were lacking in their duties with poor work performance for about one month.

I had to execute my no tolerance policy. After I got them from work and collected my weak trap I extended it right back to them as we pulled up to their apartment building. They mumbled under their breath complaining, acting as if they did nothing wrong.

I turned the radio down to catch a whiff of what they were saying and silence filled the car. I went back to the task at hand and said, "You're a day late and a dollar short. It's not the end of the world but your time with me is up. This is your last day. Pack all your things and be gone by tomorrow morning." Their eyes welled up.

Maya watched my staggering delivery as I fired them. She appeared curious but didn't ask why. Both broads started to cry what I would describe as crocodile tears. I was unmoved by their shenanigans and had no time to waste. My two new chicks were moving in the next day with Joann who already lived in the same apartment.

They got out of my car then Maya and I pulled off. I examined her for some gesture of body movement. I even looked in her eyes to see if they batted or her pupils dilated. They remained large and didn't match her reaction. I reached to see if it bought her any measurement of concern with ideas about not getting out of line. Only time would tell.

After that incident, Maya appeared to ascend higher than the stars, working even harder to stay in rhythm with me. She was always very cautious of being on my good side. We had a solid relationship and the next few months things were pretty smooth with her.

One morning, I picked only Maya up for work and handed her 15 crisp $100 bills. Spreading extra love for her hard work and dedication, it was a reward for her diligent efforts. She cast her eyes on the cash like it was disturbing and said, "I'm good." I placed the money in her hand anyway as I pulled up to Grandma's Breakfast Restaurant. I said, "Go in and get my order. Grandma knows what I want." She hung her head and turned her face away from me.

Maya sat there, frozen, not moving for several seconds. "Maya, what are you waiting on, go ahead and get my food."

She stared at me and blurted out, "No."

It felt like an unspeakable betrayal. I turned in my seat, looked directly at her and asked, "What's wrong?"

Her eyes turned tender and her face was pale, her voice trembled, "Are you about to leave me?"

"Why do you say that?"

"You just gave me money for no reason and said get out the car. I really don't want us to be apart."

At that moment, I knew how afraid she was of losing me. Maya was truly down and had built a sense of love for me. Her level of respect, honor and investment showed that she was in my corner.

"Baby, I'm sorry you feel this way but that's not the plan. Whatever you deposit in me, you'll always get double back in return, in every way, in that order."

She swung her face over towards mine, puckered up and landed her lips on my cheek. It made a smacking sound as the color in her face returned with a warm glow. She said, "Ok, since you're being so generous, can I go shopping at J-Hawk's boutique today?"

"Yes, but right now you need to go and get my breakfast." She rarely smiled with her lips. It was her eyes that drew me into her present state of pure delight as she said, "Ok."

Later that afternoon, we went to J-Hawk's and Maya purchased some nice gear. She saw a beautiful, cleverly designed, turquoise fitted, above the knee dress with a navy-blue sequin pattern. Of course, J-Hawk had all the matching accessories needed to complete the look.

J-Hawk said, "I knew she had taste when she walked straight to that dress. Go and try it on Scooter (a pet name for very pretty girls). That dress is going to fit you perfectly."

When Maya walked out of the dressing room, J-Hawk scrunched his face and said, "Man you look flawless in that dress. She looks like Hollywood off guard. I only had two of these dresses and I sold the other one to the congressman's wife yesterday."

"I love it, I'm buying it and I want all the accessories too."

"Baby, grab whatever you want, Earthquake got this!"

"I can't wait to wear it!"

I grabbed her hand, turned her around and said, "We're going out on one of your off days," as I winked at J-Hawk. Maya worked a lot but when she didn't, she loved just talking to me and I adored listening.

On Maya's day with me, we enjoyed the sweet sounds of the Ohio Players. That night was priceless and the vibe was so sensual. The song "Heaven Must Be Like This" played in perfect pitch. While I laid on my stomach in our king size waterbed, Maya walked over and rested on my back. There was a calm wave of motion happening as she gently held me around my neck and relaxed her head on my shoulder. She whispered softly in my ear as the water carried us like waves in the ocean.

"This feels like heaven."

Her words resonated into the fabrics of my mind as I responded, "There's nothing closer to heaven then this."

Her eyes slid half closed in a calm oasis and then she asked, "Can a prostitute and a pimp go to heaven?"

"Yes, the first person who saw Jesus after he was resurrected was Mary Magdalene, a prostitute and when they tried to condemn her, Jesus said, 'He that is without sin among you, let him cast the first stone at her."

"Who told you that?"

"I learned that in bible study when I was 6 years old."

Maya stared at my feet and then took my socks off. One of her little quirks was her thing about holes in clothing. She kept me equipped with more than enough socks. If I had a loose stitch, she'd take them off my feet. During the middle of the conversation she replaced them while sharing the most intimate details about work.

I learned a lot about how her dates enjoyed some off-beat activities. Maya said, "I have some of the most bizarre trick encounters." She slapped the waterbed as she demonstrated and said, "A few of my customers like me to slap them in the face. This other one paid me to walk all over him in my pointed, stiletto heels."

I lifted my arm and rested the side of my face on my hand, "What kind of pleasure do they find in that?"

"I don't know, but another one likes me to stick him with a bobby pin in his groin."

I gave off a chest squeezing laugh while she had a straight look on her face, telling every detail. Still cracking up I said, "Man, you know you could be a dominatrix."

She pondered and said, "I could see that. I really enjoy my work. I find it fascinating."

Maya appeared to play a character when she worked and seemed to love the role. I loved that she loved her job and loved me as well. She had the best of both worlds. It might not be a thing of beauty, but it's a beautiful thing, in that order!

"Let's change the subject. When was the first time that you had sex?"

"When I was 14 years old," as she laid down on her back. "My step-father molested me. He came in the room, got on top of me and initiated sex. He put his hand over my mouth told me to be quiet."

"Did he hurt you?"

"Yeah, but it felt good, even though I knew that it was wrong. I told my mother and it drastically changed their relationship. He accused her of siding with me, like we were against him. After that, I avoided being alone with him and always locked my bedroom door, secured with a chair under the knob. I got out of the house when I turned 17 years old."

I was thinking this was the first time that a girl told me that being molested felt good when she knew it was wrong. I thought to myself, 'This girl is so honest.'

On our next date night, Maya and I went to the Godfather Club to have a little fun. She sat at a two-seat table, on the side of the small dance floor as I mingled and socialized. She was wearing her new turquoise dress, looking beautiful and savvy, not like the typical club hopper. Out of all the people in this city, who walks in but Lucifer?

He headed straight over by me. I liked Lucifer. He was a cool clever looking cat and I respected his pimping. Lucifer took a quick glance at Maya and acted as if it didn't faze him. He stayed in my space as if he had a personal invitation, just chopping it up with me for about 10 minutes.

Suddenly, Maya walked over and said to me in a low tone, loud enough for Lucifer to hear her clearly, "I love you. I love you so much and I'm never gonna leave you. I'll always do whatever you want me too." I felt really odd because that was the first time that she had ever told me that she loved me. She seemed to always tell me things like that at the strangest moments. I thought to myself, *'Why not while we are making love or at home alone.'*

"Ok, thank you. I appreciate the information. I understand." She went and sat back down. That felt real odd, but I had to admit, it did give me a streak of confidence. I popped my collar and went back over to Maya. She touched my hand with a light stroke and then let it go. Lucifer looked over at us, smiled and turned his eyes away. We enjoyed the rest of the evening then picked up the girls from work after we left the club. I liked the way she handled situations, like a trooper. She was very impressive so far.

The time was moving swiftly. There were some good and bad days which ultimately turned into one long nightfall. Before I noticed, 6 months had passed. Maya positioned herself to be one of my star players, sacrificing the most. She was always trying to hit the bullseye.

On this night, I was at the house just laid-back waiting on my traps. I heard the ruckus of loud voices as my hookers came in the door so I got up, went down stairs and sat on the couch. Becky came in first. She shook her keys as the girls trailed behind her. Everyone handed me my trap.

Maya walked in last. She handed hers with an additional $1,000. She said, "A trick asked me to be a witness in court, testifying that I was with his friend on a particular night. If I did, he would give me $20,000. I told him I would ask my man. If you want me to, I'll do it."

I bombarded her with questions.

"Is he a white guy?"

"Yes, an Italian."

"Where's he from? What does he do?"

"I don't know but he's been a regular for about 6 months."

"Nope. Something is very wrong with that picture. I don't know them, and I can't take that chance. Tell him to find another girl."

Maya collapsed on the couch, rested her head and said, "Ok."

"See, I would never put you in an unpredictable situation. We're already getting money so I'm sticking to what I know. I don't fix nothing that ain't broke."

The next morning after Maya came in from work, she noticed that a sweater was missing. She went to take a shower to wash the night away. When she returned, out of the corner of her eye, in a fraction of a second, she spotted her sweater back in its original place. It was obvious that it had been returned when she was in the bathroom. The only person who had worn her clothes without permission before was Geisha, who had just arrived home.

Maya went downstairs to the living room, to engage in a conversation with Geisha. She called down to Geisha and asked her to come up from the basement. Geisha stomped up the stairs hard and intimidating. She came to the living room and they had a few words about her wearing Maya's clothing. Geisha played the situation like it was trivial. "Don't say anything to me about a sweater, that's stupid. Why are you making a big deal out of it? I won't wear it any more. You're tripping!"

Maya's cheeks didn't raise nor did her face relinquish a frown as she said, "I hear you but don't let it happen again." Everybody knew that talking to Geisha was like talking to a brick wall. She gave Maya a nasty, dismissive look, projecting anger in her demeanor and said, "You need to get a grip," as she went back downstairs.

Geisha and Maya had never gotten into a conflict because Geisha understood that I didn't play about my business. It was the best way to get fired, especially about one of my main girls and Maya had become my bottom. A bottom girl gives you the least amount of problems and is always helping to grow the business.

She is your general, your eyes and ears and she has the ability to follow instructions as well as lead. The new girls follow and pattern themselves after her. Geisha had a star role, a special place on the team but she was not the girl who you wanted your other hoes to imitate because you can't be a bottom broad if you cause a lot of problems. That was definitely a no, no!

I had to immediately nip small problems in the bud because if you don't they'll spread like cancer. Big problems take care of themselves, but small problems become monumental. Small problems can grow undetected and they often turn fatal.

I conditioned myself to know that a problem big or small should never be underestimated and all problems should be treated with the same effort. My mind drifted back to a place where a small problem turned fatal.

One of my girls had a younger sister who said she had a small problem and wanted to talk about it. My girl told her she was tired and would discuss it later. A few hours passed, my girl went into the basement and found her sister had hung herself. She never found out what her sister wanted to talk about, but that small problem became monumental and had a fatal outcome. Missing the opportunity to respond was a minor request. The pain haunted her from something so simple yet so hard to understand.

When I arrived home, Maya said, "I had a few words with Geisha about my sweater." I knew that they rarely wore each other's clothing. I went downstairs, and Geisha handed me my trap with a puppy dog look on her face, speaking to me without saying a word. I didn't have any questions because she wouldn't have had the right answers. I told her in a low but stern voice, "Don't let me hear about any kind of conflict with Maya. Is that understood?"

Geisha spoke in a way that sounded remorseful, but she looked puzzled, like she didn't have a clue what I was talking about. "Ok. Yes sir."

"I got an idea." I swept the lint off Geisha 's bed with the back of my hand. It was a hint to show how lonely she'd be tonight. "Although this was our time to spend together, since you've caused this incident, I'm going back upstairs to give you some time to think." I gave her the nastiest look and went on my way. Geisha knew that she was skating on thin ice.

I went back to the bedroom. Maya said, "Oh yeah, this hoe name Rita at the club wants to choose you. She's a renegade, that's cool with me."

As I took off my diamond rings and set them on the dresser I said, "What does she look like?"

"She's tall, about 5'10" with coco brown skin, soft facial features and a big smile. You've seen her at the club. You just didn't know her name. She's kind of shapely and thick."

Rita chose me, and she turned out to be a remarkable piece of work, always down for the cause. It had been 6 months and she never gave me any trouble. Things were working out well. I went to pick up Rita from Dreamland. My plan was to spend time with her on her off day. We would pick up my hoes working up North, drop them off at home and head back North. Kentucky Becky would take the hookers working the strip joints home. Maya got in the back seat to hand me my trap while Rita and I were discussing the next move. Maya started talking tough, cursing at me so I asked, "Have you been taking acid or something?"

She said, "You're talking crazy, I know what I'm saying." Now this took me by surprise. That behavior was so unexpected from any of my broads, especially her. I was blown away and thought to myself, 'I would hate to have to check Maya. Let me give her a chance. Maybe she's just depressed about something and this is her way of reaching out for help.' I couldn't figure it out. It had been nearly two years that she'd been with me and she never reacted like that. She just kept rattling off at the mouth.

Kentucky Becky came to the window and handed me my money. I told her to take Rita home. I looked over at Rita and said, "This is what I need you to do. When you get home, tell Amelia and Wonnie to work a double and spend a night with you. I'll see you tomorrow." Rita folded her lips and nodded yes, making sure to keep her own emotions in check. Maya rode home with me.

I pointed my finger an inch from her face warning her, "I'm checking you when we get home."

"Well, do what you gotta do." The pressure in my head laid heavy on my foot as I pressed the accelerator and the speedometer reached 75 mph on the expressway. I was anxious to medicate this problem. When we arrived home, I immediately went to see if Geisha was in and she wasn't. I didn't want her to know that I had to check Maya. It would've decreased Maya's value with Geisha, allowing her to push the envelope.

I walked into the room, snatched Maya by the arm, slung her so hard that she flew through the air and landed on the bed. I took the 6-inch stiletto off her foot and busted her in the top of the head, not realizing that it broke her skin and blood gushed out.

"I'm sorry, I won't do it again. I didn't mean it. Please, I learned my lesson," as the blood ran down her face.

I slammed the shoe on the floor and said, "If you're planning to act like this then you're gonna have to leave."

"I won't ever do that again, I promise," as she put her hands together in a prayer.

While she was still bleeding, I didn't even look back. I just walked out of the bedroom and left the house. That was one of the hardest things that I had to do in this pimp life, knowing that Maya wasn't really cut from that cloth. She was a Poodle. On the other hand, Geisha was a Pit-bull. Geisha could take it because she dished out violent nature while Maya did not. However, when she displayed this type of tough talk she too had to take her medicine.

When I returned to the house the next day, I was in a cold state of mind. Maya was sitting on the edge of the bed with her eyes focused on the floor. I said, "You're still here?"

She looked up and said, "Can I talk to you? I apologize. I just wanted to see how far I could go. I tested you because I wanted to see what I could get away with. I just wanted to see what girls get out of that. I never got beat up before although Lucifer choked me."

I extended my hand in friendship. "You're forgiven and I'm gonna forget that this day ever happened."

"You don't ever have to worry about me doing that again. I experienced it once and now I know."

"Yeah, cause I love you just the way you are, even though you are corny," and we both laughed.

Women tried to test me, but I was always up for the challenge.

CHAPTER 25

After a Haughty Spirit Comes a Fall

SOMEONE KNOCKED ON the door and I whizzed downstairs like a mack in full effect and answered. The postman delivered a registered letter that I had to sign for and that was no problem. I reached in the mailbox and got everything else out. I scanned through the envelopes. Reno's mom Jean usually picked it up. Since there was a brown envelope with red writing on the front of the one I signed for, I immediately opened it. My eyes widened as I read. It was a foreclosure letter on the house that we'd been renting from Reno's mother for nearly two years.

Standing there bewildered, I'm thinking, *'She comes and collects the rent money every single month. She'll be here in a few days to collect the rent again and then we'll resolve this matter. It's probably a mistake on the mortgage people's part.'* A few days passed, and Jean arrived like clockwork. She came in as if nothing was wrong and said, "I'm here to collect the rent."

"Jean have a seat. I received a certified foreclosure letter on the property showing that you haven't paid the mortgage this entire time."

I tossed the letter on the couch next to her. Wonnie walked out of the kitchen and said, "Earthquake, the gas is off too and the water ain't working."

Everything was rising to the surface. Jean said, "Well, I had a few setbacks and I was waiting for my 401K and pension to come through. My plan was to pay the house off."

I knew she was dragging (lying) by the way she talked. Her body language told a story I didn't want to see, sinking in the lowest direction because she was like a mother to me.

"What happened to all the rent payments and bill money that we gave you every month?"

Her mouth twitched as she said, "I've been helping my boyfriend with his bills or else I would've had to come live with y'all."

"Jean, what do you expect to happen now?"

As her eyes bulged out, she twisted her mouth and sucked through her teeth, she said, "Well, maybe you could buy the house!" I knew at that moment that she had a serious drug problem and was on a downward spiral fast.

There was no time to waste. That afternoon, I called my attorney who assisted with getting a realtor and we worked to obtain a quick deed. We negotiated a very fair deal. I immediately paid a $5,000 deposit on the past due amount of $9,000 and they forgave the $20,000 principal, interest and fees that had accumulated. At the closing, I paid the final $4,000 and took ownership of the house. I also paid all the bills and put them in my name. This was an unexpected hit and my girls kicked in like soldiers. Everything flowed like a smooth ride.

I didn't miss a beat. Now that everything was back in order, it was time to go celebrate. After sealing the deal with my attorney, I went to the house to get dressed since I was going out to kick it with my crew. I immediately saw that two of my diamond rings were missing.

I knew that Reno's mom had stolen them, but I didn't accuse her because no one saw her do it. The next day, a homie who sold drugs and pimped girls from the Jeffrey Manor said that he recognized some jewelry that came in the day before. Reno's mom brought the jewelry to him in exchange for drugs.

"I did the exchange so that Reno's mom wouldn't sell the jewelry somewhere else and this way I could give it back to you."

I lifted my eyebrows, with a surprised look and asked him what the value of the exchange was, and he said, "It was $500 but you don't' owe me anything." I gave him $300 to show my appreciation.

I told Maya what Jean had done and she shared a secret, letting me know that she had been saving money each week to get me a special gift for my 21st birthday. She had designed a $15,000 diamond studded ring which was still in the lay-a-way with a balance due of only $2,500. She showed her hand drawing of this beautiful, over the top, 3 karat cut stone, with baguette diamonds shaped like a globe of the world. I told her to give me the ticket and promised her that I wouldn't pay the balance and pick it up. I'd allow her to keep paying for it. Maya wanted it to be a true gift from her.

I changed all the locks on the doors so that only the people who resided in the home had keys. Reno's girl Barbie had a 17-year-old sister, Lia, who had just been kicked out of their mom's house, so she came to live with us. For a couple of months, she watched the house during the night when we weren't there and a few months later she returned home.

That morning, Geisha 's grandma asked her to house sit the first-floor apartment when she went out of town. After work, she called me from her grandmother's house and asked me to pick up my trap. After a 40-minute phone conversation at 4:00 a.m., as I sat in front of her grandma's house, she convinced me to stay with her until noon. I usually wouldn't stay at someone's house but since we hadn't spent time together, I decided to do so. The house was very clean and quiet. We went straight into her old bedroom and relaxed on the full-size bed. Geisha looked very comfortable in her white, oversized t-shirt and gray, loose fitting jogging pants. We listened to old school R&B slow jams and just laid back. The song "Let Me Down Easy" by the Isley Brothers was the last melody that I heard as we fell asleep.

After about four hours of Geisha spooning me, I woke up ready to leave. She seemed to be satisfied. I said I would see her at home and informed her that there would be no more spending a night for me. She stretched and yawned as she smiled and said, "Cool, I'll be home tomorrow anyway." She walked me to the door while I got my keys out of my pocket. She opened the door and I sharpened my eyes, slightly closing them from the bright glare of sunlight. I stepped onto the front porch, looked at my car and instantly got angry. I ran down the stairs to my vehicle. My driver side back window was busted, and the television and phone were missing. I could clearly see the destruction from where they ripped out the custom-made bar paneling to remove the items.

Geisha yelled from the door, "What happened?" I walked back onto the porch and told her. She got hysterical and I tried to calm her down. As we stood on her porch, I saw a dude walking along the sidewalk, past the house. Geisha ran down the stairs screaming, "Hey Butch, did you break his window?" He just looked at her. Geisha said, "You know who busted the window, and if you didn't, I know you know who did." Butch said, "Folks don't tell on Folks." I immediately replied in an angry, rough voice, "Tell folks if I catch them by my car, I'm gonna shoot them in the head."

Geisha ran down off the porch and stepped up to his face and yelled, "Yeah punk!" I told Geisha to shut up and get out of his face. With a mean frown on her face, Geisha hesitated and slowly backed away.

Butch yelled, "Yeah, this hoe better get out of my face before I knock her out."

I hurried down the stairs towards Butch, while taking off my rings. I stepped to him with an irate tone saying, "You little mark, Imma bust your face!"

He started backing up and trotted off saying, "I'll be back, wait right here."

I told him that I would be waiting but Geisha suggested that I leave. I stood there in a solid stance and said, "I'm not going nowhere," a small decision that became monumental.

Geisha kept looking around in a paranoid way, repeating herself saying, "Earthquake just leave." With a stubborn arrogance, I just ignored her. About 10 minutes later, I saw three guys walking nonchalantly down the sidewalk. As they slowly walked past, appearing nonthreatening, each of them spoke in a friendly manner. Suddenly, a royal blue Chevy swiftly pulled up next to my car and five guys jumped out. The guy who jumped out the front passenger seat was holding a 2-foot-thick oak stick. At the same time, I saw Butch with another guy carrying a small lead pipe, walking from the back alley of the house two doors down.

Geisha jumped in front of me and ran toward Butch and the guy. The guy with the lead pipe punched Geisha straight in her jaw, with a force so strong that it knocked her down. Simultaneously, I got tackled from the back by two of the "friendly, nonthreatening guys."

From the impact, my body shifted forward while my head jerked backwards. As my knees crashed into the concrete, I threw my hands forward, harshly smacking the ground to avoid falling on my face. Then I felt the mighty force of a foot kicking me dead in the nose and mouth. Next, a punch came out of nowhere and landed on the side of my jaw while the oak stick broke as it struck me on the back of my head. I used my arms to pivot and got up on one knee while throwing two guys over my back. Those two guys landed on the ground in front of me. As they got up, I punched one of them in the face and then I got hit with the lead pipe on the side of my jaw.

I caught my balance enough to swing back. I landed a solid punch on another goon. Then I ran to the front of Geisha 's grandma's building, positioning my back against the wall so no one could get behind me. I kept swinging fiercely with power and fury behind each punch. I got madder and madder, thinking about how they just stole my property and came back to jump me. At the height of my rage, they reluctantly started retreating and slowly backed off me. These wimps had the nerve to holler "Mob." Some of them ran through the alley while the rest of them got in the Chevy and drove off. These were renegade goons who were imitating the Mob.

During the fight, Geisha's family members who were in the 2nd floor apartment, rushed outside. She was hysterical, screaming and hollering as five of her relatives held her down until she passed out. She regained consciousness a minute or two later and ran over to me repeating, "They're dead. All of them. We're gonna get them, I swear!" Still crying, barely able to gain her composure, I turned away without answering and jumped into my car as the police pulled up.

An officer walked over to me and asked if I wanted to make a report and I said, "No." All I could think about was killing them and getting the satisfaction of cutting their throats as I watched them bleed to death. Then I pulled off without acknowledging anyone else.

When I got about two blocks away, a police car pulled me over with a suspect in their back seat. An officer walked to my driver's side and asked, "Is this one of the guys who assaulted you?" I swung my eyes towards him. The pain of seeing him but not being able to touch him made me wrestle with my sanity. I told the officer, "No, let him go."

At that moment, Wilfred, one of the old neighborhood homies whom I admired, drove past, then abruptly pulled over and parked. It was ironic that I hadn't seen him in 10 years, but we still recognized each other. He came to my passenger side window and whispered "What's going on? Did somebody jump you?"

"Something like that."

"What you want to do?"

"Naw, I'm gonna handle this."

Wilfred gave me his number saying, "I'm late for work but if you need me, call me." I extended my hand and grabbed his number and said, "Ok."

The police officer reiterated, "If this is one of them, tell me so we can lock him up." It was him, but I stuck to the same answer. I had already decided they were dead men.

Next, I drove to the apartment on South Shore Drive and Pow Wow was there. He looked at my face and asked what happened, so I told him everything. He tumbled into a deep vengeance, completely stricken with fury as he paced the floor. My sore knees had dents in them as I limped into the bathroom, stared in the mirror, revenge settled inside and the rage escalated. My right eye was red, nose swollen, front tooth loose and left jaw puffy with a lump on the top of my head that pounded like a sledgehammer hit it.

Just the thought of those marks made me want to watch their souls evaporate from their bodies. Pow Wow called the entire crew letting everybody know what happened and people started contacting us with information about those bums.

Larry, a friend of my cousin Chevy, was visiting his associate Nonie. They were bragging and boasting about beating up a pimp name Earthquake.

"You don't know who y'all just beat up, they gonna get at you," Larry said.

"Man, he just a pimp," Nonie replied.

"Naw, he more than just a pimp. You got some big problems coming, I'm out of here, bye." Larry hurried out of his house and called us with the info. Within a day, we knew where all of them lived and hung out. After that, we took daily shifts lurking their neighborhood.

Those marks were like ghosts in their own hood. We stalked every location that they frequented. The power of hatred blinded my purpose of being a player. I wasn't thinking about pimping or hoes, but I always checked my trap. Beyond that I thought of nothing but bloodshed. I was focused on getting revenge. I became a killer in the midst of the chaos and was in such a savage state of mind that I felt no pain. I didn't even think about going to the doctor. After the long hunt, I went home.

Finally, Pow Wow came to the house and said, "I almost killed one of them. We caught up with that mark. He got a dope spot where they sell weed, so me, Bozo and Jim flew over to that location. We scoped out the 2-flat building, peeped their secret code and headed to the 2nd floor. Bozo did their knock and yelled, 'I need an ounce (of weed).' As soon as the dealer opened, I lifted that automatic pump shotgun and he slammed the door quick, but I started blasting through anyway. Man, we heard all those chumps scattering and running through the place like hoes.

We went back to the car and discreetly ducked down, incognito waiting for that punk to leave the building. I was close enough to hear the conversation when the police arrived. Dude busted out the door and ran straight up to the officer, practically screaming, 'I have marijuana on me'. The cops grabbed the weed, handcuffed him and placed that sucker under arrest."

It was ironic that 48-hours later, he was released from jail and murdered the same day, in an unrelated incident. It had been 2 weeks and he was the first one dead.

Twenty-four hours later, my crew member, Lil Rail, befriended one of the marks so we could set him up. The plan was to get him alone so that I could kill him. That afternoon on a winter school day, Lil Rail tried to convince the mark to walk around the corner from his house and help him repair a flat tire. The mark just wouldn't go beyond a few feet from his front door.

After 3 failed attempts, Lil Rail snatched the mark while I ran out from behind a tree with the pump shotgun. The mark broke away and ran towards his house. As I aimed directly at him, his father walked out and was too close in proximity for me to shoot. I didn't want to accidentally miss, hit his father or even shoot him in front of his dad, but I still had a thirst to kill him. As odd as it sounds, knowing we were that close to assassinating one of them made me more determined than ever to complete the task.

A month had passed, and my anger still raged out of control. I remained anxious to kill them. That murdering spirit had possessed me, and it was all that I could think about. Poochie-Slim was visiting with me at the house when he got a call from Nonie asking to purchase some work (dope).

When I heard the name, I asked Poochie-Slim questions to confirm that this was the same mark who jumped me. Once we confirmed that it was, I said, "Poochie-Slim set him up."

"Ok, no doubt."

We came up with a plan. Poochie-Slim knew Nonie through his sister, who he had just started dating. The plan was to create a social environment so that they would leave the residence and head to the liquor store.

That night at around 7:00 p.m., 8 of us were parked down the street near a vacant lot on the block. I was holding the pump shotgun, posted in the back seat of a dark blue Honda with 2 crew members sitting in the front. We had 8 pistols on the back floor of the car. The rest of the crew were in Mike D's black Chevy.

We were all wearing black gear with skull caps, as we sat tucked in the car, similar to army men in a ditch in enemy's territory. Our bodies were cramped up while our joints stiffened as we patiently waited 3-hours for Poochie-Slim and Nonie. When the door opened, an unidentified guy walked down the street to the liquor store and came back with a case of beer in his hand. He went into the residence. Mike D motioned his hand signaling us to follow. We pulled up next to him. He said, "It's getting late, they ain't about to come out. We'll try tomorrow."

I wondered why Poochie-Slim didn't go with the plan. My anger was boiling with evilness and vengeance. I had never been this diabolical in my entire life. It was hard for me to wake up every day knowing that they were still alive. On the ride back, I thought, *'It's been way too long for them to stay alive.'*

We made it to the house and unloaded all the guns from the car. I placed them in the back of my bedroom closet and told the crew, "We're going to try again tomorrow, even if we have to home invade. We gotta kill at least one of them." The crew left and Pow Wow and I were the only ones in the residence. Reno arrived and asked, "Did y'all get them?" We told him the story.

Pow Wow and Reno started to gamble, playing cards. Reno was losing lots of money at $200 per hand. I went to my main bedroom, sat on the bed as my thoughts swirled through my head. *'Why wasn't it working out for me to kill them?'* To lighten my mood, I decided to go out to a club at around 11:30 p.m. I breezed through the closet and selected one of my slick outfits, a black and mustard color, tailor-made, pull-over jacket and pants, along with my black mink coat. As I laid it out on the bed to get a visual of my look, I heard a hard knock on the front door.

It was Reno's mother, Jean. When she stormed into the house, I could hear her ask him for some money, but he refused. Jean said, "You gonna give me some money because I need to help my boyfriend pay rent."

"Ma, I'm not giving you any money for drugs. I'll buy you something to eat but that's it."

Jean left but returned about an hour later, asking for groceries and Reno said no again. He gave her $20 to get something to eat. She left and returned about an hour later, for the 3rd time. You could hear the screeching from the tires as Jean drove across our lawn and straight up to the front door. She banged on the door in desperation. Reno let her in. I could hear them arguing, she was yelling at him.

"I sold y'all my house for nothing. For only $9,000 and I know it's already paid off. I can't get $125 from you? After y'all just took my house!" She was tweaking (feening for dope). "I gotta give my boyfriend the money or he's gonna get kicked out. He's depending on me. I'm staying here then, I'm sleeping on the floor!"

Reno said, "It doesn't make me no difference but I'm not giving you a dollar. Look Ma, I bought you something to eat and gave you a few dollars but I'm not buying you no drugs." Reno held his ground. "I'll give you anything, but I'm not giving you no money to get high. You can forget it."

At 2:00 a.m., I came out of my room and walked down the stairs. Jean stormed out of the house. She jumped into the driver seat of her boyfriend's car and burnt rubber on our lawn, leaving deep track marks, screeching the tires and speeding down the street, driving crazy. I walked to the front door where Reno was. We had just paid the gardener to plant pine trees. I'm looking at Reno like man, she just tore up the lawn. What is this? I walked back into the house while Reno stood there looking at it.

With all that was going on, I was there but I wasn't there. I couldn't shake that evil sense of what happened to me, that awful mood that I was in, so I decided not to go to the club.

Reno went upstairs to his room. I walked into the kitchen and asked Pow Wow, "What's up, are y'all still playing cards?"

"Yeah but Reno's mother is cracked out and she's begging him for money, I'm already $2,000 in his pocket. I want her to keep coming back because she's distracting him and I'm breaking him. I'm about to buy a home and a brome (Cadillac) off this dude."

I asked if he was ready to go over to the apartment and Pow Wow quickly replied, "No, not yet. I'm staying here."

I told him that I was going back upstairs and to let me know when he was ready. Reno swiftly came downstairs with a thirsty look on his face, anxious to win his money back. He pulled out more money and they continued to gamble.

I went back upstairs and sat on the edge of the bed. I was still thinking about why Poochie-Slim didn't bring that mark outside so that I could kill him tonight. All I was focused on was how they did me. How dare anyone put their hands on me for no reason! Nobody touches me and lives. I'm mad and I want to kill this dude so bad that I can taste it. My spirit was haughty. I couldn't rise above my circumstance. I called my driver Derek and told him to pick up the girls from work. It was about 4:30a.m. and he dropped everyone off at their spots and then arrived at the main house with my girls. Maya walked in the bedroom, handed me my trap and spoke.

We heard a car pull up fast and there was a hard knock on the door again. It was Jean. She was back and screaming.

"Reno, I told you I need that money!"

"I'm not giving you no money."

It went on like that for a while.

"What going on?" Maya asked.

"They've been arguing all night."

"Arguing about what?"

"Jean is on drugs bad. She's been storming over here all night. I know you don't want to hear all of this confusion."

"I really don't."

"I'm going to pick my money up at the apartment. I'll be back in a little while. You wanna ride over there with me Maya?" I grabbed my coat.

"No. Our jewelry and fur coats are here. I'm not leaving our stuff so she can steal it."

I thought to myself, '*I didn't think about the fact that Jean can steal something again.*' I asked, "Are you sure?" She walked slowly to the closet to hang up her coat and turned her head in my direction.

"I'm going to stay. Who's going to look out for our stuff if I don't?" I looked over at her as I was leaving. I hesitated as if I wanted something and went downstairs.

I didn't want any of the other girls to ride with me and Geisha hadn't made it in. I asked Pow Wow if he was ready to go and he finally said yes. I took him to my apartment where his two girls were waiting on him. I checked my trap from my girls then my driver Derek and I headed back to the main house. As we drove towards the Jeffrey Manor we could see black smoke. I said, "Dag man, it's a fire in the Manor." Derek agreed and said that it looked bad.

A few minutes later I said, "Somebody's house is burning up. I hope the family got out because that's a bad blaze. I wonder who crib that is?"

I thought, '*Man, it's close to our house.*' We were four blocks away, as we got closer, I realized that it was our block. "Hurry up, man we gotta get there. It's Harrell's house next door."

"It's Harrell's house?"

As we pulled up, I looked in horror realizing it was our house. There were two ambulances, detective vehicles, fire trucks, police cars, forensics, and the Cook County Sheriffs. They've got yellow tape around the property outside while they were inside, removing items onto the lawn. The house was burnt to a crisp. The firemen tore the roof off and hosed the entire infrastructure, so it was apparent that there was nothing left. I jumped out of the car and ran to the first ambulance to see who was hurt. It was Reno and they were treating his second-degree burns. His arm was still smoking, and he hollered from the pain.

"Reno who burnt the house down?"

"My mama."

"Man, why did she do that?"

"I don't know man, I'm hurt."

I ran to the next ambulance and saw Reno's girl Wendy as the paramedics were fitting her into a back and neck brace. Then I saw Barbie on the side of the first ambulance, standing there in shock. I asked Barbie where Maya was and got no answer. Barbie just stood there in a daze. I ran around to the door of the ambulance and asked Reno again.

"Where is Maya?"

"I don't know."

I spotted a black body bag on the front lawn. It was still smoking, and blonde hair was sticking out. Who else could have been in the house? My broad got blonde hair, but I know it couldn't be her. As I walked towards it, the detectives came over and said, "Hey you, you can't open that body bag."

I looked up and asked, "Who's in there?"

"A young lady."

I ran to the ambulance and asked Reno, "Where is Maya?"

He said, in a voice of excruciating pain, "Maya didn't make it."

I ran back to the body bag and then I was going in the house and a detective yelled, "Come out of there!" So, they pulled me out of the house.

"Why are you going in there, do you stay here?"

"Yeah, I stay here. Can y'all tell me who's in the body bag?"

"Maya Ferretti."

"That's my girl."

"Did she live here?"

"Yes."

"We need to ask you one question. Which room is yours?"

I told them where my room was.

"We need to take you down to the police station," and they placed me under arrest.

"Sorry about your girl but you have to go with us," the detective said.

They handcuffed me, placed me in the car and drove to the police station. I'm thinking, *'Man I can't process anything. I'm tore up.'* I said to myself, *'Let this be a dream, wake up!'* But this was no dream.

When I arrived at the police station, I saw Jean handcuffed sitting in a chair, looking all spaced out. They handcuffed me on the wall across from her. The detectives left us in the room alone. I was like man, what just happened? She apologized profusely. I asked her, "Why did Maya have to die?" She said, "I was standing on the stairs realizing what I had done, and I just wanted to die. I asked God to take me because I couldn't deal with the problems my addiction was causing."

"It was like God had answered my prayer. I felt a power release upon me, a sort of entity, some unknown force. It was the death angel and I was ready go. Then Maya rushed into the house and walked right past me. That death angel jumped straight off me and latched onto Maya. Then some force pushed me out the door."

The detective came back in and asked, "What's your name?"

After what I'd heard, I couldn't speak. They asked again but I didn't say anything because I was still trying to process everything. They placed me in an interrogation room where they asked my name again, but I still couldn't respond. The detective finger printed me and said, "We'll find out who you are once your prints come back."

The detectives started asking me if those were my guns. Reality started to set in.

"I don't know anything about no guns."

The detective repeated, "Those were your guns. Do you know that you had a state trooper's gun in there? Where did you get that shotgun pump?"

"I don't know anything about no shotgun pump."

They interrogated me for about 24-hours, grilling me, asking, "Where did you get that state trooper's gun?"

"The guns were in your room."

I replied, with a blank look on my face, "I don't know nothing about those guns being in there. We just bought the house. They haven't even moved their furniture out yet."

"Are these Reno's mother's guns?"

"I don't know who they belong to because she was renting the house while she was living with her boyfriend. So, I don't know who was renting the house or what, but I don't know anything about no guns."

"We are charging you with gun possession!"

They transported me to the Cook County Jail and I went to court the next day. The judge gave me a bond and I bonded out a few hours later. Pow Wow came to pick me up. With compassion he said, "Man I got your car from your driver."

"Did you get my money from him?"

"No, Derek didn't mention your money."

I was thinking my driver was holding about $2,000 for me.

"By the way, your two girls from Kentucky left and went back home. We're going to the apartment where everyone is waiting."

When we arrived, Geisha was downstairs. The last time I saw her, she was walking toward the scene of the fire while I was being placed in the detective car. She looked despondent and confused. When I had my first chance to talk with her, she asked what happened. I told her what I knew.

"I'm sorry about Maya. I didn't mean to say mean things. We had our little differences, but I never thought that she would be dead. She was my wife-in-law and I loved her." Geisha broke down and started crying a deep cry, like she had lost a sister. I had never seen her cry as hard as she cried that day.

After talking with Geisha, I decided to call Reno before going upstairs. He was in the hospital. I asked him his version of what happened, and Reno told me that when I left, his mom came back and said she wasn't leaving until he gave her some money. Reno said, "I don't care." He then went to bed and left his mom downstairs while the others were in their rooms. His mom Jean was hollering the same old, same old, "I'll burn this house down right now if you don't give me some money!" Jean lit the curtains on fire and Maya went upstairs to tell Reno. He ran downstairs, put the fire out and went to bed. Jean did it again. Maya hurried and put out the fiery curtains and told Reno that his mom lit the curtains on fire for the third time. Frustrated, Reno ran downstairs, put out the fire and said, "Ma, I don't care, do whatever you going to do," and he went back upstairs to bed.

This time, Jean lit the curtains near a plug and it started an electrical fire. The walls went up in flames as the house quickly burned. Maya went upstairs and told Reno that his mother started a fire and announced to everyone that they needed to get out.

Everybody who was down in the basement ran out. Reno's girl Barbie ran down the stairs and out the door. His girl Wendy stayed upstairs with him, frantically gathering their valuables. Maya went upstairs and opened the window because she heard them struggling and having trouble with it.

Reno and Wendy threw their valuables out the window as the fire gained momentum. Maya made it outside and stood on the sidewalk with Barbie. Jean was still in the house, in a daze, just standing there on the stairs. The house was burning up and Maya says, 'Man, I'm go back and get my black diamond mink coat.' Barbie said, "You shouldn't go back in there.' "I'm going to get my coat. I'll be right back!' Maya said, and quickly ran back into the house.

We surmised that Maya made it upstairs, got the coat but with smoke inhalation she passed out at the top of the stairs. The coat was laying right on the step where Maya's body was found.

After the Fire

I thought back on the last time I saw Maya. I asked her, "Do you want to come with me?" She said no, as she hung up her mink coat in the closet. I don't want to go because I need to watch our things. Something was pulling at me, nudging me to make her come with me so I gave her that look, like, you wanna go, and she said no again. My mind said, go tell her you'll be back and go give her a kiss. Then I thought, *'Naw, I'll be back, and I went on out the door.'* We took my brother to my apartment, dropped him off and headed back to the main house.

After speaking to Geisha and then talking with entire crew, who were all at the apartment, there were mixed feelings about everything. Everyone was so emotional and sad. We took turns expressing our thoughts and feelings. So many people broke down, so I had to stay strong because they were all relying on me to be the rock, to get them through this, especially my girls. They were watching me very closely. A few hours later, I retreated to my room and took some time alone, trying to digest everything and reflected on the entire situation.

All the anger was released from me. My spirit had become so humble in those moments and I was able to see things clearly. A voice whispered to my conscience, it was a reflection of what had happened. I took from you because I needed her. It was fate that brought you together. You will see her again.

For now, you must drink from this cup because you chose it. Vengeance is not yours. If you would have killed those guys, things would have turned out very different. You would have received life in jail or been killed, so I blocked it because that cup would have been worse. Live by the sword, die by the sword. This revelation was the start of me controlling my anger.

It was extremely important that I maintained my cool because when you are angry you can't see clearly. Your thinking is distorted. My anger was in control of my position. I had to condition my mind to know too much anger could also be a giant in your life. It could become monumental. Just the pain of not being able to see that coming was so devastating.

Playing it over and over in my mind, I should have saw that coming. My mind was tied in knots. Why didn't Reno get everyone out of the house? I didn't get a chance to say goodbye. I believe she would have been with me forever. All of this was hard to swallow and on top of all that, I lost my house, all my possessions and had a gun charge with a court case, while my jaw was still fractured.

At least Maya was a buffer at times, taking my mind away from issues. Now she's gone. I was weary, but I had to press on even when I didn't want to, and never forget to practice controlling anger. I had to tell myself to do this behavior until it became easy and repetitive. I couldn't let my circumstances overtake me. I had to rise above them. This pain was like a double death.

The greatest deed that anyone could do is to sacrifice their life to save the life of someone else. I couldn't stop thinking about Maya and how she made sure that everyone got out of the burning house. That was such an unselfish act, ensuring that they were safe before going back to retrieve her valuables.

Reno, Barbie, Wendy, my girls and Jean could have all died in the fire if wasn't for Maya. Had she thought about herself first, it could have turned out very differently. She was an extraordinary person, such a prize. In my mind, she was very heroic and that made me love her even deeper. It was like a part of me was lost, never to be found again. I guess it was just the whole situation. I had two pills that I could swallow: be Distracted or be Dynamic.

TO BE CONTINUED.......

Earthquake age 14

Earthquake age 16

Earthquake age 18

Earthquake age 20

Pow Wow age 15

Pow Wow age 16

Lucky age 14 with Aunt Tea

Mom in the 70's

Coming Soon

---ˁ⁊---

Human Earthquake Book II
Human Earthquake Book III

The author welcomes you to continue your experience with this series. Be sure to follow him on Facebook to get the latest news and perspectives, at Human Earthquake. Ramon welcomes your comments and questions! Website going live soon... be sure to stay tuned. Thank you for taking the beginning of this spiritual journey with me, I look forward to you riding all the way!

For any questions, press inquiries or to schedule a speaking engagement, contact the author via email at humanearthquake123@gmail.com.